WRITING ON THE EDGE

Also by Robert Daley

NOVELS

The Whole Truth
Only a Game
A Priest and a Girl
Strong Wine Red as Blood
To Kill a Cop
The Fast One
Year of the Dragon
The Dangerous Edge
Hands of a Stranger
Man With a Gun
A Faint Cold Fear
Tainted Evidence
Wall of Brass
Nowhere to Run
The Innocents Within
The Enemy of God
Pictures
The Red Squad

NON-FICTION

The World Beneath the City
Cars at Speed
The Bizarre World of European Sport
The Cruel Sport
The Swords of Spain
A Star in the Family
Target Blue
Treasure
Prince of the City
An American Saga – Juan Trippe and His Pan Am Empire
Portraits of France
Writing On The Edge

Library of Congress Cataloging in Publication Data
Daley, Robert.

WRITING ON THE EDGE Title/Robert Daley.
Cover design: Leslie Daley

Cover photo:
The Monte Carlo parking lot after the Grand Prix:
Writing The Story. Photo by Robert Riger

WRITING ON THE EDGE

The Ups and Downs of a Freelance Career

A Memoir

ROBERT DALEY

Table of Contents:

Prologue

May 10, 2000, Nice, France

From my work room I can look down on the orange rooftops of this Riviera town, and at that segment of the blue, blue Mediterranean that slaps at its edge. We live in a big, airy apartment in a hundred year old former hotel, Victorian in style, built at a time when the English upper classes owned, or thought they owned, the French Riviera, a time when Queen Victoria had her court here part of each year. There are wedding cake ceilings in all our rooms, and a working fireplace in our bedroom that we have never used.

Nice is a place I never knew existed until I was twenty three years old. No one I knew in New York City, which is where I grew up and did every day of my schooling, had ever spoken to me about it, much less been here, but this is where, in any real sense of the word, I became a man: I was married here, I began my career here. Every lifespan is a series of improbabilities. Nonetheless, if you choose to consider my improbabilities, Nice might be an interesting one on which to start.

Today is my birthday, and my principal reaction at my new age, not unique to me I'm sure, is bafflement. How did such a thing ever happen? How did I not see it coming?

The year of my birth the world thought itself at peace even as the

Nazi party finished second in elections in Germany. This made Hitler so obviously a comer that an English translation of *Mein Kampf* was published; in Britain its profits went to the Red Cross. France, undeluded, began that year to build the Maginot Line, a row of impregnable forts along its border that surely would keep it forever safe from the German hordes.

In science, meanwhile, astronomers discovered a new planet they called Pluto, and an American, Wallace Carrothers, invented a new synthetic fiber called nylon. The depression was tightening its grip world wide but a baseball player named Babe Ruth signed a contract with the Yankees for $80,000 for the season, more money than the nation paid President Hoover; but then as Ruth put it, "I had a better year than he did."

Prohibition would not end for two more years, but people seemed to have plenty to drink, some of which they were said to concoct in bathtubs. Nearly every adult smoked, often two or more packs a day, and not filter tips either, as did a good many children; no one knew yet that nicotine was addictive. Everyone listened to the radio, and nearly everyone's favorite program was Amos and Andy. People laughed at the comical antics of these characters who were called Negroes then, or colored, not yet blacks or African-Americans, played by white actors. No one considered this a racist show, unless Blacks did, silently. Radio was big, and getting bigger.

Boxing was already incredibly big, no one talked of head injuries yet, the boxers were all white, and when Max Schmeling beat Jack Sharkey to win the heavyweight championship left vacant by the retirement of Gene Tunney, this was front page news all over the world. Greta Garbo starred in her first talkie, Anna Christie, and a song called "On The Sunny Side of the Street" topped the Hit Parade. It was the year in which the composer Stephen Sondheim was born, and the conductor Loren Maazel, not to mention Clint Eastwood, Steve McQueen, Joanne Woodward, Sean Connery and Robert Wagner, all of whom would grow up to be movie stars; also Neil Armstrong and Buzz Aldrin, who would grow up to walk on the moon. And in a hospital on 110th Street in Manhattan a 19 year old girl née Betty Blake gave birth to a ten pound boy who would grow up to be me. My father was a 25 year old sports reporter on *The New York Times* earning $75 a week, soon to be cut ten percent, as the depression lengthened, to $67.50. The focus of my life, the first part anyway, was preordained: sports, and *The New York Times*. And the Catholic Church. In time I went away from all three, but not right away.

My life span so far represents a good deal of past tense, most of my part of which is as vivid to me now as it was at each step, partly, or perhaps mostly, because of my trade. I have been over and over my life looking for scenes I could use, and I have found them and written them, some of them over and over; anyone who has read me has read a dozen versions of everything I ever heard, saw, tasted or experienced. Some of these scenes came out in fiction word for word as they had actually happened, and I will show you some examples later; I gave up long ago worrying about embarrassing myself, embarrassing others. No one would ever be able to tell what was fact and what I had made up, or so I told myself—again and again—and in any case the whole purpose of fiction was to present truth, was it not? A bigger, truer truth than real life, and to get to such a level of truth as that you must start close to your front door.

If an author's books are to have any value, and especially if they are to have lasting value, he must also have lived many lives, or so it seemed to me from the beginning and still does. He cannot afford just to sit in a room writing for forty or fifty years. If he does he will run out of invention, he will run out of resonance, and he won't continue to interest readers or continue to get contracts. Since a writer, just like everyone else, must support himself and his loved ones every day of his life, contracts are important. The writer's life is not all literary art. An awful lot of it is scrambling.

And so I have not sat in a room for forty or fifty years, or at least not the same room, but have lived a number of lives, more than other writers I have known. I have moved in some curious circles in a number of countries, and have known some strange people who were sometimes famous and sometimes not. I have been inside a number of particular worlds, often deep inside, worlds that were fascinating to me then and may be to you now if I can describe them well: pro football, treasure diving, opera, wine, the newspaper world of course, the movies, grand prix car racing, bullfighting. At crime scenes, during the time I was a New York police official, I could and did duck under the police lines, the better to get close to the victims and the spreading blood. Except for a few detectives, everyone else was outside.

The material that came from all these lives I have used. Not once but several times, as I have said.

As soon as I was old enough to read, I read. There were summer days when I read all day every day, until my father would come by, take the book away from me, and order me to go outside and play. Reading gave me such pleasure that I began to long to give such pleasure to others. At twelve I started to write my first novel. My father said I could use his typewriter if I would learn to type with all ten fingers, so I did. My novel reached 112 pages in length before I decided it was childish, and tore it up, but I knew I could do better next time, and from then on I never wanted to be anything but a writer.

Or, rather, I wanted to become the greatest writer who ever lived, an ambition that would seem to any 12 year old, not just me, not only worthwhile but also attainable. A kid's ambition, fierce, trusting, embarrassing when you look back, but rather touching, too. An ambition that is absolutely vital, I think: without it, or something akin to it, no one goes very far in any line of work.

Think of the past as a series of yesterdays that can be seen clearly at last—fairly clearly. One's triumphs and disasters lying there spread out on a table. They can be seen as if pickled, or half pickled, ready to be picked over. Yesterdays that once were linked together—now you can undo the links. The emotion now is different of course. The first time around, a writer—anybody, in fact—experiences life through a veil of suspense that sometimes approaches terror. Viewed from the rear this suspense is gone; therefore the terror is absent as well. One's past life is more likely to seem enthralling, even amusing. Often what terrified you then seems now to have been charming.

No, I never became the greatest writer who ever lived. But never mind, no one else ever did either, and I did have some successes; I published 28 books before this one, and much else as well, and there were a number of films made, some of which resembled my underlying book virtually word for word, and some not at all; one movie kept only four of my lines. These were spoken by a French actor named Yves Montand, a nice man, I liked him a lot, principally, I suppose, because he told me how much he had enjoyed my book. Fortunately we could talk to each other in French, which by then I spoke, because his accent in English was, to put it kindly, execrable. Not many viewers could have understood my four lines as Montand spoke them in the movie. That is, understood even that little bit of what I had worked a year or more to get down on paper.

For a while in Hollywood my books were in vogue, who knows why? Eight of them were bought outright, and six of the eight were filmed. Then the vogue ended, who knows why? But insofar as I became what counts, in the writing game, as a rich writer, it was the movies tha t did it, not the books.

I once appeared on a book panel with a man named Norman Podhoretz, the editor of Commentary and author of a kind of autobiography called "Making It." When the panel ended we each signed our books to the other.

In the flyleaf of mine, before signing it, and handing it to Norman, I wrote: "For Norman—no one ever makes it."

And no one ever does. The road up was hard. The road staying up was harder still, and I will tell you about some of it if you care to listen. James Michener once said: "You can make a killing as a writer, you just can't make a living." At different times I did both, and believe me, the one was much more fun than the other.

1.
No Girls Allowed

I went to the fiftieth reunion of my high school graduating class. I had never been to a reunion before, any kind of reunion, and had not intended to go to this one. You can't relive old memories, only ruin them, I felt, wrongly as it would turn out, for much deeper emotions were about to be stirred up than I had bargained for, and for some hours that reunion forced me to question my life.

When the committee chairman first phoned I told him I couldn't go, and gave some excuse. Then I got a second call from my best friend during those high school years. On graduation day, we swore the way boys do that we would never lose touch with each other, would be best friends always. But we went to different colleges, and then into military service on opposite sides of the world. About fifteen years later we did run into each other once, as accidental a meeting as ever there was, for it took place on a street corner in Switzerland, if you can believe it, both of us rushing in different directions, and that was that. One ten minute conversation since high school.

But he was going to the reunion, he said into the phone from New Jersey. Was I?

Our high school was Fordham Prep which since its inception had consisted of a single four-story building, about twenty classrooms for about 600 boys, on the Fordham University campus in the Bronx. The teachers were mostly Jesuit priests and scholastics, though there were a number of laymen too, Catholic laymen of course, most of them with big big families. My algebra teacher, who was also the swimming coach (and one of the great men in my life) had nine kids.

Fordham Prep was no preparatory school in the classic sense. It did not ready somewhat older boys for Harvard, Yale or some other prestigious place. Rather it was an ordinary high school, but run by Jesuits. We had four years of Latin every day, four of religion every day, two years of a modern language, plus math, history, science and the rest. Attendance at religious services in the University church was both mandatory and frequent, and most of us after graduation would not leave the campus at all but would go on to Fordham College, whose reputation at the time was not for studies but for football.

Since the late '20s the Fordham Rams had been one of the powerhouses of the country, all the Catholic colleges were, and the explanation for this was not hard to find. The great Fordham players were students named Ritinski and Jacunski, both ends, and Wojciechowicz, who played center and linebacker and who had the hardest of all these names to spell, and who is in the pro football hall of fame today—the sports writers learned to refer to him as Wojie; also Babartsky, who later changed his name to Bart, and Wiesnewski and Pieculewicz, a tough quarterback whose first name was the almost girlish Claude, and who succeeded the graduating Krywicki; and Filipowicz who later played linebacker for the football Giants and catcher for the baseball Giants, one of the few athletes ever to play at that level in both sports; and running backs like Cheverko, Andrejko, Ososki and my own personal favorite Eshmont, whose name at least everyone could pronounce, and who later played for the Giants and, after the war, for the Forty Niners. Eshmont, known as the Rapid Ram, was five-ten, 165 pounds—about average for the great college running backs of the period.

These were Catholic boys all, tough boys, most of them the sons of Polish coal miners from Pennsylvania which was where coaches from Fordham and the other Catholic colleges did most of their recruiting. This source later seemed to dry up, but it hadn't then, and so Fordham played home games in the Polo Grounds against the toughest opponents imaginable, won almost always, and because my father was a sports writer with access to free tickets, most of the home games when I was a boy I saw. Fordham went to the Cotton Bowl on New Years Day 1941 and lost, but won in the Sugar Bowl the following year. By then the war was on, the real war, the players went into the army, and football stopped, not to be resumed until 1947, when it started over, a freshman team only. But football at Fordham was never to be the same again, even though the freshman coach that year was Vince Lombardi, a Fordham boy himself, who would make a name for himself later.

Lombardi does not really come into this story yet, but will.

Shortly after I graduated from college Fordham dropped big time football forever.

When I got to the campus during the war we Prep boys had the use of much more than the one building. The university had virtually shut down. There were some military programs, and the college still had a few students with bad limps or real thick glasses, and the graduate school was populated mostly by nuns. As a result we were given the run of the place, the college gym, pool, cafeteria, and theater, and of course the church. There was a Prep marching band that was given former college instruments to play, and was outfitted in former college uniforms that were already going moldy. The uniforms had the letters F. U. emblazoned on the capes, but it was still the Prep band underneath, and after listening to its music one of my classmates joked: "They ought to change that F.U. to pee yew."

I thought those uniforms pretty snazzy, I had seen them marching up and down the Polo Grounds at half time, but I think my real motivation for what happened next was that I wanted to become a big man on campus. Now 13 years old, weighing just over 100 pounds, and knowing nothing about music, any kind of music, I decided to go out for band. Specifically, I put myself down as a cymbals player. I was accorded one of those uniforms, and for about a week marched along in practice parades banging the cymbals together whenever I felt like it. At the end of that week I was relieved of my instrument(s) and uniform by the moderator, who suggested that I might find it more congenial if I went out for something else.

Driving onto the campus for the reunion I could have found the old Prep building blindfolded, but there was a new one now, I didn't know where it was and so had to ask directions. I had to be shown where to park also. As I walked from my car to the Prep building a strange emotion began to set in that I wasn't prepared for. I wasn't walking back into the past, I told myself, and yet I was.

The old Prep building had been in the heart of the campus; the new one was down by the Metro North railroad tracks, known as the New York Central tracks in my day. It was big and modern-looking from the outside, not fake Gothic like most of the rest of the buildings, and inside it had its own cafeteria which was where our reunion was to start off. There was a desk by the door manned by 16 year-old boy students, still no girls here, who checked us off as we entered and stuck name tags to our lapels. Having to wear a name tag had always seemed to me a good enough reason to avoid reunions, but now I submitted, and when I turned around I saw that there were about sixty of us in the room already, out of a class of probably twice that, all men of the same age, and as I glanced around, the first individual I perceived was John Nowak. He was gray-haired and walking with a cane, and he looked, as always, lonely. The sight of him caused me to experience a burst of shame that I also was not prepared for.

In senior year Nowak had played quarterback on the football team, and I found myself remembering a game against one of our arch rivals, St. Francis Xavier, I think. I doubted he had forgotten that day, or ever would. I know I hadn't. Probably it had been eating at him for fifty years.

At that age boys vie with each other to bait their teachers, if they think they can get away with it, and though most of us did not dare bait one of the Jesuits, the lay teachers were fair game, and woe to any of them too young, weak or unsure to put a stop to the baiting at once.

Across the room I spied such a teacher now, Martin Hessian. Since he was here, still walking around, he couldn't have been much older than we were back then, a recent college graduate most likely, a young man with acne scars on his face, and immediately the rumor circulated that his problem was syphilis. This rumor was launched by one of the boys of course, which one I do not know, but certainly one of the cleverer ones, and ever afterwards Mr. Hessian was known to us as Syph Marty the Great. Not to his face, obviously, but he must have overheard it at some point.

One day a boy named Bothner put a snake in Mr. Hessian's chalk drawer before class.

Syph Marty came in and opened the drawer. And stepped back rigid, unable to move.

How we laughed at that one.

At least Hessian had been old enough to take care of himself, or should have been. But Nowak out there on the football field was only 16.

Any boy who did not bait such teachers as were baitable, any boy who cozied up to one of them, who was even seen talking to one outside the classroom, was called by the other boys an ass kisser, and since the word ass was considered a risqué word at that time, even a dirty word, this was usually shortened to A.K. So-and-so's an A.K. It was the worst label that could be hung on a boy by his classmates. One had to perform very many disreputable acts to overcome such a stigma.

The football game took place on what had been the college practice field behind the college gym. There were bleachers to one side, and since this was the make or break game of the season, these were full. There may have been a thousand people present. Most of the student body was there, and most of the Jesuits who resided in Faculty Hall, plus parents, alumni, even the girlfriends of any of the boys who knew a girl well enough to ask for a date.

Nowak was an earnest, dogged kind of boy but, however hard he tried, only a second stringer until this particular day when, because another boy had been hurt, he was being given his big chance. He wasn't exactly making the most of it. His passes were too short or too long, and when he tried running plays they were thrown back. We were losing the game.

And now the chant went up: N-O-W...***A.K***. Accent on the final two letters. N-O-W...***A.K***. What seemed like a thousand voices in unison. Over and over again. The parents present may have thought this was some kind of applause. Poor Nowak could have been under no such illusion, and although he never looked toward the bleachers, and appeared outwardly to take no notice, this repeated chanting by his classmates, as it grew ever stronger and more raucous, seemed to make him frantic. He wasn't throwing passes anymore, he was flinging them, and when he tried to run the ball himself he was thrown for huge losses.

"N-O-W...***A.K***."

A.K. Ugly, destructive. It echoed and echoed: ***A.K***.

Some of us were giggling so much we could hardly chant.

Who started this chant, which lasted off and on for the rest of the game, I do not know, but I took part in it. Willingly. And afterwards laughed and laughed. It was even funnier than the snake in Mr. Hessian's chalk drawer.

How long does a public humiliation of that kind stay with a 16 year old boy? How does he ever come back from it?

I did not know the answer to this question, and I looked across the room at the gray haired man leaning on his cane and felt ashamed. I thought of going over and apologizing for my part in that afternoon, but Nowak and I had been in different sections, took no classes together, we weren't pals, didn't even know each other very well. So I merely gazed across at him but did nothing, never spoke to him then, nor the rest of the day, except that at some point we said hello to each other and as we shook hands I noticed him reading my name off my name tag.

Could I have said something? What? How can one apologize fifty years after the fact?

Instead I joined a group of men whose conversation, it turned out, concerned the Korean War. This was our war, insofar as we had one. The war nobody remembers. The invisible war. No one else ever talks of it, and I can't remember ever doing so myself after it ended. The group I had joined contained my once best friend, Joe Armas, and Ken Flavia, and Ned Curran who had been on the high school paper with me, and later on the college paper as well. Armas had been a B-26 pilot in Korea, he said, which I hadn't known. Flavia had been an Air Force pilot too, and this surprised me because in school he was considered a fruity guy. Fruit was the big word then. Haven't heard it since. When it became my turn to speak I admitted I had been in the Air Force too, but had spent most of my time helping edit the base newspaper in Ohio.

Next to me Ned Curran said he hadn't served at all. Rheumatic heart.

I hadn't expected Ned to be here today. I hadn't heard from him or of him in many, many years, and given his heart history imagined he must have died. Several years after college he and I went to Europe together, traveling third class in a cabin for eight on D deck, on a rusty Italian tub called the *Saturnia.* The sea was rough all the way. It took fourteen wallowing days to get from New York to the French Riviera. At first the ship's corridors had smelled of rust and diesel fuel, which is a sickening enough mixture, but which, with the ship pitching this way and that, soon got overlaid by the rich aroma of vomit. There were corridors that got too slippery to walk.

In Nice I met a French girl that first day, and a day or two later Ned fell down in the street from a heart attack. He was 24 years old. Soon after being released from the British-American Hospital on the Basse Corniche he went back to America. Thoroughly enamored of the French girl I stayed on alone. Ned and I didn't talk about any of this today, I don't know why. It may be that the discrepancy of our two experiences made the subject difficult for him. For me too, perhaps.

Lunch was served, but not cocktails—which is what everyone drank way back then—which were promised for supper. At lunch there was water only. This is not important in itself perhaps, a detail, but it is such details that define the culture of a time and place, define a lifetime, a history. Nearly always such details, which seem tiny, are lost to history, which is a pity. Any writer, any artist, knows where the emotions are: in the details. Tiny doesn't matter. A writer spends a lifetime collecting them.

At lunch I didn't recognize some of the men, the bald ones, the fat ones. Kilsheimer was now so tall; he had been a little guy. Meise was short and fat then, now he was thin and almost as tall as I.

I was interested in all of them, where they had been, who was still working, who not. A strong emotion, a kind of love, seemed to flow through this cafeteria. It was as if we all imagined we had liked each other so much back then, though of course we hadn't. But for four years we were here together, not in this exact room of course, but part of each other's lives for four years, and I assume everyone remembered nearly every day of it, I know I did, the way you remember your grandmother's phone number from when you were a small boy.

"We were so alike," someone said across the table.

"There were not even any elective subjects then to separate us," said someone else.

"Four years of Latin," said the first man, "who's going to believe that now?"

"We're not old," I said, for this is what I was determined to believe.

To which Ned Curran replied: "We're old, Bob."

In those days the world around us seemed such a safe secure place. The truth was known, we were told every day. All we had to do was pay attention and it would be imparted to us. Then we came out and found a world as unknown as it must have seemed to Columbus—suddenly so much bigger. And as we talked about this now, we were trying, I soon realized, to comprehend time. Which is impossible.

We talked of the one or two classmates who had been killed in Korea, and of the several others known to have died. We talked of others who were not present, though still alive, as far as anyone knew. Henning was remembered for bringing the prettiest girls to the school dances, the rest of us hardly knowing any girls at all, so where did he find them? And Vredenburg, who had been the smartest kid in the class, best marks anyway, and the only non-Catholic. Voted most likely to succeed. Seen many years later working as a clerk in an office. No one knew what had happened to him since. If he was a clerk at fifty he couldn't have done much better after that, could he?

I hadn't intended to stay past lunch, but I stayed, and in the afternoon went for a long slow walk through the campus with the Prep's president (he's not called the principal anymore) a gray-haired Jesuit of whom I would have been terrified fifty years previously. His name was Joe Parkes and as we walked, as he pointed out what was new, he twice dropped hints about money. That's the purpose of these reunions, I guess: to raise money. This seemed such an obvious idea that I wondered why it hadn't come to me sooner. Parkes sounded like a good fund raiser. The principals of my boyhood must have been good too. That's probably why they were chosen, not to terrify us kids, and this was another idea that had never occurred to me until now.

I only half listened to Father Parkes, for my thoughts were elsewhere, and they made me uncomfortable. To begin with, everything looked different. On this campus I knew so well, I was having trouble orienting myself. Entire vistas were cut off by new buildings, entry to which was restricted by security guards. Security guards had not existed in my time, not here and almost not anywhere.

The elm trees along the paths looked unchanged. The elms had survived better than some of the ideas that were inculcated in us here. This place, although we hadn't realized it back then, had always been an enclave cut off from the world around it. Nonetheless, it was here I had put down my roots, and now I had come back to them. As I walked along I could almost feel them extending down into the earth, and I could no more pull them up than I could uproot one of the great trees. Everything that happened to me afterwards was rooted here. I was rooted here. They get you young and they form you, and some of it you can throw off later—the incidentals only. You can forget the Latin, stop thinking that priests are special beings, you can quit going to mass, but most of the rest of it is there until you die. All that was important is there until you die: you can't shake the need to distinguish between good and evil, nor the sense of duty and of discipline, the notion that there is a right thing to do in any given situation and you must do it—all this, and much else too, is in there forever.

An hour later a 16 year old guide provided by Father Parkes showed a group of us through the new Prep building, stopping first at the computer room. There were 120 computer posts, he said. How long did it take a kid like him to learn computers, we asked. We had many questions for him, but that was the first of them, for it had taken us, coming to computers late, ages of hard, hard learning to grasp how they worked, and if we went away for a month, on vacation say, we tended to forget most of it by the time we came back. Did kids forget also? This kid's answers were of course unsatisfactory; he didn't appear to know what we were talking about, or why. So we talked to each other, and Dr. Carroll said he had refused to learn computers, wouldn't have anything to do with them. Fat Gerry Carroll from fifty years ago, almost unchanged now except he was a doctor with white hair.

The guide walked us into the gymnasium, a sparkling place, high-ceilinged, regulation sized. An astonishing place to us, compared to what we had known, for on the ground floor of the old Prep building there had been two exceptionally narrow basketball courts, half width, actually, whose baskets were ten feet high as baskets are supposed to be, under a ceiling that was twelve feet high. This made for quite a problem. If we wanted to score we had to shoot line drives. That is, the apex of the shot had to fit between the ceiling and the rim, which sounds impossible to me now, and sometimes proved to be then. I started to tell the kid about playing on our low ceiling courts, but turned away from him when I realized what I was doing. What would he know or care about how basketball was for us?

Instead I asked him if the old pool still existed? This had been a cold, clammy place whose ceiling also was very low.

"You mean the dungeon?" the kid said.

On my way over to it I stopped at the old Prep building. How small it seemed for so many unruly boys. It had seemed big enough then, of course. I went in and glanced around. There used to be a trophy case lining the staircase all the way up, but it was gone. It had contained many trophies, a dozen or more of which I had helped win, and I wondered what had happened to them. What do you do with fifty year old athletic trophies?

The old pool is in the old college gym, relics both. Why did I want to see it again? I knew exactly what it would look like, smell like. To get to it I had to walk down a corridor lined with rows of plaques honoring the heroes of Fordham's past, not only all those boys with Polish names, but newer heroes I had never heard of. There were plaques also in the names of big donors to athletic programs, as if they were equally important, which perhaps they were.

An attendant let me into the pool, and as I gazed around I tried to make small talk with him. The pool hadn't been heated in my day, I told him, but this comment failed to arouse his interest. "It is now, I see," I told him. But he was picking his nose. You can certainly tell when someone's not interested, can't you? I thanked him, and left.

When I got back a movie was being shown—newsreels from our four Prep years that someone had spliced together. Eisenhower talking about some illness he was having. He was head of NATO at the time. I was a bit late and didn't hear it all. Didn't remember any such illness. Of course Eisenhower wasn't important to me that year. We didn't know he would one day be president, and wouldn't have cared. Later, when he was in the White House, he got sick twice more, and we came to know more about his insides than his outsides. Next came part of one of Truman's State of the Union addresses. A great president perhaps, but a droning, monotonous voice. I had forgotten. Scenes of actors testifying before the un-American Activities Committee. Field Marshal Montgomery on a tour shaking hands with Stalin in Moscow. The young actor Jimmy Stewart asking Americans to eat less to feed the starving world.

Before dinner there was to be a mass. I hadn't intended to go, but went. Padded knee rests now. Chapel so much more handsome than I remembered. Much standing now, minimum of kneeling. I was assailed by memories of Father Shea, the prefect of discipline. During the interminable masses in this place he would patrol the aisles signaling us to kneel up straight, and never mind the way the edge cut into the soft part of our knees. One of the masses we were compelled to attend was the so called Mass of the Holy Ghost at the start of each school year. An account of this mass was also the mandatory lead article each year in the Rampart, the school newspaper, and we editors once discussed running the Holy Ghost's picture on the front page. It would be a blank space, of course, and under it would be the caption: H. Ghost.

We could be irreverent about our religion from time to time, but there is no question that we believed it. Believed it all. How could we not?

The mass was in English now. Piano and guitars played. The names of the dead from our class were read out. Hymns were sung, new ones I guess, for I only knew one of them. One of the celebrants was the Rev. Gregory Lyttle, son of my swimming coach. I didn't know him, and hadn't spoken to him. But I looked at him up there on the altar and wished I had come back to the Prep at least once over the years to see his father, to tell his father how much he had meant to my life. But I didn't know enough to do this, and then he died.

Holy Communion was distributed by my former classmate, Father Joe Neville. Except for weddings and funerals I hadn't attended a church service in thirty or more years. After hesitating I went up to the altar rail and received, though I hardly knew how to do it anymore. No need for fasting from midnight these days, or even confession. You don't even have to be Catholic, I'm told. Neville nodded and smiled at me. He was a randy kid. He used to bring salacious poems to class. Poems certain to cause impure thoughts. Straight arrow that I was I wouldn't look at them. Of course at that age everything causes impure thoughts. After graduation, aged 17, Neville went into the seminary. When I talked to him later he seemed happy with his lot. A number of his side teeth were missing, I noted. I called him Joe, not Father, but didn't dare ask him how his life had been for fear the question itself, reminding him of all he might have missed, might make him unhappy.

An hour later I came out into the vivid night. The grass under the lampposts was vividly green, the air could be smelt. I found my car and drove home.

2.
Venice, Virginity and Religion

May 17, 2000. The Grand Canal, Venice.

I am in a hotel room in Venice. It is very early. Behind me Peggy is still asleep. I fold the shutters back, and peer out at the lagoon. In the dawn light it is smooth as glass. Directly below is a promenade, a few isolated figures crossing it, men on their way to work, perhaps. Later, when the tourists have swarmed you won't be able to see the pavement for the shoes.

From behind the Lido an edge of sun suddenly peeps up. A moment later it strikes the surface of the water turning it red, a glancing blow at first, then with great force.

Presently work boats appear—first one, then several. They begin to slice up the water. One of the wakes curves in toward this hotel and ties up. An open barge. Carts are pushed up close, and bags of garbage are heaved down into the barge. The barge withdraws and a scow ties up. Men begin off-loading trays and boxes of produce

The delivery trucks of Venice at work early. There are no *vaporettos* yet, no gondolas. Work boats only.

A week has gone by since the last time I wrote in this journal, and I don't seem to be doing much writing now. To write takes a great deal of time during most of which an author's fingers don't move because nothing is happening in his head, nothing. This is something all authors know, but most people don't.

Mostly I have been standing at the window this past hour, only occasionally turning to put down the lines you have just read. A writer can choose his words just as well in a window as at a table, but in either place they most often present themselves in no usable sequence. Before they can be of use they must be untangled. There is a rhyme in one of the songs in Candide (lyrics by the poet Richard Wilbur, music by Leonard Bernstein) that has always charmed me and I once quoted it back at Wilbur: "Afford it and aboard it," I told him, "Where do you get such rhymes."

The poet answered: "You...wait."

We writers all wait. I have worked eight hours a day nearly every working day of my career. I have kept hours no different from any honest laborer, but an entire day's output—a good day's output—could probably be typed up in twenty minutes.

A short distance down the promenade another work boat has been moored to the pier. From its stern a crane has unfolded itself. It begins lifting bed linens and towels in great racks down onto the promenade. The racks are on rollers, and I watch men roll them toward the famous hotels down the line.

The month of May is by no means high season here. Nonetheless the city seems to me clogged with tourists, most of them in groups, sometimes huge groups. Sixty or more, all following a single guide. You can't get past them to get over the bridges. The guides have a trick, I have noted. They carry a furled umbrella high above their heads. Their groups follow the umbrella, not the guide. One guide yesterday, a woman, had stuck a rose in the umbrella's ferrule. No doubt her group had learned to ignore all the other hoisted umbrellas, and to zero in on the rose. There are of course no hills in Venice. The highest peaks, the Everests of the town, are the crowns of the bridges over the canals. Whenever a guide's group gets too dispersed, he or she stands on the crown of a bridge, umbrella upthrust, and waits for sixty or more people to gather round. Fine idea, but all other traffic, us, for instance, can't cross the bridge until they finally move on.

Why do people want to travel in groups anyway, especially such huge groups?

For safety, of course. For help with the menu as well. Obvious enough reasons. But Venice, a city that wants and needs tourists, wants more and more of them. It must be the most user friendly place on earth. Safety? It is impossible to get lost here, and there are no ruffians in sight. Nearly everyone with whom a tourist comes in contact has some English, and most of the menus I've seen are written not only in Italian and English, but in German and French as well. Is there danger of being mugged, raped? As one who was well acquainted with crime and criminals at one stage of my life, I would say: not much. Can there be other problems to confront? Certain ones, yes. Italy is a place where taxi drivers (gondola drivers here) will charge you preposterous fares if they can. Also you must always count your change. But in such areas as these a guide is not much help.

To me, to Peggy as well, the idea of group travel is unattractive to the point of being inconceivable. Of course we have been to Venice before, been most places (at least in Europe) before. We both have two languages, and parts of two others, so obviously my comments are not entirely fair. But more than this we also know how to find what interests us; that is, we know how to read guide books. We don't need guides with memorized spiels. We don't need to be herded into places whether we want to go there or not. Most of all we don't need to wait in a pack on top of bridges, trying to spot one upraised umbrella out of several.

Venice, May 18.

Yesterday, thirty minutes before the basilica San Marco opened, a line began to form outside. In the course of the day I came back from time to time, but the lines had only got longer. Finally the lines were gone, but by then it was late afternoon and the basilica had closed for the day.

Earlier, I had discovered a side entrance. It had a guard on duty, and according to a sign posted over his head, it was restricted to worshipers who wished to enter to pray.

That's me, I told myself, thinking that once inside I could gawk to my heart's content at the basilica's mosaics, some of which date from before 1100 AD.

My hands clasped in prayer as if I was still the altar boy I once had been, I went in past the guard. He seemed to look at me balefully, but he let me pass.

I found myself in a badly lit chapel in one of the apses. About forty people were present in pews, and a mass was in progress. The chapel, I saw, was cut off from the rest of the church by barriers, the far side of which was patrolled by a sacristan or guard or whatever he was. Up and down he marched. Getting out into the rest of the church was not going to be easy, it seemed. In the meantime the mass continued.

So here I was in a church again, gawking at those mosaics I could see, though the light was bad, and attending mass in a manner of speaking, and as I waited to see if the guard/sacristan would go away I tried to equate the Italian words of the priest on the altar to responses I had had to memorize as a little kid desperate to become an altar boy. When I started I was about eight years old. I wanted to wear the red and white cassock and serve at mass.

Catholicism has changed a good deal in the years since, how much I do not really know. How is it being taught these days? Is it still as sin oriented, or perhaps hell oriented would be more accurate, as it was then? The Catholicism I learned was extremely sex oriented as well, I have since come to believe. But then sex, sin and hell go very well together, always have, and since time began the priests of every religion have always tried to exert control, first of all, over the bedroom. Now, as I stood peering out into the basilica proper at dim mosaics, I began to remember without even trying some of the regulations my black-robed teachers preached to me and my schoolmates. They were celibate men one and all, or at least they were supposed to be, and some of the metaphors they got off were designed to impress us forever, and did so. They certainly impressed me, for I have remembered them all these years.

If one committed a mortal sin, and died unshriven, one went straight to hell for all eternity. This was dogma, and seemed obvious to us all, and was the bedrock of Catholic teaching, but how were we boys to understand what a mortal sin was, what eternity was? Well, missing mass on Sunday or eating meat on Friday were of course mortal. Straight to hell for either one. Then came murder, grand larceny, idolatry, and coveting ones neighbor's wife, sins so far beyond the reach of most of us that not much time was spent on them. Under murder came fighting, a venial sin, and under larceny came petty theft, also venial.

Adultery was another story. The sixth commandment was by far the heaviest of the ten, we were made to feel. Adultery itself was scarcely mentioned, but under it came all other sexual sins of whatever kind, from impure thoughts to fornication. Presumably one could tell if he was about to fornicate, and could probably prevent it if he wished, but impure thoughts could come upon a boy unbidden, and once in his head it was hard to keep them at bay: any sexual thought was of course impure. I once heard someone describe the Catholic Church as an organization that tried to police people's thoughts—an idea that never occurred to me in those days. Control the boy's thoughts and you control the boy. And after him the man, most likely.

My last year in high school we all went on a spiritual retreat to the Jesuit retreat house at Mount Manresa on Staten Island. The retreat would occupy three days, was obligatory, and I was concerned because there was to be a championship swimming meet that Saturday, and I did not think I could afford to miss three days of practice.

The retreat turned out to be an intoxicating experience, though it was some years before I was able to discern why I had found it so. It was sex of course. For three days we engaged in the frankest discussion of sex any of us had ever had. For three days the heat was turned way up.

Now it must be understood that in the circles most of us frequented sex was most often accorded absolute silence. There were no nudie magazines then; *Playboy* and its imitators did not yet exist. Sex was never mentioned in polite families, and many girls, and boys too, received no sexual instruction whatever. The vulgar words so common today were never used in mixed company. The silence surrounding sex was compounded by the songs teenagers loved—adults too—such as *Don't Sit Under the Apple Tree With Anyone Else But Me*, as if apple trees was all there was to it. There were many such songs. It was compounded too by the movies which dominated the popular culture of the day. Out in Hollywood the Legion of Decency, a censorship group that ruled on whether specific films could be seen by Catholics, came into existence, and there began to be films like the syrupy Going My Way, in which Bing Crosby and Barry Fitzgerald played priests, and which swept the Oscars in 1944. The Hollywood studios were run one and all by Jewish moguls, many of them immigrants from more sophisticated countries, but these men had caved in totally to the Legion. For a film to get a good rating, essential if it was to make a profit, they believed, certain rules had to be followed. Double beds could not be shown, much less married couples getting into them. Kisses could not last more than a second or two, and the mouths must be closed. Sinners must always be punished in the last reel, and the word whore could not be used. A bad girl was called a tramp. I remember not being able to figure out what the word was trying to convey. Many other ordinary English words, pregnancy for one, were equally proscribed.

This was the mood of the country then, and since it reinforced the perceptions we were given in our all-boys Catholic school, it was difficult to see past it. Most of us, incidentally, had never sat in classrooms with girls in our lives, and never would.

And so the three day spiritual retreat was something new because in order to come down hard on sexual sins, it was necessary for the priest leading each discussion to enumerate and describe them. This was exciting enough, but some of the boys then asked exciting questions. What about soul kissing, one boy wanted to know. The obvious answer came back: mortal sin. What about peeking in through the bathhouse window where a girl might be getting into her swim suit? "Looking upon the unclothed body of an adult female is a mortal sin," the priest replied. How about touching your girl friend on the, you know, sweater? Well, most of us didn't have any girl friends, but the idea was nice, even though the answer, as we had expected, was the same as all the others so far. A girl's chest was sacred, it seemed. What about artificial insemination, another boy asked. Where this idea came from I do not know, we were all of us 16 years old that year, but I remember the priest's answer to this day: "The emission of seed is always a mortal sin except inside the body of your own wife and not wearing a protector."

To us, pretty racy stuff.

Virginity was a big subject too. This priest and others considered that virginity before marriage was essential, not only for girls, but for us boys too. A girl must guard her precious virginity, her holy purity, above all things, and so must we. Your chaste bride will love you even more for having been chaste too, we were told. A girl who came to you in marriage, having lost her virginity previously, being therefore less than pure, less than chaste, was a lesser package than you had hoped for and deserved. It might be impossible to continue to love her once you found out, or to trust her to be faithful, and these heavy notions, I see now, were likely to cause some of us heartache in the future. Certainly they governed our conduct for a time, and even now, with grown daughters of my own, the echo of them remains. To put it crudely, they were telling us we had to get into a girl's pants before anyone else did, or be seriously diminished. In a world where sexual morality seems to have turned 180 degrees teaching of this kind may seem difficult to believe, but there it was.

On the subject of sex the priests at the retreat (and others elsewhere) spoke always with fervor, and they were categorical. It was categorically impossible, it seemed, to commit a venial sin where sex was involved. Venereal pleasure—that was the technical name we were given—was everywhere and always mortally sinful. Become dead following venereal pleasure and you went straight to hell. For all eternity.

And what was eternity?

On the dais the Jesuit in his black cassock seemed to be searching for a metaphor. And he found one. Found it so quickly he must have used it on every graduating class for the past twenty years. "Imagine the planet earth enlarged a thousand times and made not out of dirt and rock and water, but of reinforced concrete," he told us. "Then imagine a bird, a tiny bird, that flies by every hundred years and brushes the planet with its wing. When the day comes that the wing of this tiny bird has entirely worn away our thousand times larger, reinforced concrete planet, well, on that particular day eternity will be just beginning."

To illustrate his point further he told us the following story. It seems that a certain girl allowed herself to be seduced by her boy friend. They did this deed beside their car parked off the road. When they had finished, and got to their feet, the girl remarked to the boy: "I don't think I've ever committed a mortal sin before." They were still brushing themselves off, when a car came over the hill at great speed and killed her. Not only did that girl go straight to hell for all eternity for the only mortal sin she had ever been guilty of, but her boy friend had to live the rest of his life knowing he had sent her there.

This impressed all of us, the fornication aspect and the eternity aspect both. Even on the second and third hearing, in fact. For it turned out to be a favorite of several of the priests over the years, and each one, upon coming to the end, always swore that he knew the story to be true, the seduced girl had actually been killed and gone to hell just that way.

Three days of sky high libido and no swimming practice, but on Saturday I won two gold medals anyway.

Now in this thousand year old basilica in Venice the priest turned from the altar and launched into a sermon. In Italian obviously. My hearing is not what it was, nor my Italian either, and I didn't get much of it, apart from the operatic words, the ones sung in every aria. Per pieta. Patria mia. Andiamo. Addio. Either of the last two would have been a good idea, but I couldn't walk out on the man while he was speaking, and from time to time, it seemed, staring directly at me, as if he could tell I had no business there. Also, although the guard/sacristan appeared determined to stay where he was for the duration of the mass, he might yet wander off, allowing me to step over the barrier and see the rest of the mosaics.

Anyway, I stayed, and since I wasn't captivated by the sermon my mind went off again.

The same kind of teaching had continued into college. It got a little subtler, perhaps, but not much. I could have had a swimming scholarship to Yale, then the national powerhouse in the sport. I went there to meet the coach, who wanted me, and a Yale degree on my resume might have given me a leg up in life. But my parents were locked into their sports/Catholic world. They knew nothing about legs up, and so I was sent to Fordham. I moved to the other side of the campus—there was very little other change. We were not allowed electives until the final two years, at which time I opted for English Literature as my major. However, courses in Scholastic Philosophy were mandatory, these occupied eight hours a week, and my English courses when I added them up totaled only seven.

Scholasticism was the work of St. Thomas Aquinas, an Italian theologian in Paris, who figured out about thirty proofs of the existence of God, and went on from there. Thomas died in 1274, having also proved, or those teaching these courses believed him to have proved, the existence of a natural law which governed all things and all beings. The natural law was particularly applicable to sexual matters. For instance, birth control, which frustrated the purpose of a natural act, was for this reason everywhere and always a great evil and (again) a mortal sin. Masturbation, which I had not yet practiced, was also an unnatural act, an evil act, as evil as any other unnatural act, such as, say, murder. Evil is evil and there are no degrees to it, we were led to understand.

Well—

As graduation approached we were also told that we were about to go out into real life. Most of us, I believed then and still believe, had not yet, as the euphemism has it, known woman. There was much else we did not know either, but out in real life, we were also told, it was important to bear witness to our faith every day in every way we could think of. The Korean War was now on, and real life for most of us was going to be the army. Two weeks after graduation I was a private in south Georgia in a barracks inhabited, apart from me, exclusively by red neck World War II veterans who had been kicked out by 1946 but who, because of this new war, had been allowed to come back in. These re-enlistees were again enjoying the best job they had ever had. They were a rough lot, foul mouthed, raucous, and when night came I knelt down beside my bed to say my prayers, deliberately bearing witness to my faith as I had been instructed to do, and the barracks noise stopped instantly, not a sound, not a movement, until I had finished and stood up again. I did this a few more nights to much less effect, and then, figuring I had borne enough witness, stopped.

Up on the altar the sermon seemed endless, which surprised me. It wasn't Sunday, wasn't a feast day. It was an ordinary Wednesday in May. To walk out on the sermon seemed out of the question. The congregation was too small, there was no way the priest could overlook me as I left. Meanwhile, I could see that the day was waning fast, for in the main part of the church the mosaics were fading out. Even if I could escape this pen I was in I wouldn't be able to see much of them now.

At last the sermon ended. Not until the priest resumed the mass did I feel I could sidle toward the door. When I had sneaked out into what was left of the sunlight I cursed myself—and not for the first time in my life—for having behaved tonight like such a jerk.

Morning again, though later than yesterday. Sunny, hot. The *vaporettos* are already carving up the lagoon. Through our window we can hear the town. Peggy is packing. It won't take her long, for we don't have much with us. I've already paid the bill. In a few minutes we will board the No. 78 *vaporetto* for the ride down the canal to where our car is parked, and we will drive home. Nice is under six hours away, but we will stop somewhere for lunch, possibly Cremona which has a medieval cathedral we've never seen.

People sometimes ask why we keep an apartment in Europe, why we spend so much time here. The easy answer is because a writer, as they say, can write anywhere, so why not. Of course you have to have achieved a certain level of success to pay for it, and such a level is rare among writers, even so called "successful" ones. Most writers can't afford to give up their day jobs, much less live half the year abroad.

But the pleasures to us are considerable. Italy is so close, and in the other direction Spain, with France all around us. There are so many places to go, so much to see. But there is more to it than that. When I was a private in Georgia I hated being there, hated the red earth and the flatness, the thin pine trees and brown rivers, the southern accents. I hated all that was different from what I was used to. I wanted to leave but, unless I wished to go to prison, couldn't. In a very real sense I was a prisoner, and felt myself one, and I swore that once I got home I would never go anywhere again. But I served at two other bases after that, and when I was discharged I went with two pals to live in Mexico for two months, climbed Popocatepetl, which is 17,887 feet high, and started on a novel which I later finished but which is still in a drawer somewhere, as it deserves to be. I also looked for short stories I might write, and then tried to write them, but they were never to be published either.

Six months after that, realizing that I was not nearly as hooked on home as I had once imagined, I sailed for Europe for the first time. It took every cent I had ever saved. Once there I wrote more short stories that were never to be published. More importantly, I met the girl in Nice I mentioned earlier. It was mid afternoon, my first day in France. I was sipping Coca Cola at the bar in her father's place. It was not the dinner hour. The restaurant tables were empty. Her mother was at the cash desk. There was a barman behind the bar. And she came in through the door. Josette Peggy Ernest. I was never introduced to her. I introduced myself. We began spending every day together and three months later, on no money, we got married. And my whole world opened up.

To be a writer, at least the type of writer I hoped to become, I knew I would have to learn a lot, and quickly. I was trying to grow up as fast as I could, I was trying to learn, and the best way to do this would be, it seemed to me, to keep myself perpetually off balance, for that is when one's powers of observation are at their keenest. One is scrambling the whole time, and it is all so vivid it sticks. I didn't actually decide on this as a way of life, I only realized afterwards that it's what I was doing; there's nothing better than a foreign country for throwing a man off balance, for keeping him on his nerves. You have to live in the foreign place though. You can't simply be passing through.

And so we have kept a life in America, and a life here too. It has become habit, and I would not want it any other way.

3.
Six Seasons with the Giants

July 26, 2000, Albany, New York

Training Camp. The State University campus. The offensive players wear blue jerseys, the defense white. The quarterbacks wear yellow so that no one will smash into them by mistake. They are not so much people as finely tuned, expensive and oh so fragile machines. Money rides on them, millions. The season. Careers too. The careers of all of the coaches, certainly. Of some players. Even certain front office personnel, probably. Ordinary young men can blast into each other if they like, but when they come near the quarterbacks they stop. The game turns into touch football.

I watch all this, and much that I see excites me, but I feel terribly uncomfortable too, as if I have no right to be here. From time to time the players and the things they do, take me out of myself. I had forgotten how hard quarterbacks throw the ball, and how flat. I had forgotten how loudly the ball slaps into hands. I had forgotten the violence with which punters punt the ball, the speed of the leg action, the height to which the ball rises.

My discomfort comes from something else, and at first I am not sure what it is.

When I was 23 years old I became Publicity Director of this team. Do not be impressed with this as a title, although I was. Letterheads were printed up with New York Football Giants on top, and under that the new director's name, mine. The job had never existed before, and I had never held any job before. Being the first Publicity Director the team had ever had, or felt any need for, wasn't what I wanted, but I thought because of the title it might lead to something. Magazine editors might get to know my name, might buy something I wrote. Pro football as a subject might entice someone. I wanted to be a writer and that's all I wanted to be. I needed to get published any way I could.

Pro football was then at a low ebb, unlike now, and the Giants, who would win only three games all season, were at an even lower one. Although other teams had had full time publicity men for years, and some had staffs, the Giants' had made do on a part-time basis with one or another of the sportswriters who covered the team—the year I arrived it was the turn of Joe King of the World-Telegram. If the Giants needed a press release, Joe King would come in and write it.

Then I was hired. I was the Publicity Director, not Joe, but he stood at my back, and was paid, I believe, the same salary as always. Of course I didn't want him there, but it would be some time before anyone was confident enough about me to move him out. So among the disadvantages with which I started was not only Joe King, but what he symbolized. My presence was going to cost certain of the men who covered the Giants, my very clientele so to speak, money.

I got paid $65 a week. Not great, but I had been in no position to hold out for more. My mother was tired of listening to my typewriter clacking all day upstairs as I wrote one unpublished opus after another. She had told me I had to get a job. She wanted me out of the house.

I had recently finished my first attempt at a full scale novel. It was about a young man like me who finds himself a private on a base in Georgia. An editor at Random House whom my father knew, a man named Saxe Commins, had read it and had sent back the kindest possible letter of rejection which I, however, refused to accept for what it was. I tore the letter to shreds. Wanting to hear him explain himself, if he could, to my face, I phoned him and he agreed to see me. William Faulkner was leaving his office as I was going in, and he introduced us.

"Oh Mr. Faulkner," I said, "I've read three of your books."

To which the great man replied: "You're young yet."

Commins encouraged me to keep trying, even promised to read the manuscript again if I rewrote it, and then sent me on my way. He was really a very kind man, much kinder than I realized at the time.

So I had had to get a job, Publicity Director of the Giants was the only offer I had, and at length I took it. I thought it had two major advantages. The grand title, which at the very least would look good on my resume, was one. The other was that in the off season I would have time to write my novels. Once they started selling, and the millions came rolling in, I could quit and write full time.

It is curious to look to the rear from time to time. I don't know how many millions I expected back then, and I haven't counted up my total income lately, but I doubt I have earned in my career, which has not been entirely unsuccessful, as much as certain of the players out there on the field today earn in a single year. The new No. 1 draft choice, for instance. There he is, wearing number 27, a short, chunky guy, 5'-10", 251 pounds. A running back. He signed last week for a $4.5 million bonus, and a five year contract worth $7.14 million, plus incentive clauses that could push it higher. His name is Ron Dayne, he is 22, and he has not yet carried the ball even one time as a pro. I made a million dollars one year, and one only. I was 60 years old at the time.

But as I continue to watch practice it is not money that makes me feel so uncomfortable. It's something else that I can't quite put my finger on.

Publicity Director. I knew pro football, and I knew the Giants. My father was the Times' sports columnist by then, but previously he had not only covered the team, but had been their public address announcer at the Polo Grounds as well. So I had watched home games for years. Otherwise I was without experience, and publicizing a loser is not easy, especially, it would turn out, this particular loser. For as defeat followed defeat, the New York sportswriters began to attack the Mara Family, who owned the team, as cheapskates. Not only were they too cheap to hire high priced players, but they even saved money by hiring a publicity man with no experience whatsoever. Namely guess who.

The Maras as a family were not liked by the press, and this was going to be a burden for me. They were of Irish extraction, and there were three of them.

Tim Mara, 66 years old when I arrived, had founded the team in 1925. Formerly a bookmaker at the New York tracks when this occupation was legal, he was a tall, ruddy, narrow shouldered man of minimal formal education who could add a column of figures as fast as any computer. He spoke with the strong New York street accent common among the lower classes when he was growing up—for "thirty third" he said "toidy toid," for instance. He really did. He had been in a number of businesses, but now only football was left. He went to mass and communion almost every day, came to work every day too, letting himself into the empty offices even on Saturdays, and he had heart trouble. He was a paternalistic employer who liked to give bonuses to his employees, for which he liked to be thanked. He could be generous, or vindictive. Cross him and he would ruin you if he could. He could be petty. When Arnie Weinmeister, an All-Pro tackle, jumped the Giants for the Canadian League, I was ordered to take his name out of our press guide, and never to mention him again as a former Giants' star. "I'm not giving no publicity to that bum." When a sports writer named Gene Ward wrote an anti-Giant series in the Daily News, I was ordered not to let the bum in the press box next Sunday. If the bum called up for information, I was not to give it to him. Since the Daily News at that time was the largest of New York's eight newspapers, circulation over two million, I knew, young as I was, that it was essential that I—that the Giants—continue to be correct toward Gene Ward.

Mr. Mara was always nice to me, but my own role with the team was not important to him, and he told me this often enough in one way or another. "You win, you get all the publicity you need," he would say. "I don't need to go out looking for it." And then: "When you got a winner you can go to dinner." I heard this phrase several times over the years, for it was one of his favorites, and if it somewhat demoralized his new publicity director he did not seem to notice.

There were other times I felt demoralized too. The sports editor of the Daily News was a man named Jimmy Powers, who had begun to moonlight as a television announcer at the Friday Night fights. The infant TV industry had recently discovered boxing, which seemed made for it. Although you couldn't see the color of the blood you could see the punches well enough, and a great many mediocre fighters became famous during this period. So did Jimmy Powers—to the point where he didn't have time to write his column, or couldn't be bothered. I learned that if someone like me sent him "notes" he would "use" them. So I began to write columns for him—I saw myself as polishing my writing skills as well—sending him about one column a week together with a memo saying: "Hope you can use these notes." One of my columns purported to be a "scouting report" in which I described each of twenty two Giant players as the greatest at his position the game had yet seen.

This and other columns began to appear word for word under Powers' byline the day after I sent them over. I couldn't believe that a columnist could be so careless, or imagine he could get away with this very long. (And Jimmy didn't get away with it very long.) I also couldn't believe that Tim Mara would be totally unimpressed with what I had done, was doing. But he was. I never had the nerve to point out to him how much such free advertising would have cost him, if he had had to pay for it, but knew very well what he would have replied: When you got a winner, you can go to dinner.

True up to a point, but not exactly exhaustive on the subject.

Mr. Mara knew how many tickets had been sold each day; he walked around with the figures on a piece of paper and kept adding them up in his head. It was true that he held the players' payroll tight; it was also true that there wasn't that much money coming in. The big television contracts were far in the future. TV of the Giants' games existed, but in black and white, and on the twelve inch screens of the day football did not come across very well. There were too many players crowding the small screen, and they all wore dark jerseys. Red, green and blue all looked the same, and you couldn't tell which team was which. Anyway, most people did not yet own TV sets. Fans who wished to watch the Giants in action on TV went to a bar. Or listened on radio. The largest home crowd the team would draw in 1953 was 30,000 people.

Ostensibly the old man had turned active management over to his two sons. In fact he still ruled behind the scenes, and when major decisions had to be made he made them.

Both sons had graduated from Fordham, like my father, like me, and the older one, Jack, who was a friend of my father, had a law degree, though he had never practiced. It was Jack who ran the office, worried about the budget, paid the bills, hired the training camp each summer, made the deals for the exhibition games. And it was Jack who had hired me. He was a friendly, nice kind of man, whom everyone liked.

A good many people did not like his brother, Wellington Timothy Mara, who ran the football side of the operation. Well Mara was a modern, somewhat more polished version of his father. He too was a daily communicant, and he had a gorgeous smile, so that he seemed very attractive at first. But he had a sharp, sometimes vicious tongue, and his sense of humor, usually directed toward the weaknesses of others, could be caustic and cruel.

Well Mara attended every practice. Wearing a sweat suit he engaged in calisthenics with the players, then walked up and down the sidelines observing every move they made. He attended most meetings of the coaches. In them he was never loathe to offer suggestions, and when he commented on the abilities of players he was often amusing, and sometimes clever enough to affect a particular young man's chances of making the team. One year there was a pass receiver named Jeff Newton, dubbed Fig Newton by Well Mara. "He isn't an end, he's the end," I heard him say in a meeting once. Newton was soon cut.

Well Mara made all the trades, and many of them, as the years passed, were brilliant. He studied films like any coach, and during games sat in the press box connected to the bench by telephone, with one of the assistant coaches beside him usually, the two of them sending down alignments and suggesting plays to try. In almost every sense Well was an extra coach, and he had been since he was a teenager. His knowledge of football was keen, no one could deny this, and no coach, to my knowledge ever objected to his presence. It was, after all, his team. The press did object often enough, accusing him of interfering. But like his father Well had no use for the press, and he ignored all criticism. He was 38 that year, and unmarried. When he did marry during the next off season, he commenced fathering eleven children.

I heard some criticism earlier today that the State University campus here at Albany is too far from New York, that the players want to be closer, and certainly the press wants to be closer.

I sympathize. Most of the training camps I went to were as far from New York as the team could get. The campus of Willamette University in Salem, Oregon, was one. And the exhibition games were played in distant cities also: Portland, Seattle, Spokane, Des Moines. In theory this was to protect the team's season ticket sale. The Giants each year had been selling about 7,000 season tickets, but if reports got into the New York papers that the team was bad, its prospects bad, then some or many of these holders might cancel. And so the Maras favored training camps that were too far away for cynical New York sports writers to get to them. Distant enough also that exhibition games would end too late for reports of any crushing defeats to get into the New York papers at all.

Training camp my first summer was at Gustavus Adolphus College in St. Peter, Minnesota, which is not next door to anywhere. The opening of the camp did attract a few members of the sporting press from the Chicago area, very few, and these had to be put up for as long as they stayed because St. Peter is not famous for its hotels, and one of them, a radio reporter, was directed to my room. His name was Harold Grange—the famous Red Grange—and now he was my roommate. Grange had been the most celebrated college football star of the twenties, a decade of sports heroes that was spoken of in hushed tones, for in addition to Grange it had produced Babe Ruth, Jack Dempsey, Bill Tilden, Johnny Weissmuller, and Bobby Jones. It was as if there had never been stars of that magnitude in any other decade, and never would be again. Playing for Illinois, Grange had once scored five touchdowns in a single game. This was in 1925, only

28 years previously, and he had been a pro football star after that.

But to me as he moved into my room and began unpacking, he was old and a has-been. He dated from before I was born. Youth is callow, a notion I did not invent, and came to recognize only later. Grange was 51 that year. To me he was past tense, and I was focused on newer stars, Kyle Rote, for instance, or the other halfback, Frank Gifford. I was not, I'm ashamed to say, interested in Grange in the slightest. Besides, he snored. As a player he had been known as the Galloping Ghost, but he didn't snore like a ghost. In the dark he snorted and rumbled like a truck with a defective engine, and I could not sleep. I took no pleasure in this close brush with this famous man, asked him nothing about his past exploits, and was glad when he left.

As an aside, I have found that athletes have no memory. The stars of yesteryear might as well not have existed. Each athlete seems to be interested only in those he himself has played with or against. I who had watched Giant games for years sometimes mentioned great Giant players of the past. From the current players the names drew blank stares. One of my teachers at Fordham had played quarterback at Southern Methodist six years before Rote matriculated there. Rote had never heard of him. Nor was I the only one in camp disinterested in Red Grange. I never saw any player pay the slightest attention to him. Only the owners and coaches did, whose contemporary he was.

Since most times there were few reporters on hand for me to squire around, often none, my principal job as Publicity Director became to buy beer, booze and ice for the coaches' meetings after the last practice session ended each day. These meetings, which came to be known as the Five Thirty Club, were attended also by Well Mara, by the team doctor, and sometimes by ex players from before the war. Because I provided the makings I got to attend them myself.

The Five Thirty Club meetings lasted each evening for an hour, sometimes more. Discussions were amazingly frank. Appraisals of our own players and other team's players. Gossip from around the league. I was fascinated, I sopped it all up. In later years when I was trying to get a job on *Life* or *Sports Illustrated*, any kind of a job that might help me get away from being a publicist and become a writer, I would sometimes arrange to be invited to lunch with the editors of these magazines, and I would regale them with all this inside stuff. They too were fascinated. They too sopped it all up, and I thought this meant they would offer me a job, but they never did. To them, I would realize when I was older, these lunches were brain-picking sessions, neither more nor less. It was my own fault for not realizing this, and for hoping for so much more, and I would go back to work and wait for phone calls that never came.

The head coach that year was Steve Owen, known as Stout Steve, a man from Oklahoma who was rarely seen without a wad of snuff under his upper lip. He was a big, baldish man who wore pale-rimmed glasses. A former lineman, he was bulky all over, whatever clothes he wore didn't look good on him, and he had been coach 23 years. He had taken over the Giants the year I was born, but had never had a contract. I was unimpressed by his lack of a contract, or his 23 years as coach. As I have said, I knew nothing yet of the volatility of the sport and of life itself. I accepted the fact that Tim Mara never fired anybody. One of the people he never fired was Steve Owen, and I assumed he never would. As did Steve, I believe.

Stout Steve was 53 years old, and he took no interest in me. Of course I took no interest in him either. His salary was $15,000 a year. In the course of the season I went to many affairs with him at which he always made the same speech, always told the one joke he seemed comfortable with. The crowd always laughed politely, which seemed to be enough for Steve.

The season to come was probably already doomed, for the team needed new blood, and there was precious little on hand. But we didn't know this yet. The Giants' scouting system was breaking down. This system amounted to a number of former players who "kept their eyes open" plus a single scout who was full time, sort of. A former tackle for Notre Dame, he was a jovial fat man named Jack Lavelle who made his principal income as a raconteur at banquets. He was the funniest joke teller most people had ever heard. Obviously he was scrambling to make a living, perhaps the Giants didn't pay him very well, for he also had a third job as the starter at track meets, especially indoor meets at Madison Square Garden.

That year the scouting system had turned up several new quarterback candidates. One of them turned out to be five feet eight inches tall, and another five feet seven. Both came from small colleges. The first opted to go home after being hit by six or seven hundred pounds of onrushing linemen, a quantity of beef that did not exist on the small college circuit. The other quit after someone lying on the turf batted down one of his passes. The third rookie quarterback was a former West Point star named Arnold Galiffa who had just finished his mandatory three years as an army officer. He was three or four years older than all the other rookies, and he sustained a broken transverse process of the spine mid way through the season. His stretcher was passed in through the window of the train that waited in the station to take us back to New York. He was off loaded the same way, and that was the last most of us ever saw of him.

The game was changing in ways that Stout Steve Owen apparently never imagined. He had become known as a defensive genius, had invented the umbrella defense, but the crowds of 1953 did not care about defense. That they would come to care a great deal about defense later on, that from one day to the next defensive players would become stars too, was unknown to us that year.

From Steve Owen in the early fifties the crowds wanted offense, at which he or the Giants or both were poor. The crowds wanted spectacular plays which only the visiting teams seemed able to provide. Steve Owen was partial to the old fashioned single wing offense, a variation of which he had invented, calling it the A formation. For a few series of plays the Giants would try the T formation that everybody else used and which, in its multiple variations, is still used today, but as soon as the going got tough Steve would relapse into the A. The team's passing attack amounted to the quarterback in the huddle ordering four or five guys to run out for a pass, he would hit whoever was open. Most times nobody was.

The quarterback was a taciturn Mississippian named Charlie Conerly. The book on Conerly was that he could not throw the long ball. I asked him about this one day. He said: "I can throw it, we just haven't got anybody who can run under it."

For Conerly, who rarely spoke, this amounted to an oration. The crowds blamed him for the Giants' lack of offense, and every year new college phenoms were brought to camp to replace him. None ever did. "I ain't seen anybody yet," said Conerly, another speech. As soon as some good receivers had been hired he showed he could throw the long ball perfectly well. He was a star for fourteen years, and ought to be in the Hall of Fame, but isn't. His jersey number, 42, has been retired; no Giant will ever wear it again. Charlie and his wife Perian visited us in Nice once, after I had left the team. We took them to Monte Carlo where Charlie got drunk and complained to the owner of a night club that the nude dancers didn't have big enough tits. I learned more about this man who rarely spoke in one day on the Cote d'Azur than I had during my six years with the team.

At the end of the disastrous 1953 season Stout Steve Owen got fired. He came out of Jack Mara's office with his upper lip puffed out, wearing his usual ill fitting suit. Looking stricken, he went into his own office, and Jack came into mine to tell me I had a press release to write: Steve was retiring, which I understood to be fiction, but would stay on as a scout, also fiction. When Steve came out of his office finally I asked him what he would do now. He looked me over for a moment, then said:

"I was looking for a job when I found this one."

Steve Owen is in the pro football Hall of Fame today, which didn't help him get through that particular day.

I went home thinking: I can write a short story about this. I was excited. The curtain line would be Steve's curtain line, what could be better:

I was looking for a job when I found this one.

And I did try to write this story, but I was 23, not 53. I did not know what it was like to lose such a prominent job after holding it that long. How was he going to go into the restaurants and bars he frequented, how was he to face people who had always treated him as a celebrity? I did not know what it was like to be Steve's age, and wonder what the future held, if anything. All I had was a curtain line. I got nowhere with the story. Eventually I gave it up, and never thought of it again until today. Possibly I know enough about life to write it now, but it has lost its immediacy. The only way a story can be written, at least by me, is if I want to write it above all things. Concentration has to be so intense that the people in the story become vivid, more real than real, so real they begin to act and to speak. The writer, me anyway, has little to do once this level of concentration is achieved, except write it all down. And then achieve the same level of concentration the next day, and the next, and the next.

At today's stage of my life I don't think I would be able to do that with a story from so long ago.

After my first season, having saved nearly every cent I had earned, I asked Jack Mara if I could take five months off. He readily agreed, for the team had no need of me in the off season, and my absence, to him, meant one less salary to pay.

Carrying in my pocket my entire wealth to that point, $500, most of it in $10 travelers checks, I sailed to the south of France with my friend Ned Curran, who soon got sick and went home. My plan was to become a great writer before the money ran out. As soon as this happened, I would send a letter resigning from the Giants, and stay in Nice permanently.

Ned and I rented a hotel room and my share was $2 per night, which of course would double when Ned left. You can imagine the quality of the hotel. That was all right. That was living. Experience of that kind was good for an author. It was something that could go into a short story or novel, possibly disguised, possibly not.

I did not think then, and do not think now, that fiction was something to be made up in the brilliance of the author's head. If it was to be any good it had to be in some measure lived. Or, if you prefer the journalistic term, reported. What I had not yet worked out was how much living an author had to have done to be worth reading. At 23 I was confident that I had lived more than long enough, and had much to impart that the world was waiting eagerly to receive. The Steve Owen story had not worked out, but other stories were sure to, and a spot as exotic as the Riviera was certain to improve my writing, give it the lights and shadows needed to set it off, a certain eclat, a setting for the jewel.

Nice's Mardi Gras carnival was on, and on its last afternoon as I watched the end of it, as the floats passed by, some ideas came to me and I went right back to my room and began a story. It was about love and art, and about a young man who was disoriented, as I was disoriented in France, and who was tugged two ways at once. Since the story played out against a background of the carnival, the title was easy: CARNIVAL. And I thought the story would be easy too, but again it was a more ambitious theme by far than I then realized, or was then able to accomplish.

My $500 ran out. I hadn't become a great writer yet but could stay in

Nice no longer. But there was the girl I mentioned earlier. I did not want to go back to America without her. We began to talk about getting married. I was alone in France. I had no friend to explain myself to, no one from whom to seek advice, and I had no money left. But what had happened to me here, was happening, seemed to me the most exquisite possible accident. A collision of worlds had occurred. Her world and mine which, if we went forward, would become one. I told myself I had no misgivings, no doubts, but knew I had a few. Marriage is forever, the Jesuits had taught me; there could be no divorce. In other words, my decision had better be the right one. I had been led to believe also that a boy in love had no sense, and perhaps this description fit me. Did it?

To these misgivings and others I attempted to apply the wisdom of all 23 of my years. She had been to boarding school in England and art school in Nice, she spoke two languages without accent—in English she sounded like the queen. She knew so much I didn't know. We had grown up 4,000 miles apart—how had we ever even run into each other? I was not only in love, I also liked her better than anyone I knew, and it seemed to me that she was offering me not only herself but the essense of France, the essence of a continent.

I didn't see that I had anything at all to offer her in return.

What it came down to was the conviction that nothing as good as this girl would ever come my way again. If I did not take her I would regret it the rest of my life.

Considered in this light I had no choice, I believed.

And so we did it.

Together we went home to New York, I went back to work for the Giants, and this foreign girl's introduction to America was a month at a pro football training camp in Oregon, and then another month following the team's exhibition games back to New York. Oregon was salmon country, a country for huge ripe peaches. We rented the apartment of a professor gone elsewhere for the summer, and slept on a Murphy bed that pulled down from the wall, which seemed to us exotic, and at dinner time she asked if she should start the potatoes in cold water, or in water already boiling. Her mother wasn't there to be asked, and I didn't know either. To my shame I never realized how alone she might have felt cooking the potatoes that night—might have felt every night in Oregon. She was 22 years old. On all that vast continent she knew no one except me.

The practice sessions were like two great gashes across the day, especially the scrimmages each afternoon, and she would stand or sit with the few other wives on hand, and flinch at all the battering that was going on, and try to understand what American football was all about. The players were much taken by her, and they ragged me unmercifully.

From Oregon, after playing two exhibition games on the west coast, we moved to Wisconsin and there set up a second camp on the fairway of a golf course, which became the practice field. We were assigned individual cabins along the fairway, and I had just moved in when a carload of wives, including mine arrived.

They had driven across country to meet us here, and along the way she had seen bears begging for handouts from the cars, and real Indians, and towns with wooden sidewalks like in the movies. She was almost giddy reporting this, and just then practice ended, and here came the players in their wet, mud-stained uniforms, each toward his own cabin, and in front of the cabin next to ours stopped Roosevelt Brown and Bobby Epps. Brown was six feet three inches tall, weighed 245, and had a 32 inch waist. Epps was shorter, but built similarly, and they ripped off their sodden jerseys, their pads, and stood there swilling water, their dark faces wet with sweat, their slick torsos glistening in the late sun, and the eyes of this foreign girl, who had never seen physiques like this before, got big as footballs.

Rosie Brown is here in Albany, studying the rookie linemen during the drills, and I go over and talk to him. His first year was my first year also, and insofar as offensive tackles can be called stars, he was a star from the beginning, played thirteen seasons, coached the line afterwards, was elected to the Hall of Fame as soon as he was eligible, and is an aging Giants scout now—that's 47 years with this team.

He greets me with a big grin, his teeth as big and white as ever, and tells me that, apart from the gray hair, I look unchanged, a nice lie. I say the same to him, and he does look fine, except that his knees are ruined and he tells me he must move between the field and the locker room in a golf cart.

He leads me over to where Ken Kavanaugh, now an aging scout also, stands watching the new ends. Kavanaugh came in as end coach my third year, and stayed and stayed. Now, as the three of us peer across at the new running back, Dayne, who is waiting his turn to run through plays—waiting at $100 a minute, or however it works out—we talk mostly about money, which is only normal, I suppose. Almost $12 million for playing football is hard to ignore. The kid is already rich, and what will this mean to his desire to play, to his willingness to accept the punishment pro football dishes out? Kavanaugh gives a laugh and says that after college he signed with the Chicago Bears for $300 a game. "We had to buy our own shoes. Hell, we had to buy our own jock straps. They'd wash them for us, but we had to buy them." Brown, whom Frank Gifford, the Giants' star that year and for many years to come, once called the best athlete on the team, earned I think $4700 his first season, the starting salary for linemen if they were black. White linemen got a bit more. Neither Brown nor Kavanaugh begrudges the money the new players are paid, so they tell me. Inasmuch as the players draw in the fans, they deserve what they get.

But then Rosie turns a bit bitter. Money is ruining the game, he says.

A man ought to play because he loves it, but too many of those guys out there—he gestures toward the blue jerseys, the white jerseys, the few yellow ones—don't love it, they play only for the money. There's no love at all. Some money is fine, but there is far too much. "It's a $3,000 fine if you lose your playbook," Rosie says, "but now some of these guys can't find their playbooks."

I find I don't care much about the money modern players earn. I went off and earned my own money, theirs has nothing to do with me. Nonetheless I am aware of it, can see money in every direction I look, starting with the thirteen assistant coaches—in my day there were four. At either end of the field atop two collapsible towers, each about four stories high, stand videotape operators with their machines; everything that happens here is videotaped. There are a dozen or more employees scampering about—college boys in official Giants T-shirts—who move the small crowd back, or fetch balls or water. They even help move the goalposts, which are on wheels so they can be dragged to wherever on the field an assistant coach wants them. They work ball machines that spit out perfect spirals that are harder, flatter, more accurate than any quarterback can throw, and more difficult to catch as well, judging from the number that are dropped.

None of this did we have.

The man who holds my old job, Pat Hanlon, has numerous assistants. He has a better title, too: vice president of communications. Whereas I of course was alone, and not nearly as appreciated as he seems to be.

I wrote a novelette about pro football while I was still with the team, and a novel long after I had left it, but never used anything else of my Giant experience in fiction. The idea of writing some fresh new football story has of course occurred to me, but it is an idea I discarded at once because two monumental changes have come into the game since my time, and these I do not understand at all. The first of them is money in vast amounts, and the second is race. Most of today's players get very rich very fast, and most are black—on some teams some years eighty percent. Rosie was only the second black player the Giants ever had, and there were never more than five. For all his size Rosie was, and is, a sweet and gentle man, but not all the modern ones are, I'm told. Football is only a game, but money is not a game, nor race either, and no writer, in my opinion, has a right to do exploratory surgery on subjects as serious as money and race without acquiring a good deal more first hand knowledge than I am likely to acquire now.

Left alone, I watch practice and ask myself why I feel so uncomfortable here. In the presence of Brown and Kavanaugh my discomfort only increased. Is it because I don't know any of those players out there, where once I knew them all? Is it because my head is filled with players I remember, but no one else remembers? Players who, in memory, are still the same age I was then.

Newly married and back in New York I began sending out to magazines the stories I had written in Europe.

All of them were beyond my then powers as a writer, all the stories I wrote during this period were, but I didn't know this, or else refused to believe it, it would take years and years to get them right, but I kept sending them out, each time being sure to enclose the requisite stamped, self addressed manila envelope. A few days later the return envelope in my handwriting would be dropped on my desk by Jack or Well Mara, or one of the coaches, accompanied by a comical remark, or what I read as a smug smile. It got so I took to waiting out in the corridor to catch the mailman before anyone else did.

Scores of magazines published fiction at that time. There was a hierarchy, and young writers like me went down the list. As fast as a story came back you sent it out again. Buying stamps and new envelopes to self address you could go broke, there were so many magazines. You needed fresh envelopes for each submission or the next editor would know that the story had already been rejected by the last one. You needed a thick skin too.

That very year the Giants began a dynasty that was to last ten seasons. At first a little, then a lot, the team learned to win.

I had once asked Well Mara who among Steve Owen's assistants would make the best head coach. "Jim Lee Howell," he answered at once. Howell had been a Marine officer during the war. "Jim Lee can command by raising an eyebrow." And so Jim Lee was the new head coach.

But what would he be able to do with the wretched team that he had inherited?

Howell was six feet five inches tall, a farm boy from the University of Arkansas, a bone crushing end who had come up to the Giants in 1937, and had stayed. Back home in Lonoke he still owned a farm, and farming was what he really liked, he told me once, but it was impossible to make a living at it.

He had a big booming laugh, was the same age as Well Mara, and like Well had just married for the first time. Both new wives were 25, but after that they were different. Ann Mara had been a secretary and was content to have married the boss; Sue Howell was a pianist with concert aspirations, and a lover of art in all forms, and she never seemed comfortable as a football wife. Also, she was my age, not her husband's. It was perhaps for these reason that my new wife and I found ourselves courted by Jim Lee. We went to restaurants with the Howells, were invited to their house across the bridge in New Jersey. Jim Lee must have looked over the football world in which he stood, the only New York world he knew, searching for friends for his young wife, and there was no one but us. He saw, perhaps for the first time, that most football people were focused on football, other sports, and football again. And nothing more. I am exaggerating slightly, but not much. I do not remember a single discussion, in the Five Thirty Club or in hotel dining rooms, or anywhere else, about religion or politics, or even World War II, much less art. I am not suggesting that these men were stupid. Football at that level is an art and a science too, and they were focused on it to the exclusion of all else.

They were not usually sympathetic to those with an artistic bent, although perhaps now Jim Lee was learning to be.

I don't claim to have been very sensitive to other peoples' feelings at this stage of my life, but if I imagined I understood Sue Howell's, at least to some extent, it was because I felt the same lack of sympathy toward myself.

The New York Times's sports desk had formed the policy of running one feature story each day. All the previous season I had been bringing football players in to be interviewed for such a story. The features editor was a man named Frank Blunk. He was about 60, baldish, a former copy editor who had only now got himself promoted off the anonymity of the copy desk. His face was stern. When I would bring in a player he would gaze across the desk at us with one eye half closed, and then fob the player and me off on a reporter.

But as the 1955 season neared its end, being a still unpublished writer and becoming desperate about it, I approached him. If I could get another leave of absence from the Giants, I said, and if next January I paid my own way to the winter Olympics in Italy, and if I wrote a preview story just before the events started, would he use it? He said he would.

And if I wrote additional feature stories during the games?

Possibly he would use them too, he said, if they were good enough. He would pay me $50 for each story the Times published. Of course, he added, an experienced sportswriter would be there to write the lead story each day.

On that basis I asked for the leave of absence, and got it, and we sailed third class to Europe, all three of us, again spending every cent I had saved. My wife and our daughter Theresa, six-months old, stayed with her family in Nice, while I took a train across the top of Italy, sitting up all night in a third class carriage worrying about money. The train pulled into Venice at 6 a.m. the winter night still pitch dark, the canals empty, the streets as well. Cortina d'Ampezzo in the Dolomite mountains, site of the Olympics that year, was still ninety miles north, I had an hour between trains, so I checked my bag and typewriter, went out of the station and moved through streets, crossed over bridges. I was reluctant to stray too far from the station for fear I wouldn't be able to find it again. It was too dark to see anything. I was hoping to come upon one of the landmarks I had read about, St. Marks Square, for instance, but never did. I got back on the train.

In Cortina, because I was several days early, there was still a room available in the press hotel at $15 a day—the Winter Olympics, like pro football, was another event that had not yet really caught on. But to get this room I had to guarantee that I would stay for all seventeen days of the games—and sign a paper to this effect. A guarantee of $255. This was an enormous amount of money to me that year. If I got five pieces into the Times I still wouldn't break even, and never mind the cost of the ship from New York and the train from Nice. Could I even do that well? I remember thinking that I was making an investment in my future as a writer, but I had never made an investment of any kind before. I was 25 now, and I hesitated. Finally I signed the paper.

The experienced sports writer had not yet reached Cortina. The Winter Olympics would begin in four days time and in a few minutes I would go back to my hotel room and try to write a preview for the sports page of the Sunday New York Times.

It was a cold Saturday afternoon. I was outdoors in the dusk striding back and forth trying to concentrate myself into a mood in which the best words would be sure to come out. I could not afford a piece that was merely adequate. It had to be better than anybody else could do. Great, if possible. My one novel so far had hit a wall. No one would publish my short stories. But a newspaper was different. I had got this far. This was my chance.

The village was surrounded on all sides by craggy peaks and snow. Banks of snow leaned against the walls of buildings. The sun had started down, and slush in the streets was beginning to freeze into ruts. Church bells were tolling over the rooftops, and I had an 800 word piece to write about the village on the eve of the games.

Here I am, I thought, trying to encourage myself, at my age already a foreign correspondent. Sort of. I wasn't even an accredited journalist. I had gone to the press desk but the Italians had refused to give me credentials. Rightly so, I suppose. The American athletes had arrived by now, and so had a man named Dan Ferris, who was head of the AAU, initials that once everybody knew. Amateur Athletic Union. It was he who ruled on the amateur status of every American athlete. If Ferris blackballed you for real or imagined professional dealings, you were out, there was no appeal, and never mind that most of the young men and women competing for other countries were amateurs in name only.

I had gone to see Ferris. Could he help me get credentials? He knew my father and he had listened to my story and told me to come back the next day.

But it turned out he couldn't get me press accreditation either. When I returned he had handed me, perhaps out of embarrassment, credentials as an *Ufficiale*, part of the U.S. delegation. I would not have press privileges, I thought as I thanked him, but I would be able to get into the events. Probably I would be able to interview the athletes. I would be able to write my pieces.

Though sunlight still touched the highest peaks, the village was nearly dark. The air was getting very cold very fast. I went back to my room and during the next two hours wrote my preview, read it over about twenty times, then carried it to the press room for transmission to New York.

There, it was gone. I wouldn't know for several days if anyone liked it, if it even got into the paper, if I had earned anything for it.

The next day there was a speed skating race at which a Russian broke the world's record. I wrote this up and sent it to New York also. So if they used this too, perhaps I had earned $100 already. Better still, magazine editors would be seeing my byline. Perhaps when this was over one of them would buy one of my short stories. Or offer me a job as a writer.

No word came back from New York.

By the time the experienced sportswriter arrived I had written and sent four pieces. I told him over dinner that of course he would write the lead article each day, that I was there only to help. I told him that bobsledding, which I had never seen before, excited me, that I had taken to going up to the starting line each dawn to watch practice. The run was a glazed ice trench, very steep, one violent turn after another, the worst of them banked. The sleds weighed half a ton. High up on the banking they hit speeds of sixty miles an hour. The noise, as the sleds were dropped out of the trucks, as they were push started, as the riders jumped aboard, as they were thrown high up on the banking, as they rattled and banged all the way down—the noise, I said, reminded me of football scrimmages. Except that bobsledding was very much more dangerous.

I told him I had met and interviewed one of the bobsledders, Alfonso

Cabeza de Vaca y Leighton, Conde de Carvajal, Marques de Portago. Knowing nothing about bobsledding Portago had bought a pair of $1,000 sleds, recruited some cousins from Madrid, and entered the Olympics. He was Spain's only entrant, only chance for a medal. During one of his first descents he had lost control and at great speed was slung out. He could have been killed, but walked away. Now, only a few days later, he had the fourth fastest practice time.

I had no notion of the impact Portago was to have on my life and career, nor that he would alter its direction in ways undreamed of by me.

Portago was 26, I told the experienced sportswriter, was enormously rich, spoke four languages, and was a racing driver, actually, under contract to Ferrari. He gave outrageously quotable answers to every question I put to him. How had he met his American wife: "One does not meet an American girl, she meets you." What did she think of him racing bobsleds and cars: "I do not ask her, I am Spanish." He was unshaven, chain smoked, and was dressed all in black except for the white helmet. He looked like a pirate, or like one of his famous ancestors, Nuñez Cabeza de Vaca, a 16th century conquistador whose name and title he still bore. He once flew a plane under a bridge to collect a $500 bet. He said he would win the racing drivers' world championship before he was 30, then retire. His friend Gurner Nelson standing beside me in the dark and cold said: "I doubt he'll live to be 30. Every time he comes in from a race the front of his car is wrinkled where he's been nudging other cars out of his way at 130 miles an hours."

"That's your feature story for tomorrow," said the experienced sportswriter.

I went back to my room, wrote the story, and sent it to New York. People were going to notice this piece about Portago, I told myself. They would see my name on top of it and maybe, just maybe, it would jump start my career.

From Cortina I wrote also about figure skaters, ski jumpers, downhill racers. I interviewed and wrote about a 20 year old Austrian named Toni Sailer who won all three Alpine events. I wrote fourteen articles in all, fourteen bylines I believed, and then the games ended.

As I started back to Nice I imagined that I had pulled it off. I had got to an exotic place, got accredited, done the work, and got out, having earned much more than my expenses. And those bylines would certainly have impressed editors.

In Nice the clippings were waiting, together with an apologetic letter from Blunk. All fourteen pieces had been published, but after the fourth day the sports editor had ordered my byline removed, the letter read, and had also decreed that I was to be paid only half of the agreed upon $50 per story. The sports editor at that time was an arbitrary, despotic individual who was hated and feared by most of his staff. Blunk was very sorry, his letter read. He had tried hard for me but there was nothing further he could do.

I wrote letters to everyone I could think of begging for the money I thought was owed me. To no effect. I could do nothing about my missing byline.

We sailed back to America, and I went back to work for the Giants.

As the next football season progressed I found, as I opened the sports pages each day, that I had begun to look for the results of car races, a sport that had never interested me before, and to search out the name of the Marquis de Portago. In a sense I had discovered him although, since my byline had not appeared on the Times article, no one knew this but me.

Portago was mentioned often enough, for he drove factory Ferraris in races at the Nurburgring, LeMans and elsewhere in Europe, and when the cold weather set in and the fast car circus moved to Buenos Aires, Nassau and Havana, he raced there too. Always Ferraris. Grand prix cars and sports cars both—as yet I did not know there was a difference. He was almost always highly placed at the finish, and in the long distance races he sometimes shared the wheel with drivers who were among the biggest names in the sport.

He moved about the world, while I, a publicity man, stayed where I was.

Much that happens to a writer's career is luck—sometimes good sometimes bad. Now I chanced to meet a freelance writer named Martin Gross, who was a few years older than I, and who made his living writing articles on a variety of subjects for a variety of magazines, and when I began to ask him to divulge to me what another writer might have considered trade secrets, he responded generously. At the time I thought such generosity normal; I know better now.

When in need of an assignment his technique was to go through the newspapers looking for ideas for magazine articles, Gross told me. Reports that left him, the reader, wanting to know more—something he could flesh out in a full length magazine piece. Or he looked for some sports or entertainment or political figure in the news who might make a full length profile.

Gross could find five or six such ideas any day of the week, he said.

After that he would call up some editor whom he thought, based on the type articles the editor had already published, might be interested in one or several of these ideas, and he would invite him to lunch. The editor would pay for the lunch, don't worry about that, he said; that's what editors were for. During this lunch Gross would pitch his ideas. Editors were men who had to have articles, and most of them didn't have a clue how to find ideas of their own, he said. So most often the lunch ended with an assignment.

And he began to give me the names and telephone numbers of editors of major magazines.

I told him I didn't think I could call up such important editors, and invite myself to lunch.

"You can do it," he encouraged me.

With my background in sports I should probably start with one of the men's magazines, he advised me.

A number of them were being published at that time. They were not girlie magazines, which did not yet exist. Bare bosoms would have got everybody arrested, girls and editors both. Instead, men's magazines featured articles about guns, fishing, mountaineering, open ocean sailing, together with profiles of wildcatters, home run hitters and stunt pilots. These were mainstream magazines, and their success, it was theorized, was due to World War II. The seven or eight million young men spilled out by the war, who were now in their thirties, had survived the grandest adventure of their lives, would never have another that was comparable, and were in the mood now to read about the adventures of others. It would also be theorized fifteen years later, after these magazines had one and all gone out of business, that the now paunchy ex-servicemen had lost their taste for adventure and had instead learned to face real life.

Among the many men's magazines of those days, *True* and *Argosy* had the biggest circulations, and paid the most money, but I found that I did not dare call up the editors of such prestigious publications who were no doubt men of prestige themselves.

One step down were other possibilities. Second tier magazines, Gross had called them. If I would be more comfortable with one of them, then start there, he had suggested. The second tier editors were not hounded by name writers, and weren't as picky. Of course they didn't pay as well either. Among them was a magazine called *Cavalier*, whose phone number he had given me, along with the name of its editor.

Telephoning this man was hard. It was worse than telephoning girls to ask for a date when I was a teenager, but finally I forced myself to do it. As I talked to him I got more and more nervous, to the point where I could hear the cursed tremble in my voice, and hoped he couldn't.

He agreed to meet me for lunch.

He turned out to be not much older than I, and probably not much better fixed in the adult world. Not very sure of himself. Hoping for better in the future. I wasn't nervous now but felt like most actors claim to feel: the moment they step on stage the nervousness stops. I offered the editor several ideas, one of them a profile of Portago, and I passed my New York Times clipping, datelined Cortina d'Ampezzo, across the table. No byline, but I said I wrote it, and he believed me. He said he did, anyway.

Portago would be racing in Florida in the Twelve Hours of Sebring in a few days time, I added. I could go there and interview him and get more material.

The editor nodded, paid the check, and said he would get back to me.

He phoned that afternoon. By all means try the Portago profile, he said. Go to Sebring. If he bought the piece he would pay $400. Of course, he added cautiously, he could not pay any expenses, and he waited to hear my reaction.

It never occurred to me that expenses might be negotiable, and I wanted the assignment too much to risk jeopardizing it.

"Okay," I said.

I bought a ticket to Tampa on a flight in the middle of the night when rates were cheapest, landing there at about 4 a.m.. After sleeping for an hour or two in a cheap motel, I took a bus across the waist of Florida to Sebring.

I found Portago's hotel, and he agreed to come downstairs and talk to me. We sat in the bar. I was so inexperienced that I did not really know what to ask him. "Every curve has a theoretical speed limit," he said. "Let's say a certain curve can be taken at a hundred miles an hour. A great driver like Fangio will take that curve at 99.9 every single time."

Fangio was the reigning world champion that year.

"I'm not as good as Fangio," Portago continued. "I'll take that curve one time at 97, another time at 98, and a third time at maybe 101." He smiled. "If I take it at 101, I go off the road."

He was as always a patient, well mannered young man. We talked for a while, then he left to go to practice. The race circuit was a disused airfield outside of town. I was too new and unsure of myself to ask for a ride out there with him, but instead waited for him to leave, then cadged a ride with someone else.

Once at the circuit I found that the race had drawn not only the most famous drivers and race cars in the world, but also, if I can use the word loosely, some of the most famous magazine writers as well. There were men from *Life*, *True*, *Esquire*, *Sports Illustrated*, all of whom were preparing profiles on, and were clustered around, Portago. Lots of photographers too. And me from *Cavalier*.

Partly this interest was due to the sports car craze then sweeping America. I use the words "craze" and "sweeping" in the magazine sense. Magazine editors then and now must continually introduce their readers to the new and exciting, or what can be made to seem new and exciting. The latest music, dance, matinee idol, the latest ideas, the latest fad. The latest sports car driver. This is their stock in trade. To justify the new thing, whatever it is, they normally introduce it as a "craze." Better still, as a craze that is "sweeping" the country.

In truth the American interest in sports cars was both real and sudden. A part of the American market was tired of the usual Detroit behemoths that waddled around corners, tired also of the Indianapolis oval track, where racing seemed based on brute speed and bravery. Indy racing had no chic at all.

Chevrolet and Ford had recently come out with sports cars, the Corvette and the new two passenger Thunderbird, examples of both of which were entered in the Twelve Hours endurance race I had come to Sebring to see. Imported MGs and Triumphs were selling briskly, and the luxury car market had been invaded by passenger Ferraris costing as much as $15,000 apiece, an outrageously high price at the time. Road circuits had sprung up from California to Connecticut. Even *The New York Times* had taken note of all this—Frank Blunk had promoted a regular car column to be written by himself, promising his bosses that it would bring in car ads, which it did.

As if to feed this sports car "craze" there had now appeared, racing for the first time in America, the glamorous Portago.

In those years big time motor racing was a murderous sport, as I would soon enough learn. The excessive danger weeded out the timid, and all the drivers were brave, though none quite as brave, if that is the word, as Portago. According to certain of his rivals, he wasn't skilled at all, what he was instead was fearless. He courted risks not acceptable to them.

Being a flat, featureless former airfield, Sebring was not a particularly dangerous place, but most of the rest of the year these men raced at great speed on open roads bordered by things to hit—trees, fences, houses—and those who made serious mistakes did not usually survive them. The death rate was high. Among the not more than fifteen men each year, the elite of the sport, of whom Portago was now one, it worked out to about two dead drivers every season. And so his rivals would shake their heads when talking about him.

Some of them prophesied that they would soon be attending his funeral, perhaps before the present season ended.

In the paddock during practice, as the race cars boomed by, I heard such comments for the first time.

There was an extravagance to Portago, a physical magnetism. It was in the way he held his body and used it, in the way his mouth moved, his head. There was a feeling of danger about him. He had big white teeth and a dazzling smile. He had only to climb into a race car to draw all eyes. Girls and women flocked around him—with the result that his name often enough appeared in gossip columns too. He did seem to have more than his share of girls. Was this at least part of the reason his rivals spoke of him the way they did?

Many of the girls were groupies, but not all. According to the gossip columns there were two other women in Portago's life, in addition to his wife, and they were as celebrated as he. One was Dorian Leigh, the top model of the day, who had borne him a child, (he had two with his wife) and the other was the beautiful Linda Christian, a minor actress who had once been married to a major actor named Tyrone Power. Portago's wife, no lesser a beauty than the other two, had been with him in Cortina, and I had interviewed her, but I did not see her at Sebring.

All three of Portago's principal women, if I can call them that, were in their mid thirties—about eight years older than he was. Which was possibly significant, though no one could say in what way; at 26, my age at this time, I certainly couldn't.

At 10 a.m. the next morning the race began, fifty five cars, 110 drivers, lapping a circuit that was a bit more than five miles around, and for the next twelve hours the booming noise never stopped. In some previous life the terrain had been scalped. It was totally bald, not a house, not a tree anywhere. In many places its curves were delineated only by painted lines, straw bales or rubber pylons, like roads under construction. A few temporary bleachers rose up here and there, otherwise nothing. Sebring was not only the least dangerous place where these men raced, it was also by far the least interesting, though not to me. I had a pit pass and could move anywhere, talk to anyone, and did so. For twelve hours I was enthralled.

By what exactly I do not know. By the speed and danger, obviously. By the beauty of the cars. By the spectacle of men trying to master machines they had themselves created but could not fully control. Brave young men. Beautiful, deadly machines.

By this new, extravagant world suddenly revealed to me, about which I wanted to know more.

The cars went round and round. The noise was stupendous. At a certain point it gave me a headache. I was enthralled anyway. At about 7 p.m. the headlights came on, and three hours later under the lights the race ended. The winning car had lapped that stupid circuit 197 times. Portago's car, which spent nine laps in the pits for repairs, and had had no brakes since noon, finished seventh.

I went up and talked to him.

"I drove nine of the twelve hours," he told me. "My co-driver, Musso, was sick. Castellotti's death upset him, I think." Castellotti, another of Ferrari's contract drivers, had been killed a month before, and Musso would be killed the following year.

I did not say goodbye to Portago, for by then he was surrounded by journalists much bigger and more important than I.

I went home and began to write my article. So did they, I assume. I don't know how long theirs took to write. Mine took more than six weeks, for I saw almost as soon as I started that my research was defective: I had not asked nearly enough questions, had not acquired nearly enough quotes. I made phone calls, searched out obscure references to Portago that had appeared in the public press. I wrote one draft, then another. An article under Portago's own byline appeared in *Sports Illustrated*, ghost written I assumed, lighthearted, exactly as I had judged him to be. In it he joked that the life expectancy of race car drivers on his level was about the same as that of Kremlin bigwigs, who at that time were being regularly stood up and shot. I revised again and again. I worked during those slow off-season days at the Giants, I worked nights and weekends. I wrote and rewrote, for it seemed to me that my entire magazine career rode on this one article for *Cavalier*.

Finally I turned it in. And waited for the editor's reaction. I did not have to wait long.

The Twelve Hours of Sebring had been run on March 23. Portago had no races scheduled until the Mille Miglia on May 12, to be followed a week later by the Grand Prix de Monaco and then the entire European season.

Point to point open road racing was the way the sport had begun, the first race being from Paris to Rouen in 1894, ninety miles, won at the breathtaking average speed of over eleven miles per hour. That year, and for many years to come, the driver had a mechanic with him, for tires regularly blew out, engines regularly broke down, and it took two men working feverishly to keep each machine moving. The roads were dirt, often badly rutted, and they were studded with nails jarred loose from horseshoes. The two men rode high up, steering at first with a tiller, only later with a wheel that had to be manhandled. Along the route waited hundreds of thousands of awed spectators. Speeds got up to 60 mph, making the cars virtually uncontrollable in turns, or when bounding out of potholes, and once they got into or near the towns, they had to be pointed through alleys of spectators pinched so narrow a bicyclist could scarcely have got through.

There were many of these open road races, more every year, most of them starting from Paris, the capital of cars: Paris-Berlin, Paris-Vienna. The most famous was Paris-Madrid in 1903 which resulted in many separate accidents, many wrecked machines, and more than a dozen corpses. Afterwards such an outcry against the new sport rose up that it was believed there would never be another open road race.

But there were. Many.

And in 1927 Italy started the Mille Miglia, the greatest of them all, a thousand mile sports car race over open roads. It drew each year hundreds of entrants, millions of fans. The race plunged through villages, through major cities, it twice crossed the country's tortured central spine. All the major factories entered cars, and so did scores of individuals, some of whom were skilled. Others frightened everybody. Because of this, because of the twisting terrain as well, and given its sheer length, the Mille Miglia was the most dangerous of all the races, and the most difficult, and winning it the supreme achievement in the sport.

Portago did not want to enter that year but Enzo Ferrari assigned him a car, informed him he was driving, and that was that. He wrote a letter to Dorian Leigh in which he commented: "My early death may well come next Sunday."

Think of the route as a broken rectangle standing on end. The start was at the northern city of Brescia. From there the route headed east, plunging south at Padua and angling toward the Adriatic coast. When it got there it ran behind the beaches for more than 200 miles before turning west and crossing the mountains to Rome, where it turned north to Florence, climbing up and over the high Futa and Raticosa passes, and crossing the Apennines a second time, then coming down into Bologna where the road flattened out, stretching flat and fast the rest of the way back to Brescia again.

The race began at midnight. There were 301 cars entered. The smaller cars went off first, starting at intervals. These cars and their amateur drivers were going to be strung out on the road all the way to Rome before the big factory cars even went off. Portago's turn did not come until 5:31 in the morning. It was still dark and his headlights threw their beams far out as he surged down the ramp onto the street and off toward the coast.

The ordinary roads of Italy on a Sunday in May. In theory the side roads had been closed off, but there was still plenty to hit: lampposts, bollards, curbs that could tear off a wheel, houses, fences, walls, embankments, alleys of spectators, a stray dog perhaps, or some amateur enthusiast's car sideways in a blind turn.

Portago was not alone. In the passenger seat rode Gurner Nelson, who was later described as his co-driver, which he was not. In the tradition of the old open road races many drivers carried passengers that day, pals usually, navigators sometimes, company of course, and perhaps useful as muscle if the car slid into a ditch. Nelson had been an elevator operator in one of the hotels frequented by Portago and his mother, and had latched on to the boy. Though older, he had become a friend. A major domo as well. I had stood with him at Cortina. I had found him fascinating too, for he said as many quotable things as Portago himself. I had made Nelson out to be a man who watched the world go by with a cynical smile on his lips, making no effort to control his own life or anyone else's.

The Ferrari team had fuel and tire depots at Ravenna, Pescara and Rome, which were official checkpoints as well, so Portago knew all day where he stood. As he came down out of the mountains he could see the spires of Rome ahead, and he pulled into the Ferrari depot, took on fuel and was told he lay fifth. Linda Christian, his current girlfriend, was there. Dirty and sweaty as he was he pulled her down over the cockpit and kissed her. This kiss lasted long enough for a photographer to run up and snap a memorable photo that would be published around the world. How romantic.

There was another depot at Florence—he was still fifth—and the final one at Bologna, by which time he was fourth. A little later he was third and gaining. Could he have won the race?

Beyond Bologna he had the pedal floored. He rocketed through Goito, and was making top speed, about 170 mph, as the faded walls of Guidizzollo came into sight. He had come more than 960 miles. The finish line was now about thirty miles ahead, the road so straight and flat he could almost see it. The car could go no faster than this. In less than ten minutes he would be there.

It was late afternoon. The sun had started down. In a fraction of a second a good many things and people came to an end. Though I was 4,000 miles away, something ended for me too, or so I learned the next day, and something else went deep into my soul, so that afterwards I would never again look at life in quite the same way.

According to witnesses the car inexplicably swerved left and shot off the road. I have seen a number of explanations. A blown tire was one. A cracked half axle, damaged when the car slid into a curb many miles back, was another. Portago, it was said, knew about the weakened half axle, the tire rubbing on the frame or fender of the car, making an eventual blowout inevitable, but chose to bet he could make the finish line first. Was he that daring, that mindless?

Again according to witnesses the car's tail walloped the embankment, uprooting milestone 21, before guillotining a telephone pole and leaping into the air.

The car evidently careened across the road and up the opposite embankment, where it scythed down two boys. It was in the air now, and it sailed back to the other side where it slaughtered seven or eight more, all of whom were standing. Others, who were seated on the embankment were missed completely; the car went right over them. Finally it dropped low enough to be caught and held by the drainage ditch.

Ten or eleven spectators had been killed; I have seen both figures given. The Mille Miglia had been killed too. As an open road race it was never run again.

Portago and Nelson had been flung out. There were no seat belts in race cars in those days. When a car collided with something its driver or drivers went flying. The machine itself disintegrated as well, and men and spare parts danced on the air. Nelson was found in a field to the left.

Portago was found twice. That is, the hood of the car had lashed back and he was in two pieces.

I heard the news on the radio in mid afternoon, New York time. I was listening to hear who had won the race. In my head I had been living with Portago night and day for weeks, and the shock and grief I felt were as personal as if he had been my brother. So young, so full of life. Alive one second, dead the next. How could this be? These are cosmic questions that everyone gets to consider sooner or later. In my case I was asking them of myself for the first time, and I lay awake most of the night mourning this man I had hardly known, and trying with tortured reasoning to find answers.

I had not immediately considered how his death might affect my profile of him, but the next day my phone rang at work and a secretary at *Cavalier* said she was mailing the manuscript back. To what address, she asked, did I want it sent?

I didn't want it sent where the Maras or the coaches might see it, so I told her to address it to me at home.

I was living in Mount Vernon, N.Y., at the time, commuting every day to the Giants' offices on Columbus Circle. I would take the 8:18 into Grand Central each morning, and most days walk uptown from there. Evenings as I walked back to Grand Central I would look into the windows of the art galleries and travel agencies along the way and wonder if I would ever become a successful writer. Maybe I just wasn't good enough.

The American magazine industry was not much interested in dead men, it seemed. The big name writers who had hounded Portago at Sebring had fared no better than I. *Life* eventually published only three or four pictures, with brief captions, under the headline: "Death Finally Takes a Man Who Courted It."

The pieces submitted to *Esquire* and *True* were rejected outright, and never mind the prestige of the men who had written them. But I didn't realize this at the time, and I doubt that knowing it would have helped me much. My magazine career seemed to me over before it had even started, and I did not know what to do next.

As a publicity man my job grew as I grew, and as the team got stronger. I learned to go into cities in advance of the team, not only the smaller cities of the exhibition games, but the league cities as well. I had a repertoire of anecdotes about players, and I gave them out in dozens and dozens of interviews in newspaper offices, and on radio and TV, and the men who interviewed me always seemed pleased.

I got to see much of the country, and ticket sales improved as well. Back in New York I would call up columnists and offer them lunch with one of the star players at a popular restaurant, usually Toots Shor's. I would bring in the player, sit there listening to the interview, and then, young as I was, pick up the check. That same afternoon I would write up my expense account. Lunch for three. The cost to the Giants of a column about, say, Conerly in *The Herald Tribune* or the *Journal American* therefore might come to as much as $25, a sum I was always afraid Mr. Mara might refuse to pay since, as I have said, he didn't believe he needed publicity. If you've got a winner—

Under Jim Lee Howell something new in coaching was being tried. Whether this was Howell's idea, or Well Mara's, or just happened I never knew, but the new backfield coach, Vince Lombardi, was given exclusive control of the offense, and defensive coach Tom Landry, who had been a player-coach the year before, was given complete control of the defense. Howell himself functioned almost as chairman of the board. He was definitely and obviously in control, he could and did command with a raised eyebrow at times, but he allowed the two other men enormous latitude. They were men of ideas. Left alone they flourished, and as time went on they got stronger and stronger. There also was a new end coach to replace Howell himself, a man named Bill Swiacki, who came from the Detroit Lions, the best team in the league the previous two years, and he brought with him the Lions' passing attack, the first passing attack the Giants had ever had. Swiacki only lasted one year, and he worked under Lombardi.

But now, it could be said, there were two distinct teams wearing Giant uniforms, the offensive team under Lombardi and the defensive team under Landry. They watched game films separately, held separate meetings in separate rooms. They took calisthenics together before each day's work began, and shared the shower room afterwards. Otherwise it was as if they hardly knew each others' names.

The new system worked.

Landry was then 30 years old, a tall, former defensive back from the university of Texas. He was balding, and he had already taken to wearing those small brimmed fedoras that were popular in the early fifties. This style soon began to seem dated, but Landry stuck with it decade after decade. He was a silent man. In social settings he rarely spoke. At meetings of the Five Thirty Club he would sip a beer and say nothing, at dinner the same. When the team won he never showed glee, and when it lost you could not tell this from his face or demeanor. I ate scores of meals with him, spent hundreds of hours in his presence but never had a conversation with him. He was, if possible, an even more taciturn man than Quarterback Conerly; a conversation between the two of them would have been interesting to overhear.

In the army during World War II Landry had gone to flight school and become an Air Corps pilot, but you would have to find this out from someone else, you were not going to hear it from him. The height limit for fighter pilots was five feet ten, so Landry, who was six-two, 190 pounds, was assigned to bombers, and he flew Flying Fortresses in combat over

Germany, and on some raids ten percent of the planes or more did not get back. He never talked of this, or alluded to it in any way. I once asked if it had bothered him to drop bombs on civilians, on cities. The answer came back: No, that's what the bombs were for. End of conversation.

What else did I ever learn about him? His wife's name was Alicia. He called himself a Christian, and apparently had strong religious beliefs. For breakfast he drank water. How this subject came up I do not know. Not tea or coffee or juice, just water. When I questioned him about this (probably what I said was: "Really?") he did not try to justify his choice or explain why he made it, he merely fell silent. No, I cannot say I ever knew him.

It was impossible to believe that if he ever became a head coach he would be capable of inspiring players, but when the Dallas Cowboys came into existence in 1960 he was their first, and for twenty nine years, only head coach. When he patrolled the sidelines during games he could be recognized by his hat, and he won more games than all but two other coaches in League history.

Nonetheless, he never really caught on with the public, and prior to what would have been his thirtieth season the team was sold and the new owner dumped him. It was the Steve Owen story all over again, but few tears were shed for Tom Landry. He was not the type man who attracted an emotional response.

The one who did capture the public fancy was Lombardi, who would very soon become the most famous coach in America, one of the two or three most famous in the history of the game, literally a legend in his own time, and this is something that mystified me then and still does.

Well Mara once said: "You could hear Vince laughing from two blocks away. You couldn't hear Landry if you were in the next chair.

Lombardi was 41 years old his first year with the Giants, and if he was looking for a career break-through, it was not in sight. He had come from college football where he had worked as an assistant coach at West Point, so he was not even going to be familiar with the pro game. Jim Lee Howell didn't know him, and can't be said to have hired him. Usually head coaches choose their assistants, but it was Well Mara who chose Lombardi, and Howell did not have much choice except to approve the choice. Well Mara and Lombardi had been classmates at Fordham in the thirties. Though not very big for a lineman—five-nine, and about 170 pounds—Lombardi had played guard on the great Fordham teams of that era, had been one of the so-called Seven Blocks of Granite, and Well Mara had remembered him now.

Immediately Lombardi locked himself up with game films so as to study current Giants players. He charted every player on every play, and he did not come out for months. This was a pattern that would hold throughout his career. He would prove to be the hardest worker anyone had ever seen.

Training camp opened, and we began to learn who he was. Like the Maras he went to mass and communion every day. Unlike Landry he was an emotional man. What he was feeling showed on his face and in his voice. He hid, it seemed, nothing. He drove his players hard, praising them for good plays, screaming at them when they made mistakes. He was always tense, a man leaning forward on the balls of his feet, and he smoked too much. His voice was distinctive. It was loud, raspy and could be heard all over the practice field. He had some pet phrases. "Run to daylight", for instance. Nobody objected to this one, but also he kept urging backs and ends to "run with abandon." After a few days on the team bulletin board someone tacked up a hand drawn sketch of a naked woman. She had tremendous breasts. Her name, emblazoned on the thin sash which was all she wore, was ABANDON, and in the bubble over her head she was saying: "Come Run With Me."

The entire camp was laughing, though not Lombardi. He said nothing about it that I recall but on the field never again advised anyone about who to run with.

He always seemed to me vulnerable to this kind of ragging. At West Point none of the cadets had dared do it, perhaps, but this was the pros, and he was a man who did not spend enough time protecting himself.

He was always well groomed. He had his hair cut once a week, a habit he had learned at West Point where it was obligatory for cadets. He was barrel-chested and had a lovely smile but was not a handsome man, and there were gaps between his two front teeth top and bottom, and between some of the others as well. One columnist described him as having teeth like tank traps. Another wrote: "Lombardi smiled showing all forty eight teeth." Later, when he had become a god, this kind of thing perhaps did not bother him, but he wasn't a god yet, and I assume it hurt.

I always had the feeling he wasn't all that sure of himself. He grew up in an era when Americans of Italian extraction, even if not immigrants themselves, were at best the sons of immigrants, sons of the laboring classes, and Italians in general were often disparaged. People mocked the way immigrant Italians spoke English, adding a vowel at the end of every word. There were hundreds of Italian jokes, and often Italians heard themselves referred to as Ginnies, Wops, Dagos. Any second generation Italian had experienced a lot of this. Lombardi had too, of course, it was obviously a confidence buster, and as he tried to make his way in life he had had to get past it many times.

In private he was a talkative man, but soft spoken. The big voice he kept muted, and there was no sign of the brash confidence he displayed on the field. Still, he came across as gruff, and as a man who seemed socially unsure of himself. Socially, he lacked finesse.

And since at first the Giants paid him only $8,500 a year, the going rate for backfield coaches, Lombardi was obliged to work at a second job selling life insurance. One of his clients was me—I still have two policies at home, the first I ever bought, with his name on them. He did not give me a hard sell. At the age I was then death was of no concern, but Lombardi very quietly taught me that I needed insurance, and I bought.

On the field he was a man of energy and drive, the big loud voice could be heard from a hundred yards away, and when he was trying to teach players what he wanted them to learn any complexes he may have harbored disappeared. He let Jim Lee Howell make the speeches, deal with the press, deal with Well Mara, and he himself got on with the job of fashioning a group of disparate young men into an offense that was exciting, that could score points, that could win games, and at the end of the 1956 season, his third as backfield coach, the Giants beat the Chicago Bears in the championship game by 47-7.

With Lombardi what you saw was what you got. His feelings always showed. When a play worked he chortled with delight. When one failed he visibly suffered. He said what he thought, didn't know how to lie or dissimulate, and was amazingly frank at times, even to me. One afternoon in training camp Jim Lee got mad at the players, told them off for not working hard enough, and then kept them out scrimmaging an extra hour under a broiling sun.

This was the second workout of the day, and he pushed them to exhaustion. When he finally sent them to the showers, Lombardi muttered to me: "He just killed the season. This team's not going anywhere now." He meant, I think, that the punishment just inflicted had taken the heart out of the team, and heart did not grow back. I was surprised, did not believe he could be serious, for the season hadn't even started yet, but he proved to be right, and that year the Giants ran completely out of steam at the end, lost the final three games, and finished only second. Was it this ability to perceive so acutely the moods and emotions of his players, their needs that they didn't even know they had, that made Lombardi in the end such a great coach?

One year there were two more quarterback hopefuls. One was from a major college, had a major reputation, and proved to have many qualities, the ability to throw a football long and accurately not among them. The other was a 27th round draft choice from a small college, tall, blond, and a brilliant passer, even in a league full of same, but he wore his blond hair long in an era of crew cuts, and complained often of minor injuries which the others took stoically. He seemed not tough enough. Almost at once the other players nicknamed him Elvis, after the first of the long haired singers who was just becoming popular, and after that they ragged him day and night, and the ragging was not always kind. The question soon became: how long could he stand it. The coaches, who might have protected him, who might have shut the ragging down, did nothing.

There came a Sunday when Conerly was hurt, and Elvis, everybody called him that now, not only started at quarterback but completed 21 of 27 passes for two touchdowns, while leading the team to an easy victory. How that boy could throw the ball!

Even this did not stop the ragging, and Elvis was put into games less and less often, and then cut.

This troubled me, and I had several long talks with Lombardi about it. Why hadn't the coaches nourished such talent, I asked, why throw him to the wolves? Why lose him?

Lombardi the teacher began to ask rhetorical questions, including this one. What was the most important quality a player needed?

I offered several answers, but not the one he and the other coaches looked for first in every player.

"Desire," he said.

"Not talent?"

"No, desire."

A player, Lombardi said patiently, quietly, has to want to play the game above all things, must want to give of himself at all times. He has to love everything about the game. The blond boy, according to Lombardi, didn't have enough desire. Neither did Fig Newton, a few years ago, even though he could catch any ball thrown near him and could run the hundred in 9.6 as well. Coaches could give various kinds of help to players, but desire had to come from within. There was nothing a coach could do.

Despite what Lombardi had said, the story of the blond quarterback intrigued me, and I began to write a short story based rather loosely on his short career, a kind of football tragedy. Suppose he suffered a bad injury, but no one believed him, and he went on playing? I wrote this story during the off season of 1957. It came out longer than I intended, about 42 typewritten pages, but after a time it was as good as my then equipment allowed me to make it, and I got ready to send it around to the magazines. Lombardi was in the office a lot that winter, but I did not tell him about it, and in fact did not tell anyone. The story was about football; therefore someone might demand to see it. Or worse, favor me with a new round of smart remarks or smug smirks. Lombardi had never done this, but he had never encouraged me either. I was about to be 27 years old, but I had still never been published except in newspapers.

Most of the magazines to whom I sent my stories don't exist anymore, or else are so changed as to be unrecognizable. *The New Yorker* used to publish several stories every week, *Esquire* several every month. *Cosmopolitan*'s specialty was literary fiction, which was what I thought I was doing.

At the top of the heap were *Colliers* and *The Saturday Evening Post.* The Post, which boasted a paid circulation of over five million, meaning about fifteen million readers for each issue, published four short stories and a serialized novel every week, and sometimes a novelette as well, and paid, it was said, terrific money.

How many stories were being published in magazines in America then? Where did people find time to read them all?

Now I typed a title on the story about the blond quarterback: *The Touchdown Makers*. The two novels I had written had not sold, nor the twenty or so previous stories, but this one was the best I had done so far, I thought. Maybe this one—

After some thought I decided to send it to the sports editor of *The Saturday Evening Post*, because he had once hit me up for free tickets to a Giants game. Perhaps he might think he owed me a favor. I asked him to forward the story to the fiction editor, and he sent a note back saying he had done so.

The manuscript was rejected quickly enough, but this time there was a letter attached, signed by E.N. Brandt, the fiction editor. My story was quite long, Brandt noted, the length the Post called a novelette, of which they had too many on inventory already. However, once they had used some of them up they'd be happy to look at the story again.

To me this was just another rejection, more polite than most, and I was desolate. I sent the story around to other places. No one took it, or even sent more than a printed rejection slip. One day I talked to my father's plumber, a sympathetic man my father's age. "Isn't anyone ever going to publish me?" I said, almost in tears.

"Maybe," he answered, "you just aren't old enough yet."

What does he know, I thought, he's just a plumber.

Tales of rejection any author can tell you—any artist of any kind. Some cannot take the rejection, and those are the ones who never get to be heard.

It takes time, and I wish I had known this then. Literary talent does not emerge from the marble in polished form. Truths have to be found that are different in quality and weight from those that other authors have found before. And when the young author has managed finally to write something publishable, he has to learn still another skill, this one completely different from everything so far: how to sell it.

The championship game that the Giants had just won had played to over 5,000 empty seats, for pro football did not have much of a grip on the public imagination as yet, and during the off season no one, it seemed, thought of the game or the Giants at all. Our phones did not ring, and there wasn't much for any of us to do, so when the coaches were in the office we would sit around talking football most of the day. However, if Lombardi happened to come in alone, he and I would sometimes have long talks. Already he wanted a head coaching job badly. "I want my own team," he said often enough. Perhaps I was a sounding board. He was telling me what he didn't yet wish to tell Well Mara.

So we both wanted something that apparently we could not have.

For me the waiting went on and on. In reality it was not such a long time perhaps, but time counts differently when you are that age. It seemed an eternity to me.

As the 1957 season progressed I kept my eye on the Post each week, and as soon as an issue appeared with a novelette in it, I mailed off *The Touchdown Makers* a second time.

Two mornings later my phone rang, and the caller identified himself: "This is Mr. Brandt—"

As soon as I heard the name I got chills, and the hairs stood up on my hands.

"—From Philadelphia," he said, "from *The Saturday Evening Post.* Well—"

A rivulet of sweat was running down my back.

"The last thing in the world we need is another novelette, but, well—"

I knew he hadn't called to give me still another rejection, and my head had gone so light I thought I might faint.

"Well, we're buying it."

A start, a start. At last a start.

"We'll pay you $2,500. That's our beginning rate for new authors. Is that all right?"

All right? It was almost half a year's pay.

I'm surprised I was able to answer him at all.

When I could talk again I phoned my wife and went through the whole charade.

"I just had a call from Mr. Brandt," I said.

"Yes?"

"From Philadelphia."

"Yes?"

"From *The Saturday Evening Post*."

"Yes?"

"They're taking it."

There was a shocked silence, and then: "Oh I'm so happy for you."

The check arrived two days after that. No one ever paid as fast as *The Saturday Evening Post*. I thought it would be gauche to show such a big check around, but Jack Mara asked to see it, and after that I showed it to everybody.

The story was not to be published until the following season, and as the date approached I began to worry about how the Maras would take it, for the villain of the piece was the team owner, and Well Mara might decide it was based on him.

Finally the issue appeared. Nobody ever said anything to me about it. But after that I was never invited along when the Maras went out to lunch, as I frequently had been previously.

That was the year of the so-called greatest game ever played. Having won their division the Giants met the Baltimore Colts in Yankee Stadium for the national championship. It was a game played with terrible intensity on an unseasonably warm December day with both teams, except for one or two big plays, scarcely able to make a first down. With under two minutes left the Giants led by 17-14, but the Colts marched almost the length of the field, and with seven seconds to play kicked a tying field goal. Then came the first sudden death overtime playoff in league history. Having won the toss, having received the kickoff, the Giants failed to make a first down. A titanic punt put the Colts on their own 18 yard line. Once again they came the length of the field, it took them eighteen plays, six or seven minutes of agony for me, and once again they scored, and the game was over. The Giants had lost it 23-17.

It was said later that this one sudden-death game was what put pro football into orbit, leading to the astonishing popularity the game enjoys today.

Previously I had died a little every time the team lost; that day I died a lot. I was by now 28, was plainly going nowhere as Publicity Director of the New York Football Giants, and since I was unable to read the future it seemed to me that the game itself was going nowhere just as fast. I was earning $125 a week, and I asked Jack Mara for a raise, citing among other arguments that I ought to be paid for the suffering I went through, watching the team win some games and lose others, unable to affect the outcome in any way, my whole life tied to the next completed pass, the next first down.

But his answer was curt. "The job pays $125 a week, Bob."

I was thinking of going out on my own as a freelance, I told him.

Jack Mara said nothing, and I paused because a decision was about to be made, and I was going over it again in my head. Since selling *The Touchdown Makers* I had, writing in my spare time, sold a few other magazine pieces—only a few. A freelance existence was precarious to say the least, and I had a wife and two little girls to support. I had some possible assignments. Ideas in which editors had expressed interest. If the stories worked out I would be paid for them. If they didn't I would get nothing. The assignments all lay in Europe, which seemed to me unexploited territory for a freelance writer, but no one was willing to pay my passage across. I would have to pay it myself, and all other expenses as well. Even if the first assignments worked out, was I so sure there would be others? Could I support myself long term?

Jack Mara watched me, and waited.

Probably I bit down on my lip a time or two. Ahead was no security at all. Yet Europe seemed to me the best possible chance to make a name for myself.

The next season—training camp—didn't start until July. "If it doesn't work out," I asked Jack Mara, "can I come back?"

"No," he said.

This reply may have had something to do with *The Touchdown Makers*, or perhaps it did not. I have often wondered what I would have done if he had upped my salary, told me how important I was to him and Well and his father, and to the fortunes of the team, how much everyone wanted me to stay.

He didn't. Which seemed to leave me with no choice at all, so I resigned.

Two months later Vince Lombardi resigned also.

Many assistant coaches get head coaching jobs these days, but there are thirty two teams; jobs open up all the time. That year, Lombardi's crucial year, there were twelve teams only, and the sole job vacant was as coach of the Green Bay Packers, a team which, in the season just past, even as the Giants and Colts moved toward the greatest game ever played, had fielded the worst team and compiled the worst record in the league, winning only one game out of twelve. Its best players appeared to be no better than ordinary, and its somewhat promising quarterback, a journeyman named Bart Starr, had never even won the job outright but shared time with another.

On the whole a new head coach gets only one chance at success. If he takes over a bad team and fails to move it, he will be fired the next year, or the year after, and will be forced to revert to being an assistant somewhere else, or leave the game altogether. A second chance as head coach he probably won't get.

Lombardi knew this, and it was one of the reasons he did not want to go to Green Bay, but there were others.

He was a New Yorker, raised in Brooklyn, educated at Fordham in the Bronx. New York was home. Green Bay was to his mind the worst hick town imaginable, population under 80,000, with not much to do except drink beer in saloons or fish over an ice hole on the frozen lake. Green Bay was the poor relation of the league, and the temperature was below zero for months and months at a time. What would he do there? What would his wife do there?

Lombardi wanted the Giants.

Jim Lee Howell would hang on a bit longer, but the strain was beating him down. Clearly he would not last more than another year or two. Lombardi asked for assurances that he would succeed Howell as coach.

The Maras refused to give it to him.

Surely it was as difficult for them to imagine him as a head coach, as it was for me. Perhaps the Maras thought as I did, that Lombardi lacked a number of essential qualities, and one of them was presence. I liked him a lot, but he was not a man who could command by raising an eyebrow. He would have to shout. He was too focused, too earnest, too intense. He was an honest, honorable man, but the edges were not smooth. He was too vulnerable. His personality was too exposed. A head coach could not be a man who protected himself no better than Lombardi did.

Rejected by the Giants, deciding he had no other choice, he took the Green Bay job. If he wanted his own team, as he put it, it was Green Bay or nothing.

His amazing career began. He had a winning season the first year, won the division championship the second year, and then won five national championships in the next seven years, and the first two super bowls as well. He shouted at his players, but he gave them pride, and belief in themselves. He was voted coach of the year many times. Under Lombardi, Bart Starr became the best quarterback in football, and nine of those "ordinary" players, including Starr, are in the Hall of Fame today. As is, of course, Lombardi.

As he started to win, reporters flocked to Green Bay. The story seemed so improbable, a Brooklyn boy making good in that frozen wasteland. They turned him into a legend, and then a god. Television documentaries were made about him, in which mostly he looked embarrassed, and he was on the cover of *Time Magazine*, not to mention a number of other publications. Everything he said got quoted, starting with "Run To Daylight", which then became the title of the first book written about him, and the first documentary; and also: "Winning isn't everything, it's the only thing", which you will find in almost all the books of famous quotations. One of his players said of him: "He treats us all the same—like dirt," and this quote was widely circulated as well. People invented jokes about him, which made the rounds. One of them had his wife in bed in the night saying: "My God, your feet are cold." To which he replied: "In bed you may call me Vincent." In Green Bay an avenue soon bore his name. Thirty years after his death a book about him was on *The New York Times* best seller list for months.

If you are interested in sudden unexpected fame you might study the career of Vincent Lombardi.

Who would have thought it?

As I left the Giants I took with me a great number of sensual impressions, many of them from the various training camps, and they are vivid to me to this day.

The scrimmages. End runs that ended five feet from where I stood. The noise. The speed. The padded haunches, the swollen shoulders coming fast, the collision of helmets, bodies. Crashes that squeezed the sweat out of the uniforms, out of the faces, drops of sweat in the air, almost a mist, sparkling in the afternoon sun.

The injuries, the bad ones and the not so bad: the little halfback with the two inch gash over his eye sitting sweaty and dirty on an equipment trunk, not making a sound as the team doctor drew the gash together with needles, and sewed him up.

Balls thrown hard. Sometimes I warmed up Charlie Conerly before practice, and every ball he threw me, if I hadn't caught it, would have hit me smack in the chin. Every one. And of course he had to lunge for half the balls I threw back.

Naked hope on display, year after year. One boy wanted so badly to make the team that he ran himself into total exhaustion. He passed out, and could not immediately be revived. He was in shock, and I looked down on him and wondered if he was still breathing. At the Five Thirty Club later the doctor said that the next time this happened the boy might die, so the coaches cut him.

"The Turk is out." This whisper occupied the halls many times each summer: "The Turk is out." It meant that assistant coaches were searching for certain players, who were about to be cut. Some boys, knowing they were on the edge, hid. The assistant would find them anyway and say: "Coach wants to see you." And the boy knew, and his head would drop.

Some years he would be sent along to me afterwards, and I would collect his playbook and sign the travel voucher home and hand it to him. A player cut from the team during training camp during those years received no pay for the days or weeks he had put in; he got the voucher, nothing else. Most times as I handed it over nothing was said.

The overloaded elevators. In one hotel I came down in one whose capacity was eight passengers—so said the wall plaque when we turned to look at it. But the other seven were linemen and the weight was such that the cabin came to a stop ten inches below the sill. The doors would not open and we had to be rescued.

Game days. The 10 a.m. breakfasts in hotels. The mostly overcooked steaks piled high in the center of the tables beside pitchers of orange juice beaded on the outside. The chefs had always been instructed that the steaks and baked potatoes had to be there ready when the players came in, that the players were big eaters, but fast eaters, and would not wait.

The locker room. The kickoff twenty minutes away. The tense young faces. Tension that seemed stifling, and then here came the equipment manager moving along the dressing stalls with a box, collecting bridgework. Clumps of teeth rattled down into the box, leaving twenty or more partly vacant mouths. Most of the linemen and almost all the backs had played without face guards at earlier stages of their lives. Now, though not much more than boys, they showed the caved in cheeks and sudden gums of old old men.

There are many other such memories, but these are some. Yes I loved the football. It was just that I wanted something else more.

I saw Lombardi only once while he was coaching Green Bay. It happened that I was going to be in Cleveland one Sunday when the Packers would be there playing the Browns, so I phoned him. Eight years had passed, and he was now as famous as any man in America except possibly the president, but immediately he offered me tickets, which I refused, for I had already cadged them from my former counterpart on the Browns, and after that he invited my wife and me to the Packers' version of the Five Thirty Club the night before the game. I accepted, and as I came into the crowded hotel suite he ran across to greet me grinning from ear to ear, saying: "I knew you would become a great writer."

This was gratifying, of course. I only wished he had said it back then when I was struggling so hard, for it might have helped. He must have seen, they all should have seen, how hard I was trying. In players they looked for desire first, and I had certainly shown them that.

We went out to dinner together, talked of the Maras, talked of players, talked of the novel I was writing about pro football, for which I had received an advance of $15,000, the best contract I had had to that point. When dinner ended Lombardi paid, or rather the Packers, a rich team now, paid, and afterwards we said goodbye, and I never saw him again.

He coached in all nine years in Green Bay, stayed on one more year as general manager, then decided he wanted to coach again, though not there. Again he wanted the Giants, and the job was open, or would be soon, for the glory years were over and the Giants were back in the doldrums. But Lombardi was famous now, and he wanted not only the head coaching job but equity in the team, and this the Maras would not give him.

So he went to the Washington Redskins, which gave him everything he asked for, except what he wanted most, which was New York. But almost immediately he came down with colon cancer. Many Packer players came to the hospital to see him, for they had heard he was dying. They called him "Coach," and gazed down at him with reverence. He told them: "I'm going to beat this thing."

But he didn't. He was 57 years old.

My first year with the Giants, my first training camp, I had come up from Mexico bearing my typewriter in its wooden box, and a suitcase that contained my clothes and my never to be published manuscripts. The last part of the trip north from Minneapolis airport to St. Peter was in a Greyhound bus containing mostly players. Like me, they were reporting to camp, and among them was Kyle Rote, the star halfback, to whom I introduced myself. Rote was all of 25, two years older than I was, but coming from Mexico I had not shaved in a day and a half, and was embarrassed to be meeting such a great player, looking, I imagined, scruffy.

In a way Rote represents the beginning and the end of my football career. He turned out to be, to me, the most interesting of all the players, the wittiest, the kindest, a great running back, a great receiver, the Giants' captain, a brilliant natural athlete in all sports, and an after dinner speaker of enormous charm—by far the best on the team; I can attest to this because I was the one who scheduled the players' appearances, and sometimes accompanied them to them. Rote was also a writer of short stories, some of which somewhat shyly he gave me to read. His stories were at least as good as the ones I was writing at the time, maybe better. Naturally he did not show them to his teammates. He drew amusing cartoons as well that he also showed me.

Life did not turn out well for him.

A Texan from San Antonio, he was one of the best known athletes of the day. At Southern Methodist he had been on everybody's All American team. The SMU-Notre Dame game when he was a senior was broadcast on national radio. This was in 1950. Rote ran, passed, kicked, he was a one man team, it was Rote against Notre Dame, and in the end he lost. But his performance that day had put his name on the lips of everyone who cared about football. In the articles written about him one learned that, young as he was, he was already married, that he tried always to do and say what was expected of him, to be what was expected of him. An All American on the field and off. One of the finest young men in the country.

In the winter draft the Giants drew the bonus pick and immediately picked Rote, as any other team would have done also. He signed for a $5,000 bonus, plus $15,000 a season, unheard of sums for any player, much less a rookie. Quarterback Conerly in his fourth season got only a bit more, $16,000, and Frank Gifford, whose life and career in many ways paralleled Rote's, would sign the following year for $8,500.

Rote made a brilliant start, then suffered torn knee cartilages twice in successive years, and his days as a running back were over. His career would have been over, had he been a lesser player than he was. Instead he became a receiver, played on all the big teams of the fifties, and lasted altogether eleven seasons.

But after football there was—nothing. He became a football commentator on NBC, as Gifford did on CBS. But Rote on television, and on radio as well, was wooden. The easy warmth he showed from the speaker's platform, the ability to charm people, was nowhere in evidence, and every time I heard him I found myself asking: But where did it go?

As a commentator, Rote did not last.

His marriage did not last either. He got involved with a former Miss America, Sharon K. Ritchie. She was married too, and after each of them got divorced they married each other. The All American Girl and the All American Boy. They came to our house to dinner. Sharon fussed over my daughters—thrilling to them—which was sweet of her. At a later dinner she said that winning the Miss America contest had been the high point of her life—she was then about 35—and everything since had been downhill. Rote could have said much the same, perhaps, though he was as charming as always, a delight to be with.

But his marriage to Miss America did not last either, and later there was a third marriage. During part of this time he had been a Giants' assistant coach, but the straitlaced Maras considered his conduct immoral, and they did not renew his contract. Gifford did much the same thing later, or even worse, for his first wife came down with multiple sclerosis. He divorced her anyway, and married another, then divorced this second wife to marry a television star.

But none of this, apparently, hurt Gifford with the Maras. On television he was just as wooden as Rote, maybe more so, but in 1971 he switched to ABC and became a commentator on Monday Night Football on which he lasted until 1998. He became a rich man. Rote by then was drinking too much, and was heavily in debt. His drinking began while he was still a player, I believe. I always supposed, maybe I am wrong, that he drank to dull the pain in his knees, that his knees, though he said nothing about it to anyone, hurt him all the time.

Gifford always seemed to me a much harder man than Rote. He was, during my years with the Giants, a loner, which is odd for a man in a team sport. After dinner in the training camps he never joined in the gabfests or bridge games, but wandered around by himself. The two of us once stood together in the night on a street corner in Excelsior Springs, Missouri, looking for girls. We didn't go out together, we met on the street corner by accident. Even then I did not have the feeling that we shared anything, not even the moment. I just happened to be standing next to him, nothing more. He was not a big star as yet. We were both 23, he was already married, and no girls came by. Eventually we went back to the dormitory. That night, as always, he seemed to me self absorbed, rather humorless, not a warm young man at all.

He was not very good at public speaking, though I believe he became good later, and I used him as little as possible.

One day long afterwards a mutual friend set up a tennis match with him.

He lived in Greenwich then, as I did, and had his own court. This was just before he dropped his second wife and married his third. I had not seen him in many, many years, and wanted only to talk over those seasons of our youth, the time when we were boys together. But this idea did not interest Gifford, and there was no such conversation. Gifford wanted only to play tennis. And once on the court he wanted only to win.

If I had to describe a single image of him as a player, it would be from early in his career. During Steve Owen's last year the Giants were so bad that, in a game in the Polo Grounds against the Cleveland Browns, Gifford found himself playing offense and defense both. Late in the game he intercepted a pass and ran it back until there was no one between him and the goal line but the Brown's quarterback, Otto Graham. Graham was the heart and soul of the Browns' team, and Gifford made no attempt to elude him. At full speed he tried to run over him. There was a massive collision, and both men went down, and when I asked Gifford afterwards why he had done this he said he had thought that if he hurt Graham and knocked him out of the game, this would be more valuable to the Giants by far than scoring a touchdown.

Maybe, but Rote would have run around him. And scored.

The novel I wrote, the one I had mentioned to Lombardi, was called *Only A Game* and sales were slow until I was interviewed on the Today Show by a man named Joe Garagiola, who told viewers, and me as well, that one Giants star had called up another Giants star, and said: "It's you, but with my body."

The allusion was to Gifford phoning Rote.

The next day the novel sold 3,000 copies, and although it never became a big best seller, it went through several printings, acquired cult status, and kept me afloat for a year or two. *Sports Illustrated* in 2002 called it one of the top sports books of all time.

It did one other thing, it finished me with the Giants. First I received a letter from Well Mara. He had not read my book, and would not, he began, after which he castigated me for two single spaced pages. He had thought I was an honorable man, Galahad on a white horse, but my book proved that my steed was stained, and my lance a dripping reed.

You can laugh at the imagery, but the man was very upset.

In my novel, after the hero falls in love with another woman, his wife attempts suicide. I would not have written these scenes so callously, Well Mara wrote, if I had looked into Betty Rote's face when they carried her out of her house on a stretcher, or had been with him when he took Kyle to the hospital.

Of course many of the scenes in the book did actually happen but not that one, I had thought. That one I had imagined to be pure invention by me. The story line had called for it, and so I had made it up. Apparently I was wrong. It too had actually happened. Apparently I had invented the truth.

So I wrote Well back. I tried to explain that I had known nothing about any actual suicide attempt, nothing at that time about the Rotes' marriage. I tried to apologize where I could.

And a letter came back from him which began: "Your letter like your book will remain unread by me."

Until that time I had continued to receive press credentials, and to watch home games from the press box in Yankee Stadium, Giants Stadium in New Jersey being still some years in the future. The press box hung below the mezzanine. A short, iron staircase led down to it, at the top of which was stationed a guard. This is where, at the next game, I was intercepted by the team's general manager who demanded my credentials back, and then instructed the guard not to let me in the press box ever again.

I never went to another Giants game. Nor to a training camp. Until today.

Some years ago I ran into Rote in the grill room of the Four Seasons, the New York restaurant favored by the publishing business. I was there with Michael Korda, my editor at the time. Why Rote was there I do not know, perhaps only to have lunch, but he came forward with his hand outstretched saying: "Bob, I'm Kyle Rote."

This man's face had been on magazine covers, so I was struck by a wave of sadness.

I said: "Oh, Kyle, you don't have to tell me you're Kyle Rote."

Last year at a Fordham dinner honoring my father I encountered Well Mara. Old Tim Mara was by now long dead, as was Jack Mara, and of course my father too. Well Mara was 83 years of age, he told me somewhat proudly, and we talked about old players and old games for most of an hour, which perhaps meant that all was forgiven, I hoped that's what it meant. In any case, it was because of that meeting that I felt able to make arrangements to visit the Albany training camp today.

I expected Well Mara to be here, but don't see him, and as I stand at the edge of the field watching practice I am surprised how uneasy it makes me feel to keep looking around for him. Finally the morning session ends and a number of us troop toward the cafeteria on the ground floor of the Indian Quad dormitory, which is where the players are housed, and here comes Well along the path, hand outstretched, smiling. Which proves, I suppose, that on attaining a certain age it becomes hard to hold grudges any longer.

We go into the cafeteria together, and through the line together, players in front of us and behind, overly large young men wearing shorts, T-shirts and sandals for the most part, and heaping their plates higher than we do. The luncheon fare is much the same as in my time: cold roast beef and turkey, pasta salads, rice salads, raw vegetables, rolls.

Well heads for a table already occupied by the team's general manager and one of the assistant coaches, and motions me to the seat beside him, and during lunch he asks after my family, and I after his. The last of his children, he tells me, is getting married this summer. “I’m almost free,” he remarks with a smile.

After that we all talk football. The atmosphere is cordial enough, but as I try to eat, try to listen, try to respond from time to time, I try also to cope with those insistent, persistent emotions I mentioned earlier. It is not just Well Mara who makes me uncomfortable, it is all of them. And it is then I realize there can be no place for me among these football people. Once long ago they nurtured me—not these same men perhaps, with the exception of Well, but men just like them. And then I spurned them. That’s what my discomfort is all about. I am like a onetime lover who long ago walked out. Once having turned away from what they hold dearest in life I can’t come back.

I stay for afternoon practice, the booming, bashing part of the day’s work. At last the whistle blows, the players straggle toward the locker room, the small crowd drifts away, and the college boys in the T-shirts gather up all the balls.

Now will come the July 2000 version of the Five Thirty Club, to which I have been invited. Strangely, or perhaps not so strangely, I do not wish to go. With fourteen coaches present, plus others, it will be a cocktail party, not the somewhat intimate gatherings of my time with the team. I don’t know these people. I was introduced to Head Coach Fassell at lunch but did not realize at first whose hand I was shaking.

My general discomfort is no less strong this minute than it has been all day. It is as if, by going away from the game and finding a different life, I betrayed them all. I proved that my values were not and are not their values, have not been for many years. Would they feel this, if I turn up at the Five Thirty Club? I don’t know, but I would.

So I walk off the field, find my car and drive home.

4.
The Best Job in the World

October 5, 2000, Nice

We stand in the road looking through the fence at the villa, and for a time neither of us speaks. The windows are open, but we don't know who lives there, and it does not occur to us to ring the bell.

It is not a big house, does not look comfortable, nor is it handsome. Its style is Mediterranean, but it's not an attractive version. Square, two stories. Beige stucco walls. Green shutters under an orange tile roof that, like a hat with too wide a brim, overhangs too much on all sides. The result looks heavy, overly prominent. There are windows but they seem a bit too narrow and there are not enough of them. Off the bedrooms hang two balconies but they are small too. They once commanded an extraordinary view of town and sea, but major apartment buildings have been built on both sides, and in front. To admire the view today you must peer through shelves of balconies descending the hill.

In short, no one but us is likely to stare in at this house, would look at it twice.

We are nearly at the top of the Chemin de Fabron on the north western outskirts of the city, and the road up here is, as it has always been, tortuous.

The house seems not to have changed over the years. Like most houses hereabouts it has a name that can be read on its gatepost: Villa Nina. It was built between the two wars by a Russian named Kroubitch. Nina was his wife. One day the Gestapo broke down the door and arrested Kroubitch for the crime of being a Jew. Nina never saw him again. Afterwards she could not bear to live in the house, nor sell it either, and so moved items she cared about into a single room, locked the door, and rented the rest of it out year by year, until finally we were there looking for a place to live, and for $85 a month she rented it to us: three bedrooms, living room, dining room, kitchen, a small garden. In America I had quit my job with the Giants. We had sold our car, sublet our apartment, emptied our bank accounts, such as they were. France was home now, or so we pretended. I was out of the football business, out of the publicity business, our ties to America had been cut. I was a professional writer, I told myself, though as yet this was by no means clear. What I really was was a young man with a wife and two small children. Suppose as a writer I did not succeed? We had no money. We had spent nearly every cent just to get here.

And so this afternoon we stand in the road in front of the Villa Nina, both of us reaching back for the facts and emotions of that time. The facts—details, actually—are easy enough to remember. How the rooms were laid out. How shabby most of the furniture was. How the kids looked, one of them five, her sister not quite four, neither yet speaking French, holding hands and leaving the house for the communal school in the valley for the first time.

The top of the Chemin de Fabron was rural then, and the Villa Nina stood in a crowd of carnation farms. In summer the fields around us were a fireworks of color; in winter we lived amidst a huge flashing mirror, for the flowers then grew under glass. Winter and summer the cut flowers went down the hill to the market in the early mornings in baskets in carts dragged by the busses. Mostly our children's classmates came from the farms. The communal school was two rooms for eight grades.

When you are young and just starting out, as we were then, such details stay with you forever. But the emotions that accompanied them are proving today much harder to conjure up. However carefully I stare in at the Villa Nina I don't seem able to feel them very much and when I look over at Peggy, I don't think she does either. The details are in place in both our heads, or nearly so, and that's about all.

I ought to be better at the conjuring up of emotions, because it is what I do every day. A novel is a succession of specific scenes, each one designed to evoke in the reader's head whatever emotions the novelist is trying to put there. To the reader these emotions may seem to occur spontaneously, and if the novelist is good enough so they should, but the process is calculated. In each scene the novelist selects and arranges the details that make the emotion, and the job would be easy if the details he needed were properly labeled. But they are not. Some will work, and some won't. Figuring out which do, which don't, and which order to put them in—that's what's hard. A novelist is a man who tries to twist and hammer details into emotion. He can work all day on a single paragraph only to conclude that the details in hand won't do what he wants them to do. They're the wrong ones, or he doesn't have enough of them, and everything stops while he dredges up some more. The emotion—I've said this before, but it can't be said often enough—is in the details. This is everywhere and always true in fiction, but even in non-fiction articles one seeks to evoke an emotional response from the reader, or at least I do. Perhaps I had a bit too much Scholastic philosophy as a boy. I am not interested in wowing the reader with the speed and intricacy of my steel trap mind. To fill a book or article or story with intellectual tricks seems to me a spurious way of doing business.

The purpose of literature is to make people feel—feel first, and think only afterwards. If the emotions evoked are genuine, plenty of ideas will be implicit in them. After putting the book down the reader will—or at least should—brood about whatever emotions have just moved him. The thoughts and ideas should then come by themselves. The author must attack through the nerve endings, not the brain cells. Emotion first, thought later. This is hard enough to do. To reverse the order is, most times, nearly always in fact, impossible. Literature is an art form, not an intellectual exercise. Art is the communication of emotion from the artist to the recipient. And that, to me, is the only goal an artist ought to have.

There was no desk for me in the Villa Nina, nor any table I could use. I went down to the open market, found an apple crate and brought it home. When I turned it on its side I could get my knees under it. I built shelves into the sides. I unfolded an Esso road map of Europe, trimmed it to fit, and smoothed it out on top. I bought a piece of glass cut to the proper size to cover the map. I put my typewriter out on the glass, pulled up a chair, and that was my office.

After Portago was killed and my article rejected by *Cavalier*, weeks had gone by during which I had sat in my cubicle at the Giants unable to write anything, had lacked the will to try. When Coach Lombardi would come in we would, on occasion, talk of his possible future, not mine, for I did not seem to have one, a secret so shameful that I tried to keep it to myself. Did it show sometimes on my face? Probably. A writer's block as severe as this happened to me only one other time, much later in my career. It too had a specific cause, but an account of it in its proper place comes later.

But finally that winter I got out Martin Gross's list of magazines and editors and looked at it. Just looked—I had no intention of calling anyone.

The next name down was *Coronet*, a small format magazine, a second tier *Reader's Digest*. The editor was named, his phone number noted. A day or two later I forced myself to dial this man. I told him I was a freelance writer with some ideas for his magazine that might interest him. He was cordial, said to come on over, so I did.

I did have some ideas—culled from the daily newspapers, as Martin Gross had advised. Although this new editor was again not much older than I, and although I was trying to project confidence, I nonetheless called him Mister.

I named an actress, Claire Bloom, who had played opposite Charlie Chaplin in Limelight, and who was about to start a new movie based on The Brothers Karamazov. An English actress, an American movie, a Russian classic. Chaplin's last leading lady. I offered the editor a profile of Claire Bloom and—

This suggestion failed to hold his attention. Nor did my next two or three. So I showed him my Portago press clipping from the Winter Olympics. I doubt I had any real hope of interesting him in this subject; rather I was making a somewhat desperate attempt to impress him with my credentials, the only ones I had: see, I am a published writer, even if only a short article in *The New York Times*.

But immediately he looked alert. His magazine might be interested in a story on the dead Spanish Marquis, he said. "Call it *Death of a Nobleman*—how does that sound?" If I wanted to try writing such an article, that's what my slant should be, he said, and dismissed me.

I went home and worked another six weeks. "Alfonso de Portago was in love with life," I wrote, and for 3,000 words I mourned him. I quoted another driver, Jean Behra. "Only those who do not move do not die," said Behra who, incidentally, was about to be killed himself. "But are they not already dead?" I tried to write a straightforward article, but it filled up with grief. Grief for this dazzling young man dead so young. Grief probably for myself as well—not at all the focus I had intended, but certainly the way the story came out. Today I see clearly enough that Portago was a fool rushing toward violent destruction with a grin on his face and a cigarette dangling from the corner of his mouth. To put it most simply, he was not a meteor whose flame, after a minute, flamed out, he was, and had always been, a car crash waiting to happen. But that wasn't the way I saw him then. Last year when one of the glossy car magazines asked permission to reprint this article I reread it still again. Though not something I am particularly proud of, I took their money and let them do it.

When my manuscript was finally finished I carried it over to *Coronet* and turned it in. Several weeks passed during which I heard nothing. Finally, forcing myself, I screwed up enough nerve to phone the editor. He didn't think the article was good enough, he told me as gently as he could, but he had passed it on to the other editors. We would wait to see what they had to say.

It was while waiting, feeling pretty much bereft of hope, that I sent *The Touchdown Makers* off to *The Saturday Evening Post* for the second time.

I was on the road with the Giants when a letter finally came from *Coronet*. The verve and feeling with which I had written about Portago, the editor wrote, had overcome his original misgivings. They were buying the article for $500. Congratulations.

Two sales, one right after the other. Wow!

Also, *Coronet* now decided that a profile of Claire Bloom was just what they needed. Would I write it for them?

Since I was on my way to Los Angeles where the Giants were to play the Rams, they could get the piece without paying expenses. In giving me the assignment, was this what had appealed to them most?

I met the actress on the set of *The Brothers Karamazov*. She was wearing a white, 19th century ball gown. It exposed most of her breasts—it fit her perfectly. She wore jewelry. She was exquisitely made up. I had never seen anyone more beautiful. We were introduced, I shook her small hand, then watched her shoot a scene or two while growing more and more nervous because in a few minutes I would have to interview her.

The scene finished, she invited me into her dressing room, offered me coffee. As I took it from her, my hand was trembling. I began the interview, but my cup was rattling so loudly on the saucer I could hardly hear my questions, or her answers. I don't remember a thing she told me, but I must have remembered it then for I reread that article recently too, and it isn't bad.

About ten years ago I found myself standing next to Claire Bloom on 77th Street, part of the crowd watching the start of the Thanksgiving Day parade. She was with Philip Roth, to whom she was then married. I had one of my granddaughters on my shoulders. I recognized Roth but didn't know him, and had no interest in him, for he was only a writer like me, but I stared at Claire and deliberated talking to her. I would remind her of our interview and—

However vividly I remembered her, she was unlikely to remember me. Unless the rattling coffee cup had stuck in her mind. So I did nothing. Presently she and Roth walked away.

With these two sales we had enough money to support us for six months while I again tried to get a full fledged writing career going. As soon as that season ended I got another leave of absence from the Giants, my third in five seasons, and we boarded a Pan Am Constellation for Nice, a 16-hour flight with stops in Lisbon and Barcelona en route, but enough room between the rows in those days, even in tourist class, for the children to sleep on the floor.

I had two assignments from *Coronet*, one of which, since it was about an Italian gangster (another of those supposedly Robin Hood type gangsters, of course) took me to Rome for the first time. The second was about a French Jesuit whose mission was to play his guitar and sing songs of his own composition in cafes. When people had gathered, he would answer their questions about God, if they had any. His guitar strapped to his back, he traveled through France on a motorcycle, so I was able to interview him when he stopped one day in Nice. He sold me two of his records on the spot.

In addition I had arranged to cover three Grand Prix car races (Monaco, Belgium, Holland) and three major sports car races (LeMans, Nurburgring, Monza) for the Times on the same basis as at Cortina d'Ampezzo: my expenses were my own, but the Times would pay me $50 for each of two stories per weekend. There was a new sports editor now, the despot had been deposed by management, so this time I was assured both of a byline and of getting paid.

All this work I did, and was paid for, and then we had come home, and I had gone back to work for the Giants once more.

The New York Times was, and as I write still is, at 229 West 43rd Street, though a new site is planned. It is a fourteen story building, squat by New York standards, extending from 43rd through to 44th streets, with its presses anchored to the bedrock underneath it. These presses churned out about 800,000 copies every night, 1.2 million on Sunday.

The publisher and his closest subordinates worked on the top floor in elegant suites of offices reached usually by express elevator. Other executives—advertising, circulation, distribution etc.—were grouped on the floors immediately below. Between the paper's business side and the block-long newsroom on the third floor, where nobody had an office except the managing editor, there was, figuratively speaking, an iron wall, in whose existence everyone on both sides professed to believe, and which so far as I know, was never breached. Business never tampered with the news.

At that time, and still, I knew almost nothing about any of the executives, or what they did in their fancy offices upstairs, but I knew who everybody was who actually put the paper out—where they sat in that vast open space, and what they did there, and I had known all this from childhood on, for my father started bringing me in there from time to time when I was still in short pants. He showed me the mighty presses rumbling in their heavy closed space, the noise so powerful we could not hear each other speak. He took me up to the composing room on the fourth floor to watch the linotype operators work, their clattering machines dropping lines of hot type into trays in columns. He showed me the makeup tables, which were made of steel, on which lay tomorrow's pages, thousands of lead lines in steel frames. These pages could even be read, if you could read backwards, which most of the makeup men could. I learned early on to recognize the keen smell of hot lead, of hot ink. I loved the way the fourth floor smelled.

I started working for the Times in high school, earning fifty cents a week for calling in the scores of Fordham Prep football games, of which there were never more than six a year. In college, after waiting for the kid who had the job to graduate, I wrote accounts of Fordham games in various sports for slightly more money, and truncated versions of these were printed. At that time the first edition of the Sunday paper closed Saturday evening at about 6:30, and sometimes, as the editors waited for important games to finish, my prose, and that of other young men like me on other campuses, was used to hold open a certain amount of space that, in the editions to come, these late reports would need. Sometimes I even got a byline. Nineteen years old with bylines in *The New York Times*. I took this as a matter of course, not yet realizing how precious a byline would later seem to be.

After my junior year in college I worked at the Times at the front of the newsroom as a copyboy on the 8 p.m.–4 a.m. shift for a salary of $29 a week, plus a night differential of $2.50—less money than any previous summer job had ever paid. But this job was more serious than the others. I was working toward my future now. So said my father, and I believed him.

Much about the job—not all—I loved. Carrying copy up to the fourth floor, into that odor of hot ink and hot lead, was always a pleasure. The mechanics of putting out the paper intrigued me. And the sudden quiet that descended on the newsroom as each edition closed, nobody hurrying anywhere any longer, nobody calling out, most of the desks empty, all work stopped—this always came as a bit of a shock. But almost immediately there would follow the rumble of the presses underfoot, a pulsation felt throughout the building. To be in possession of important news long before anyone else heard it—the start of the Korean War, for instance, or the outcome of the vicious battles that followed—this was exciting too.

The night managing editor would give us the good night at 3:40 a.m., and the paper would close down. This live, vibrant thing would close down. I would go out onto Broadway, and glance around in the dim light. No traffic. Broadway totally empty of cars. The city as quiet as it ever got. To me, a born New Yorker, it would seem absolutely quiet. Except for the cats at the garbage cans there was no sound or movement anywhere. A city finally asleep, and *The New York Times*, now, finally, slept too.

But there was much I didn't like about the job as well. As a copyboy one responded to cries of "Boy!" The cries came from editors on the various desks, from reporters on night rewrite. Boy, fetch this, fetch that. Boy, carry this or that here or there. Boy, sharpen my pencils, get me some coffee.

"Boy!"

This cry was very little more palatable to a white twenty year old than it would have been to a black twenty year old. And the job, most of the time, was boring. I wanted something that would stretch my talents, whatever they were, give me a chance to shine, but this wasn't it.

In addition, I looked around at the other copyboys, there must have been about ten of us on duty at any one time, and I did not like what I saw. All hoped to become reporters, all were waiting to be promoted, but some were nearing thirty, and it wasn't happening. The career path had been laid out by someone: three years as a copy boy was the norm, followed by another three, most likely, as a clerk, which was the next step up, and then finally the big jump to reporter. The starting salary for reporters was only $55 a week, not nearly enough on which to get married and start a family. Even at twenty I was able to think that far ahead.

I couldn't bear the notion that this was to be my immediate future, and if it wasn't, what was I doing here answering cries of "Boy!"

To stay out of the draft, to avoid the Korean War altogether, I hoped, I joined the Air Force reserve—only to have my unit called to active duty ten days later. Although I was given a delay to finish college, I would be inducted two weeks after graduation. This further clouded my future, and I quit *The New York Times*, having been a copyboy by then for ten months.

When the Air Force finally let go of me, and I came home, when my mother at last forced me get a job, I considered, though only briefly, reapplying to *The New York Times*. But I could not face the prospect of being a copyboy again, and waiting all those years to make reporter.

And so I took the job of publicity director of the Giants, and never went back into the Times building until I started taking Giants players in there to be interviewed. It was while sitting listening to one of these interviews that an idea began to root itself in my head. A big idea, I thought.

Suppose, suppose—

In the newsroom, then as now, the reporters sat at rows and rows of desks, most of them occupied by the city staffers, of whom there were legions. The sports department was on the 44th Street side of the building, rows of open desks also, though not as many, with financial, society and other such departments nearby.

In all that vast space there was only the managing editor's one full fledged office. Even the assistant managing editors sat out in the open. There was a row of them on the 43rd Street side facing the rows of city reporters, who sat facing back at them. The foreign, national and city editors did not have offices either, nor did the sports or financial or society editors. There were however several glass cubicles toward the rear of the floor, one of which, once he became the sports columnist, was occupied by my father.

My father was like a man on an island. Isolated in his glass cubicle he was not really part of the sports department. No one ever told him what games or athletes to cover, what to write or not write, and his daily column, "Sports of the Times," By Arthur Daley, was never altered by editors, not a word. He turned it in, and that's the way it was printed. Along with the editorial page columnists, and the executives, he was on a separate payroll that depended directly from the publisher. He wrote seven columns a week, and supervised no one, exerted no influence over the department. Given the number of games he attended, the interviews he did, plus seven columns a week—my God, seven!—he had no time to exert influence, even if he had known he had any, which he did not seem to, or knew how to use it, which he did not seem to, or wished to do so—he did not seem to. He was a modest man, somewhat aloof, rather shy, unsophisticated in the extreme, mostly well liked, totally unaware of office politics, mostly unaware of the esteem in which he was held by the public, or the rampant jealousy of some of his colleagues.

It was now the start of my sixth season with the Giants, the season-to-be of the greatest game ever played, and my big idea was still there in my head. I did not go to my father with it, nor did I ask his advice. I was now 28, and one afternoon, leaving my football player with a sports writer to be interviewed, I went out into the newsroom, and sat down beside the desk of the assistant managing editor for administration, and broached my big idea to him.

I was bolder now than I had been. The Post had bought *The Touchdown Makers*, *Coronet* had bought *Death of a Nobleman* and three other articles as well. I had written three pieces for *The New York Times Magazine*, including a long study of Bingo, the gambling game which was then keeping many of the city's Catholic parishes afloat. Now I suggested to this middle-aged administrator, this man who did the hiring of reporters, that I go to Europe and report regularly from there on whatever major sporting events took place. I would be the Times' European sports correspondent.

From the administrator, whose name was Richard Burritt, this idea evoked a hostile, almost violent reaction. He seemed personally affronted, and he began to attack both my idea and me. The standards of the Times were rigid, as I would have known if I cared anything at all about the paper, he said. If I wanted to be a Times reporter I should work my way up, like everyone else. My motives were transparent. I was just trying to use the paper to get a free trip to Europe. He knew my kind. I cared nothing about the paper. My idea was not going to be considered by him or anyone. By now the administrator was almost snarling.

As an aside, this same man a few years later said to me: "We're proud of you, I knew you could do it."

Well—

To me this was just another rejection—I was better able to cope with rejections now than I had been. Rejections could be reversed. I would just have to find a way around this one. And I got up from his desk, walked back to the sports department, collected my football player, and together we left the building.

The way to get around Burritt, I decided, was to go over his head.

The following week I stepped up to the counter in the Times morgue. During my time as a copyboy I had been sent dozens of times to fetch folders for reporters, so I knew all the men who worked back there. After shaking hands with the one who waited on me, I asked for my byline folder. Everyone who wrote for the Times had one; mine was merely slimmer than most. In a few minutes he came back and handed it over.

Back in the newsroom I sat down at an empty desk, got out my few clippings, all of which had been date-stamped by morgue clerks, and I arranged them in a folder so that they showed to advantage. I had determined to approach the managing editor himself. His name was Turner Catledge. He too had once been a reporter, but now ran the news side of greatest newspaper in the world. I had only to wait until he came out of his office, and—

There he was, talking to his secretary. I went up and asked if he would see me for a moment.

He invited me into his office, and I passed my folder across the desk.

He glanced into it. He had seemed cordial until then, but at once his manner hardened. As I suggested myself as the paper's European sports correspondent his mouth got thin as a razor blade. He let me talk for less than a minute, before saying in a cold, hard voice:

"Where did these clippings come from?"

He knew where they had come from, for he could see the date stamps on them.

"They were in my byline folder, and—"

"Morgue folders are never to be removed from the morgue except by reporters working on stories."

"Yes, sir."

"Clippings are never to be removed from the folders for any other purpose."

"I intended to put them back."

"See that you do."

"Yes, sir."

"Now."

"Yes, sir."

So that was the end of that interview.

Some days passed before I approached the new sports editor. If I paid my own way to Europe, I said to him, and if I paid my own way to major sporting events in the various countries, to the car races, fights, horse races, tennis tournaments as I had already done a few times, could I cover these events for the Times on a regular basis at $50 per story?

He said he liked the idea, and would talk to them "outside."

Outside meant Catledge, Burritt and the others.

He wrote out the proposal, pointing out that I had done a good deal of work of this kind for the paper already, and in me now the Times would have a full time European sports correspondent, the first ever, which would be good for the paper's prestige. But I would not be on the staff, meaning that there would be no insurance or pension obligations, and if I did not work out they would have no further obligation to me of any kind. The risk, he suggested, was very little compared to the possible large return.

He sent this proposal forward, and it was approved immediately.

Why? Well, he was new. The sports pages now looked better and read better than they ever had before. The staff liked him. Morale was up. As far as the bosses were concerned he was much easier to get along with than the despot had been. Most likely they wanted to give him confidence, were unwilling so early on to squash any of his ideas.

His name was James Roach. He was a tall thin man with thinning red hair and he wore, now, half glasses on the end of his nose. If he took such a chance on me and for me—and he did—he must have believed I could do the job. Certainly he had read all of my Times articles, and possibly some other work besides. But there may have been other reasons. He was my father's age. Although not close friends they had been young reporters together, had known each other twenty five or more years, and Roach had probably known me since I was a very small boy, for he had once courted and proposed marriage to my mother's younger sister who, however, had turned him down and married someone else. Perhaps I had said or done something nice to him when I was a child. He had married for the first time only a few years previously; his young wife was my age, and he had two small daughters the same ages as mine. Perhaps he felt some kinship because of this. He may even have seen me as the son he supposed now he would never have.

Who can say exactly what he was thinking?

When he called me in to give me the news he suggested that, in addition to covering events, I write a column called Sports in Europe for the Tuesday paper each week. This would give me, most weeks, three paydays. He would also, he said, try to throw some expenses my way from time to time.

It was on this shaky basis that I quit the Giants, that we sold or gave away everything we owned that we could not take with us, that we emptied our bank account, that we spent nearly all of this money on first class tickets for four on a luxury liner sailing in early January from New York to the Cote d'Azur. I was absolutely certain that a big and lasting success lay ahead, whereas my parents were appalled, begged me to reconsider, were sure we would starve. Nonetheless, they were among those who came to the going-away party we threw in our stateroom in the hour before our ship would be tugged backwards into the ice strewn Hudson River, and our voyage into the future would begin. Now that I have grown children myself I know how much my parents must have worried about us, but I did not realize this at the time, only laughed at their fears. And then my parents and everyone went ashore, and the four of us stood on the deck in a biting wind. Peggy and the children went below almost at once, but I stayed at the rail feeling no fear whatever, and watched an entire continent, disappear behind me.

And that is how the Villa Nina came into our lives. In the street now we stand looking in at it, the first house we ever had together. It had, still has, a small garden in which in our time grew, all piled together, a miniature orchard. We had three orange, three tangerine and three lemon trees, most of which touched, or almost touched, the walls of the house. There was a single pear tree crammed in as well. In season so much edible fruit came forth that we could not eat it all, but had to search out people to give it to. Today there seem to be fewer fruit trees than there were. Grapes still grow along the south fence, however, and the purple bougainvillea still climbs toward the balconies. Under the trees and along the paths the grass looks lush. We tried to grow grass too, but American seed varieties were imported into France only later, and the local strain then available was unsuited. Our grass came up so scraggly that Peggy kept it trimmed with a scissors. The public gardens down in the city did no better: beautiful flowers, but thin grass, and always the sign: Forbidden to Enter Upon the Lawn.

From the small balcony outside our bedroom window we could see, it sometimes seemed, from Italy to Spain. The sunsets could be glorious, bruised skies hanging above the sea or, on more flamboyant nights, streaks and blotches of every color of red there was.

From the Villa Nina I would set out each weekend to sporting events in one corner of Europe or another, and write my stories, and come home and rest up for a day or two, and then go out again. I felt myself grow more and more confident about my role as a man, my place in the world, and the big career I had so long hoped for, and had almost, by then, ceased to believe in, took root.

"They've changed the front entrance," notes Peggy.

"I don't really remember."

"And they've walled up the entrance to the garage and made a room out of it."

That first weekend, only hours after getting ourselves and our trunks off the ship and into Nice, I was on a train en route to the world bobsledding championship in St. Moritz. Again I rode sitting up all night in a crowded third class compartment—I was getting used to rides like this, and would make many more. The lighted stations, the lights of farms, of isolated houses. The train crossed northern Italy and started up into the Alps. Though passengers got on and off the compartment remained full all night. Some of the people beside me had food and drink which they pressed on me. That night was the first time I ever drank grappa. It was four a.m., a long swallow to be polite. My Adam's apple nearly popped out of my neck. *Grazie*, I said, and from then on feigned sleep.

As at the Olympics the sleds went off in the dawn light. Same tension, same clattering and banging, same danger as when Portago had raced. It was dark and very cold. Our exhalations hovered like smoke. There were hardly any spectators, and no money involved, but the contestants were as intense and as concentrated as any driver at Indianapolis or LeMans.

It seemed to me that I could write well about this kind of scene. I did not much care who won, and assumed my readers would not either, but I could describe the faces, the noise, the speed, the way the surrounding peaks looked when the sun finally struck them. I could make the reader feel he was there, or believed I could, make him see and hear what I wanted him to—this was what a writer did and it was what I wanted to do.

It was also the way I would work for the next six years. In New York 4,000 miles away there was little or no fan interest in the events I was reporting, so I could not focus on the outcome of the game, whatever it was—if I did, who would read me?

I would focus instead, as much as I could, on what each of these sports cost the players. I would focus on the endless training, the injuries, the pain, the risk, the fear that went into winning. I would focus on the darker side of sport, the damage that winning—trying to win—did to men's bodies, to their psyches, and to their ability, on occasion, to keep from getting killed. There would be times—many times, it turned out—when I would be writing on the sports page about death. Sports in Europe had given me the leeway, I saw, to write about sports in a new way. It was leeway I could not have got in the sports department in New York, or indeed in any other place in the paper, and I took it. This was not an arbitrary decision, but was determined by the need to grab distant readers who had no pre-existing interest in my subjects. Also, it was the way I myself had come to feel about sports—don't ask me why. Sports was serious business, or it was not worth writing about at all. I was not interested, as most reporters were, in investigative reporting or getting on the front page, only in writing with deep and accurate emotion—day after day writing just as well as I could.

The championship for two man sleds was decided one weekend, the four man championship the next. In between I went home to Nice, then came back, three more all night train rides. I had no money. Going home was cheaper than staying on in a hotel.

Portago's sleds were entered in both races. A cousin named Vincente Sartorius who had been on his team at Cortina, had inherited not only the sleds but also the dead man's seat at the wheel. It was while sipping cognac in a restaurant after the second race, which like the first he did not win, that Sartorius claimed he could eat glass, had done so many times. When I told him this was impossible, he drained his cognac, chewed off the side of the snifter, and chomped it into small bits. I could hear his teeth grinding. He swallowed this first morsel, and then chewed off another, and so forth, until the glass had disappeared. Why he did this, or what happened to him afterwards, I do not know.

The shooting war had been over, by now, for fourteen years, but in Western Europe the American passport was still king; everybody else needed visas to move around but Americans did not. The dollar was still king too; in France, payment in dollars brought an automatic 20% discount.

But the iron curtain was still down, and behind it was a different world. The world hockey championships that year were in Prague, a handsome old city not much touched by the war, though the people were poor and wore drab clothes. The stadium was down by the river, and it was filled night and day by screaming Czechs. The American team flunked out quickly, the Canadian amateurs soon after. The match of the tournament was Czechoslovakia against Russia. These were the two most powerful teams. One or the other would be world champion. The referee threw the puck to the ice. Two young men slashed at it.

The Czechs against their Russian masters. Skates curved and carved. Bodies crashed into the boards. Pucks were slammed at goalies. There was a different quality to the screaming now, and to the ferocity of the Czech players. Russia controlled their country, tried to control their very thoughts, but could not control Czech skates and sticks, Czech ice. Behind me in the stands the roar never stopped, nor the pounding feet. An earthquake of noise. The whole arena shook, noise so loud and sustained one could hear nothing else.

I had witnessed a good many sporting events, but never a display of such raw emotion as this. The Russians had taken Czech sovereignty, their right to live as they chose. What the Czech players were fighting for transcended any trophy.

They lost the game, and the final score is in my story, but mostly I wrote about what the hours in that hall felt like, tried to describe the sounds, sights, smells, the weight that a hockey match could carry.

The Times had a contact in Prague. He was middle-aged, formerly a journalist, only recently released from jail, living with his wife in a small apartment near the center of the city. I had been told he would forward my copy.

I went to him and he took the pages and went out. He was gone so long I worried about him, imagined him thrown back in jail because of something I had written. When he at last returned his wife served tea and cakes, and we talked, and I saw how starved they were for contact with the outside world. We talked most of that night, and the succeeding nights as well, a lonely, middle aged couple and a 28 year old American with very little experience of the world, and none at all of the world as they knew it.

I met another such man later in the Times office in Warsaw, a fortyish Polish count. He was full of cheer and energy. He answered my questions about Poland and told me where to buy records of Polish folk songs. He too had been in jail for years, and most of the teeth on one side of his face had been knocked out. The world forgets, perhaps has forgotten already, that such people as this, such suffering as they knew, ever existed.

In Nice I was my own assignment editor, my own appointments secretary, made my own travel arrangements. Regularly I wrote Jim Roach to advise him of what I planned to write for as far ahead as I could. He never disputed my schedule, even let me do stories on subjects of which he did not approve, bullfighting, for instance. If the distance was far I flew, or took the train. I bought a small car, a Renault Dauphine, top speed about 70 miles an hour, and in it drove into all the neighboring countries, drove thousands of miles. Sometimes Peggy came with me; sometimes all four of us went. There were less than 100 miles of four-lane roads in France at this time, about the same in Italy, and in impoverished Spain even the major roads were sometimes not paved. I drove not around villages, but through them at low speed, through the major cities at low speed too. I could never average more than 40 miles per hour, could cover 400 miles a day if between towns I drove as fast as the little car would go.

I had no press card, only a pile of Times letterheads that I had scooped up in the office before leaving New York, and that no one knew I had. I used the letterheads to write ahead for credentials. I did have a credit card for cabling my stories to New York. In those days before instantaneous communication via modem, the reporter in a foreign country had three jobs, to get the story, to write it, and then to get it to his paper, and the last of these was frequently the hardest. My credit card had been issued by one of the several international cable companies then in existence. Supposedly I could go into any post office in any city in any country, step up to the telegraph desk, show this card, and hand over my copy. Supposedly it would be accepted and telegraphed on. But in practice almost no post office clerk had ever seen such a card or knew what to do with it. Often I would have waited a long time on line even to reach him, with a line of people still behind me. Often then he was surly, occasionally tried to brush me aside, and supervisors almost always had to be sent for, sometimes only after I had done considerable screaming. Usually the supervisors would have to make some calls themselves. Ultimately the card was always accepted, but I spent an awful lot of time in post offices.

I went to Sicily for a car race, went there year after year, in fact. I am the only person I know who has been to Sicily that many times. The event was the Targa Florio, oldest race in the world, having started at a time when 30 miles an hour was breakneck speed. The circuit was public road, 45 miles per lap, miserable little roads for the most powerful sports cars in the world. The cars raced through three villages, crossed narrow bridges built by the Romans. The villages were poor, the hills between them, for the most part, uninhabited. There were no forests, only individual trees. There were so few trees, I wrote, that if someone were to cut one down, everyone else would miss it at once.

The race started in the dark and went on past supper time. In Palermo afterwards four of us—the drivers Phil Hill and Cliff Allison, and the journalist Jesse Alexander, who worked for the magazine then called Sports Cars Illustrated—rented a horse drawn carriage and had the coachman drive us slowly through the lighted streets, past the palaces, the churches, the piazzas with their fountains, the cafes brim full of people and life.

I got an assignment from *Esquire* for a profile of Enzo Ferrari, whose cars since the war had won more races than any other marque, and killed more drivers too, and I went to Modena hoping to interview him. Ferrari never attended races, rarely gave interviews, and was something of a recluse. Since I had no appointment I was apprehensive.

Phil Hill, who would soon be Ferrari's No.1 driver as those ahead of him got killed, was testing cars at the Autodromo as I arrived. I watched this for a while, and when he had finished he drove me around the track as fast as my Dauphine would go, not slowing down for the corners but sliding them all. The windows were open. We both wore short sleeved shirts. I held onto the seat with both hands. Once he looked over and laughed at me: "That kind of thing doesn't even tickle my tummy anymore," he said. "Relax," he said, "it won't tip over, it will slide."

Phil was 31, from Santa Monica, California. I asked him who I should call to get in to see Enzo Ferrari. He said he didn't know, and disappeared for a time. “He’ll see you at three o’clock tomorrow,” he said, when he came back.

The interview took place in Ferrari’s office at his factory. It was one of the most vivid of my life. The Commendatore, the rank to which Ferrari had been raised by the Italian king before the war, was then 71, but carried himself with the force of a man years younger. He was a big, robust man with a long nose, tinted glasses, and a domineering manner. He had no English, at least none that he showed me, but spoke excellent French. He answered every question succinctly and, from my point of view, perfectly. He had no trouble whatever phrasing exactly what he wanted to say, and most of it shocked me.

On a sideboard beside his desk stood six, black framed photos of his last six dead drivers, one of them Portago, and I kept glancing at them as he answered my questions. Finally I asked him: “Why do you not go to races?”

The legend was that he loved his drivers like sons, could not bear to watch the risks they took. But his answer was quite different.

“A man builds something,” he said, “a beautiful machine. He puts all of himself into it. And then he goes to races and sees his machine, this part of himself, being maltreated, and—” He put his hand over his heart. “And so I do not go to races because it hurts me—here.”

“You mean you suffer for the car, not the driver?”

“The driver too, of course.”

During the interview Hill had stood silently in the corner. In the street afterwards he said bitterly: “I never thought he’d say something like that in front of one of his drivers. We all like to think he loves us because we are so brave and drive so fast. But deep down I guess we always knew he cared more about his cars than he does about us.”

Flushed with this triumphant interview, flushed with the driving techniques Hill had shown me as well, I drove back to Nice faster than ever, and when I came to the Chemin de Fabron, almost home now, I climbed its twists and turns as Hill himself might have done, slicing across all the apexes, sliding all the corners.

And that's the way I drove that road from then on. It became my favorite road in the world. I had the Dauphine souped up, insofar as one could soup up a Dauphine, bought stiffer suspension, slightly more power, and inside of 8,000 miles had scrubbed the tires bald.

At Pau I watched the end of that day's stage of the Tour de France. The Pyrenees could be seen across the valley, the highest peaks still white in July. When morning came, I found a seat in an open car belonging to a bike racing magazine. We were part of a cavalcade of vehicles containing managers, mechanics, trainers, gendarmes, photographers, reporters, and we moved sometimes in front of the bikes, sometimes behind, sometimes within, and we moved all day at the speed of 110 young men with thighs like trees and faces burned the color of cinnamon. Tens of thousands of people watched us go by. We passed through Lourdes, sacred to Bernadette and to the Virgin who was said to have appeared to her there, sacred also to the millions of pilgrims who had come hoping to be cured in the years since. The bars and restaurants, I noted as we went through, were all named after saints. Store after store sold religious goods: statues, candles, whatever. Rosary beads, holy medals on chains dangled from racks, from awnings. I admit that this too shocked me, and it took a moment to refocus my thoughts on the bicycle race.

Presently we were outside the town, and climbing. Sometimes there were mountain torrents beside the road, sometimes pastures that looked extraordinarily green, in which shepherds, old men in berets for the most part, watched their sheep.

The Pyrenees in that part of the range are rust brown in color, very steep, and as we rolled along at under twenty five miles an hour I had all the time in the world to admire them. The best part of riding with a bike race is its pace—to move that slowly all day. Pace as slow as this opens the senses to every passing moment. There is time to observe the glorious scenery certainly, to inhale the purity of the air. But one notes the lesser details also, such as the size of the drops of sweat that quivered on the chins of the exhausted faces. Not to mention the sudden excitements that upset this tranquillity from time to time: the breakaways, the crashes, the fans dashing into the road to touch their heroes.

Up and up we climbed crossing finally Tourmalet Pass, highest in the Pyrenees, a road 7,000 feet high that doesn't really go anywhere, as if the sole purpose of its existence was, is and will always be, to punish the lungs and legs of the men who race the Tour de France.

In my story each night I described all this. Mostly what I wrote was landscape painting with bikes moving through it. I did not see how I could do otherwise, for few of the Times' readers would have known or cared who the riders were, or who was winning, but spectacle is spectacle to everyone, mountains are everywhere and always mountains.

Each day with the Tour was a delight, and at night there was always a real press room from which to send the stories to New York, no problem, and on the third day Peggy met me at the finish line, and as soon as my story was written and sent we drove across the Pyrenees into Spain to the fiesta at Pamplona for the first time. We stayed seven days, I ran with the bulls most mornings, we watched all the bullfights, and I wrote two stories which Jim Roach knew were coming, didn't much want, but had agreed to. I spent a lot of time in the Pamplona post office waiting to file, but it was worth it.

There were numerous assignments from magazines now, and an offer to write a book. A reporter called from *Newsweek* wanting to write a piece about me. Everything I wrote was being published, and Jim Roach was sending more expense money than I had ever hoped for. By the end of the year I would have earned twice what the Giants paid me. By our standards we were rich, so we bought a living room set for the Villa Nina: a rattan sofa with bright flowered cushions, and armchairs to match, and a gold rug for the floor, cheaply made furniture perhaps, but it picked up the villa enormously. We hired a local peasant woman with whom we could leave the children, and now Peggy could come with me most weekends: to most of the car races, back to Spain for more bullfights, to Rome for a preview of the Olympics, which were now less than a year away. I wanted her to know the people and things that excited me. I wanted us to share them. I did not see how you could have a marriage any other way.

We have moved around the Villa Nina and stand looking at the villa next door, one of the finest examples of Provencal architecture you could find. Today it too looks submerged amid the high rises, but back then it was brand new. In it lived a young couple and their little boy Denis, who played with our two, and a grandfather who walked all three children down to school each morning, and back each afternoon. One day we found the three kids showing each other in which way boys differed from girls, Denis in his garden, the girls in ours, a wire fence in between.

"It's a very nice house still," Peggy says.

The husband was some sort of minor city official, yet he had been able to build this wonderful villa. The corruption at city hall was only suspected at that time; it was later proven to exist at a level that staggered everybody. The mayor back then stayed mayor for 28 years, and when he finally died his son succeeded him for 25 more, at the end of which the son got caught, was extradited from Uruguay where he had fled, and went to jail. Denis' father, if he was part of city hall, would have been expected to partake of whatever was handed out. It is the only way corrupt officials can assure the loyalty of those around them.

"We rarely saw him," Peggy says. "He left his wife alone for long periods."

"I always supposed he had this villa built by city workers on city time out of city materials."

"His wife never went anywhere. She envied me my life, and I envied her her house."

An organization called Baseball for Italy sent Yogi Berra and his wife to Rome, and Jim Roach suggested I meet them there. Peggy and I both went, not knowing the Berras, not knowing what we would find. Carmen turned out to be bright and extremely pretty, the Yankee catcher as homely a man as his pictures suggested, but warm and friendly with a lovely smile. He had been accorded a minivan and guide by Alitalia, and he invited us to go touring with them. The guide took us to the Roman Forum, the Coliseum and other such places, and Yogi kept pointing out to Carmen and to us sights he had seen sixteen years previously in the next to last year of World War II. The warship he was on had docked at Naples, and he had hitchhiked up to Rome in his sailor suit catching rides on American jeeps and trucks, for only the Americans had gas that year. The countryside he passed through was devastated, and there was nothing to eat. In Rome his stomach was growling the whole time. The city itself had not been touched and he gawked at sights he did not understand, and promised himself that some day he would find a way to come back. He saw everything a boy his age could see, given how few hours he was there, then hitchhiked back to Naples and his ship.

We ate meals with the Berras, spent most of two days with them. Yogi kept trying to use me as his interpreter though I had very little Italian—not nearly as much as I imagined he had. I kept urging him to bring forth his own Italian, but he wouldn't. He wouldn't say why, either. Finally

I understood that the Italian he had learned as a boy in St. Louis was the dialect of his peasant forebears, not proper Italian at all, and he refused to speak it now, lest he be taken for a lout and a fool.

Then 34, he had already been voted the American League's most valuable player three times. He was already famous for his malapropisms too, most of which were not a bit stupid. In the outfield at Yankee Stadium, he said once, "it gets late early." And another time, probably his most famous one: "The game isn't over till it's over." Yogi and Carmen were received by Pope John XXIII, who gave them rosary beads for their children. At dinner that night Yogi said that the beads for his son were too small. When Carmen laughed at him, he insisted stubbornly: "A big boy needs big beads." You could call this a malapropism too, but I knew very well what he meant. The wisdom of Yogi Berra, it seemed to me, was more wise than anyone ever gave him credit for.

We got back to Nice into a storm that had struck in ferocious proportions, and had stayed on. Tons of rain had fallen, fell still. Wind and waves had thrown tons of beach stones up onto the Promenade, had covered it two inches deep; eventually the street would have to be cleared with plows. A parked car had been wafted across the sidewalk into the glass door of American Express, which it broke. Our phone rang. It was the Times' Paris bureau chief. Forty miles down the coast at Frejus a dam had burst, he said. Some people were reported dead. Could I get down there at once?

I could not, I told him when I rang back. All the roads were cut. But I could rent a plane and write what the devastation looked like from the air. It would cost the Times the equivalent of $120. Did I have his permission?

Too expensive, he said, the paper would never approve it.

"The paper just paid my way to Rome and back to write about Yogi Berra," I said. "Is this story more important than that, or not? I think the paper will approve it?"

Finally he said: "Rent the plane."

The only plane I could get sat eight, so we both went. So did a pal of the pilot's, riding free on *The New York Times*.

The dam had broken in shards like a flower pot. The shards were enormous chunks of concrete, some like blockhouses, some the size of ships, and the force of the water had driven them, floated them, hundreds of yards down the valley where they now lay, presumably forever. Except for a trickle in the center of the valley the vast former lake was gone, its high water line visible all the way around. Further down toward the town the flood had spared a few houses and trees but mostly had flattened everything it touched. The new, modern section of Frejus had been erased, leaving, in most places, not even a smudge. The railroad tracks ended on one side of a vast gap, and resumed on the other. But the Roman arena, which stood on slightly higher ground, had survived still again, and would continue to last for who knew how many centuries more. The medieval old town on its hill was intact also. More than 400 people were dead.

We flew back to Nice, and I wrote my story. A day or two later, as soon as the roads opened again, we drove back there, and parked. In the town square the wooden coffins were piled higher than my head, and I wrote this too.

A bit further up the Chemin de Fabron there is a lane I know of. It goes off to the left and runs along the crest with the sea visible to the south, and the Alps to the north. Directly below in the center of the steep valley runs the Var River. We go looking for this lane now, but with the flower farms gone, and the glut of high rises, I have difficulty finding it.

At last I do. I pull the car off to the side and we get out. Whenever I was writing something and had a problem to work out I used to walk up here and along the crest mulling it over. The view today is much as it always was, except that both sides of the valley, I note, have filled up with houses.

I stand in silence for a time in more or less the same spot where I stood so often so long ago. Particularly I remember days in December at the end of that first year. Fall comes late here. The leaves don't change much, it isn't New England, but there is some color, plus the big view, and the reason I particularly remember those days is because I was so happy. I would stand here breathing in the air, and I kept asking myself: why am I so happy?

5. The Cruel Sport

November 13, 2000, Monaco

Places do play roles in people's lives, and this place, emotionally speaking, has played a big one in mine.

Tonight, though late in the year, it is mild enough for tables to have been set up outside on the terrace. We are under an awning, and there are heaters to be lit if necessary. We are at a restaurant called La Saliere in Fontvieille, which is a new section of the town. The terrace is really part of the quay, and we are looking at masses of moored yachts. To our left is a sight that surprises me—amazes me might be more accurate—each time I see it. Rising straight up out of the harbor is a cliff high as any skyscraper, part of the gigantic rock that is Monaco. At the top of it sits most of the original town: the prince's palace, various public buildings, and hundreds of souvenir shops.

Grace Kelly of Philadelphia who became Princess Grace, and who used to live in that palace, once said that the only direction in which Monaco could grow was up. Not true. Of course there are dozens and dozens of skyscrapers now, (and nowhere else on the coast), some with enough bulk and height to challenge the surrounding mountains in grandeur; so many that people sometimes speak of Monaco as Hong Kong on the Mediterranean.

But the town has also grown outwards into the sea. It has been filling in the sea for the last forty years, and one of the places this has been done is under the table at which we are dining. The Mediterranean is extremely deep along this coast, and the workers had to break up entire mountains inland (in France, of course) to get the rock to do it. Fontvielle, which used not to exist at all is, therefore, an engineering marvel. To either side of us are more restaurants. Behind us are blocks and blocks of extremely expensive flats with, at street level, luxury stores. The yacht harbor we are looking at is crowded, every slot full.

To our left, floodlit, is the towering cliff. The lights delineate its veins and ribs all the way up. The palace on top is floodlit too. Huge and overbearing, it seems to hang over us. It is supposed to have more than a hundred rooms, which may seem a bit large for a place this tiny—in area Monaco is half the size of Central Park for 29,000 residents. Only about 8,000 of these "residents" are Monegasques. Many of the rest are concert artists, tennis players and bankers, foreigners all, who are almost never here. The town's golf club, tennis club and cemetery are all in France, its gas and electricity come from France, and its police chief and many other officials must be French according to the treaty by which France permits Monaco to exist. Though it has much to recommend it, Monaco's claims to sovereignty, to royal stature, sometimes seem pretentious to some people, or even ludicrous.

Monaco is 12 miles from Nice. Even so, we don't come here much. To a restaurant from time to time. To the opera, if we can get tickets—the Monaco opera house seats only 500 people. And of course friends and family from America always want us to lead them here, to the Palace on one side of the town, and the Casino on the other.

Then there is the Grand Prix in May. The first Grand Prix I ever saw was here, the last as well. I used to come for it every year but that is over. Never again.

The race through the streets of the city, the race around the houses—I watched eleven of them in all. It was here, as a very young man, that I began to learn what this sport, if it is a sport, is all about, and how much it weighed on the people in it. It was here, well before my time, that I began to learn about death.

From the beginning I was half fascinated, half horrified by Grand Prix racing, and still am, I suppose. I went to many races in many countries, which formed the basis for a good number of newspaper and magazine articles, and for a novel and two other books. Probably from the beginning I was trying, as I wrote, to explain to myself what I had seen, and what I felt about it. Probably also I have not been able to come to any valid conclusion yet.

Some years ago two drivers were killed at a Grand Prix meeting. One was an unknown, the other a three time world champion. This was in Italy, and it sent the country into an orgy of bereavement and, simultaneously, an orgy of investigations. The Italians have always been terrific at both. They hadn't had much practice recently but had had plenty in the past, and remembered just how to do it. Italian television ran specials, parts of which were shown on American news programs. For the most part the little known driver was ignored. The covered over stretcher moving though silent crowds was the star's; the wrecked race car we were shown was the star's.

Next came the doctors' press conference (in Italy there are always many doctors at such times, never just one); followed by attempted interviews with rival drivers who refused to answer questions, and with the dead hero's girlfriend. She was about 25, gorgeous, weeping. She seemed unable to speak. The front pages of the next day's newspapers were bordered in black. The accompanying articles speculated that something must have broken on the car, for such a genius driver could never have made any ordinary man's mistake. He could not have been, simply, going too fast.

The picture magazines when they appeared devoted a quarter of their pages, in some cases more, to the dead star and his crash. Photos showed him on his estate with his gardeners, and in his bedroom with its closets where he stood in front of innumerable designer suits. Turn the page and see him playing his guitar in a nightclub, or at the helm of one of his speedboats or his cruiser. In almost every photo the girlfriend was shown as well, either this girl or an earlier one. The girlfriends were interchangeable: young, blond, big busted and wearing clothes or bikinis a size or two too small.

Already there had been speeches in various parliaments; Grand Prix racing should be stopped, it was not sport but murder.

I was following the story closely, and was not surprised.

Meanwhile, the carabinieri had detained the surviving drivers, some of whom, waiting their turn to be interrogated, were kept over night. Furiously angry, they vowed they would never race in Italy again, though they all did. The polizia nazionale, which is a different agency, had impounded the wreckage, the star's corpse as well. By the second day the two police agencies were engaged in a public, quite noisy dispute over who had jurisdiction. To prove its rights, the polizia held onto the corpse and did not release it until pressure by the race organizers got too strong to bear. The organizers had already scheduled, and had had to keep postponing, the funeral. It was held finally, the first of three, the church overflowing.

The other two funerals were in the late world champion's home country—he was from Brazil.

I had to laugh—not at the deaths of these young men but at the fuss that was made, as if this tragedy was something the world had never seen before. The funerals. The weeping girlfriend. The politicians crying stop the slaughter.

Nothing was unique to these particular deaths except, these days, their extreme rarity. Because of the improved solidity of the cars, and the construction of new circuits devoid of anything the cars might crash into, there had been no fatalities in eight seasons, and no star had been killed in twelve.

Whereas, in the first Grand Prix race I ever saw—here in Monaco as I have said—there were sixteen starters, of whom four were dead before the year was out, and four more in subsequent years. Two others would be injured so badly in crashes that they never raced again.

Stop motor racing indeed. The organizers, owners and drivers of my time had to cope with that kind of pressure every other week. Doesn't anybody remember? This is not ancient history I am talking about. The fathers of today's drivers were in those cars.

That first year I was feeling my way. The Times had Frank Blunk's car column on Wednesday, which generated ads, and which seemed to constitute approval of my covering these races. Now all I had to do was write interesting copy. Which meant getting to know the circuits, and the drivers. Nearly all European races were run on public roads or streets, sometimes streets with tram tracks in them. These circuits framed the cars and drivers, the speed and noise, and this frame was lined with fences, ditches, curbs, lampposts, trees, houses. In my Times pieces I described them, sometimes poetically, or at least as poetically as I could manage.

More importantly I thought I had to become as intimate as I could with the drivers. I needed to know what they were thinking, saying. I needed to describe what was happening from their point of view. At that time, at the age I was then, it was not good for one's psyche to get to know drivers.

Peter Collins was 27. He agreed to an interview but not graciously. A somewhat surly young man, it seemed to me. He and his young American wife lived on his boat in Monaco harbor. I went to look at it one night.

The boat was smaller than a trailer and moved up and down as the water did. But the idea of it sounded romantic. Collins always wore a brown fiberboard helmet. There were no space helmets then, no seat belts, and no fireproof coveralls. The drivers wore street clothes, sat loosely in big roomy cockpits, and nobody wore a helmet any more serious than the one Collins did. On the day in Germany that his Ferrari went into the forest, catapulting him into the air en route, he was wearing, apparently, a blue polo shirt because witnesses described the red car mowing down real estate, and the "blue blur" overhead that sailed head first into a tree.

Luigi Musso, also a Ferrari driver, spoke no English and only a few words of French. I never said much more to him than "Bonjour". Estranged from his wife, he traveled with his long time girl friend and they seemed devoted to each other. Since there was no divorce in Italy at that time this was the best relationship that would ever be available to them, unless the wife died. Instead, Musso died. He went off into a wheat field in France. The car climbed the embankment and at one point, according to witnesses, was three stories in the air with Musso floating above it. The kinetic energy stored up in race cars at speed is quite astounding. Musso's wife locked and blocked all his possessions. The girlfriend went back to Italy to ask Enzo Ferrari if there was not something, an insurance policy, anything. Ferrari knew vulnerability when he saw it, and kept her for many years.

Stuart Lewis-Evans was a little guy, no bigger than a jockey. No better than an also-ran, either, so I never got around to talking to him. He crashed in Morocco in the final race of the season. The car caught fire and he did not get out of it. He was flown back to England where he lingered some weeks in a burn ward.

The world champion that year was the Ferrari driver Mike Hawthorn, a tall, blond young man who always wore a bow tie when racing. Always.

He considered this important. It was his style, so to speak. Being new to the sport I didn't know this, and asked him about it. Apparently I phrased the question badly. "How come you're wearing a bow tie today?" I said.

"You don't notice much, do you?" he answered curtly, and walked away.

Reporters frequently get snubbed, especially by athletes who don't see that anyone contributes to their fame and fortune but themselves. Politicians and entertainers, who know better, snub reporters much less often. Asking questions entails certain risks to one's ego, and a reporter had best get used to it. Hawthorn, driving a Jaguar, a saloon car as the British call them, was killed drag racing a friend on a public road near London. It was just past noon. He skidded into the back of a truck coming the other way.

That was that year. There were two more the next, six of the sixteen gone already. Harry Schell, who was killed testing a car in the rain at Silverstone, was always described as an American living in Paris—he ran a bar there, or someone ran it for him. I interviewed him at a back table. We talked of Portago for a time. They had been great friends, had once shared a car at the 24 Hours of LeMans. Portago had picked this famous race for his debut in motor racing, but he didn't yet know how to shift gears. Schell had had to show him. American or not, Harry Schell spoke English with a strong French accent. He was one of the oldest drivers, 39. He told me that Grand Prix racing was not dangerous at all if you knew your limit, and stayed within it, as he did, and I noted this down. Over the years a number of drivers said the same to me, or something similar, an attitude that doubtless saved the lives of some of them, though it did not help Harry.

You almost couldn't tell, but Jean Behra had a plastic ear, the original having been rubbed off the side of his head in a crash. He was a Ferrari contract driver but got in an argument with the team manager, which ended when Behra, call him a fiery Frenchman as others did at the time, slapped the manager's face. Enzo Ferrari had no choice but to fire him.

The German Grand Prix was held on the pre-war Avus track in Berlin that year. Behra was driving his own Porsche in a preliminary race when killed. One end of the track was banked. The car entered the banking on the proper line, but immediately began sliding higher. The animal was trying to get out of its cage. Behra wrestled with it. Higher and higher it slid. In a moment it had wrested control from its driver. A second or so after that it threw him out altogether. The top of the banking was lined with flagpoles, one of which Behra hit about halfway up. It broke him almost in two. I didn't see this. I went rushing back to the circuit where I scurried around interviewing people who did, and then sent still another grim report to *The New York Times*.

By this time I was acquiring a certain reputation in the small and insular motor racing world, and not one to my liking. It must be understood that the enthusiast magazines—they are legion in all the countries—concentrate on cam shafts and gear boxes, not crashes. Fatal accidents are scarcely mentioned and never described, never dwelt on. One sentence is usually enough. On lap three, or lap ten, so-and-so had a shunt that proved fatal. Shunt is a British word. No one ever crashes, they have shunts.

Whereas I was writing something else entirely, and in a journal with weight, and certain of my colleagues were distressed. I was "hurting" motor racing, they felt, and behind my back I was sometimes referred to by some of them—the journalists, not the drivers—as Death Daley.

The drivers' attitude was quite different. Often they talked about getting killed. The nearness of death was what made them special, they felt, and Stirling Moss, the greatest driver of that period, liked to expound on this subject. He liked the danger being there, he said. "Without it," he said, "what would be the point? Anybody could do it."

The day after Behra's death the Berlin papers carried a photo of him in his open coffin, plastic ear in place, his face serene. Beside the coffin stands Count Von Trips, his hand on the dead man's cheek. A photographer must have led Trips, who had won the race, to the funeral home and posed him.

This picture chilled me. I'm not superstitious, never have been, never expect to be, but felt as chilled as if I had seen a future I was not supposed to see. That there was death all around me, I knew very well. That these young men got much too close to it was obvious as well. Some of them would get out alive and smiling. Perhaps not very many, but some. Others would die, one of whom, the photo in some way made clear to me, would be Count Von Trips. Forgive me, but it was as if I saw that photo as his death warrant.

He was not quite the next to go, but almost. Two rookie drivers, replacements for those who had been killed already, were killed during the Grand Prix of Belgium the following season. Then it was Trips' turn. When he went he took fourteen spectators with him.

The night before the race I had sat with him in a cafe. Previously I had talked to him many times in many countries. He spoke English without accent, and had much charm. He could describe with great good humor certain of his past crashes. He was another of those who spoke without being prodded of getting killed, or almost getting killed.

Now, with the season almost over, he was in the lead in points, and if he did well the following day he would win the world championship. He didn't even have to win the race, just finishing high up would clinch it for him. He expected to manage this. At the same time he realized the sharpness of the edge on which he stood. On which they all stood. "That's the thing about this business," he said. "It could all end tomorrow. You never know." My article on him appeared in the Times the next morning, but before most New Yorkers read it, given the time difference, he was dead.

I was having trouble comprehending all this. Grand Prix racing was a world in which skill did not protect a man, it put him closer to the hole. Sport was supposed to be fun. This was fun? Why were we permitted to go on with it? I could not understand any of it from any angle, had begun to see it as an insult to the world. Each of these men made a thousand judgments in every race, any one of which, if only slightly inaccurate, would send him off the road at great speed. Which, depending on how solid the object he eventually hit, could kill him. How could they keep doing this? It certainly wasn't for money. Normally each driver got a small retainer from whichever factory had him under contract. This amounted to hundreds of dollars a month, not thousands. Normally he then got half of whatever starting money promoters offered, and half of the prize money, assuming he won any. But starting money was rarely more than $2,000 per car, and first prize was usually worth about the same. Nor were endorsement contracts to be had, for advertisers at that time had no interest in building a campaign around a young man who might not live out the week, much less the season. A driver who earned $25,000 in a year was having a big year.

One day I wondered in print how motor racing could survive the loss of so many of its stars in so short a time. I wasn't thinking of legislation that the politicians might bring, but of a sport that was in the process of devouring itself. Stars big enough to draw crowds did not emerge overnight, it took years, whereas to kill one of them took only an instant, and each time this happened a replacement came in who was a nobody, and who would remain one a good long time. No entertainment medium could prosper very long under conditions like that.

As I watched all these young men die, it became harder and harder to see their sport as sport. What they did had nothing to do with laughter or love or pleasure or even pain. Its excitement was based on the tendency of human beings to make mistakes, and on the extreme fragility of human life. And as my view of motor racing changed, so in subtle ways did my very character. I felt myself becoming pessimistic, even morbid, and did not like myself for it. At the start of each race I now wondered not who would win, but which driver or drivers would be dead before it ended. I found myself counting the cars every time around. Whose funeral would be next?

Such macabre thoughts as these were with me always, and to some extent have stayed.

Worse, I had by then become fond of Phil Hill. He had got mc that interview with Enzo Ferrari, though I hadn't known him well at the time, and hadn't really asked him to do it. From then on I was in his camp, and in each race I worried about him as I would have worried about my brother. He seemed to feel as ambivalent about car racing as I did, and his conversation reflected this ambivalence: he loved it and feared it both.

He became the one from whom I got most of my information. He let me get close to the world in which he lived. I learned about the financial aspects of a driver's life from him, and which of his colieagues were fastest, and why. Of one fellow Ferrari driver he once said: "If he lives, I'll be surprised," and that particular driver, Ricardo Rodriguez, 20, was dead within the year. I learned much else from Hill as well. Every reporter (every detective too, I was to learn later) must find an informant who is in close himself, and who will bring the reporter in with him. A reporter is not obliged to find a hundred, or a dozen, or even four or five sources. He just has to find one who can tell him what he needs to know, and whose information he can trust. Or at least that is what I felt then, and still feel, about the reporting trade. I talked to other drivers as well, and checked Phil's information out often enough, and never found him wrong.

In addition, most of what he said was quotable, sometimes shockingly so, making him for me, and for *The New York Times*, marvelous copy. On the subject of danger: "It depends how much glorification your ego needs.

If it needs enough, you don't think of that at all." On owners: "Most of them see us as funny little psychopaths who sooner or later become too scared to stick our shoe in it." Once in the Grand Prix of Belgium in heavy rain a number of cars went off the road. The ambulances were out there on the course. The remaining cars went past them on every lap. When the race ended and Phil pulled into the pits he was exhausted, dispirited, soaked, and he looked up at me and said: "Well, who got killed?"

He lived part of the year in Modena, had learned to speak creditable Italian, and he loved going to the opera. He was not a grease monkey type. He was by no means hard as nails, either. He was a very fast driver, but very careful, never brutalized the machinery, almost never went off the road, and was never hurt. He loved to race in the rain. Ever since he was a little boy, he said, he had felt secure in the rain.

He was not married, did not think a racing driver had a right to marry, and did not marry himself until his racing days were over. He would look at the drivers' wives sitting on pit counters working their stop watches, apparently calm, apparently unaware of the risks their husbands were taking, and this amazed him. He thought these women must all be stupid.

He was not easy to know. In my own case, he let me in close some days, and rebuffed me on others, but then he treated everybody this way. Most of us thought him an enigma, and around restaurant tables the conversation was often about Hill. Who was Phil Hill, really?

It was a question that demanded multiple answers, most of which elude me to this day, but if anything ever happened to him, I came to feel, I would never be able to go near a car race again. When Von Trips was killed, leaving the world championship to Hill, who had won the race, I pleaded with him to retire because I could not bear to think of him one day lying in the road like Trips, as disarticulated as a bundle of laundry. But he brushed my pleading off. "When I love motor racing less," he said coldly, "my own life will become worth more to me and I will be less willing to risk it."

I began to prepare a book about Grand Prix racing. It would be a big picture book and it would be beautiful, I hoped. Almost the last thing Jim Roach had said to me before I left New York was: "Get a camera. We pay $15 for every photo we publish." That sounded like big money to me, so I did get a camera, and the Times began to publish my photos which, in addition to the extra money, dressed up my stories; and then other publications bought photos from me too: *Esquire*, *Sports Illustrated*, *The Saturday Evening Post*. I had a cover on *Newsweek* once. I continued to write my articles and columns, but I became more and more enamored of this new art form I had discovered, bought better and better cameras, and day by day took, I think, better and better pictures.

Now I began to imagine that I could translate car racing into images that would have value. This would not be as simple as it might sound, because the three principal elements, speed, danger and noise, cannot be photographed. But I would try. The book would be nine by twelve in size, my text, my design, 165 of my photos. I would begin with page after page of portraits of drivers, most of whom were dead, or soon would be. And the title would be: *The Cruel Sport.*

Shortly after the book came out a driver named Bruce McLaren asked me to sign his copy. McLaren was from New Zealand, and he had a game leg from a schoolboy accident—he had fallen from a horse. A nice young man. Opening to the flyleaf I wrote: "When you are an old man I hope this book will help you remember how it was when you were young." Then I thought, as I handed the book back to him: but he won't live to be an old man.

And he didn't.

La Saliere is an Italian restaurant—Italian waiters and cuisine. The Italian frontier is only about ten miles further down the coast. Sometimes it is a bit difficult being understood here, for most of the waiters don't speak proper French. But we dine on wonderful antipasti: tiny pizzas, crespelles stuffed with rabiola cheese, fried mozzarella croquettes, and slices of Parma ham. We each order a salad tre colori. For the main course Peggy has ordered grilled shrimps with sautéed spinach, and I the spaghetti Bolognaise. We have drunk a fine Chianti Classico.

Afterwards we walk along the quay looking at the yachts. Peggy hates the whole idea of yachts, but I tend to ogle them the way a man might ogle girls. I have never wanted to own one, or even sail on one, but I do like to look at them, perhaps because of the freedom and luxury they seem to represent, if you don't look too closely. In actuality, most of them rarely go to sea, and they don't represent anything, except great expense.

But presently we come to a yacht moored stern first to the quay, which represents, at least to me, a great deal more. It is a long, high-masted sailing vessel with scrubbed teak decks named the Zaca. It has the lines of the great Clipper ships that once raced across oceans.

I first saw it after we had dined in this same restaurant in the company of a couple we had known a while. The man was our age, more or less, the woman he was with was thirty years younger, and as we came out onto the quay afterwards he pointed out the Zaca and said it had once belonged to Errol Flynn.

To which the young woman replied: "Who's Errol Flynn?"

Flynn was one of the most swashbuckling figures ever to blaze across the American sky, and if you caught him young—he as a young man, me as a boy—he was Captain Blood, he was Robin Hood in Technicolor, he was the hero all of us yearned to be. He had charm, incredible good looks, a neat British accent (though in fact he was Australian) and he got to kiss girls like Olivia De Haviland, like Maureen O'Hara, each one more beautiful than the next. He earned $300,000 a year at a time when $100 a week was a fortune.

Then came his trial for the statutory rape of two girls, both of whom, separately, had thrown themselves at him, and both of whom had turned out to be under age. This trial was unimaginably tawdry, but lubricious too. The tabloid newspapers carried every word. The war was over by then, but America hadn't grown up that much, and sex in polite company was a taboo subject still. Flynn, who was about 37 at the time, beat the rap, but from then on he aged fast.

He spent a good deal of time here on the coast. His third and final marriage was celebrated in the cathedral in Nice. The reporters and paparazzi turned the ceremony into a circus, and the traffic outside was backed up for blocks. That marriage failed quickly, after which Flynn sailed around, and wandered around, fleeing his creditors, hoping for acting jobs. No one in my lifetime was more instantly recognizable by name or face than Errol Flynn, but he took his great gift and great good luck and squandered it. He was not at all a nose-to-the-grindstone type, which is what I suppose I am, and he cut his gaudy swath, then drank himself to death at fifty, leaving behind three ex-wives, many debts and the Zaca. I don't know who owns the Zaca now, and don't much care, but each time we come to dinner here I like to walk over and look at it.

We get back into our car, and because it is late and there is no traffic, we take a turn around the race circuit. We can't drive all of it, because some of the streets are one way against us, and a large section, part of the promenade around the harbor, is closed to vehicular traffic. But we cross the starting line and drive up the hill to the casino, swinging left in front of the Hotel de Paris, and then right again and downhill through sharp turns to the tunnel under Loews Hotel. At the exit from the tunnel there begins a fast sweeping bend toward the harbor front where, on race days, there is always a chicane designed to slow the cars down before they must make a quick left hand jog onto the promenade, followed by an equally quick right hand jog, unless they wish to plunge into the water.

This has happened, and those yachts normally moored against the quay were—and are—obliged to move back into the harbor a minimum of ten meters by law before the race. Frogmen on launches are stationed among them, ready to plunge down if necessary and extract the errant driver before he drowns. Driving a race car into the harbor is a neat trick, for the barriers there are formidable, but two men over the years have performed it. Both made it to the surface without help, both were unhurt, and both as they swam to shore were blushing with shame. One was Alberto Ascari, who had already won the world championship twice. The other was a much lesser driver whose name I've forgotten, though I stood there the following morning to watch his dripping race car hoisted out.

It was my habit at all of these races to acquire a photographer's brassard, not a press ticket. This allowed me to move anywhere on the circuit. I would do my interviews before the start of the race, and again after the winner had won, but during the race I would prowl about watching the way different drivers took different curves, at the same time looking for photos.

I always watched part of the time at the chicane, where the cars were slowed enough for me to photograph faces; in addition I could try for race cars in the foreground and yachts and girls in bikinis in the background—a nice juxtaposition, I thought. At the chicane, I also knew, there had been interesting pileups in the past. But no one had ever been hurt there prior to the crash I am about to describe, and hardly anyone had ever been hurt anywhere else on this circuit either, for the Grand Prix de Monaco was and is too slow a race. Only the other races killed drivers, we all believed. It took decades for the winning car here to average over eighty miles an hour, and even today no one has reached ninety. For a race car that is creeping. At such relative slowness the car can always be stopped before great damage is done. Almost always.

In the absence of great speed and the danger that rides speed's back, the Grand Prix de Monaco was, and for most spectators still is, celebrated mostly for its setting. It is the race through the streets. The race around the houses. There are those who call it the most cherished and exciting of all the races—but the excitement doesn't have much to do with the race itself. Monaco is an enclave of riches, and during race week all this wealth and luxury is there to see: the women in jewelry, the elegant girls, the curbs lined with Rolls Royces, Ferraris, Lamborghinis, the crowded lobbies, the parties. While outside in the street those uncouth, brilliant machines ravage the silence of the town. A race to be watched, if possible, while sipping champagne. A unique race in a unique setting, the air so electric that one sometimes feels it is difficult to breathe.

Never mind that the circuit through the streets is so tight and twisty that high speeds are impossible, passing a rival driver is virtually impossible, and the machinery can't stand it. Most often more cars break down than finish the race.

The first time I came here, as I picked up my credentials, I was wildly excited. There was no ESPN as yet, the race had not yet been televised in America, and all I knew about it was what I had read. I walked through the empty streets, the engines already revving behind me, and saw that there were people in every window, on every balcony. The temporary bleachers were packed. So were the steps of the most famous casino in the world, and the terrace of the Hotel de Paris, and the decks of the yachts in the harbor.

Crowds of course are relative. Other races draw more spectators but have places to put them. They have room. In Monaco—Monte Carlo—there is no room. Everything is jammed in tight. I had never seen a place that felt so crowded.

But the cars as they raced through the city were going to be obscured by the city, I realized, by hotels and houses, by rows of trees, by the bleachers, by people. From the press box, once the race started, I could see very little.

So the next year and in the years following I applied for a photographer's badge, not a press pass, and so was able to move freely. Before long I had become so enamored of photography that I was seeing much of this race (of all the races in fact) through lenses. What had started out almost as a con became a hobby, then a profession. I was on my feet and moving around for nearly three hours, and I got close enough to be physically assaulted by the noise and speed. If I gave up worrying about personal safety and leaned out over the street, I could get close-ups no one else had thought to try for. And I saw exactly how dangerous, even here, this sport could be.

In this way I watched nine of these Monaco Grand Prix, and nothing bad happened. But the tenth time the bill was presented here too.

A Ferrari driver named Lorenzo Bandini paid it. I watched him pay it.

It was late in the race. Bandini was perhaps tired. That he had become slightly less accurate in placing his car is certain. He came though the chicane cleanly enough but once on the harbor front never got properly straightened out. The barrier there was a row of straw bales braced with telephone poles. It was designed to keep errant cars from plunging into the harbor. The Ferrari's left wheels touched this barrier, then clawed their way up it, and as the car climbed, it capsized. Then it was in the air upside down, flying. It flew quite far.

If it had flown into the water Bandini might be alive today, but it didn't. Instead, it came down on the pavement on top of him. There was an audible whoosh, like a giant expelling all his air, and then it burst into flames. Sometimes the flames parted and Bandini's helmet could be seen, underneath everything.

I stood in horror, my cameras forgotten, while the flag marshals tried to get the fire out and succeeded for a moment, during which they lifted up the car, got it half off him, but when the flames burst forth again they dropped it on top of him and jumped away. Other men came with other extinguishers. It seemed to take forever. Probably it lasted three or four minutes. A long time if you are burning to death. When the fire was reduced to a sputter, they again tried to lift the car, but again the flames flared up, and again they dropped it and ran. All this time the race continued. The other cars kept coming through. They were slowed by the smoke and flames and foam, but they kept coming through.

At a certain point I gave myself a lecture. Take the picture, I told myself. But I'm watching a man die, I told myself. I don't care, I told myself. Set the aperture, set the speed, and take the picture. You're a professional. Take it, take it.

So finally I did. One photo from that series later hung in museums (The Art Institute of Chicago, The Baltimore Museum, the New York Gallery of Modern Art) as part of a Man in Sport exhibition. Which proves, as is true of many of the great photos of the world, that I happened to be standing in that particular spot. Nothing much else.

The death of Bandini must have marked me more than I knew. Although I have been a professional writer all my adult life, I have never described it in prose until now. Sometimes I have asked myself why. There had been many previous deaths—too many, as I have said—but this one marked me in a different and more profound way than all previous ones. Suddenly, finally, I had had enough. I didn't want to see anything like that again. I couldn't bear to go back, not to Monaco, not to anywhere else the fast cars ran.

Eleven years passed before this emotion dimmed enough for me to accept another assignment to the Monaco Grand Prix. There was international TV now. The drivers had become rich, their faces known far and wide. When not in their cars they hid out in trailers like film stars. The same electricity was in the air, however, and although for me much of the romance was missing, perhaps gone forever, still everyone else seemed to feel it. The crowds, I saw, stirred to the spectacle in the same old way. The setting had not changed either: the parties, the yachts, the fancy motor cars, the girls in bikinis. In limitless amounts the champagne still flowed.

It seemed clear to me then, and still does, that the Monaco race will stand always in its special place and role, unchanged and unchallenged at the pinnacle of the Grand Prix world, but for me personally it was over. I have never gone back and do not think I ever will.

6.
Time Off to Enjoy

November 24, 2000, Lyon

Today we have driven up here from Nice in a bit over four hours. The French autoroutes are designed to be very fast roads, but are so expensive they are under-used, in some stretches almost empty. The result, if you are on one of them, can be somewhat scary. I tried to hold the car at 140 km/h all the way—about 87 mph. This is ten kilometers above the speed limit, and it felt very fast to me, but from time to time cars went by me like jet aircraft. And not even high powered cars. Renaults, Peugeots, Citroens. Whoosh. This tends to shake one's aplomb. Anyway, it shook mine.

We drive into the city, take a hotel room on the Place des Celestins, and go out sight seeing. The best part of being a tourist, to me, is just walking along looking at buildings, and pretty squares, at churches that date back 600 or more years. One studies the stone doorways, the lintels carved in stone, the great wooden doors, the wrought iron balconies, one looks through the tall windows at vaulted or beamed ceilings—details that for the most part do not exist in America.

Because of the Alps on one side and the Massif Central on the other, Lyon is the great crossroads of France. Almost any north-south journey must go through here. In the years I worked for the paper there were no autoroutes yet, I was on the road most weeks, and I probably drove through here forty or fifty times and never stopped once. Never had time, was always rushing somewhere. Now we do have time, or else make time. As time begins to close in, one has less of it in some respects, more in others.

But Lyon is a dazzling place, we see now. It is as beautiful as Paris but, because it lies at the confluence of the Rhone and Saone, it seems much more open, much more user-friendly. There are many bridges, many pedestrian bridges also. The city center between the two rivers is an elongated peninsula that reminds me of Manhattan, though it is narrower, only seven or eight blocks across, and unlike Manhattan, there are many walking streets, meaning no cars allowed. The buildings are only four or five stories high, some are palaces, most are centuries old and almost all bear the architectural decorations of a former time.

In the evening we walk through the streets to the opera house which turns out to be as dazzling as the rest of the city. Though it's auditorium seats only 1120 people, it is the equivalent of eight stories high. Garishly lit up, with people milling around outside, it looks to me like two separate buildings, one of which sits on top of the other. The bottom half is a 19th century theater, its mostly marble facade richly decorated with columns, capitols and bas reliefs, with arches on top of arches, with standing statues of eight of the nine muses. It is similar to what you might see in many another French or Italian town, and it ought to end in a peaked tile roof—which it once did, I'm told. Seen from the front, the building's present top half is a great, glass-fronted, reinforced-concrete, half cylinder. It is as heavy and substantial as the part below. It is as modern as modern. One looks up at half of a gigantic hoop. Obviously at least two major architects designed this place, and they worked about a century apart.

The show we have come to see is Offenbach's *Orpheus in the Underworld*, which pretends to be a parody of the Orpheus and Euridice myth, though it resembles it hardly at all. In the Greek myth the two are so much in love that when Euridice dies, Orpheus goes down to Hades to get her back. But in this show, which is played strictly for laughs, they are married, can't stand each other, and both have lovers. Euridice evidently likes men. When she gets to Hades she forgets her husband, forgets her lover, falls in love with Jupiter and stays. All this sounds silly, and it is, but we watch it enthralled. The orchestra plays well, the singers, all of them French and all of them unknown to me, sing well, and there is a great deal of excellent comic dancing. It is odd to listen to such beautiful music wrapped around a farce. I have sometimes thought of Offenbach, who had his own theater and composed dozens and dozens of these things, perhaps as many as a hundred, as the Richard Rodgers or Jerome Kern of his day, but he was much more than that, wasn't he?

It is late when the show ends, so we have dinner in a brasserie that will stay open most of the night. Nothing fancy. I ordered slices of hot Lyonaise sausage over a bed of lentils, and we drank a Beaujolais nouveau not yet two months old. Lyon is so crowded with famous restaurants that it has long had the reputation of the best eating place in France. This may explain why dinner in an ordinary brasserie seemed to us so grand. Other towns support plenty of bad restaurants—yes, even here in France. But Lyon apparently does not. In Lyon either you are good, or you go out of business.

Lyon, November 25

It is morning and we walk along a section of Roman road. We are high on a hill from which we can look down on the city and on the two big rivers coming together. Julius Caesar had his headquarters here—perhaps they started building this road then. It is surfaced with great flat stones, most of which are big enough to be called boulders, and almost all of which are somewhat askew now, for the centuries have shoved them about. Irregular in shape, they are up to three feet long. The Romans, to make the boulders more or less flat cracked all their bellies off, placed them as close together as boulders can be made to go, then smoothed them over with sand. Every time the sand washed away, professional road menders replenished it—drayloads of sand must have got dragged up here from the coast with the regularity of a train schedule.

Nearby, is a stone and brick amphitheater, also Roman in origin, in which concerts are held in summer, and we walk to it over the ancient road. The road was, and still is, wide enough for two chariot drivers to pass each other at speed, though if they tried it today it would jar all their teeth loose.

When Rome ruled the world Lyon was the largest city in Gaul, up to a hundred thousand people, Paris being still a village then, no contest. So times have changed. But Rome's road and Rome's amphitheater are still here, almost as eternal as the two rivers below, though not quite.

Lyon, November 25

In the afternoon we drive out to Perouges, a village of old stone buildings, some of them timbered, all with tiled rooftops. A village on a hilltop, a huddled village. Partially restored, it looks much the same as it did in the middle ages.

It is tea time, so we step into the dining room of the Hostellerie du Vieux Perouges. Timbered ceiling, antique furniture, a fire burning in the hearth. The building dates from the 14th century but hanging on the wall are numerous photos of Bill and Hillary Clinton grinning at the camera. On a day off from a European summit meeting a few years ago they too stopped here for tea. It gives me a bit of a laugh. You can't go anywhere today that everybody and his brother hasn't been there before you.

Lyon, November 26

On Sunday morning the streets are empty. It is as if no one lives here. We find the oldest church in the city, St. Martin d'Ainay, which was consecrated by Pope Pascal II in 1107, and look it over. We have lunch with friends—he is a professor at the university, she is the city librarian—then get on the autoroute and start home to Nice.

Tomorrow I go back to work.

7. Knives Flashing: Foreign Bureau Intrigue

December 4, 2000, Nice

After two years here, after I had written about 300 articles for the paper, after a hundred or more of my photos had been published as well, I asked to be taken onto the staff and brought to Paris. I wrote to Jim Roach, who presented my case to Catledge, Burritt and the rest. But there was resistance, for the New York Times guarded staff positions jealously. I kept pushing, kept asking what more I had to do to prove myself. This argument at length prevailed. I was put on staff and attached to the Paris bureau. We were to move there at our earliest convenience.

That is, my wishes were granted.

Like the man says, be careful what you wish for.

My new salary would be $190 a week. This amounted to a healthy raise plus a degree of security I had not had before. There would be a cost of living allowance too, and help with the rent. The children's schooling would be paid, and half the cost of a new, bigger car. All of this worked out to about $15,000 a year, which was to me an unheard of sum. There would be Blue Cross coverage, paid vacations and all the rest. Henceforth my travel expenses would be paid in full. Paris being more centrally located, there would be fewer horrendously long drives. Members of the bureau's support staff would arrange my accreditation at events, make my hotel reservations, my plane and train reservations, would hand me tickets at my desk. I would no longer have to wait in line at the Nice post office to file stories, just hand them to the bureau's teleprinter operators for direct transmittal to New York.

All of which I had wanted, of course. But more than this, I had longed to be part of the big team, and now was. I had come up from the minors to the world champions, and it was a good feeling.

At first.

I had thought nothing else would change. I would continue to make my own assignments, travel where I wished, write whatever stories I chose to write in whatever country I chose to write them. My boss—my only boss—would remain Jim Roach in New York, with whom I corresponded by mail two or three times a week, and who always accepted my schedule.

But I had landed with both big feet in the midst of the tense and competitive world of foreign correspondents. A world of whose existence I had previously been unaware. A world that, seeing it up close for the first time, I never recognized for what it was. Did not see it clearly until years later, and to this day I ask myself: how could I have been so blind? How could I have expected other correspondents to welcome me with open arms? How could I have understood so little about the way these other men reacted to the perceived threat that I represented? Yes, I was much younger than they were. And, yes, I had been living in Nice in a cocoon. But these excuses do not serve. I should have known. I should have tailored my instincts and reactions to fit, but didn't.

In the newspaper game at that time (and still) being a foreign correspondent was a plum. Running a foreign bureau was the plum of plums, hard to get, hard to hold onto. For the bureau chiefs there was no promotion ahead. One could aspire to no higher stardom. Some bureau chiefs, as they got old and slow, became editors in New York, even high ranking editors, but the peak of their careers and lives, was always the time spent abroad, ask any of them.

These men—there were no women bureau chiefs at the time—were foreigners living in foreign countries that they did not understand very well, not having grown up there, and most of them spoke the local language poorly, or not at all. They felt themselves out on the edge, totally exposed, and they guarded their turf and their perks with a fierceness that was sometimes hidden, sometimes not even. Space in the paper, if they got it, was the only security they had, particularly space on the front page. Not only on the front page, but above the fold.

Space was limited, however, and their confidence rose and fell according to how much of each day's story the editors in New York decided to run, and where they ran it. The terrific pressure each felt himself under gave them the need not only to do well themselves, but also to outshine their colleagues in the other bureaus, and if one of these colleagues was seen to fall on his face, their own faces broke out in smiles.

But let a few days go by with no big story or, worse, with some other bureau dominating the front page, and their jobs would seem to them in jeopardy. Not only their jobs, but their allowances and prestige, their chauffeur driven bureau cars. All of them knew what was ahead if they were brought back to New York.

Years later I did a short stint in the city room in New York. Sitting at the next desk was a man named Raymond Daniell. Then over sixty and waiting out the years to retirement, he had once been a famous byline, and he had reported always from exotic places. Now he was experiencing the foreign correspondent's end of the trail. At the front of the newsroom was the city desk and on it stood a table microphone. Each morning one of the editors would reach for it, and the loud speakers on the walls would blare out our names as something came up: "Mr. Daley, city desk please." I would troop up there. "Mr. Daley, a water main has burst on 48th Street, look into it, please." That would be the day's assignment, which was almost never a very large story. Important to the paper, perhaps, but not to whoever had to report and write it. But Daniell, who was so much older and more prestigious, who had worked abroad most of his life, who had had his own bureau and had covered wars, was summoned in exactly the same way, and assigned exactly the same type stories. I couldn't stand this kind of thing very long and didn't. But Daniell had to.

What had happened to Daniell was what happened to nearly all of them.

Each bureau chief not only wanted to be in the paper every day, thereby proving his worth as a correspondent, he also wanted all his men in there too, proving his worth as bureau manager. At the time that I moved from Nice to Paris there were about forty Times bureaus overseas, some manned by a single correspondent. The important bureaus had more. In Paris there were six, sometimes seven of us, and the bureau chief, as soon I had got installed in an apartment, and got my children registered in school, began assigning me stories. His stories, not mine. It was his job to make use of me to his advantage, he believed, and if the stories he assigned were small enough it was a way to diminish the threat to his career that he may have imagined I represented.

He sent me to Rennes, a 217 mile drive, to interview the prefect there about an upcoming referendum. How was Brittany going to vote? I wrote this story while wondering how many Times readers cared how Brittany voted. And even if one or more readers did care, what difference could Brittany's relatively few votes make to the eventual outcome? I knew in advance that this story was never going to get into the paper, and it didn't.

He assigned me to write a story about the Spanish Republican Government in exile. Yes, there was one, and Paris was its headquarters—five or six old men who had been in exile now for 22 years while the Franco dictatorship ruled Spain. There had been more of them. Now only these few were left. They made their living clerking in stores or teaching Spanish to children, and they shuttled the various government ministries back and forth among themselves. The man I interviewed, Julio Just, claimed to be vice president, and also minister of the interior and immigration. In the past he had held other ministries, had even been president himself once. The present head of government lived in South America. So did the present prime minister.

General Franco would fall this year, I was assured by Señor Just. This was fact, they had operatives moving in and out of Spain regularly, and the evidence was plain, Franco was about to be overthrown, his tyranny had only a few more weeks to go, and this is what I should print.

I went back to the office and told the bureau chief that I had been listening to the wishful thinking of a bunch of old guys who hadn't set foot in Spain in 22 years. I had no story, I said.

Oh no, I was told, it was a good story, and I should write it exactly as Julio Just had explained it, quoting him as the authority.

I did as I was told, and the next day the story ran on the front page of *The New York Times*, one of the few front pagers I ever had. When the paper arrived by mail four or five days later I read my handiwork and felt half amused, half disgusted. This too was the newspaper business, I told myself.

Of course Franco's reign, despite my front page article, did not end on Julio Just's schedule. It lasted fifteen more years and ended only when the dictator died a natural death.

I didn't care about the front page, and it was becoming increasingly difficult to do the job I believed I had been sent to Paris to do. I would be away at some event from Thursday to Sunday, come back into the office to write my Monday column, only to receive one of the bureau chief's assignments for the next day.

What to do? A person with any political smarts at all would have drawn the bureau chief aside, and done some respectful explaining. My role in his bureau was supposed to be something else, I should have told him. I might have asked his understanding and forbearance. I should at least have given him a chance to back off. But I had no political smarts, so instead I wrote letters of protest directly to Jim Roach in New York, knowing he would take them "outside."

The bureau chief was about 45 years old, a stolid, relatively humorless, competent man. I had no desire to harm him, and never imagined I had it within my power to do so. To me he was a personage, rock solid in his job, a pillar of the paper. Of course he was none of these things. Paris was his first posting abroad, he spoke only halting French, and he was trying to manage one of the paper' biggest foreign bureaus. Meanwhile his wife was away caring for a sick child, and in her absence he was carrying on a liaison, it became known later, with one of the secretaries in the office. That is, he was at least as insecure as all the other bureau chiefs, and probably more so.

A letter of reprimand was sent to him signed by the managing editor. It said I was to be treated as an equal member of the bureau, on the same footing as everyone else, but that I reported not to him but to the sports editor. He was to understand this. He was not to use me as an extra correspondent except in an emergency.

I received a copy of this letter.

He never spoke to me about it, swallowed the dose and said nothing. The extra assignments stopped for a time, and I was relieved at this, even happy, and never saw the cost: one new enemy.

While working out of Nice I had impinged on certain of the other bureaus, but not seriously. I was, after all, only a stringer, and I had rarely worked under their noses. The events I wrote about took place usually in the far corners of their domains: in the Eifel Forest not Bonn, in Sicily not Rome, in Pamplona not Madrid, in the Pyrenees not Paris. But now I was suddenly one of them, equal in standing, and coming into their territory to do a story which, as they saw it, they could have, and perhaps should have, done themselves. For those who were insecure enough, or paranoid enough, it was possible to take my arrival as proof that New York was dissatisfied with them. In other words I was a threat. I never saw myself as a threat to anyone. I never imagined anyone else did either, but I see now they did.

In London the bureau chief was Drew Middleton, a slightly portly, middle aged man who affected British tweeds and smoked a pipe. He was sometimes accused of trying to appear more British than the British, and for a long time he maintained an embargo against me. Even though many major sporting events took place in England, I was not permitted to go there. But once installed in Paris I began to question this, and presently a letter came from Jim Roach saying he had spoken to them outside, and the embargo had been removed; henceforth I should feel free to go to London any time a story called for it.

In Rome the bureau chief was Arnaldo Cortesi, an elderly Italian, normally a debonair, courtly man. At first his manner was barely correct, but the next time I went to Rome I brought Peggy along. Arnaldo, who had an eye for the ladies, evidently liked what he saw, and he took us to lunch at Alfredo's, a restaurant at the height of its fame. From then on he was the perfect host, and once even drove us to Castel Gondolfo, which is quite far out in the country, where we lunched outdoors while looking across at the Pope's summer residence.

The Madrid bureau chief was Benjamin Welles, whose father, Sumner Welles, was a Washington insider who had once been under secretary of state. Benjamin Welles had a diplomat's good manners and at first meeting was perfectly correct. After that he managed to be absent when I was there. The bureau was available to me, and his secretary had evidently been instructed to be helpful if necessary. But I don't remember ever seeing Welles himself again.

These men and others whose bureaus I visited were heroes to me. I was eager to get to know them, but for the most part this did not happen.

In Paris, which cowered under its heavy cloud cover for most of each year, our children were sick regularly, so when summer came we rented a furnished apartment on the Promenade des Anglais in Nice, and there I installed Peggy and the children, Theresa who was six, and Suzanne who was five, and also our au pair, a 16 year old German girl named Heidi Vad, whom we soon came to love as much as a third daughter, to the point where we have kept in touch with her all the years since—she is a middle aged woman now. In the mornings she or all of us had only to walk the kids across the street to the beach. Of course I was not often there, for at this time, I once calculated, I was away from home all or part of 135 days a year.

The principal concern of the correspondents in Paris during those years was the war in Algeria, which France was losing. There had been atrocities on both sides. Tens of thousand of people had been killed on both sides. Many governments had fallen, De Gaulle had come to power, and that summer the war boiled over into Tunisia.

I had come over the Alps and into Nice with the Tour de France, and in a few days would fly to Warsaw for something else. I was hoping for a short rest in between, but as we walked across to the beach that morning

I bought a Nice Matin, read the big headline and feared the worst: a battle was raging in Tunisia, which was just across the Mediterranean from where I was standing. I'm the one closest to it, I thought, and the Paris bureau chief has been aching to take control of me.

When we got back to the apartment two hours later the phone was ringing. I knew what it was, I believed, and I did not answer. A war in Tunisia is not my job, I told myself.

But after that, the phone rang every ten minutes, and finally I did answer.

I should get right over to Tunis, the bureau chief told me.

"I have to be in Warsaw this weekend."

"This takes precedence. How soon can you hop over there?"

I sent a frantic message to New York. Whose idea was it to send me to North Africa to a war?

The answer came back: "Mine." It was signed by Turner Catledge, managing editor.

So I sent a message to Roach and to my father. I would come back bearing my typewriter, or upon it, I wrote. I was really upset, but a message as idiotic as this one is embarrassing to remember. I did not even pause to think that in New York all messages came off the teleprinters in a glass enclosed room beside the newsroom. They were ripped off the machines by copy boys and carried wherever they were supposed to go. The copy boys always read them en route—I used to read them myself—and if they were especially juicy, as I suppose mine was, they were passed around and read by everybody. So I was not only being forced to go to a war against my will, I was making a fool of myself in the bargain.

I got off the plane in Tunis and was met by the resident correspondent there, a man named Tom Brady. The battle was at Bizerte about forty miles away, he told me. "I'll handle the diplomatic end in Tunis," he told me, "you handle the Bizerte end. Take the bureau car and get out there as fast as you can. But for God's sake be careful, they're strafing the road."

So I drove out across the desert toward Bizerte, and before long began to pass burnt out hulks that had been pushed off into the sand. I gave each of them a quick glance. Sometimes I could see the bullet holes, sometimes not. Mostly I was driving with my head out the window looking for planes. There were occasional desiccated trees along the road, none of them leafy enough to hide under. The road was straight and flat, and I was in the desert and off to the west I could see a group of Bedouins moving along on camels with the declining sun behind them.

I came to Bizerte which is on the coast and is bisected by a channel. From across the channel came the noise of gunfire and mortar explosions, there was much smoke, and part of the city was in flames. I parked, and walked toward a group of French soldiers who, sitting on the ground behind a low wall, were eating chunks of bread and paté, and I stood over them and started asking questions, and heard popping noises beside my head, and the soldiers started shouting at me, calling me names like *cretin*, which is the same word in English, and *espece de con*, which means "species of cunt" and which is what you call someone who does something mindlessly stupid. I was, it seems, being fired at from across the channel. As it goes by ones head rifle fire does not whine as in the movies. Each bullet makes a rather loud pop. I crouched down, and from then on was careful not to expose myself. I didn't walk across gaps, I ran. I did my interviews from behind cover. I was by no means afraid. Bullets going by cannot be seen and, assuming they don't hit, are hard to take seriously.

By the time I started back to Tunis I had a fairly coherent picture of what was happening. I reached my hotel, but before I started writing I needed a beer to calm my nerves so I stepped into the bar—where I was immediately set upon and interrogated by other reporters whose habit it was to spend the entire day in the bar, where they would interview the many photographers and few reporters who had actually gone out to see the war and had now returned from it. Realizing this came as a terrific shock to me, for I knew some of their famous bylines, and had read their first person accounts from other war zones. They turned up every place where there was shooting. They liked to write about all the bombs and bullets they had had to dodge to bring back the story. Not necessarily so, I saw now. Photographers had to get in close, had to take chances, for photos can not easily be faked, but reporters didn't, and for some of the men I met in Tunisia that hotel bar was as close to the danger zone as they cared to get.

It was not a very big war, as wars go. A small Arab country fired up by a petty dictator and rising up against mighty France. An army mostly of ragged volunteers. In a few days it was over. I went into the devastated city. There were dead bodies on the terrace of a cafe. Two men came towards me pushing a wheelbarrow. Not a very big wheelbarrow, but full: a man and a woman, charred. Most of the clothing had been burned off them. The man's sex was shriveled to the size of a walnut. Broken white bones peeked through the blackened meat.

I took a turn through the town. The fires were being put out, the dead collected. Trees along the boulevards had been sheared off half way up, the bulky foliage lying in the street. I came to the hillside where a mass grave was to be dug, where 300 bodies in neat rows lay out in the sun. Many were without shoes. Some were perforated in only one spot. A single tiny little hole. A number of faces wore expressions of surprise.

I had never seen a reporter try to write what a city smelled like when the battle ended. I thought it was worth trying to do this, that if I did it well enough it would stand for the stupidity, futility, and waste of wars like the one just concluded, which was so like all the others everywhere. Bizerte reeked of smoke, of smoldering ruins, of days of uncollected garbage, of the disinfectant that the fire trucks were spraying down, of so many dead so long unburied, and of the iodine soaked masks the corpse collectors wore to kill the stenches in which they worked. It was summer, it was bakingly, implacably hot, and the various stinks competed with one another, fought for prominence in your nose. It depended on where you stood.

I wrote my story and sent it, and the foreign desk, which unlike the sports desk had not been told to leave my copy alone, toned it way down. Maybe that's what it deserved, who knows, I am not the one to ask. I was trying to evoke odor in prose, which I believed then and still believe, is impossible to do. One can write about food and the reader's taste buds will salivate. One can make the reader hear sounds, see sights. One can evoke certain types of physical contact, especially sexual contact, and cause the reader to feel palpable sensations. But one cannot evoke odor. At least I've never seen it done, and I'm not pretending I did it then, or now either.

I could now call myself a war correspondent, I realized on the plane back to Nice, and from time to time in the years since it has seemed profitable to do so. Technically I had been one, and there was no need to add that I went there under protest, or that the war in question was short. I had seen killing close up and been shot at, so why not. I never suggested that I was a very important war correspondent. There are men and women, many of them, who have got in far closer than I for a much longer time, and they are the ones who deserve the praise.

I went to Ireland to see a horse race, and into the Pyrenees to describe a salmon fishing tournament—we ate freshly caught salmon every night while there—and in London I watched the Henley regatta, two eight oared sculls racing up the Thames. In Siena I wrote two pieces about the Palio horse race. This is more pageant than race, but a very peculiar one. Horses and jockeys are hired to represent each section of the city. The track is the Campo, the main square of the city, a huge and gorgeous piazza which lies on a slant and is ringed by medieval buildings; that is, the surface is neither turf nor dirt, but cobblestones, and it is, don't forget, tilted. The sections' flags are paraded, and then the jockeys in their gaudy silks parade the horses, which are the opposite of high priced thoroughbreds. Upwards of 100,000 people watch all this. The piece de resistance, when it finally goes off, is the incomprehensible race itself. The nags slither and skid around the turns, while the jockeys flail at each other with their whips. Horses go down, jockeys go down. It's all very spectacular, it makes no sense at all, and I had great fun writing about it.

In winter I would drive into the Alps every other week for the major ski races. Usually we all went, including the au pair. At each place I would leave the kids and their mother and the girl skating, or taking ski lessons, and go up on the slopes with the racers. Once up, I had to get down again. I was not a very good skier, never had a lesson from anybody, but I came down all those famous downhill runs, not always elegantly, sometimes for hundreds of yards on my elbows and chin. The Piste Verte at Chamonix, the Hahnenkamm at Kitzbuhel. The Kandahar was raced one year at Sestriere, the highest ski village in the Alps, 6600 feet, different from other villages in that it had two round, modern hotels that were so high they could be called skyscrapers. The Lauberhorn at Wengen had a jump that the racers took in a schuss, but that I found terrifying, and skied cautiously around. The weather in these places was sometimes atrocious, frostbite cold, or so thick with fog that the village below would repeatedly vanish, only to reappear slowly, steeples first, like a fairy tale village coming back to life.

At Davos the temperature was 14 degrees below zero, and I skied down the Parsenn, a run about twelve miles long, in order to write a piece about it. The wind wafted ice crystals off the snow and blew them into my face with such force they stung like sand. I have never been so cold, and as soon as I reached the bottom I fled, took the next train into Austria where I found Kitzbuhel 3,000 feet lower and forty degrees warmer.

In Wengen one year there was insufficient snow, and the decision was made to hold the races on the north face of the Eiger, the most sinister side of the most sinister mountain in Europe, killer of hundreds and hundreds of climbers. A temporary T-bar had been rigged which tugged me upwards for two or three thousand feet until I had reached the starting line of the downhill—but once there I found that the snow under my skis was not snow at all but glare ice. I wasn't good enough to cope with this kind of thing but had to, couldn't stay up there forever. I was almost the last man off the mountain. Tense with fear, I got down sideslipping my edges most of the way.

Three times a year I dreamed up assignments that would take us to Spain. In the spring we would go to the feria in Seville, and stay for four or five bullfights on successive days, or else to Madrid for the San Isidro fights which went on for almost two weeks, though again we could stay for only a few days. The Pamplona Fiesta began each July 7, seven days of fights, and finally in October as the season ended we would go looking for three or four more wherever we could find them.

These trips constituted a problem both for me and for the paper. I had become enamored of bullfights—I had been enamored before I ever came to Europe, based on what I had read in college, meaning Hemingway mostly, and on what I had seen in Mexico. My problem was that *The New York Times* was not interested in bullfighting at all, and in fact received many poison pen letters from animal lovers whenever I wrote about it. Copies of these letters were usually sent on to me, FYI, presumably so that I would feel the same pressure Jim Roach felt. Every time I went to Spain I was afraid it would be the last time, that I would be stopped, Roach would be made to stop me.

It made me extremely careful about what I wrote. Mostly I addressed the subject as obliquely as possible, never describing any corrida, writing instead about bullfighters who came back from terrible gorings, their wounds still open, so as not to lose contracts, or about rookies being promoted too soon because the hordes of tourists who flocked to Spain in those years demanded more and more fights. In Seville there was an American bullfighter named John Fulton who was struggling and mostly failing to get contracts. I went there to write about him, and afterwards went out to ranches with him, and into bullfight cafes with him. He became a close friend and stayed one until few years ago when, aged 65, he died.

At Pamplona I wrote not about the bullfighting, but about different aspects of the fiesta. After the running of the bulls each morning, the herd having gone through the ring and out the other side into the corrals, leaving the ring still crowded with breathless runners, the authorities turned loose wild cows with padded horns to provide comedy. One morning one of them tossed me high in the air. I had seen the beast coming, had turned to run, and then been astonished to look down and see a horn projecting from between my legs, even though I was running as fast as I could. Then I was sitting on its head, and then I was flying. The stands, the other runners, were roaring with laughter; I wrote this up too, wrote it funny, though landing on that arena floor was like landing on cement. The desk put a wonderful head on it: COWED TOURIST GOES ON A FLING.

All these were stories the animal lovers could not object to too much, or so I hoped.

I had one other element in my favor, a surprising one, Hemingway himself. I only talked to him once. This was in Pamplona. When I asked him for an interview, he put his arm around my shoulder and politely refused: "We're just having fun here, Bob." Later I learned that he never gave interviews to anyone he regarded as a rival. Me, a rival? An interview might have lifted my passion onto a literary plain, thus giving me a buffer against the animal lovers.

But the mere fact that Hemingway was there proved to be all the support I needed. For this was the summer of the feud between Antonio Ordoñez and his brother in law, Miguel Gonzalez, called Dominguin, about which Hemingway later wrote a book. A series of mano-a-mano corridas had been scheduled. Hemingway was championing Ordoñez, the son of the bullfighter who had served as his model for Pedro Romero in *The Sun Also Rises*, and he was such an opinionated man and such a celebrity that this judgment carried weight. Among Ordoñez's other champions were Orson Welles, who was also in Spain that summer. On Dominguin's side were, among others, Pablo Picasso, Jean Cocteau, the poet Robert Graves, and the screen writer Peter Viertel, and his wife Deborah Kerr.

These people turned the ritual slaughter of a few bulls into what passed in the newspaper trade for an important international story. As it spilled over into the magazines, it became too big for *The New York Times* to ignore, or for the poison pen letters to get in my way.

According to the publicity the two brothers in law hated each other, which they didn't, and this was a fight to the death, which it wasn't. Nonetheless, it was fun to write about, and it supported a number of trips to Spain. Many fights were scheduled; only a few came off, for both men were gored twice and laid up. Bullfighters are rarely killed, but they take tremendous punishment from the bulls.

After two seasons the Dominguin-Ordoñez feud passed from the scene, as did Hemingway, who put a shotgun in his mouth and managed to pull both triggers. With all three gone I had to be careful again, and many times I invented reasons for going to Spain which had nothing to do with bullfighting.

I did a piece on Spanish horse racing, for instance. I was at this time capable of conversing in Spanish on bullfighting, a subject in which I knew all the words. Other than that I spoke haltingly, but now I studied up on all the arcane horse breeding terms, foals, colts, studs and so forth and did my interviews in Spanish, and to my surprise got by. That same year, or another, I took a look at the best soccer team in Europe, Real Madrid, whose star players were mostly South Americans, and whose stadium, it seemed to me, was worth an article in itself. From my years with the Giants I knew nearly every stadium in America, but had never seen one like this. It rose up four tiers high, held over 100,000 people, and it made for a nice prose picture.

My passion for bullfighting, which had only got stronger, was in need now of another international story, if I were to keep going to Spain, and very soon I had one, a penniless waif known as El Cordobes who caught the fancy of the world.

The Cordobes, who wore his hair long like the Beetles, invented what seemed a new style. He didn't so much dominate bulls as collaborate with them. They seemed to know he would never brutalize them. His picadors were ordered to do very little pic-ing, and with the muleta he rarely gave the hard, punishment passes with which others liked to break the bull down and make it less dangerous. These passes doubled the bulls within their own length, hurt their spines and loins, and took the fight out of them fast. But the bulls the Cordobes fought came to him whole. As a result his faenas lasted minutes longer than anyone else's, and therefore were scarier. Most often prettier as well.

In addition, he had a smile that showed all 32 teeth—it could be seen from the topmost row, and certainly part of his enormous appeal was this glorious smile. (As an aside, a glorious smile has been part of the appeal these past thirty years of the tenor Luciano Pavarotti as well.) Before long the Cordobes was as famous in Europe as the Beetles. A good deal of his fame then made its way to America, partly due to me and *The New York Times*.

Spain at this time was hot, poor, dusty. The civil war was more than two decades in the past, but even in the big cities you sometimes walked along potholed sidewalks. There were thousands of bootblacks who offered to shine your shoes every time you sat down in a cafe. One saw plenty of people missing an arm, or limping along on one leg and a crutch. Spain was a depressed, repressed country whose streets reeked of strong odor. Cigars, cooking oil, spilled wine, cheap fuel. Trucks moved slowly under clouds of black smoke. Part of the main road between Barcelona and Madrid, the first time I drove it, was not paved.

Spain today is as odorless as France, as modern and prosperous too, but it wasn't then. There were police everywhere. The various fiestas were a time for letting off steam, as if without them the country would explode. The poor saved up for them the whole year, blew all their savings in a week. The bullring was the only place where men could scream and not get arrested. The upper classes, some of whom bred fighting bulls, lived amid great wealth. Everyone else was hungry much of the time, none of them hungrier than most bullfighters starting out. When the novice torero put on the gold brocaded costume and strode across the arena he had left all that behind, at least for the time being, and now he too might become rich.

I saw in bullfighting, and tried to put into words, the entire country, its heat, dust, poverty, wealth—all of it, even its music, guitar music mostly, which we heard in every cafe during fiestas, not to mention the plaza band that played in the arena during the paseo and, if the fight was good, later on too. Bullfighting, to me, was Spain. In Madrid during the San Isidro we would go out to the park called the Casa de Campo where there was a restaurant with, in front of it, six or eight small corrals, each holding the six fighting bulls scheduled for each of the feria's many fights. After the lunch, sometimes before, we would walk along looking in at the bulls, seeing them up very close, seeing the horns close enough to reach out and touch, seeing how sharp the points were. The bulls were almost always black, their muscles rippling under smooth healthy coats, we could smell them, smell the power they gave off, and some had splintered horns, so that we always wondered what such a horn would do to a bullfighter if it got inside him. Then in the evening, after the corrida, we would be exhausted from the sun, the dust, the strong emotion of the corrida, and we would sit in cafes, drink Tio Pepe finos, eat tapas, and listen to Spanish guitar music.

I cannot defend bullfighting to those who consider it a horror. One cannot reach them with the argument that the bulls are butchered immediately after, and sold and eaten shortly after that, thereby fulfilling the function for which they exist—to serve as steaks on the table. And I do not deny that most fights are awful, even boring, and if they are really bad, if the bull is not dispatched quickly, they are cruel. But the one in ten or twenty or fifty that is beautiful can be a thing of such extraordinary brilliance that it will lift you out of your seat, and leave you babbling about it for years. And the work of the bullfighters themselves—great athletes every one, or great dancers, a little of both perhaps—however you wanted to see them—was lovely to watch.

I have always imagined that I happened upon bullfighting at a time when it was richer in great toreros than it had ever been before, or would be again. Diego Puerta was known as Diego Valor. A little guy, it was said that he had never stepped back from a bull. Twice in one season the horn reached his liver, and according to one of the surgeons who worked on him, he had the highest threshold of pain the surgeon had ever witnessed. Juan Garcia, called Mondeño, fought with exaggerated slowness. "Like an altar boy serving mass in a dream," Hemingway wrote. He later went into a monastery, proving Hemingway's imagery more apt than anyone could have guessed, and still later he came out of the monastery and out of the closet as well. Whatever your feelings may be on this subject, Mondeño was a beautiful, beautiful bullfighter.

Jaime Ostos was brave and popular, though sometimes inattentive. Twice I saw terrible things happen to him while his back was to the bull. Once he was walking away from a supposedly exhausted animal which then lumbered forward and speared him in the back of the thigh. He hung upright on the horn, pedaling in the air, then fell, still speared, the horn making a 180 degrees rip inside his thigh, and he hung there head down like a counterweight until the bull threw him.

Another time he was dedicating a bull to someone near us in the stands, making a short speech. The bull came at him from across the ring at a full gallop. The crowd was screaming at him, but he mistook this for applause and his short speech was not finished yet. The 1200 pound bull slammed into him at thirty miles an hour, or however fast bulls can run. He went up in the air and over the fence and crashed down on his face. The next morning I chanced to run into him in a cafe. Behind the dark glasses his face was puffy and discolored. "Look at this," he said, peeling up his shirt. One rib seemed to protrude out half an inch from under his arm all the way to his breastbone. He was not looking for sympathy. His rib and face were curiosities, nothing more. His driver waited with the car in the street, and five minutes later they left for Barcelona, where he was to fight the next day.

There were others too, El Viti who never smiled, and the Giron brothers from Venezuela, and Paco Camino whose manager had had to teach him first how to eat—he had grown up in a household so poor that his principal diet until he became a bullfighter was bread soaked in olive oil.

These men were great young athletes. In every way that counted they were indistinguishable from ballplayers, except they were physically braver, and they had better manners. I sometimes went into their hotel rooms before fights and watched them dress, a ritual. There were always many people in there, and usually a few of us were foreigners, people who could not even talk to them. We were part of the ritual too. It took me a while to realize this. They liked us in there. Upper crust Spaniards were not interested in them, whereas we were.

I never spoke to El Cordobes. Unlike all other toreros the level of adulation he inspired was so great that he had to be protected by phalanxes of police every time he arrived at or departed from an arena. One could not get close to him. The others were easily approachable, extremely polite, flattered, it seemed, that a foreign reporter was interested in them, and I talked to them in hotel lobbies, or in their rooms as they dressed in the suit of lights, or even in the patio de caballos as they waited to go out into the ring.

I knew Dominguin somewhat better than the rest, possibly because there was more to him, and most of it showed. He was a bit older, had lived his life in public for a long time, had been written about a good deal, and he spoke in quotable sentences, sometimes in passable English. I once asked him how he had learned English. “I learn from friends,” he said, adding with a laugh: “sleeping friends.” He was an extremely handsome man to whom women responded, especially actresses. His wife was an Italian film star; when he married her a Czech actress committed suicide clutching his picture. Another of his sleeping friends was Ava Gardner who took him into her house in America—she was living at Lake Tahoe at the time. But she began to demand from him the adulation she thought a movie star’s due. Dominguin was used to receiving adulation, not giving it, and soon left. She came down in the morning and went through rooms looking for him but he wasn’t there. He was on a plane back to Spain. No man had ever walked out on Ava Gardner before. Still, their relationship lasted, and every time her life fell apart, which happened regularly, she phoned Dominguin in Madrid, and he came to her on the next plane.

All these bullfighters I wrote about, not only in the paper but in *The Saturday Evening Post*, in *True* and *Esquire*, in *Vogue*, even in *Seventeen*, which ordered a profile of the new teenage sensation, Camino.

Often in later years I admitted, if the subject came up, that, yes, I had run with the bulls at Pamplona. Not once, but many times. People's eyes usually got wide, as if this demonstrated uncommon bravery, or perhaps stupidity on my part. I didn't see where it demonstrated either.

The first time I ran, yes, I was scared. I stood in the street in front of the Ayuntamiento amid hordes of other runners, some of them drunk. It was just past dawn, and already hot. When the clock in the tower touched the hour a rocket would burst overhead, the door to the corral down the street would be thrown back, and that day's six bulls, able to run faster than any man including me, would be on top of us. Should I mention the horns?

Every few years a runner got gored and killed—far more often than any matador—and in nearly every running someone got batted to the pavement by a beast weighing half a ton and coming hard, or batted against a wall, or into other runners, or got mauled on the ground or trampled—badly hurt, in other words.

This much I had read. Otherwise I did not know what to expect. Being there was an act of pure bravado, a bunch of us sitting around all night drinking, daring each other to do it.

In the street there were police lines at our backs, and also in front, the police holding the mob in place until the rocket went up. But as the hour neared, and the horns began to seem closer, the mob pushed forward, the police line ceded, and men pounded down the empty street toward the arena. I watched the crowd around me thin out fast, and though it seemed cowardly to start running so soon, the hour not yet struck, still I didn't mind jogging away from that clock.

And then the rocket burst above the town, and I ran. I ran amid hordes of men, the buildings pressing in on either side, no escape, and quickly realized that the danger was as much people as bulls. Get knocked down and the bulls might be the least of my problems. I sensed rather than saw that from windows and balconies people hung like grapes. Along the length of the run the side streets had been closed off by double wooden barriers most of them now crowded with spectators. No escape that way either.

I was running as fast as I could, listening hard, and when the hoof beats sounded as close as I cared to hear them I leaped up onto one of the barriers, perhaps knocking someone off backwards, I don't know, and watched the horns go by underneath.

Then the bulls were gone. The street was full of runners who had stopped running. I got down and stood breathing hard. Probably I was grinning hard too. From now on, I congratulated myself, I could brag that I had run with the bulls at Pamplona.

Only, according to standards I was to adopt later, I hadn't. If I really wanted to call myself a runner, I would have to get in much, much closer. As close to the horns as the real runners got. Newspaper photos each morning showed them close enough to grip the horns, sometimes even within the pack.

I would have to get in that close, or nearly.

Over the years I came to know a New York high school English teacher named Joe Distler, who became celebrated in Spain. The magazine *Cambio* once named the five greatest living runners: Distler and four Basques. Naturally such enthusiasm proved costly to Distler, who was gored twice mildly, and once badly, sustaining a twelve-stitch gash in his back, a broken arm, three broken ribs, a broken front tooth and a dislocated hip.

Why did he come to Pamplona each summer to run, I asked him once.

I knew his answer in advance. Why did I come myself? "In New York I have a very structured life," Distler answered, "but in Spain I live an insane life for five minutes every day for eight days—and I can live on that emotion for a year. There's no high like it."

I could not rival this man, never dared run as close as he did. Nonetheless, I had my adventures.

One morning, as soon as the police withdrew, I and a number of drunks ran halfway down the Calle Santo Domingo toward the overnight corral. There were about 20 of us down there. The street was very narrow. There were no barriers to climb up on, nothing but doorways and window ledges for protection. Bulls tend to avoid coming up onto sidewalks, but there was only one sidewalk, and it was much too narrow.

A dangerous place.

But I was preparing a book of text and photos of mine to be called *The Swords of Spain*; what it required, I had decided, would be the only photo ever taken, so far as I knew, on foot at street level in front of the bulls. Halfway down the Santo Domingo I set my aperture, speed and focus, and planted my feet. The rocket went off, and the bulls burst out of the pen. The early light was very poor, and I did not have a motor drive. One shot was all I would get. The bulls were coming fast. Wait, I ordered myself. Wait. They were almost on top of me. Not yet. Wait.

Now!

Actually there were still three runners between the bulls and me, the photo would later prove, but I was not able to make the count, for I had turned and was running hard. The run was uphill. I could hear the bulls, louder and louder. At the top of the street they would have to make a ninety degree turn. I was betting I could get there before they did, make a sharper turn, and they would go by me in a wide sweep.

Which in fact they did.

As for the photo, it was a good one, I thought, and fit the eventual book well, but no one ever noticed it particularly.

So much for heroic actions undertaken for commercial gain.

Another time I was trapped in the street with a lone bull. This was in the long runway between Calle Estafeta and the gates into the arena. The barrier fences to both sides were still jammed with people. I thought the bulls had all gone by, the encierro finished for the day, and was ambling along looking for a gap where I could climb out of the street and go to breakfast. But there was no such gap.

A lone bull galloped out of Calle Estafeta, and stopped. The crowd, as if with a single tense exhalation, breathed two words: "*Falta uno*."

Still one loose.

A bull in a herd will almost always go with the herd. It is this instinct that makes the encierro possible. But once separated, a bull will attack anything it sees. A bull alone is incredibly dangerous.

This bull and I stared at each other. There was no one else in the street but me—where had everybody gone? A frantic glance showed there was still no gap on the barrier, nowhere to climb out. The gates to the arena were still open. The authorities who controlled them knew well enough that one bull had not come in.

The bull launched itself into a gallop. It galloped straight for me.

If I can outrun it to the arena, I told myself, I can dart to the side and perhaps hurdle the barrera. Could I make it?. I did not think so. It was too far and a fighting bull was too fast. But it seemed the only chance I had. Start running I told myself. Don't panic. If you trip, if you fall down, you are finished.

So I ran, the bull gaining with every stride. I could hear it snort. It was so close I thought I could smell it. Magically, or perhaps mystically, a gap appeared on the barrier. I leaped for it, hauled up my legs, and as the bull went by underneath I could have counted the hairs on its back. My immense fear was followed by an exultation such as I have never known before or since. I was still alive. I had got out of it on my own two feet. I was ecstatic. I felt an intensity of emotion that was almost stupefying.

The next day I was afraid to run. It was myself I was afraid of, not the bulls. I wanted that same emotion again and was afraid that to get it I might do something really stupid, and so that day I watched from a balcony.

The day after that I took a deep breath, told myself to be careful, and ran again.

My father in law died in the night. We rushed to Orly to catch the first plane to Nice, and on the concourse ran into one of my colleagues from the Bureau, who said: "Off on another vacation, I see."

"No, my father in law died."

"My condolences," he said. "I'm very sorry." And he hurried away.

But my job wasn't all play, I wanted to tell him, not in Spain, not anywhere. I always did the work too, all of it, overcame whatever obstacles were in my way, drove sometimes two days to get where I was supposed to be, found the story and wrote it, waited sometimes hours in post offices to send it—eight hours in the Pamplona post office once waiting for my call to Paris to go through, sat or paced all day while listening to the fiesta going on outside in the street. Nearly all these trips were rushed. After the race in Monaco one year I couldn't get out of the parking lot. I wrote my story standing up, my typewriter on the hood of the car, while waiting for the jam to break. By the time it did I was finished, and I got the story in on time. I was in Seville for a day and a half during which I interviewed and photographed John Fulton, drove with him out to Concha y Sierra ranch to see and photograph bulls in the bakingly hot fields; we were all a little afraid of the bulls coming through the wire at us. Hurrying back to Seville

I went into Diego Puerta's room to interview and photograph him as he dressed for the fight, the second of two excellent corridas I saw there, both of which I also photographed. And then I flew back to Paris. All in a day and a half.

Even then I realized I was moving too fast, trying to cram too much in, and to some extent ruining for myself what ought to have been glorious. Sometimes I thought myself a fool, getting only half or less of the pleasure that was there, and that my colleagues in the bureau so envied me for. But I got the work done, all of it.

Regularly now the Sunday Magazine Section asked me to do articles on subjects unrelated to sports. I went to Aix en Provence for a full length study of French universities in turmoil. As France ceded Algeria to the Algerians, I wrote about French refugees from Algeria arriving "home." In Marseille I watched them come off a ship, some blank faced, some in tears. Most had lived in Algiers, or Oran, or wherever, their whole lives, their families had been there for generations. Most had been forced to leave behind everything they owned, and I talked to them, and wrote about their despair. In Montpellier later I listened to other refugees speaking bitterly about what they had lost—the hairdresser, for instance, who had had his own shop in Algiers but now worked for someone else.

The Times Magazine paid very badly, $250 for a full length article being a big price for articles in those years, but was said to confer enormous prestige. I knew nothing about prestige at this stage of my career, but it was accruing, I see now, at a great rate, especially within the paper itself—accruing to me, not to the Paris bureau chief, or any other bureau chief. I was the one being asked to write for the Magazine, not them, which perhaps they (once again) found threatening. Which, at the least, must have rankled.

Jim Roach wanted me to go to Moscow where a track meet was to be staged, the United States against Russia, the two super powers head to head. I should plan to stay two weeks, he suggested, covering the meet of course, and then looking around for whatever else I could find. No one, both of us knew, had ever looked into the status of sports in Russia.

I would have to go to the Russian embassy in London to apply for a journalist's visa, I learned. I did this, filled out the form, handed over the photos and money, and was then told that, unfortunately, a journalist's visa would take weeks to be accorded.

I cabled this to Roach, who went to the foreign desk with it. The foreign desk cabled Seymour Topping, Moscow bureau chief. Could he do anything to push my visa through on time?

Journalist's visas were always hard to get, Topping answered. I shouldn't worry about not getting one, but should come to Moscow on a tourist visa. A tourist visa was all I needed, he said. Nothing to worry about at all, he said.

Which sounded good to the foreign desk, and to Roach as well. But this was at the height of the Cold War and the idea of signing a false application, and then entering the Soviet Union on a false visa, made me nervous. Surely under Soviet law this constituted a crime—it did in America, did it not? The Russians had just been humiliated by the Cuban missile crisis. Who knew what mood they were in now? One humiliation perhaps deserved another. Surely they could have no interest in me personally, but if they arrested a New York Times correspondent for lying on his visa application, or for entering the country illegally, this would certainly humiliate the Times, which as all Russians knew, was a branch of the State Department. They might even decide to claim I was a spy.

Despite ideas like this, which never ceased to occupy my head, I signed my application, the visa was stamped into my passport, and in due time my plane landed in Moscow.

My job now, after I had checked into the hotel assigned me, (no choice of hotel of course) was to get to the bureau, meet Topping and pick up my credentials to the track meet. But as a tourist I had been assigned a full time Intourist guide, a fiftyish woman who attached herself to me as if by handcuffs, kept asking which sights I as a tourist wished to see, and then took me wherever she wished to go, whether I did or not. In this way we visited the Moscow subway and the Pushkin Museum, and we walked along the bank of the river like lovers looking for a spot to lie down. Perhaps I could have led her to the bureau with impunity, could have admitted to her my nefarious status, but I was too nervous to try it. For two days I could not shake her. Finally I claimed to be sick, promised to stay in my room, and she left me. I had a map of Moscow, and was able to find the bureau on my own. As I came in Topping was seated at his desk while the bureau translator explained to him what was in Pravda, the Moscow newspaper, translating for him one story after another, word by word. Topping and I shook hands and he introduced me to the bureau's second correspondent, Henry Tanner, who also spoke no Russian.

Topping had been asked by New York to prepare a program for me, and the place for me to go, he said, was Stalingrad, today called Volgograd, where there was a school for young gymnasts, and he handed me my ticket. I should spend a week there, he said. Plenty to write about down there, he said. A week wouldn't even be enough. I would come back to Moscow just in time for the track meet.

So I flew to Stalingrad, which is on the edge of Asia, in one of those two-engined Illushin jetliners that, in the air, make a lot of noise. Immediately upon landing I found myself attached to another Intourist guide, this one named Boris. Boris wanted to know what journals I wrote for, so I started lying immediately—not the best way to begin a relationship.

The next day he took me touring. There was not an old building anywhere. The two hundred day slaughter that was the Battle of Stalingrad had reduced the city to crumbs, and everything was new except the Volga River itself. As we walked the streets I noted vast open squares in which nothing grew, not a house, not a blade of grass. There were plenty of monuments, however, and around the city stood about one hundred and fifty ugly new factories making tractors, and the like. Trailing behind Boris, I got to see almost all of them.

I was still trying to find the gymnastics school, and kept asking Boris about it. I was extremely interested in gymnastics, I told him, and the Russians were the best gymnasts in the world. But he had never heard of such a school. He promised to ask all the other guides, and did so, I believe, but none of them had ever heard of it either. The gymnastics school that Topping had sent me to write about did not exist.

I told Boris that, as a tourist, I had now seen everything, and wanted to get back to Moscow. Could he arrange for an earlier flight? He could not. One could not alter airline tickets in the Soviet Union, it seemed. My reservation was for a week hence, and that was the flight I would have to take. The rules, he said firmly, were the rules.

So I stayed the full week with nothing to do but lie on my hotel bed in total boredom, sometimes feeling sorry for myself, and at other times being tormented by erotic images from another life. There were no English language book shops downtown. There was no downtown, and I had only one book with me. It was *Lie Down in Darkness*, by William Styron. I was unable to read it, which is amazing, under the circumstances. I found Styron's prose overblown, his story dull, and though I tried some of his other books later, I was never able to finish any of them. Well, he was one of those who did not write books the way I did. It was always difficult for me, reading such books, to get enthusiastic.

At times I wondered if Topping had sent me to Stalingrad only to get me out of his way. Was it possible he wanted to prevent me from finding and writing any decent stories on his turf? But I could not believe this of him. Surely he had merely made a mistake. We both worked for the same paper, did we not? He would never do such a thing, would he? No, I thought, impossible. No one would.

Sometimes in the night my paranoia got extreme and I would imagine the police coming for me. Perhaps I could get out of the hotel unobserved. Then what? No one could help me here. I would have to help myself. To escape to the west I would have to walk across half of Russia, all of Romania, all of Hungary. Only then would I be outside the Iron Curtain. Impossible, it was too far. My only chance was to steal a boat and row down the Volga until I got to the Caspian Sea. I didn't have a map. How far would that be?

It would have been quite a row, I found out later, 285 miles.

One day Boris took me to a department store where I bought a swim suit. There was only one style on sale. It came in either blue or black, and was almost as skimpy as a jock strap. I bought blue. The Volga was more than a mile wide here, and we took a ferry across to an island in the middle where there was a sandy beach on which reposed a great many shapeless and overweight people. All the men wore the same swim suit I did. The women overflowed their bikinis top and bottom. I noted no pinups.

The week in that hotel room ended finally. When I got back to Moscow I told Topping there was no gymnastic school in Stalingrad.

He pretended to be surprised. "I thought there was," he said, and busied himself with something else.

After the two day track meet ended, having returned to the bureau, I wrote my story, then reached for the telephone to call Paris, where there were now operators to take dictation. But Topping yanked the phone out of my hand. "You'll file after we file, and not before," he said, and slammed down the receiver. So I cooled my heels there for another few hours until it was my turn.

I did not blame Topping particularly. I figured he was overwrought about something, never imagining it might be me. He later became an assistant managing editor, and then a high ranking executive in The New York Times Company.

For my column that week I decided to write a piece about the Volga. Drab city, meager lives, glorious river. The river offered swimming, boating, but not sailing or ice boating, for there were no sails. And fishing, of course. Carp and pike. The sturgeon in there sometimes reached fifteen feet in length. And camping, escape. Its banks were a place lovers could go. In winter the surface froze many inches thick and there was ice fishing and skating. The ice got so thick one could drive a car across, if one had a car. Sometimes at night wolves could be heard howling over there and these and other game could be hunted.

Apart from my stories on the track meet, and another that I wrote from clippings I had compiled before leaving Paris, this was the only story I filed while in Russia. Having sent it, I had two days to myself in St. Petersburg, which was then called Leningrad, where my inevitable Intourist guide turned out to be a pretty young woman, who never asked me if I was a journalist traveling on a false visa. Instead we gawked together at the paintings in the Hermitage, and at other art treasures elsewhere, we went to the ballet and saw *Giselle*, and then I went back to Paris.

New York's reaction to my work was waiting. They were all a bit disappointed in my coverage from Russia, Jim Roach wrote. They had expected more from me. During the six years I worked for Roach this was the only criticism he ever sent me.

Sportswriters who got tired of reporting fun and games, who decided to try to create literature instead—there have been many such men in the past—turned always to boxing for subject matter. Brutality, aggression—almost every mean human trait is on display in the prize ring, men publicly distribute pain to each other, and every bout ends in tragedy for someone. Sometimes for everyone, including those watching.

In America those bouts that attracted attention, especially literary attention, took place in great arenas for enormous purses while millions watched on television. But that's not how it was for me. The bouts I got to see were, mostly, of a different sort. The tragedy enacted was of a different sort as well, much more raw, and there were times I felt like a man who worked day after day in graveyards.

In Rome I sat one afternoon in the hotel room of a fighter named Bobo Olson. Though sunlight streamed in the window, Bobo was in bed, the covers pulled up, resting for a fight the next day against an Italian named Giulio Rinaldi. If you wanted to speak to Bobo you most likely had to catch him in bed for he spent most of his time there. He tried to sleep fourteen hours a day to keep his strength up, he told me, and more hours resting. On the floor beside the bed stood a pile of lurid magazines. When he woke up he sometimes read in them. Each day also he trained in a gym, or went shopping with his wife for presents for their four children in San Francisco, or did his roadwork in Villa Borghese Park, much surprising Romans who saw him there and wondered who he was. He would be paid $5,000 for this fight, out of which would come the two airfares, ten days in a Rome hotel, the cost of sparring partners and gym space, plus a percentage to the New York agent who had got him the fight. Not much would stick to Bobo.

Once he had fought for big purses, had been middleweight champion of the world, but that money did not stick either. Having lost the title eight years previously, he had been trying for a comeback ever since. Now in Rome he was eighteen pounds heavier, nearly bald, and nearly broke. "If I could get another shot at the title," he said, "I could maybe put some money aside, maybe start a business." In America hardly anyone knew he was still alive, much less still fighting, and he could not get fights. So here he was in Rome.

He did all his own business now, he said. He knew he had no head for business, but it was the only way to keep some of the money. If he did well tomorrow night, he might be invited back, he said hopefully.

But if he beat the Italian and won the fight, I reflected, he wouldn't be.

He seemed earnest, polite, wistful, and the next night he gave his best, but the judges called the fight a draw. He didn't lose, but didn't win either. His comeback hadn't gained ground. His career was still on hold. He would have to fight again, and then again, and still again.

He had been a professional prize fighter from the age of 17. He was 34 years old, two years older than I was.

Sugar Ray Robinson came to Paris. In some ways the same story, or perhaps worse. In the fight game in his prime Ray was a god. He was called the best fighter pound for pound in the world. He was tall and slim, a sharp dresser, a dandy. He was extremely handsome, his face unscarred. He had been welterweight champion of the world, won the middleweight title as well, then decided to fight for the light heavyweight championship next. He would beat a man who outweighed him by twenty pounds, and hold three titles at once, why not. He almost pulled this off. On a night when the temperature reached 106 degrees he was felled by heat prostration when leading on points in the 13th round.

All of these were big money fights. Sugar Ray banked plenty. And spent it.

He came to France aged 43, where he told reporters, including me, that he was rich and fighting only for love of the sport. He then fought five fights in 58 days, earning himself numerous additional punches to the head, and only about $25,000 in all. Less expenses, of course.

He did not train very hard. For one fight he began training on Thursday, and knocked off on Friday. There were many cocktail parties in his honor. He liked these, liked being surrounded by foreign celebrities he had never heard of. He spoke a little French, and had a certain charm.

His opponents weren't much, but they did hit him. One of them, whom he fought twice, was a part time boxer and full time Louvre Museum guard named Armand Vanucci. Vanucci's principal role in life was guarding the Mona Lisa. I went there to see him one day. Yep, there he was keeping crowds away from the most famous painting in the world.

The Vanucci fights were at the Palace of Sports. They lasted a total of 20 round, every one of them lost by Vanucci. But Robinson couldn't put him down, much less out. Round after round Robinson would jolt him with jabs, hooks and crosses. The jabs reddened the museum guard's face. The hooks and crosses sometimes lifted him off the floor, or sent him reeling backwards. Round after round he would straighten up, then again plod forward trying to cuff the ex champion with his short arms. The mob kept chanting Vanucci's name, a rhythmic, 6,000 voice roar. Once I overheard a man say: "You got to hand it to Vanucci, he really can take it." It was a pity Vanucci couldn't fight, I reflected, for his head was made of stone. He had the head of a champion.

Robinson fought in flurries, each of which seemed to exhaust him, and for minutes at a time he would backpedal and rest. At times he looked too tired to dodge punches. The museum guard hit him with some big ones, mostly lunging right-hand leads. Sucker punches of this kind were not seen often in the company Ray used to keep.

Both times Robinson looked glad when it was over.

Then came a slightly different story. Cassius Marcellus Clay, 21 years old, who was beginning to be known in America, arrived in London, where he was not known at all, to fight a man named Henry Cooper, heavyweight champion of Great Britain and the Empire. He would knock Cooper out in the fifth round, Clay was predicting: "Henry Cooper will fall in five."

In London I walked down the long hotel corridor, and knocked on Clay's door.

"It's open," said a voice from inside.

The shades were drawn. Two young men, fully dressed, reclined on beds in the gloom.

"Which of you fellows is Cassius Clay," I asked.

The youth nearest the door said: "He is."

So I moved further into the room and tried to interview the other, who soon began giggling. Then the first youth said: "That fella you talkin' to, that's my brother, Rudy. I's Cassius, the onliest fighter that predicts the exact round. I's the one you come all this way to see."

I rarely got a word in after that. "I's the world's greatest, boldest, and most prettiest fighter, only they haven't gave me the title yet." As for Henry Cooper: "That bum will fall in five. I's going to hit that bum so fast and so regular he'll think he's surrounded. I fought a bum named George Logan. I said that bum would fall in four. That bum fell in four. I fought a bum called Charlie Powell. It was twenty below zero in Pittsburgh, but the place was sold out. I predicted that bum would fall in three. That bum fell in three. I predicted Archie Moore would fall in four. He said, `Kid, you're crazy.' He fell in four."

I spent the rest of the day with Clay, and a number of subsequent days as well. I crossed to London three times to see him, the final time for the fight itself.

I would go to the gym with him, watch him do pushups, skip rope, sock the heavy bag as if to tear it from the ceiling, rattle the light bag, rattle the teeth of sparring partners. He was beautiful to look at, his young face unmarked, all his movements fluid and quick. He was 6 feet 3 and a bit over 200 pounds, but his body was lithe, still more a boy's body than a man's.

Each day a press conference followed. I would stand to one side and watch him handle the English reporters. His wit was quick. He gave them verses, jokes and bombast, all to the effect that Cooper would fall in five, all with a twinkle in his eye. They never saw any twinkle. They were exasperated by him, even appalled, addressing him always as "Mr. Clay", but with contempt in their voices. In their reports they spoke angrily of his big mouth, and hopefully of Cooper's left hook.

Was I the only one at these press conferences who laughed at his performances, or who noted that the ticket sale became ever more brisk? Though only 21 years old, he was hyping the fight with extraordinary skill, and he was doing it all by himself. No one wrote his odes, his jokes, his doggerel, much of which was ad libbed, or so it seemed to me. His entourage consisted of a middle-aged white trainer and four well dressed young men his own age, two of whom were sparring partners, the others being his brother, Rudolph Valentino Clay, aged 19, and a boyhood pal named Ronald King, 21, whom he always introduced as his bodyguard. Ronald's function, he said, was to prevent him from laying out Cooper on the spot if they should meet in the street.

Clay loved to perform, I saw, loved to bounce his wit off an audience, loved to hear the laughter, though he got precious little of it from the English press. Toward the end he became edgy, and much less funny. Asked by one reporter how he could be so sure Cooper would fall in five, he answered: "I's the fastest living fighter. I will have reach on him, and will outweigh him by 15 or 20 pounds. He should not have agreed to fight me."

In private I found Clay a much more introspective young man than his odes and jokes suggested.

"There's nobody around telling me what to do," he said one day. "I's my own master. I have a trainer, but he does not tell me what to do. I have eleven millionaires backing me. Otherwise I's on my own. I don't need no one to make me train. I don't need no one to keep me from chasing girls. I am strong of will. I am here to fight, and that is all I's thinking of. There is no one watching me."

I asked him about segregation.

"Twice a day people ask me to take part in this. I can't. I's no leader. I never went near college." And then, after a pause: "Integration's gotta come, but somebody's gotta die first."

This reply stunned me. There had been no assassinations yet, and only Clay seemed to know there would be. I did not know what to say, so I told him I was surprised at how wise he seemed.

"I know a lot of wise people," he said quietly. "I learn from them." Then he added: "A wise man can act the fool, but a fool can't act like a wise man."

After a moment he said: "You want to know what else I know? I know who God is. You a tough man to cope with if you know that. I read the bible a lot. Do you read the bible?

"I even know when the world's going to end. The bible says the world will be one inch from destruction. That's us and the Russians, right? Who's gonna drop it first. The bible says there will be buildin' up and tearin' down like mad. Look around you. Everybody's buildin' up and tearin' down like mad. The bible says the truth will be so plain even a fool can see it. Now all you got to know is, what is truth?"

Abruptly he broke the tension. A big grin came on, and he said: "The truth is, Henry Cooper will fall in five. I is here with the truth."

I didn't know how good a fighter he was. I didn't know how the fight would turn out, and neither did he. I certainly didn't believe he could pick the exact round, as he claimed, and wasn't sure he believed it either.

I went to see the champion of Britain and the Empire. Cooper's record was 27 wins, one draw, eight defeats. He was 29, craggy faced, with scar tissue over both eyes. Not a handsome man, nor a witty one. Unlike Cassius Clay in every way.

He trained in Southeast London in the neighborhood where he was born, in a gym upstairs over a bar. I watched him train. He had a good left hook but didn't seem to use his right hand at all. Afterwards he invited me to go home with him. The house was small, not pretty. His mother let us in. That was when I realized it was her house, not his. When he started serious training for this fight five weeks before, he explained, he had cut himself off from his wife and baby, from his home on the other side of the city, from all distraction, and gone back to live with his mother, who looked after him as she did when he was a child. She cooked his food, all the good things he had liked as a boy, and watched him eat it. She cheered him when he felt lonely and blue. There was no phone.

His mother served us tea, while Cooper talked to me of certain opponents he had "stopped", and of himself being "stopped" by certain others. He did not use the phrase knocked out. He missed his family, he said, but would not see them again until he stopped Clay, or Clay stopped him.

The papers had carried all of Clay's taunts, one of them being: "Why doesn't Cooper say something, is he that scared?"

The Englishman was not so much scared as speechless—he couldn't think of anything clever to reply. Clay's latest ode ended: "But if Cooper wants some fun, I'll cut it to one.

Each of these jokes and odes landed like punches, and they hurt.

Why was Clay saying such ugly things about him, Cooper asked. Why did he keep holding him up to ridicule? The Englishman was perplexed. He had tried to hate Clay, he said, but "I know he doesn't mean it, that he's just trying to build up the gate."

A gentle, nice kind of man, I thought, not given to hating anyone.

On fight night Wembley Stadium was sold out. As the fighters came down the aisle to the ring, first Clay, then Cooper, a squad of trumpeters blared out fanfares. Clay wore a gorgeous red bathrobe with white trim, and emblazoned on the back were the words: Cassius The Greatest. On his head, cocked at a jaunty angle, rode a high, gaudy crown, hastily rented. It was brass polished to resemble gold, and studded with false precious stones, with a velvet lining and pseudo ermine trim. As he reached me Clay cracked: "This crown makes me the king-sized greatest."

In his turn Cooper entered the ring wearing a bathrobe that read: Henry Cooper, England.

Having removed his bathrobe, Clay stood naked to the waist still wearing his crown. His so-called bodyguard climbed into the ring carrying a small silk pillow on which Cassius reverently laid the crown down. Across the ring Cooper looked both angry and edgy. Cassius looked relaxed, almost smiling.

The business of the evening got under way.

At the bell Cooper rushed forth throwing left hooks, flustering Clay, forcing him backwards. Some of the Englishman's punches hit and hurt. Some strayed a bit low. Clay was screaming at Cooper to stop fouling him, screaming at the referee to make him stop it. Henry Cooper looked like the champion of Britain and the Empire, which he was, and Cassius Clay, getting the worst of it, looked surprised and scared, and I found myself wondering about all the jokes and odes I had been hearing.

In round two Cooper came out hard again, but this time Cassius too came forward, punching, not flinching. Almost at once he caught Cooper on the eye, and as the blood started to flow a disdainful expression came onto his face. A moment later he staggered Cooper with a right, the best punch of the bout so far.

Round three. Cassius stepped forward and banged five or six swift straight jabs to that eye. Each jab snapped Cooper's head back. The blood flowed. Soon the Englishman wasn't coming forward anymore. Clay kept smacking that eye.

Then abruptly he stopped fighting. He began to lope and dance around the ring. He did a ten second dodging act. He dropped his gloves and bobbed his head, daring the dazed, bleeding Englishman to hit him. Cooper began lunging recklessly forward swinging, and he caught Clay cleanly a time or two. Cassius only smirked.

One of the millionaires, Clay's manager of record, came racing around the ring from his seat, shouting at Clay's trainer: "Make him stop the funny business."

But the funny business went on until the bell.

In the fourth round Cassius got serious again, banging away at the Englishman's eye. There was a contorted, suffering, bloody grimace on Cooper's face, he seemed about to fall, whereupon the funny business resumed, the dancing act, the loping around. Cassius was thinking of his prediction, it seemed. He was going to carry Cooper one more round and knock him out, as predicted in the fifth.

But moments before the round ended, as Clay was gazing off into the distance, Cooper staggered into him and let fly a frantic left hook. The punch came from a long way back, with Cooper lunging forward as hard as he could. It caught Clay on the side of the jaw and he went over backwards through the ropes.

He rolled back into the ring, then got dazedly to his feet. He was gazing off into the distance again, but this time starry eyed, and I for one thought the fight was over. He wobbled forward, gloves low. He started to fall, but his handlers caught him. The round had ended. No one had heard the bell. Wembley Stadium was in an uproar. Cassius was dragged to his stool where his handlers worked on him.

The bell rang for found 5. On dreamstreet sixty seconds before, Clay sprang forward and laced into Henry Cooper. His first jab snapped Cooper's head back and opened that eye again as cleanly as if with a cleaver. It was followed by what seemed like a hundred other punches, rights and lefts both, so many Cooper couldn't have known where they were all coming from. Covered in gore, unprotected, trying to crouch, not even fighting back, Cooper did not go down. For a minute and fifteen seconds Cassius slugged him. Few men have ever absorbed such a beating in so short a time. There was blood everywhere. People were screaming: "Stop the fight." At last the referee did so.

Henry Cooper, as predicted, had been "stopped" in the fifth round.

The referee did not raise the victor's glove in triumph. Clay raised it himself. Then he toured the ring holding up five fingers, and this seemed in bad taste because Cooper, a few feet away, was so badly hurt.

Rudolph Valentino Clay, by now in the ring as well, grabbed the crown and attempted to sit it on his brother's head. Cassius bent to receive it but then looked across at the ravaged Cooper, appeared to realize the humor was gone, and waved the crown aside. He had beaten his man. He declined to rub it in. This decision, it seemed to me, was one of the most important he made all night.

I wrote my story about the fight, and sent it, and the next day filed another in which I tried to understand what I had seen.

"Cassius Clay is trying to do two things simultaneously," I wrote: "win the heavyweight championship as a boxer, and charm the world with his wit. Either job would be difficult alone. Together they may not be possible at all...He lacks not so much experience as maturity...He is still slightly wide-eyed with wonder at the world, at the things and people around him, at himself. And so he clowns for two rounds, and nearly gets knocked out, merely to fulfill a boast. With so much at stake, a mature man does not clown.

"Similarly, his very great charm is balanced right on the edge of bad taste. A mature man would know where bad taste began, and would avoid it. Cassius does not know yet. He obeys his instincts, which are often brilliant, but which sometimes betray him.

"Now at 21, he has no one left to fight except Floyd Patterson or Sonny Liston, both of whom probably would beat him. He has no way to polish his skills any further first, though he needs to. There is no place to go with all that charm and wit either, except to predict the defeat of older, more experienced men who know more than he does, and hit just as hard.

"His double gamble, fists and charm both, could turn sour, whether he wins the world championship or not. But it is fantastic that he has got even this far, and it is impossible not to root for him all the way."

It was days before I could get my mind off this young man. He was fast with his fists, yes, but that was the least of it. I had known a good many prize fighters by this time, not to mention famous athletes in other sports. None had ever impressed me in the way Clay did. I felt he exuded a force field of some kind. It was impossible to be close to him and not feel it. I can't say I knew in advance he would become the symbol of an age, but in some way I could not define he was special.

The world knows what happened next. Although he didn't figure to beat either Patterson or Liston he knocked out both. No sooner heavyweight champion of the world than he called a press conference at which he changed his name to Muhammad Ali—he would no longer answer to his "slave name", Cassius Clay, he said. Most of the sports writers had trouble with this. Unable to call him by either of his new names, they learned to address him as Champ. There was one exception, a raucous-voiced TV sportscaster named Howard Cosell, who was not then as famous as he would become. Born Cohen, Cosell maintained stubbornly that a man had a right to be known by the name of his choice.

Presently the champ publicly embraced the Black Muslim religion. The Muslims were seen by white America as a dangerous extremist sect, and the white reporters who had flocked so avidly around Ali, flocked just as fast in the opposite direction. All except one. Again Cosell. The TV sportscaster with the abrasive voice and manner was willing to court the disapproval of his peers, of the entire country in fact, to stand up for what he saw as another man's right to live his life as he chose.

And shortly after that, claiming to be a Black Muslim minister and therefore exempt, Muhammad Ali refused to be drafted for the Vietnam War: "I ain't got no quarrel with them Vietcong," he said. He was arrested, convicted and sentenced, but remained out of jail pending appeal. Meantime he was stripped of his title by the various boxing boards. There was no due process, it was simply done, with no possibility of appeal, and being now without official sanction he could no longer get fights. Meanwhile, his legal appeals dragged on for what should have been the most profitable years of his career, but weren't. Finally the Supreme Court ruled in his favor, eight votes to none.

During all those long years only one voice was raised in defense of Cassius Clay/Muhammad Ali—Cosell's of course.

It was on the subject of Cosell that I had my next conversation with Muhammad Ali.

The two men had much in common. Both had audiences of millions, both projected outsized egos but were perhaps not always as sure of themselves as they liked to pretend, and both dealt in superlatives. Clay/

Ali was "The Greatest." Cosell's claim was a superlative too, differing from the fighter's only in kind. Cosell was the man who "tells it like it is." As if, in the sports world, no one else did.

In truth there was an honesty about Cosell that was rare among his peers, most of whom saw no character flaws in great athletes, or in owners either. Cosell saw plenty, and his feelings were expressed over the ABC network. He did not hero-worship jocks, and he had no time for fools. The adulation that attached to the likes of Babe Ruth, Joe DiMaggio and so many others could not have occurred if Cosell had been around at the time.

So, yes, mostly he did tell it like it was, and as a result became not only one of the most famous men in the country, but also one of the most vilified. The fame, the big money he earned and the hatred all went together, but he did not see it this way. He was a man who was often deeply hurt.

I first met him the year Cassius Clay destroyed Henry Cooper. A collections of my columns and articles had been brought out by William Morrow & Co., then one of the most important publishers in New York, and a small publicity tour had been arranged, beginning with an interview with Howard Cosell on ABC.

An editor at Morrow had suggested the collection to me, and I had agreed, and had put one together. The advance was $2,000, which I was glad to have, of course. Apparently I was more of a blithe spirit than I realized at the time, for I felt no particular pride of achievement. I took it for granted that a publisher would want to bring out a collection by me, though four years previously I had been unable to get anything published at all, and I learned only later that collections usually lose money, and are therefore rare. Getting one published does not happen to every writer every day. Certainly it never happened to me again. I have been trying for years to get a collection of my short stories published, but with no success at all. They are good stories too. Well, some of them must be, certainly.

So I had come back to America, had agreed to be interviewed by Howard Cosell, whom I had never heard of, and people said to me: "You don't want to go on with that guy. You should hear the questions he asks people. He's vicious. He'll murder you."

Not so. He treated me with kindness and respect that night, and he praised the collection. It didn't sell well, there were never any royalties beyond the advance, but that wasn't Howard's fault.

After that I went on with him on one or another of his programs every time I had a book come out. Some of the interviews were quite long, the radio interviews especially. We would sit there talking seriously about whatever subjects came into our heads for thirty minutes or more.

In all, Cosell interviewed me about twenty times. I interviewed him once, by which time he was as instantly recognizable by voice or face as anyone in America. He called all ABC's boxing matches, was the acknowledged star of Monday Night Football, his autobiography (entitled, naturally, "Cosell") was six months on *The New York Times* best seller list, he was extremely funny and much in demand as an after dinner speaker, he had appeared on television as guest comedian with the great names of those years, Bob Hope, Flip Wilson, Dean Martin. He had played in comic movies, including two with Woody Allen. He had had his own prime time variety show. He was even talking of running for the Senate.

And *The New York Times* Magazine asked me to write a profile of him.

To prepare, I talked to many people who knew him or, because they worked for the same network, had spent time in his presence, and in my notebook I wrote down their comments.

"Cosell's like a comedian who has to be funny all the time, except that Howard has to be obnoxious all the time."

"He's the supreme intimidator. Intimidation is his art."

"He the last remaining figure who's not afraid to be hated."

"His real stage is the elevator. You're trapped. He takes you apart. He measures the floors."

I did not know what this comment meant, but a few days later I got into in an elevator with him, and found out.

No doubt he varied his elevator routines, but I did not see how the one that now followed could be improved upon. He stepped aboard, selected his victim, and that raspy voice rang out over the heads of fellow passengers: "Ed, I'm sorry, but that's show business. The rumor is you're out on your ass. I pity your poor wife. Of course, she could have married a talent. But take consolation, at least now you'll know if she really loves you. Eighteen months on unemployment will be the bitter test."

The elevator stopped, disgorging Howard, just as the victim was about to think up a clever rejoinder. The elevator continued up with everybody staring at him.

This was in the ABC building. We went into Howard's sixth floor office, which I had never seen before, all of our previous meetings having taken place in studios. It turned out to be an interior, windowless room and it was minuscule. Howard had to move stuff off his cluttered desk for me to get in there with him, so that I asked myself: if Howard Cosell is the towering ego everyone supposes, why does he put up with this tiny office?

His phone rang. "Don Meridith has left Monday Night Football," he said into it. "Couldn't stand being second banana to me. Dandy Don doesn't want to be Dandy Don anymore. Doesn't want to be what he is. Dandy Don, the modern Aristotle, a fugitive from life. `Hard livin' ain't that easy,' he says, as he plumbs the bottommost depths of philosophy."

Probably Cosell was the most controversial figure in America at that time, though he didn't look it. He was 54 years old, round shouldered, a former lawyer who had never played at anything physical in his life. His hand shook as he lit a foul smelling cigar, and he wore a toupee, one of twelve he owned, I was to learn, and as I sat down opposite him I asked myself a second question: How could a man like this, a mere sportscaster, which was primarily what he was, have attained such notoriety?

But I thought I knew at least part of the answer. In a country shot through with perjury at the highest level, as it was in those days, Cosell's blunt and sometimes painful honesty, coming as it did in the otherwise bland arena of sports, seemed shocking. Nearly all other sportscasters were "approved" by the owners whose games they broadcast, Even print journalists traveled, in many cases, at the expense of the team they covered. As a result, nearly every play of every game was a "great" play perpetrated by a "great" player.

Though not if you listened to Howard. Indeed not. He was not afraid to point out flaws in thinking, or execution, he was not afraid to castigate greedy players or tightwad owners, and when he interviewed these people he asked them indiscreet questions in his inimitable indiscreet voice.

To Carmen Basilio, winner of 56 fights, all of which showed in his scar tissue: "But Carmen, what about your face?"

To Brian London, who was about to be knocked stiff by Ali in the third round: "Brian, they say you're a pug, a patsy, a dirty fighter, that you have no class, that you're just in there for the fast payday, that you have no chance against Ali. Now what do you say to that?"

Every time Cosell asked questions like this the phones at ABC rang off the hook. The hate mail rained in too, he took many letters personally, and sometimes they had him near tears. He could not understand the world's reaction to him. "You hate poverty," he said, "you hate war and racial anguish, you hate narcotics addiction, but do you hate a sportscaster because he's told a few truths?"

Now, sitting opposite me, he grabbed up a pile of manuscript off his desk and in an admiring voice began reading aloud a section from his second book, which he was then writing. It was to be called, naturally, *How It Is*, and as he read he paused from time to time to chortle and remark: "This is great stuff, isn't it?" It is said that Hemingway used to read his own prose aloud in an admiring voice also.

Cosell lived in Pound Ridge, N.Y. on Old Snake Hill Road—"They named it after me"—and later I visited him there. He was a cordial, thoughtful host. The house, which stood in five acres of woods, was comfortable, but I saw nothing special about it. He also owned an apartment in an East Side high-rise, where he stayed when he had to work late. A balcony gave off the living room and I once stood with him on it for a minute or so. It was some 35 floors up, tiny, and felt so fragile that I could not get back inside fast enough. Nothing special about this apartment either. His only luxury as far as I could tell was his drawer full of toupees.

We invited him and his wife Emmy to dinner to the apartment we kept at that time in the Des Artistes on 67th Street. Among the other guests were a mezzo-soprano, an artist, an editor, a district attorney and a former chief of detectives. We liked to give eclectic dinner parties in those days. These people were delighted with Howard, and he with them.

One day in Pound Ridge with a grandson on his knee he sat beside his small pool dressed only swim suit and toupee, and he said: "My life's a success. This Sunday my wife and I will have been married thirty years. We've got two great daughters, a son in law of whom I'm very proud, two grandsons and a third grandchild on the way."

There seemed no reason to disbelieve his sincerity as he equated success with family love.

It was impossible to write about Howard Cosell without talking to Muhammad Ali about him. My father had died not long before, Ali had sent a message of condolence, which is not what one would expect from an ordinary prize fighter, or even an ordinary world champion, and after thanking him for it I brought up the name of Cosell.

"Every time Howard opens his mouth he should be arrested for air pollution."

"No, speak seriously."

"He's just a man in business, he's doing his job and he does it well. He's got a sassy sounding voice. He's got his own style, which is unique. It's designed, whether he's conscious or unconscious of it, to attack people in one way or another so that people, whether they like him or not, like him. He's had a lot of breaks. I was one of them. He followed me, talking back to him, being witty. There were a few more celebrities he did good interviews with.

"I think it took courage for him to defend me during those three and half years. Surely he had people who got on him for standing up for me. If you look at it, he really didn't lose nothing, he gained, because he represented justice which the flag and the country was supposed to represent, freedom from injustice. And although in the blindness of dislike toward me, a lot of people didn't recognize that, a lot of other people maybe did.

"He's a tricky man. One day he'll defend you, he'll talk up for you, then he'll turn right around and ask you something that, if you don't answer it right, you're in trouble with somebody. To me he's just another man who's good in his field, and I don't understand what the rage is over him, the special write-ups and the banquets.

"People say that if I had lost to the Supreme Court, Howard would have been in terrible trouble. Not really. He's going to have his job if I stopped tomorrow. He'd have lost one of his good interviews. And I'd have been in terrible trouble too, because of him rapping me. He'd have sent me out of the game with a lot of disinviteful words.

"No I don't feel he's a friend of mine. I have a lecture that I give about friendship." And he began to give this lecture now to his audience of one.

It made perfect sense, but went on a bit long. It ended: "A real friend has a deep regard for the pleasures and displeasures of his friend, making sure that no words shall hurt his friend, that no accidents shall harm him, that not the slightest shade of coldness shall fall upon his hearth.

"So we can't consider Howard Cosell a friend," he concluded.

I went back to Cosell.

"You mean Ali wouldn't say I was his friend? But he must have said something else about me, didn't he? That he respected me, or something, didn't he?"

Cosell was hurt. There was no doubting it.

"He must have said something nice about me, didn't he?"

No.

Cassius Clay/Muhammad Ali was another boxing story that concluded in tragedy. As this is written, though only 58 years old, Ali cannot walk unassisted and can barely talk. His condition is blamed on Parkinson's disease, but I have never believed it, for the symptoms he displays are too close to those of too many other fighters in the old days, men who had taken too many punches to the head, men we called *punchies*, not really understanding what had happened to them. In our ignorance we even laughed at certain of them. But it is impossible to laugh at Ali.

Cosell's story finished sadly and tragically too, though normally in every way. In time he gave up covering boxing for his network, saying he didn't believe in the sport anymore, could no longer defend it. Presently he walked away from Monday Night Football as well. He kept one or two other programs, but the glory years were over. The Howard Cosell phenomenon had played itself out.

His beloved wife Emmy died. I attended her memorial service, and so did every major sporting and television figure in New York, or so it seemed. Afterward I spoke briefly to Howard. His eyes were red, there was a stunned look on his face, and I don't think he recognized me.

He did not last long after that. When he went I was out of the country, so I never knew what kind of crowd he was able to draw at the end.

8.
How to Quit *The New York Times*

December 23, 2000, Paris

For reasons I will go into in a moment, we will spend Christmas in Paris this year.

I served under two bureau chiefs here. The second was Drew Middleton, whom New York moved over from London. He brought with him his British tweeds and his pipe, but not a word of French. Middleton had started as a sports writer, then had done some splendid reporting from the battle zones during World War II. In London he had developed high level contacts, was chummy with dukes and cabinet ministers, none of whom, unfortunately, accompanied him to Paris. When he got here he knew no one. He was about 45 then, and although he looked good in the big office with the windows looking down onto the Rue Caumartin, and although he put on a brave, rather pompous front, he was lost in Paris, lost in France. Sending such a man here seemed to me then, and still does, an unkind trick, but it was the type of thing New York did all the time. It was something I could look forward to if I stayed long enough, and I saw this too.

The man Middleton replaced had been transferred to Italy to head the Rome bureau, though he spoke no Italian. He soon left the paper, but Middleton never did. After Paris he was moved back to New York as "military correspondent," where he kept up the same brave front, the pipe and tweeds too, but he never again cut the figure he had cut in London.

Loaded down with three heavy suitcases containing presents, we flew here today on the Nice-Paris shuttle, to spend Christmas with the current Times bureau chief, who is our daughter Suzanne, and with our granddaughters Avery who is 15, and Galen who is ten. Suzanne does not have the problem Middleton and so many other past bureau chiefs have had. She did the first four years of her schooling in France, first in Nice, and then here, learned to speak French like any French kid, and when she speaks it now sounds like a Frenchwoman. She got here by coming up through the ranks: copygirl, reporter, deputy Metro editor, and then bureau chief in South Africa. When she was assigned to Paris a year and a half ago she was overjoyed not only because she had lived here as a child and was, in a sense, coming home, but because now her children would learn French too, and ever afterwards be in touch with that part of their heritage.

Apart from the publisher and his cousins on the 14th floor, who own the paper, the Daleys, so far as I know, constitute the only three generation dynasty the Times has ever had, my father for 47 years, me for six, Suzanne now for 23.

When my father graduated from Fordham in 1926 his mother told him to go out and not come back until he had a job. He had been sports editor of the Fordham Ram, so he went to the Times sports department. They hired him as, I guess, a stringer, for he was paid according to how much he wrote. He wrote so much and earned so much they put him on the staff to save money.

The day I was born he covered a fencing match in Brooklyn. Three weeks later when he was in Boston for some other event he wrote me a letter, the first of hundreds. It was really a love letter to my mother, of course. I don't think I ever saw it until she showed it to me after he died. In it he promised he would teach me to play ball when I was big enough, but when I was twelve he started writing "Sports of the Times." He had to turn in those seven columns each week, one every single day. He didn't have time to play much ball during the remaining years when I lived at home. Later when I was taken onto the Times staff myself I felt guilty about filing only three stories a week, and offered to send more. Only three were wanted, I was told. Three. I had grown up thinking seven was the norm.

He was a shy man. I don't think he thought he could do the column at first. "Of course you can do it, Arthur," my mother told him. She was the strength behind him.

He received thousands of letters from his readers; he answered them all himself, for he had no secretary. Every one. He read all the other New York papers' sports sections every day, a chore in itself, for there were eight of them. He read all the sports magazines and the Sporting News. He collected every sports book published. He filed away every clipping that interested him, filling cabinet after cabinet, the finest sports morgue in the country no doubt. When I went through his papers after his death I found clips already marked and dated on his desk, waiting to be filed, and I could not throw them away just yet, because they were so important to him.

There were no days off. He had no other life outside of sports and *The New York Times*. It was agony to try to buy him a Christmas present. He had no hobbies. He did not drink. He had been a heavy smoker as a young man, despite attacks of asthma that sometimes incapacitated him, but in middle age he gave up smoking. He played no games, though as a boy he had been athletic. As a young man he broke his right thumb playing baseball, and it healed stiff and smooth. No joint showed and as little kids we used to sit in his lap and try to make it bend.

He knew nothing about office politics and little about money. My mother handled the money. He was ingenuous in many ways. If he came to dislike a sports figure, he simply never wrote about him again. My father bad-mouthed nobody in print.

He always said Joe DiMaggio had class. Ted Williams too. At home in his den in later years there were framed photos of him with DiMaggio, Williams, Marciano, Arnold Palmer and many more. My father always thought the important figure in the photo was the athlete, but as I got older I came to see it differently. My father never thought of himself as a big hitter but he was as big as any of them, and bigger than most.

He won a number of prizes. Most surprised him. When he got the Pulitzer Prize for "Sports of the Times" in 1956 he was astonished. He had always imagined Red Smith might get it, if any sportswriter did, or one of the others. My brother Kevin told him: "They didn't give it to the cleverest guy on the sports page, but to the man who day after day wrote the best column."

He never gloated over his Pulitzer. He always wrote to each of his children every Monday when they were away, and that week's letter to me read only: "This will be short, but very, very sweet. I have just won the Pulitzer Prize. Love, Dad."

Hundreds of messages poured in (and he answered every one), including a telegram from Red Smith, who thought himself the best of the columnists, was certainly the cleverest and, since the award to my father precluded him getting one, was surely bitterly disappointed. "Congratulations," Smith's telegram read, "from now on only one column a day." He himself did not win a Pulitzer until twenty years later.

Afterwards my father never tried to parlay his prize into book or magazine contracts. He never even asked for a raise. He didn't see where his Pulitzer improved his writing. It was a relief to know that now The Times would not fire him. At least not right away.

President Kennedy once asked to meet him, and took him along in a motorcade, talking sports. Later Kennedy sent him a photo inscribed "from an avid reader." My father found it incredible that the President of the United States liked to read Arthur Daley.

I was the only one of his four children who followed in his footsteps. I fought against him and competed against him every day of my life and, especially when I was little, he could have crushed me easily, but he never did. I would never have accepted an ordinary job on the Times sports staff in New York. I was determined to make a career that would be different and more exotic than his. He was the first Times sportswriter ever sent over to report from Europe—the Berlin Olympics in 1936. I was the first ever stationed permanently abroad. I was rather proud of myself and thought I had outdone my father, but given the changes in the intervening years I don't suppose I had. It was about even, except that he had had to start from much further back. He was the son of a rope dealer, whereas I was the son of Arthur Daley.

During those first years in Europe, with a wife, two tiny kids, and no guaranteed salary, there were plenty of days when I felt vulnerable and scared. My father wrote every week to tell me how well I was doing, and he clipped and sent every single article I wrote, about 1,000 of them over six years. Every word of praise picked up around the office he sent, too, except one. One day Harrison Salisbury, an assistant managing editor, pointed to a piece I had filed and said to my father: "Arthur, you've out-bred yourself." Plenty of kings down through history had had their sons murdered for less, but my father was delighted. He went around repeating that comment to everybody, except me. My mother told me the story only after he died. He never really told me he was proud of me at all. He just gave that incredible support during those years I needed it most.

I went on to write novels he didn't approve of, and he would not have them on his bookshelf. After two of them, for periods of several weeks he wouldn't even talk to me. I had left the Times, I had given up writing about sports. I belonged now to a different world from the one he had brought me up in, and we never talked about any of this. I had once supposed that fathers and sons would be able to talk to each other, and so had he when I was born, but it isn't so. We never even talked professionally except toward the end, when he would sometimes ask my advice. I seldom told him I thought a particular column especially good. To compliment him felt presumptuous. After all, he was my father, and he was also Arthur Daley. But sometimes I would do it, and he would nod. Later my mother would tell me how pleased he had been: "It must have been a good column if Bob liked it."

My father was the only man I ever knew who was better than he thought he was. He wrote about 10,000 columns, and if a man's life is measured in the amount of pleasure he gave others, then he ranked very high.

When he began writing "Sports of the Times" he was told to write it until further notice. Further notice came 31 years later while he was walking across 43rd Street on his way to work, the next day's column moving about in his head, where it stayed.

An ambulance got him to the hospital, where doctors worked on him without success, and a paramedic, opening the dead man's wallet, looked up and said: "Oh, shit, it's Arthur Daley."

Somewhere along the line I had conceived the notion that I wanted to write "Sports of the Times" one day, and one day only. I wanted to write about my father in his space on the day that he would die.

Then the day came when he did die, suddenly, and long before any of his children were ready for it. It was January 3, 1974, and he was to retire on his seventieth birthday the following July 31. The grind had got him down by then, and on his desk calendar for the day of his death he had scribbled, "Only 89 more columns."

There weren't 89 more for him, but there was one to go for me, or so I thought in my grief. I rushed over to see my mother, then left my sister with her and came back to make the calls that had to be made. One went to A.M. Rosenthal, executive editor of the Times. I told him I wanted to write my father's column for tomorrow, and then I began to bawl.

There went any chance of being allowed to write the column. Rosenthal soothed me, then gave someone else the delicate job of calling back to say that obviously I had enough jobs to do that day, they couldn't ask me to write "Sports of the Times," too. Someone else would do it.

I wrote it anyway. I wrote it all that afternoon between friends calling to offer sympathy, and my brother calling from New York about arrangements for our father's funeral. I wrote it as if, by writing it, I could tell him before it was too late that I was glad to have been his son. It would never appear as "Sports of the Times." I wrote it anyway.

Two days later in St. Patrick's Cathedral where he and my mother had been married 45 years before, came my father's funeral. In attendance were many of his colleagues from the Times, his rival columnists from other papers, and much of the New York sporting world. A bishop officiated.

I had wanted to read what I had written from the pulpit as a eulogy for my father, but fifteen minutes before the service was to begin the rector of the cathedral, a monsignor, learned of this plan and vetoed it. Impossible, he said. I confronted him in the sacristy. Only a priest can give homilies, he informed me. Lay people are not permitted to speak during a funeral. I argued, he was adamant, and very soon voices were raised. "This is not your funeral," I cried, "it's ours. You don't own it, we do."

"Out of the question, the rule is the rule."

"It's because of men like you that people are leaving the church," I shouted.

In the end my tribute to my father, which contained much of the information you have just read, even some of the lines, was read by a priest who had taught both my brother and me at Fordham Prep. It was just as well. I choked up listening to it. What a mess I would have made trying to read it.

Suzanne was 17 years old when her grandfather died. And now she is the Paris bureau chief of *The New York Times*.

December 25, 2000, Paris

This has been a different Christmas from the ones we used to spend here, though in some ways the same. Our granddaughters rip the wrappings off much the way their mother used to—that is not what I mean. But we were usually alone in our apartment on the other side of Paris. We had family in Nice, and in America, but not here, and so despite ourselves a certain loneliness crept in. Today at least there were three generations on hand. As there should be at Christmas.

I used to shoot color slides of Theresa and Suzanne, and then of Leslie who was born here, as they opened their presents. Hanging around my neck I had a big battery pack contraption that operated the flash. You had to know a good deal about photography to get good pictures—any pictures—in color indoors. And slides were the thing. When they came back from the developer a week or two later we would wait until dark, then set up the projector and the screen and look at them.

I don't know many people who still use slides for family pictures. We haven't looked at our old ones in years—too much trouble to set up for it—and of course you can only watch at night. Today's photos were taken by Galen, aged ten, with her new Christmas present camera with contained flash. The camera cost very little, and the prints, if we take them in tomorrow morning, will be ready by afternoon—and sharp as you might wish, as well.

Suzanne's present to us was cell phones, one each. The fifteen year old Avery programmed them for us. Took her five minutes. I might have done it myself, but it would have meant hours of studying the directions. So now we are reachable any hour anywhere. I wasn't sure we needed to be, but in a short time doubtless will decide we were, and will wonder how we ever used to get by.

When I look back on the changes that have occurred in the world since my youth, it seems to me that almost all of them are in the nature of cell phones: technical and/or financial, perhaps both. Cheap cameras a child can operate. Phones that come out of your pocket.

I can think of one or two substantive changes, but not many.

During my years in Paris for the Times I never once spoke by telephone with anyone in America. Transatlantic calls were possible, but took too long to go through and cost too much. Instead, hundreds of letters passed back and forth, transmitting from one party to the other exactly the same facts and emotions, though a bit more slowly. Jet airliners fly higher, faster, cheaper than DC-7s and Constellations, but the object, after all, is to get from point A to point B, and the prop planes could to that too. I used to lug a 20 pound portable typewriter in a wooden box all over Europe, plus sheaves of paper to put in it, and was sometimes sweating through my clothes by the time I got wherever I was going.

One hot day I remember, it was the first time I ever covered the Dutch Grand Prix, I carried that heavy typewriter from the Zandvoort train station to the circuit, not knowing how far away it was—about two miles, it turned out. A computer would have been lighter, but the distance would have been the same. Everything else would have been the same also. I would have been excited to be there, excited about the race to come, and afterwards I would have worked just as hard to write a story so good that it would be judged, I hoped, exceptional.

What else has changed? Not Christmas in Paris, for here we all are again, with a tree lit up, and a turkey and some nice wines, and two happy kids. And different roles for Peggy and me that time has promoted us into.

December 27, 2000, Paris

Mid afternoon. The day is cold, gloomy. I step out the door into a fine cold mist of rain. Upstairs the girls are nursing colds. On such a day no one else wanted to go out, so I am alone. The sidewalk is narrow. Suzanne's apartment is next door to the Matignon Palace—the prime minister's residence—so the area is littered with cops and gendarmes, two or three guarding all the corners, individual cops standing and stomping in many of the doorways, police buses parked half on the sidewalk with relief crews dozing inside. I think these men work two hours on, two off, but their vans and buses leave so little sidewalk room that pedestrians must sidle past or else walk in the street.

At the corner I turn onto the Rue du Bac, and begin to pass the small, smart shops: antiques, jewelry, paintings. My face is cold and wet from the mist. This is the Paris that I remember. In winter the sun can stay hidden for weeks at a time, and you walk along under a heavy grayness, or a light drizzle, or are bathed by a wet mist like today's. It rarely rains hard here, and almost never snows.

I stop at a window where expensive wines are laid out individually in nests of straw, or fiberglass, or silvered paper, treasures one and all. I read the chateau names, the horrendous prices, then walk on. The Bon Marché, which seems to me the most chic of the Paris department stores, covers an entire block, the sidewalk here is crowded, and I am some time getting past it. The street opens onto a square framed by bare trees with wet trunks, and, to one side, the Metro entrance. I go down the stairs and put my ticket in the slot. On the corridor a man sits on the floor against the wall playing a violin. Between his legs is a beret with some coins in it.

I have decided to have a look at the Notre Dame. Surely it will be deserted on a day such as this. I will be able to sit in a pew and gawk at the stained glass, at the towering columns, or even just sit and brood. So I ride two stops to Cluny, come up on the Boulevard St. Germain, and walk toward the river. The Seine is split in two here, and I cross the bridge over this half of it onto the Ile de la Cite.

But the square in front of the cathedral, I see as I approach, is jammed with people.

The mist has turned into a drizzle, but there is a queue sixty yards long, four abreast, sometimes six abreast, almost none of them children, standing in the cold rain waiting to enter the cathedral via the south portal, while the same queue, much disordered now, is disgorged by the north portal. More hordes spill into the square even as I watch.

I find this totally disheartening, and almost turn back. It is two days after Christmas—in no way a special day. The afternoon is cold and dark. It is raining. Why would anyone queue up to enter a church on a day like this? And then my other questions: where do all these people come from? What are they looking for here? The words and phrases I can pick up are as much foreign as French, and I am reminded of my last trip to Venice—too many people there too. The answers come readily enough. In this age of affluence, of cheap airfares, of airliners coming in non stop from everywhere, the great tourist attractions are overwhelmed. What else do you expect? The solution would be to build ten more of each of them quick, and in any other business this is what would be done. Ten more (brand new) Romes, Parises, Venices to handle the crowds. That's what Disneyland did. There used to be only one Disneyland, after all. How many are there now?

Part of me, not all, wants to leave. While trying to make up my mind—stay or go—I join the queue. This is called keeping ones options open. Umbrellas in various colors dot the entire square, but many people are exposed, don't even have hats. My own umbrella shields me from the rain, most of it, but not from the cold dampness or from the cold itself. I stare over heads at the facade of the cathedral, and shuffle stolidly forward as the queue does.

The Notre Dame, begun in 1167, was the first of France's great gothic cathedrals to be built but this afternoon doesn't look it. It's facade has been recently cleaned, the patina of centuries scrubbed off, the stone now cream colored, no patina left at all. I never saw it like this. All the other cathedrals are gray and mottled. They show how old they are. This one looks brand new—looks as it must have looked nine hundred years ago. I much prefer it the way I saw it last, the way the others still are.

Also, precisely because it is so creamy and bright, I am extremely conscious of the friezes over the doors, and the life sized statues in the niches above that. I never really looked at them before, presumably because I never had to wait to get into the cathedral before. But the friezes and statues are all of them intact, not a nose or finger missing, and this too, at least to me, is not as it should be. There is no sign of the erosion caused by nine centuries of rains and storms, of wars and revolutions as well. Especially during the 1789-1794 Revolution gangs of young hoodlums amused themselves by shooting up the statuary outside, and sometimes inside, every church in France. Take a look at some of the others if you doubt me, any of the others. Not this one of course, though it happened here too. The Notre Dame, when the then world finally calmed down, was in bad shape. But in the mid 1800s a architect named Viollet le Duc was given almost unlimited funds and he "restored" it. Made it like new. Made new ears and eyes and heads for the statuary, new hands and arms. Everything. The centuries disappeared overnight. The result, I decide as I study the facade, is not to my taste, thank you.

All the time I am thinking these not so deep thoughts the queue has been shuffling forward, me with it, and then it is the turn of a number of us, pressed together like a bunch of grapes, to enter the darkness inside. And it is dark. Almost no light comes through the windows. Well, on such a gloomy day there wasn't much out there to start with.

Now I am in a river of people. The current moves me down one ambulatory, around the altar, and up the opposite one, and out again. One isn't exactly pushed along, but the flow creates an impetus of its own, and one goes with it without even wishing to. One allows oneself to be swept along. One hesitates to get outside the flow. I might fight it, of course, but choose not to, and am soon out on the square again. It has taken scarcely five minutes. Well, the conditions were wrong. The Cathedral of Notre Dame has nothing to offer me this day.

At least now, I note as I come outside, it has stopped raining.

By the time I have crossed back over the Seine I have decided against the metro, and as I stroll toward home I admire almost everything I see, the shop windows, the wrought iron balconies on the buildings along the St. Germain, the church of St. Severin, which I have never looked into before, which dates from about 1220, and which turns out to be a miniature version of a perfect gothic cathedral. Paris is a wonderful walking town. I am slightly enchanted by the famous cafes when I come to them, the Deux Magots, the Flore, the Brasserie Lipp. Can one be slightly enchanted by something? I think so. In this case it is not the cafes themselves that hold enchantment, but the idea of all the famous writers and philosophers of winters past who talked themselves almost to death over tiny cups of coffee behind those same vapor-obscured windows.

Paris itself is an enchantment, or can be, and I feel as much at home in its streets as I do in New York. We lived here all those years as a young family, and I have returned many times since, often at the behest and expense of publishers who were bringing forth novels of mine in translation. Apparently it was easy for their publicists to set up interviews. To French reporters I was a curiosity, a foreign author who spoke French. Some of them couldn't get over me, or so they pretended. The schedule the publicists made was always tight, presumably because the housing and feeding of an author night after night is expensive, and for one recent book I was subjected to eight interviews a day for three days, most of them press, but radio and TV interviews too, and then sent packing.

When we lived here I did not like Paris much. We had plenty of money and freedom, but almost no friends. I realized, at least vaguely, that I was not popular around the bureau. We were at an awkward age to make other friends, too young to be considered a catch by people of achievement, but too rich and successful for most of our contemporaries to be comfortable with. The columnists and senior correspondents who came through the bureau showed no interest in our company. Famous American writers lived in Paris, James Jones, William Saroyan, Irwin Shaw and others, and we met some of them, but how could I present myself to them as someone they might like to know when, in my own mind, I had written nothing significant yet?

Also, it was a bad time for Paris and for France. The losing war in Algeria was on everybody's mind. Torture and assassinations. Lives squandered, money. No end in sight. Algeria was a giant sore in the mouth, around which it was difficult to smile. Most people—shopkeepers, taxi drivers, salespeople—were sullen most of the time. On a more personal level, our children were often sick, chicken pox, whooping cough, and I myself was almost always working, away to events most weekends, writing books and magazine articles on the side when at home. My career was solidly based by now, but it didn't seem so to me. Looking back I can see that I ought to have relaxed, enjoyed every day, but I didn't. Having no certainty that my success, such as it was, would last, I accepted every assignment, felt I had to work doubly hard or we would be back where we had started. Besides, we were spending the money, buying antiques, buying paintings.

The last year we were here I recognized it as the last year, was determined that it would be, and I went back to events I had loved in the past and loved them again, both for themselves and for what was around them—in Amsterdam for the Dutch Grand Prix I sipped an aperitif on a terrace beside a canal, and the banks of rhododendrons and laurels were in bloom, their colors doubled by the water and I felt dazed by so much beauty; I went with the Tour de France, up and over Envalira Pass and down into Andorra, and wrote about the scenery, and about exhausted men crashing; we went again to the fiesta at Pamplona, and I ran with the bulls a few more times. I tried to enjoy every event more than I ever had, write every story better than I ever had. Time exists in three parts, memory, the present tense, and what is to come. I was living the first two now every day, and devouring both. But for me here there was to be no future, so at the same time I was saying goodbye—goodbye to these years, to this way of life.

Goodbye to all of it, and hello again to my old ambition to write novels, which had returned in full force. I had already started one, and though I later threw away a good many chapters and the central idea itself, I was burning up with the need to become a novelist. One day after finishing a sports column I got so excited I wrote fourteen pages. Novel writing was what I had always wanted to do, not daily journalism, a novelist was what I had always wanted to be. Certainly, France was seductive, the job I had was seductive. Too much so, perhaps. It was time to get back to what I had always thought of as my life's work, which meant back to New York because the action was there, not here. I needed to get enough of the novel down on paper to perhaps get a contract.

But supposing I couldn't get one, wasn't good enough?

That was a chance I would have to take.

What else was I to do, stay in Paris endlessly copying myself? I could do so if I chose. Was that all I wanted from life?

Peggy and I talked it over. We had saved $30,000. We could go back to America, put half down on a house, and the rest, if we were careful, would carry us for a year. At the end of a year we would see. I would either succeed, or not succeed.

We had a full time Spanish maid by this time—she cooked wonderful Spanish omelets among other things. We lived in an apartment with wedding cake ceilings and five marble fireplaces, one in each room, and enjoyed many other perks. We would have to give all that up. Would have to give up France, and perhaps not be able to get back.

Peggy agreed it was what we should do, or perhaps I only talked her into it. There, it was decided.

I was due that year for home leave. Without telling New York we packed everything up, emptied out and gave up the apartment, and got on a plane to New York. I might have asked permission first, but feared the answer might be no, and so didn't. I chose to confront the Times with a fait accompli, and take my chances.

In New York I would have to work in the City room, as one did on home leave, but I was entitled to a three week vacation first, and we used it to find a house, stone and stucco, with a slate roof, on three quarters of an acre in Greenwich, Ct., $15,000 down payment, a $30,000 mortgage—the same house that recently, long after we left it, sold for $1,25 million.

It was within walking distance of the grade school, and the train station as well, in case my big plans did not work out and I had to commute. I might have to commute for the rest of my life, and I knew this, and faced it, or thought I did. Pretended to myself that it couldn't happen.

With the house papers signed, I took the train in to the Times, went to work in the city room and after a week got my nerve up and announced that I had bought a house and wasn't going back to Paris.

Jim Roach looked betrayed when I told him. His whole face fell. I didn't care about betraying the Times. The Times was a corporation and had no feelings. But I did care about Roach, and tried to explain, but he only kept nodding his head. I didn't want to write about sports anymore, either, I said. He got up and left me there, and I felt ashamed and miserable.

Since I had no contracts yet, I went to the brand new Metro editor, Rosenthal in his first big post, and told him I needed a job. Rosenthal had been expelled, some years before, from Poland, supposedly for "probing too deeply" into Polish affairs, and had been temporarily assigned to Geneva, which was where I had first met him. In fact Peggy and I had happened to be having dinner in his house the night he won the Pulitzer Prize for his Polish coverage, and he went around the room unable to stop grinning, socking everyone in the arm.

Now he was trying to strengthen the Metro staff he had inherited, and he said I was one of the two or three young reporters he had been hoping to get. He gave me an immediate $25 a week raise, and two more weeks off, which I used to paint my new house. I painted rooms for eleven straight days. Later, when Rosenthal became managing editor, and then executive editor, he would abolish all the Times' various fiefdoms—the Sunday Magazine, the Washington Bureau, etc.—until all power was consolidated in his own hands. He would become the most powerful newspaper man in the country. He would also become a tyrant hated by most of his staff. But he wasn't all that then. He was smiling, rubbing his hands together, glad to get me. I still had every intention of quitting the paper as soon as I got the book contracts I was after. If I got them. But I did not tell Rosenthal this, nor anyone.

What I was hoping for was two contracts, not one. I had come home with six years of bullfight photos, mostly in black and white, but some in color, out of which I wished to make a big picture book I would call *The Swords of Spain*. It would be similar in format to *The Cruel Sport*. The thought of them as companion volumes gave me pleasure. Swords might even outdo *Death in the Afternoon*, the previous best work on bullfighting, because both text and photos would be by me, whereas Hemingway had culled his photos from various agencies.

The second book would be a novel about foreign correspondents in Paris. I imagined a young correspondent who spoke French and was at ease in Paris, and an older man, the bureau chief, who didn't and wasn't. The young man would fall in love with a French girl, and the bureau chief would be involved in a rather sordid love affair with a secretary. In the background would be the paper itself. I would call the novel *The Whole Truth.*

A cynical person reading the above might remark that I hadn't looked far for a plot, might even conclude that I was planning something ugly. I would answer that the object of any novel is not to expose someone, or offend someone—at least it shouldn't be. Instead novelists take something they know well, and people they know well, and they throw it all into a soup which must be allowed to bubble for a while. Eventually it hardens into a lump which they hold up to the light. They try to see what they've got, examine it from every aspect. They begin to finger this lump all over, slowly manipulating it into the shape they want the way a sculptor molds clay. Finally they sit down and write.

That is what novelists do, if they are any good. The result will be a novel, not a documentary, though probably it will have a certain number of verifiable details in it, perhaps a great many. What it must also have, and this is the real justification for doing it in the first place, is truth. The reader must recognize its truth, and be moved by it. Truth cannot be made up. A novel which pretends to have value cannot be entirely made up. It must be based however loosely on real people and real events. Or so I have always believed.

Does this sound self serving, even reprehensible? Maybe. I don't think so. I hope not. In any case, a novelist does not really have much choice. If truth is the place he is trying for, and it should be, there is no other street I know of that will get him there.

When *The Whole Truth* was published two years later—I had long since quit the paper—it offended a good many people at the Times who felt it belittled the paper's role and stature in the world. Included in this group, unfortunately, was the daily reviewer who, as he wrote at great length, found little in the novel that was praiseworthy, or worth a reader's time and money. He saw it principally as a betrayal. Betrayal of the paper which had nurtured me, betrayal of the trusted, inside look at itself that it had permitted me. He condemned *The Whole Truth* and crushed its young author. Betrayal is such a heavy word. He made me feel guilty. He made me feel unskilled, as well. That the novel got some fine reviews elsewhere in the country in no way assuaged this guilt, or lifted my morale. *The Whole Truth* today is the only one of my books that I never look into. I will pick up any of the others from time to time and read a page or two, but never that one.

At the time of which I write this first novel of mine did not yet exist, I didn't have a contract yet. I was working every day in the city room, and from there I would make appointments with publishers. I would go into their offices, lay my bullfight photos out on the floor, describe what I meant to do with them, and await a reaction. Usually the reaction was swift enough. No thank you. I would scoop up my photos and leave.

I came to the Dial Press, which was one of the smaller houses, and showed my photos to its editor in chief, a man my age named E.L. Doctorow. Doctorow, who would become an important figure in American letters, and a rich writer as well, had already written a novel or two that didn't sell. He was a long way from making a living at writing. It was his day job, editing, that supported him.

Doctorow liked both my ideas, offered a $2000 advance on *The Swords of Spain*, and $4,000 on *The Whole Truth*. The contract was ready a few days later, and I signed it.

My hours at the Times were eleven to seven, but I formed the habit of reaching the office at 9 a.m., which gave me a minimum of two hours each day to work on *The Swords of Spain*. I would sit at my desk writing short profiles of bullfighters, and captions for the pictures, and I would write until the table mike on the Metro desk would blare out my name, and I would be given an assignment. But some days this might not happen until noon or later. One day I was not called until 5 p.m., when I was given a short obituary to write. So by Christmas *The Swords of Spain* was finished.

Only one assignment of note had interrupted it during this entire period. About two weeks before the election I was sent out to accompany Bobby Kennedy, who was campaigning for the senate. I spent only one day with him, about eight hours in all. He made many speeches, never the same one twice. He was charming, self deprecating, funny. He is Saint Bobby now, but he wasn't then. He was known as hard edged, controversial, and he was not a New Yorker, but after a day in his presence I thought he would win the election, and if he did, it was his charm and humor that would do it for him. Most Americans, most New York voters, had no idea that he was anything except a hardliner. And so in my story that night, reading from my notes, I wrote about how amusing he was, how his speeches were fun to listen to, and that this was possibly important. I tried to get the charm in. However, the desk made me rewrite the story, confining it to what he had said about the issues. No jokes.

In its next issue *Time Magazine* ran a photo, shot sometime during that day, of Kennedy and me side by side, me looking deadpan, or even glum. Kennedy sent me a copy of this photo. On it he had written, "I hope before the day was out you smiled. It was another two weeks before I did."

Swords was finished. It was time to begin work on *The Whole Truth*. It was time also, if I was ever going to do it, to quit *The New York Times*.

There were two other young reporters who sat at desks near mine, Gay Talese and David Halberstam, both of whom had already published small books that had attracted little notice. In addition Halberstam had won a Pulitzer Prize in Vietnam. Both wanted to quit the paper and freelance, or said they did, wanted the freedom to write big books, and we used to talk about this. I was determined to resign, I said. So were they, they said. They would do it soon, they promised. But the days passed, the weeks, and none of us did it, had the nerve to do it. The paper represented prestige, secure income. But we wanted to make our own prestige, and we wanted more income than the paper paid us. The paper was mother, we were safe close to the bosom of mother, a notion none of us put into words, but that we all felt. You can't cast off mother. It was fearful even to think of doing such a thing—more fearful perhaps to me than to them because the paper had stood behind the family in which I had grown up, and for which my father still worked.

Was survival possible without the paper? Who could say? How could one be sure? The three of us were all watching each other.

It was clear to me that neither of them was going to make the move.

It was clear to me that one of us would have to go first.

I called Rosenthal aside. It was evening. The day's stint had ended. I would have a short piece in tomorrow morning's paper. We stood beside my desk in the city room. I told him I had a novel contract now and wished to resign from the Times to devote full time to it. I made, in other words, a rather long nervous speech.

Rosenthal tried to talk me out of it. Assistant Managing Editor Salisbury came over. I didn't have to resign, he told me, plenty of reporters wrote books without quitting the paper. The paper didn't want to lose me.

No, I said, I want to resign.

Rosenthal told me to write a letter of resignation and give it to him. I did this, and became his first defection. According to Talese in *The Power and the Glory*, the book he later wrote about the Times, Rosenthal took my letter and went into the men's room and started to cry.

I went off to dinner in a Greenwich Village restaurant with my wife and some friends. I felt enormously light, and at the same time more weighted down than I had ever been. Could I survive without *The New York Times*?

We would see.

And now Suzanne is bureau chief, and I am grateful to her for being here in Paris, and for us all being together in her house this Christmas. At the same time I see that she is doing exactly what I did when we lived here, concentrating too hard, trying to be too perfect, not appreciating either Paris or her children as much as she should. I keep telling her she is one of the paper's stars, something I never quite believed about myself, and that my father never believed about himself either although it was certainly true in his case and, looking back, perhaps in mine as well. They don't have all that many stars, I tell Suzanne, her career is solidly on track. But she only smiles and nods. I wish I could do the worrying for her, I would be able to do it so much better now.

In any case, having her here seems to have given me back the city as we knew it then, though in a more enjoyable form. It's given me back the bureau too, her bureau—I can go in there any time I want. Watching her it is almost as if I am a young reporter again, working out of the Paris bureau once more.

And that, I think is the principal reason for the enchantment I feel right now strolling along the Boulevard St. Germain, the principal reason for the gratitude I feel toward my daughter. Because of her I feel attached, however tenuously, to *The New York Times* again.

Reattached to mother? Perhaps. Sounds a bit silly, doesn't it?

In two days time we fly back to America.

9.
The Race to Make the Racing Car Movie

January 12, 2001, Connecticut

I had no sooner quit the paper and begun working out of our new house in Greenwich, than the race to make the racing car movie heated up, and my phone rang. Unbeknownst to me the race had been going on for some months already, it was getting ugly, and if you had told me I would have a role to play in it, I would have laughed. As things turned out, my role didn't last very long, and the laughs didn't either.

There are rules for dealing with Hollywood, but this was my first movie experience, so I didn't know them.

The phone calls, two of them, came from John Frankenheimer in Hollywood. My wife, who answered both times, said I was not home, so Frankenheimer no doubt thought I was ducking him. Hollywood is a place where most phone calls are not returned. These people treat each other very badly. When you are hot everyone will take your calls, but as soon as your grosses drop no one will. Since you can't ever be sure about your own hotness, not really, unreturned phone calls make you bite your nails. Frankenheimer's must have been down to the quick.

When I got home I was too tired to call operator 56 in Hollywood. An hour later Frankenheimer called still again. "I have 10 million dollars to make a movie on Grand Prix motor racing," he began. "I want to talk you about writing the script."

Hollywood people get what they want by waving money. Most times they don't actually pay it. Just waving it is enough. People start grasping, as if trying to snatch flies out of the air.

But the money mentioned by Frankenheimer had nothing to do with me as yet, and it sounded so crass I was amused.

I knew his name in a vague way. He had made a reputation in TV in the early days of live drama, a boy wonder who directed plays month after month on live shows like Studio One, Playhouse 90 and such. By the time I first talked to him he had moved to Hollywood, and had directed seven rather big movies: *Birdman of Alcatraz, Seven Days in May, The Manchurian Candidate, The Train*, and others.

Now he praised *The Cruel Sport.* Best book on car racing ever written, he said. He wanted me in Hollywood on Monday, all expenses paid.

The free trip to Hollywood, it seemed, was supposed to make writers—anybody in fact—fall all over themselves. But after my years in Europe, four or five days a week on the road nearly every week, I had settled down in Connecticut, and had a novel to write. Hollywood was more travel. I did not want go, and so told Frankenheimer that if he wanted to see me, he could come to New York.

Which so flustered him that he began to plead. Although I didn't know him, I sensed this was an unusual role for him, and I enjoyed hearing him play it. Watch closely, because for about another ten paragraphs, I do everything right as far as Hollywood is concerned. Then, like everyone else—

"All right, if it means that much to you, I'll come to California."

"Come Monday."

"I'll come in a week."

"Come Monday."

"No."

"All right, a week from Monday," he said.

Without knowing it, I continued to handle Hollywood brilliantly. "I'll come a week from Tuesday," I said, and on that note rang off.

I phoned my agent, still Sterling Lord, to report all this. There was a pause, then he said: "There's something we haven't been telling you. Steve McQueen and John Sturges are doing a car racing movie too. They want to call theirs *The Cruel Sport*. They've been negotiating to buy your book, and the deal is nearly complete."

"How much do they want to pay?"

"It's a non fiction book. They only want your title."

"How much?"

"Five thousand."

I thought: We can live in relative luxury for three or four months on that. Does a reaction such as this sound unworthy of me? I didn't think so then, and don't now. I was a brand new freelance writer with three children. I had a novel contract, yes, but the advance was only $4,000. Like most, maybe all, freelancers, I had no idea where any money would come from after that.

I said to Lord: "What do I do now?"

It was decided that I should fly to Hollywood, find out what Frankenheimer was offering, and stall him until the McQueen-Sturges deal was on the table.

"Suppose Sturges finds out I'm in Hollywood?"

"Stall him, too."

At the Los Angeles airport, I was met by Frankenheimer's secretary, and driven to the Beverly Hills Hotel, the film world's poshest, and lodged overlooking the gardens in a room costing Paramount Pictures some enormous sum.

Morning came, and with it Edward Lewis, partner of Kirk Douglas (Douglas-Lewis Productions Inc.) and producer-to-be of Frankenheimer's race car movie. The day was already warm, and instead of the banks of snow I had left behind there were banks of flowers, and the mist of early morning hung above the lawns.

As we drove north along the winding Pacific coastline towards Frankenheimer's house in Malibu, Lewis told me that most of the elite stars of the world were clamoring to be in this film, which was to be called *Grand Prix*. "Steve McQueen wants to be in it so bad he can taste it."

I gave Lewis a sharp look.

As they waited for me to agree to write the script he and Frankenheimer were stalling everybody, he said, McQueen and everyone else.

"Hmm," I said. A lot of people were stalling a lot of people, it seemed.

Lewis was about 48, swarthy, tough looking, a former prize fighter. His hobby was poker, he informed me during the long drive. He could play poker all night without ever changing the expression on his face, he said. I studied his profile.

The plan, he told me, was to pair me with William Inge to do their screenplay. Inge the famous playwright, and me the famous car racing expert.

Still playing my cards perfectly, I answered that I was under contract for a novel, and didn't know if I could take on another assignment; in any case I would not work with Inge or anyone else. And I would do the job at home or nowhere, travel was out.

"I plan to be known as one of the greatest writers who ever lived," I told Lewis. "I don't collaborate."

It sounded horrendous. I don't know why I said it. But it was, in

Hollywood, and especially with former prize fighters turned movie producers, exactly the perfect thing to say.

Lewis nodded soberly.

Frankenheimer's house was a bright, airy place opening out onto the beach. The houses along that beach were almost all owned by film directors, producers and stars and they cost a fortune. That I was supposed to be impressed by the house and its location, I know now but didn't then, and so wasn't. Lewis and I sat beside the pool and were served coffee. After a moment, Frankenheimer came down wearing ragged clothes, his bare feet shoved halfway into ragged moccasins. He was 6 feet 3 inches tall, thin, narrow shouldered, and he carried himself stooped, but leaning aggressively forward. He had sensuous lips and soulful eyes, and at 35, a bit older than I, his hair was already graying.

Lewis told him: "He says he won't collaborate with Inge."

"Christ, Inge is coming out here for lunch."

"I'm sorry," said I, "that's the way it is."

They were both nodding soberly now. It is interesting to speculate on what might have happened had I been able to maintain this kind of cool all the way.

"Well," said Frankenheimer, "we'll just have to break the news to Inge."

He began to talk about the movie he wanted to do. He had got interested in the subject by racing and wrecking a Triumph Spitfire at nearby Riverside. He had since read all the books, had seen an American race of two, and had brain-picked many of the top drivers, one of whom, former world champion Graham Hill, had said patronizingly: "You say you want to take some shots with your cine camera?"

"You should have seen his attitude change once he heard the credits," said Frankenheimer, with a note of triumph in his voice.

He wanted to do a three hour Cinerama movie in two parts, he said. He would begin with the rear of a car, engine roaring, filling the screen from side to side. Then this engine speeds away and we show fifteen minutes of racing through the streets of Monte Carlo. There should be five or six drivers in the story, plus their women of course, and the first part of the film should end with a titanic race around the Nurburgring in the Grand Prix of Germany, in which one of the drivers should get killed. He looked up at me, as if for applause.

Frankenheimer had never seen the Nurburgring, nor Monaco either.

The death scene would be followed by a grisly funeral like that of Count Von Trips, buried three funerals later, the third at graveside on a muddy knoll in pouring rain, the coffin having been lugged up there by eight soaked, slipping drivers.

After the intermission the film should show the remaining drivers engaged in a struggle to be world champion.

I had virtually forgotten the projected sale of my book to John Sturges and Steve McQueen. Instead I found myself being seduced by Frankenheimer. It was clear that nearly everything he knew about car racing he had got out of my books and articles, including the description of the Trips funeral. Most of his images and ideas were my images and ideas. He even seemed humble in the face of my knowledge, experience and feelings on the subject. This was flattering. Yes indeed.

We were beginning to build the movie scene by scene when Frankenheimer was summoned by his butler to the phone.

He came back looking stunned.

"Variety has a story that Sturges and McQueen have bought *The Cruel Sport*."

I nearly pitched over into the pool. "What?"

"Is it true?"

First I thought: I hope it's true, because with that out of the way I won't have to stall Frankenheimer anymore.

"We can't have you writing our movie if Sturges's movie is based on your book," said Lewis.

I had realized this myself. "I don't know if it's true or not."

"Call your agent and find out."

"It can't be true."

"Are you sure?"

"I think so."

"You think so?"

"Yes. No. I didn't sign anything."

"How much were they going to pay?" cried Lewis. "We'll top it."

I had the vague thought that I could say $25,000, perhaps more, and Lewis would agree. But on the one hand I was not used to the movie business, and on the other I was not used to lying. So I told him the truth.

"Consider our offer better."

Looking back, this is one of the funny moments. But no one laughed. Instead we shook hands solemnly all around.

Meanwhile, back at the Beverly Hills Hotel two phone messages and a telegram, all from John Sturges, were piling up. I didn't know this. Although John Frankenheimer was a big director at that time, Sturges was far bigger. I wouldn't have known this either.

William Inge was the author of a number of Broadway plays including *Picnic*, which had won a Pulitzer Prize, *Come Back Little Sheba*, and *Bus Stop*, all of which had become movies.

As he sat down to lunch Lewis said to him: "You're a prize winning dramatist, and this young man, who has never written in the dramatic form before, refuses to collaborate with you."

He sounded a bit self conscious as he said this.

Inge nodded. No doubt he had no desire to collaborate either. He was middle-aged, portly, slow moving, soft speaking, a gentle kind of man, and a future suicide.

"This isn't my type of movie anyway," he said gently. "I've never even been out of the country."

Nonetheless, as the rest of us talked, he listened intently and asked perceptive questions, while at the same time thumbing through Frankenheimer's copy of *The Cruel Sport.*

Lunch ended. As he stood up to go he addressed Frankenheimer. "You don't need me," he said in his kind, gentle way. "You've already got your writer."

We saw him out the door, then went on talking about the movie. My mind was in a fevered state in which whole scenes bloomed. Frankenheimer said he loved them all; he invented a few himself, and they were good. I felt we understood each other. This would be our movie.

About 5 p.m. Lewis said: "John and I don't even have to talk this out in private. You will write the movie. I had another writer coming out in a few days, frankly. But I'll call and tell him not to come."

I went for a walk on the beach hoping to calm my nerves. I walked a mile or more down toward Los Angeles, not even knowing that the houses I passed, which looked ordinary to me and which were jammed in virtually wall to wall, were all frightfully expensive, and were owned, most of them, by film stars and film heavyweights like Frankenheimer. The light began to fail as I walked, and by the time I had turned around and got back to the house it was dusk.

"You haven't changed your mind?" cried Lewis as I came in.

"No," I said. "No, of course not."

At dinner Frankenheimer talked about Frankenheimer. I learned about the private detective work that had gone into his divorce, and that he had been under analysis for seven years. I learned how he had become a TV genius at the age of 23, but had priced himself out of TV and had come to Hollywood. He now earned half a million dollars a year, he asserted.

Since we were buddies sharing confidences, I told him I had been averaging between $25,000 and $30,000 per year for the past several years. I had always been rather proud of this income, which was as much or more than any other journalist was earning, but was surprised to hear how puny it must have sounded to John Frankenheimer. Immediately I wished I had kept my big mouth shut.

(Later I learned that John Sturges, who had directed *The Great Escape, Gunfight At the OK Corral, The Old Man and the Sea,* and other blockbusters, paid half a million a year in income taxes. There must be subjects these people never mention, but money isn't one of them.)

Sensing how much ground was being lost and seeking to regain it, I told Frankenheimer he had an unrealistic attitude toward money. He assured me I was wrong, and made me come into the garage to see his Ferrari and his Rolls Royce. He hadn't even paid for them, he bragged. United Artists had given them to him for directing his most recent picture, *The Train.* It didn't occur to me to suggest that he might have had the money instead.

I realized I had begun to lose points all along the line, and I guess he realized this too, for he fastened his eyes on mine and told me that if, while writing his picture, I stood up to him, we would get along. If I did not, he would "crap all over" me.

This is a rather unusual thing to be told, and I didn't know quite what to say. Meantime, the sensual mouth had turned hard, and the soulful eyes were boring into me. A contest was on—who was going to drop his eyes first?

Should I stare him down?

Could I stare him down?

It seemed to me that I was cooked either way.

Then I got angry and for the first time entertained serious misgivings about him and his project. This is infantile, I thought. Have I got mixed up with a child, or what?

I attempted to give a nonchalant shrug, while averting my eyes. Frankenheimer's face glowed with triumph. I noted this well enough, and for a moment felt disgusted with him and his project both. Then I told myself: no, I still think he's a helluva nice guy, and we will do a great movie together.

He told me I would clear at least $100,000 on this movie, and passed me his copy of *The Cruel Sport* to sign. I wrote: "With admiration for *The Train*, and in the hope that *Grand Prix* will be something important in the lives of both of us." And I signed it.

They sent a man to the Beverly Hills Hotel to clear me out of my room, and booked a seat for me on the midnight plane to New York. They were sending me home on the red-eye to get me out of town fast, but I didn't realize this. I don't know what happened to the phone messages and telegram from John Sturges.

While waiting for the limousine to take me to the airport, we talked about Frankenheimer again. I learned that one of his parents was Jewish, one Catholic. He had gone through a stage growing up when he wanted to become a priest, and another when he decided to become a rabbi instead.

On the plane I was too excited to sleep. Scenes from the movie were writing themselves in my head. I made some notes, and watched the dawn come up someplace over Pittsburgh. It never occurred to me to wonder about Sturges, and I did not learn about his messages until he told me of them more than a year later. But I probably wouldn't have called him. Frankenheimer and Lewis were promising to do the film I wanted to do, and to pay me so much money, that I wouldn't have wanted to risk offending them.

The lavish promise technique is used all the time in Hollywood, and as many writers lose their virtue to it as starlets.

In a little under four weeks I wrote an 85 page detailed treatment of the movie Frankenheimer and I had worked out that day. Frankenheimer called several times, and I would outline what I had done, and he would cast the part in my ear. Mastroianni would play the Italian driver, and Sophia Loren his consort. Belmondo would be the French driver. DeSica would play the Ferrari-type owner, and the English personnel would be played by Sellers, O'Toole and Ustinov. Frankenheimer had no actor in mind for the American driver because he had counted on McQueen, whom he had now resolved to destroy, if he could.

Back in Connecticut I wrote. The days seemed glorious. With all those stars in it—Frankenheimer never got any of them, of course—I figured we would have a great movie and I was absolutely confident about my script, because we had talked it over all the way. Every scene was where he wanted it.

So I flew to California and sat at the bar of a restaurant with Phil Hill, while waiting for Frankenheimer to read the script and arrive for dinner. The European season was over, Hill was back home in California, and he had agreed to work as a technical adviser on Frankenheimer's film.

But he said now: "John Frankenheimer is the most unpredictable man I've ever met."

At dinner Evie Frankenheimer made a fourth. This was in a French restaurant in Santa Monica, and Frankenheimer talked only to Hill. After about an hour of this, it was clear he didn't like the script.

But no verdict was announced, so I went back home to await it. It never came. Frankenheimer neither phoned nor wrote; nor did Lewis.

At length the various options ran out. Several times I thought of phoning

Frankenheimer, not because I was in any doubt about his decision, but because I couldn't understand what had gone wrong. I never did call him. That first day beside his pool he had admitted modestly that he had been "combing people out of my ass since I was 23 years old." I didn't feel the need to phone and get combed.

Meanwhile I was being sued for breach of contract by John Sturges and Steve McQueen. This didn't worry me overmuch, and the suit was later dropped. But it worried me greatly to learn that McQueen was trying to find out where I lived. According to people who knew him, he was liable to do something drastic. Then at the top of his fame, McQueen was considered an eccentric even by Hollywood standards, and he had played in a lot of cowboy movies. I joked to friends that he might ride up on his motorcycle and let me have it with one of those sawed off rifles he used to use on TV. Twice my phone rang and some woman asked if this was the home of Robert Daley, the author of..." And she would name one of my books, but never *The Cruel Sport.* I would answer yes, and she would say thank you, and hang up.

I was concerned enough to talk to the lawyer who lived next door. What should my attitude be if confronted by an irate Steve McQueen?

The phone rang again. "Daley, my name's McQueen. You screwed me, Buddy. I won't forget it."

The voice paused long enough for me to feel a chill, then began to giggle, and I recognized who it was: my lawyer amusing himself at my expense. Ha ha.

There were no more phone calls after that, not from McQueen, and certainly not from Frankenheimer. It was the silence that crushed me. It could be said that my defeat was in no way personal, that I had merely got caught in a Hollywood power struggle, but if I realized this it was only dimly, and I was so ashamed at not having protected myself even a little, that it did not help. Several weeks went by during which I could not make myself work, and to pass the days I concentrated on dandelions. For hours at a time I would squat on my lawn rooting out dandelions one after the other, and brooding with great bitterness about Frankenheimer. Was this a stupid waste of energy? Yes. But I seemed unable to do anything else, and this was the second and final time in my career that I suffered from writer's block. Frankenheimer had paid me $15,500 for less than four weeks work. My first year as a freelance writer was therefore assured, which should have helped, but didn't. Nothing in any way helped.

Several months passed. It was now May, I was feeling better, and I wanted to go to the San Isidro bullfights in Madrid, and then to the Grand Prix de Monaco. Europe was my turf, and that year, and for several more years to come it was easy to get magazine assignments that would take me there.

At Monte Carlo, when I reached the pit area, I saw that Frankenheimer stood at one end of the row passing out tracts, while Sturges and McQueen watched him from the other.

Frankenheimer's tracts announced all the famous drivers and race circuits he had signed for his film, which would start shooting at this very circuit next year. The message he was trying to get across was that Sturges and McQueen, some of whose long ago planted publicity articles still called their movie *The Cruel Sport,* were soundly beaten. Not only had they lost their title, but they could not use Frankenheimer's drivers or circuits either.

During the three days of practice preceding the race Frankenheimer would not look either Sturges or McQueen in the eye, and when he happened to walk past me several times, he pretended I wasn't there either. Finally I went up to him and said, "John, good to see you again. How do you like your first race in Europe?"

He mumbled something, nodded, and hurried off the other way.

I decided to speak to Sturges but at first couldn't find him, and so asked a man in McQueen's entourage where he was.

"Who are you?"

I told him.

The man's eyes went wide. "Well," he said. "Well. Would you like to meet Steve McQueen?"

"No," I told him, "just Sturges."

Sturges and I watched most of the race together. "Frankenheimer seems to have this vendetta against us," he said as we moved from corner to corner. "I don't think he ever intended to use your script. His only purpose was to get you away from us."

If so, then Sturges had lost that battle, and most of the circuits and most of the drivers. But he seemed a decent, cordial man, and perhaps he would win the war. McQueen was not exactly following us, but was never far away. Each time I glanced in his direction I found him eyeing me. But he did not come in my direction and I did not go in his.

Frankenheimer and Sturges went back to California to work on their movies.

Suddenly Paramount Pictures dropped *Grand Prix*. Down the drain went Frankenheimer's $10 million backing. He still had no stars and no script. But he seemed to be a ferocious competitor, and he quickly lined up MGM for financing, though for only $7 million. And at length James Garner and Toshiro Mifune signed to do the film. Garner that year was only a mid-level star, and could not be counted on to sell great numbers of tickets even in America, but Mifune, in Japan, was a giant. He could carry the film there all by himself. The John Wayne of Japan, was the way Frankenheimer described him.

Sturges was being backed by Warner Bros., and by now had lined up

Stirling Moss, Jim Clark, John Surtees, Jackie Stewart and others—as impressive a list of drivers as Frankenheimer's, perhaps more so. Sturges had bought, and intended to use, a lot of the previous season's race cars; Frankenheimer had bought up old Formula 3 cars, and had had plastic shells constructed to make them exactly resemble the latest models; he would splice them into actual race footage.

This is supposed to have cost him $300,000. It and other such gestures, I read, had thrown him so far over budget that he had had to agree to work without salary. His pay would come out of profits from the film, if any.

More importantly, it precipitated another legal battle when the factory owners demanded stiff fees for the use of their names in the two films.

There was no case against Sturges who owned all his race cars outright, his lawyers pointed out. He could use them legally in the same way he could have used a Chevrolet or Cadillac. Frankenheimer, however, only owned models. The owners suit against him meant still more costs he hadn't counted on.

The following spring, anxious to get back to Europe still again, I got together new magazine assignments to pay my way, among them a *Sports Illustrated* profile of Jackie Stewart, who was the most promising of the new drivers; a wine story for *Esquire*; and a *Vogue* article on Frankenheimer's movie as it began shooting. I had accepted the *Vogue* assignment without telling them of my connection to the movie, of my possible conflict of interest. This was probably unethical of me. But I believed I could report and write some sort of neutral article. I would have to, if I hoped to have the magazine buy it. Neutral, in a magazine contest, meant pro-Frankenheimer and pro-movie. This was not the way I felt, but there was no way around it.

Frankenheimer reached Monte Carlo with a team of 200, and there staged a spectacular if improbable collision between Garner, playing a wise guy American driver, and the English actor, Brian Bedford, playing a dedicated Britisher with a high class accent.

Nominally the two men are teammates, but when Bedford tries to overtake his wise guy teammate, Garner will not move over, their wheels touch, and this precipitates Bedford's car into the cliff at high speed, and Garner's into the Mediterranean even faster.

I watched them make this scene. Dummy cars with dummy drivers were fired by a special effects expert via compressed air exploding out their tails. While seven cameras rolled, one car climbed the wall, and the other made a tremendous splash.

So far so good. Oozing gore, Bedford replaced the dummy in the wreck at the foot of the cliff, and Frankenheimer ran up with a blood bottle—a plastic, Ketchup type thing—and squeezed additional blood all over him, squeezed blood everywhere. Then with cameras grinding, and other race cars booming past—for the race, cinematically speaking was still on—some real Monaco firemen threw themselves on the wreck. With the actor "unconscious" they cut the car to pieces. Since this particular car was completely hollow inside it came apart rather too quickly.

Worse, the scene brought on still another lawsuit.

The car that had been shot into the cliff was BRM No. 12, a perfect replica of Jackie Stewart's car in the actual race. Furthermore, the actor "driving" it, Bedford, had been outfitted with a Scotch plaid helmet exactly like Stewart's. The driver professed to be irate that people would think he had ever crashed into a wall, and since Stewart was under contract not to Frankenheimer but to Sturges, here came Sturges' lawyers.

Although Frankenheimer had bought from the organizers legal rights to film the race, he had no legal right to splice in footage that seemed to show Stewart in a crash. "We'll just injunct him," Sturges told me, when I asked him about it later. He spoke with a combination of amusement and pride.

"He'll have to take the Stewart footage out. How could he have been so stupid as to try something like that?"

The scene following, which was to take place on the other side of the harbor, involved a lawsuit also.

While it was being set up, a company press agent confronted me. I would have to leave, he said.

"Why?"

"Frankenheimer doesn't want you around."

Since the scene was being shot on a public street with a crowd by bystanders of whom I was one, this command sounded preposterous. If I refused to leave, the press agent said, he would call the police and have me ejected.

I stormed over to Lewis.

"What's this about trying to run me off?"

"Who's trying to run you off?"

"Your press agent."

He was gazing off into the distance. "Speak to him about it, not me."

"You're in charge here."

"You've been up Frankenheimer ass all day."

These people, I thought irrelevantly, are very anal minded.

"Just try it, Eddie, just try it."

I stormed back to the harbor front but was no longer at ease. To be able to work in places like Monte Carlo, a movie company distributes a little money at the top but a great deal at the bottom to race officials, the police and such. If Frankenheimer objected to my presence in the crowd, he theoretically could do nothing about it. But if he owned the nearest cop—

If the cop then told me to leave, I would be obliged to defend the rights of any citizen to the public streets and those of a journalist to observe; obliged, that is, to refuse to move, and then I might find myself in a

Monaco jail.

Now I climbed on top of a concrete block where Frankenheimer would see me every time he turned around. I wanted to bug him of course. I was worried about what nearby cops might do, but I was furious too.

No cop ever came toward me. Perhaps Lewis had lost his nerve. Perhaps the police had obeyed one of the first rules of French law enforcement: never get mixed up in a quarrel between foreigners—a rule I knew about and had hopefully counted on.

The scene being set up was this one. Garner has been fished out of the harbor, and Bedford has been run across the road on a stretcher, and the two of them are loaded onto the same launch to be rushed across the harbor to an ambulance.

But as the camera rolled and the launch docked a committee of Monaco merchants bulled their way forward and ruined the scene. The head merchant, a man named Voorzanger, operator of a bar on the port, screamed that Frankenheimer had had the streets closed off for ten days, he was losing a fortune because patrons could not get through the roadblocks to his bar, and he and the other merchants had had enough, they wanted to be paid, or they would stop the film.

It took a while, but by promising payment, and credit in the film as well, Frankenheimer got the guy partially quieted down. But Voorzanger still would not get out from in front of the cameras.

During this dispute Garner had had to keep jumping into the water so as to stay soaked. Now he stuck his face to within inches of the suddenly frightened Frenchman. “I’m freezing my ass off,” he bellowed. “How much money do you want? I’ll pay you myself. Now get the hell out of here. Get going. You hear me?”

The Frenchman slunk into the crowd, but not before advising the surrounding extras to “wave at the camera, spoil the movie, they’re nothing but foreigners and they're ruining us small businessmen."

Before the extras could soak up this idea, Frankenheimer yelled "roll em," and the scene was played once again. But one of the actors had the misfortune to pass too close to Voorzanger who planted a tremendous kick in his buttocks which left him limping for two days.

When the scene ended I confronted Frankenheimer. "What's all this crap about trying to run me off?" I shouted. "Who the hell do you think you are?" He was a man who took any kind of politeness or decency as a sign of weakness, I had decided.

"It's not my fault," he said, "it was Eddie Lewis. Eddie said you were going to write an article blasting us. He said, why make it easy for him? I said, don't do it Eddie."

He turned on his charm, or tried to. It had never been his idea, he said. He was sorry. It was a misunderstanding. Before I could react he had his arm around me and was telling everyone within earshot that I was to be accorded all courtesy.

As I shrugged him off Lewis came over. "I see that you and John have made up."

I gave him a hard look. My hardest, in fact. Which didn't appear to faze him in the slightest.

"I was just trying to protect John," he said, and shrugged.

That afternoon Garner, who had the body of the professional baseball player he once thought to become, and perhaps a ballplayer's outlook on life as well, shot a 69 on the Monte Carlo golf course, while Bedford, the Shakespearean actor who had once played Hamlet, negotiated to purchase a Vlaminck for $9,000 dollars. Yves Montand went home to the Colombes d'Or at St. Paul de Vence, which was where he and his wife, Simone Signoret, lived when on the Riviera. And I went to see Voorzanger in his bar.

Negotiations with Lewis about payment to the merchants had dragged on and on until finally Lewis had offered only $360 a day, Voorzanger told me. This was completely unacceptable.

"But Garner's a nice fellow, don't you think?" I said.

"He's a total cheap skate. Comes into my bar every day for lunch but orders only coffee."

That evening I sat over drinks with the actors. Garner was there, Bedford, some of the supporting players. Montand stopped in, but did not stay long.

I told Garner that Voorzanger had called him a cheapskate who ordered only coffee for lunch.

"Everybody knows I never eat lunch," the actor said.

"Everybody?" I said.

"Every time I went in there he tried to show me his card tricks. I guess he didn't like it that I showed him a few of my own."

No one present thought Voorzanger would ever get paid anything at all. Lewis would stall and stall. Before the merchant could file a lawsuit or injunction, the company would be finished and out of town. That was the way the movies worked. Tough on the Voorzangers of the world, but, well—

"Europe is not for me," Garner remarked. "Even though I've spent three of the last four summers in Europe making movies."

"How many do you make a year, Jim?" asked Bedford.

About two and a half, Garner said. "Takes up about eight months. The other four months I devote to my business interests."

"What kind of businesses are you in?" asked Bedford.

"Oh," said Garner, who was then 38 years old, "I have some oil wells, some apartment houses, a chain of garages, an electronics company, I'm president of a bank."

The Shakespearean actor nodded. "I see," he said.

Though Garner had never attended car races in the past, he had followed them, he said: "When I read the sports pages, I read everything." He realized "*Grand Prix*" would be 90 percent cars, only 10 percent people. This was fine with him, and he thought he had improved the script in several places by inserting a number of wise guy remarks for himself to make. That is, he had changed the role into what was already his screen persona. His off screen persona did not seem to me much different. Often his remarks were amusing. His only complaint—and I got this from others, not him—took the form of a question. Where were all the international co-stars Frankenheimer had promised him. Where were Monica Vitti, Ingrid Bergman, and all the others?

Garner knew about the Steve McQueen film that was being planned, and in fact had had a letter from McQueen, who was still delayed in Hong Kong, where his current film, *The Sand Pebbles*, was sixteen weeks behind schedule. "You don't know what a job it is to get Steve to write a letter. When Steve writes you letter, you know things are going really wrong for him."

I invited Ken Purdy, author of Sturges' screenplay, to dinner in my hotel, the Voile d'Or in St. Jean Cap Ferrat. The hotel was splendid and new that year, and we sipped our wine, gazed down on the tiny harbor full of yachts, and Purdy talked of Frankenheimer's script, which nobody seemed to like. Some of his actors thought it absurd, Purdy said, as did Sturges, who had read a pirated edition months ago. But other people had seen the rushes, which were almost all of speeding race cars filling the screen from wall to wall, and the effect, in Cinerama, was three dimensional. Purdy, who was on his way to London to meet Sturges, was worried. "I'm going to tell him that it is absolutely essential we come out first. Frankenheimer is going to have the most visually spectacular footage on race cars ever shot."

But Sturges could not start shooting until McQueen reported for work—July 5 at the earliest. Frankenheimer would have six weeks head start.

The two movies had now been engaged in battle, legal and otherwise for eighteen months.

We all went on to Belgium, the second of the eight races that would appear in *Grand Prix*.

For three weeks Garner was lodged in a small hotel in Malmedy. There were only six rooms, for Garner, Montand, Toshiro Mifune and an Italian actor named Antonio Sabato; and also for the dialogue coach whose job it was to make the three foreigners speak comprehensible English. The final room was for Garner's stand in and gofer, a man named Louis Delgado: "I forgot my cigarettes, Louie, they're on my dresser upstairs. Run up and get them for me, will you?" Garner was distressed about having no one to talk to: "We come down in the morning and Montand says bonjour, Sabato says buongiorno, I say good morning, and Mifune says whatever you say in Japanese."

A setup like this, drivers and owners representing four nationalities and unable to talk to each other, was common in international car racing. It is a situation pregnant with unspoken tensions, and is potentially dramatic. But it is also subtle. There were no subtleties in the *Grand Prix* script, and no thought of putting any in there.

During the first three days in Belgium Frankenheimer shot the preliminary footage he would need, much of it of Garner who, driving a white Japanese car owned by the John Wayne of Japan, wins the race. Frankenheimer had of course made sure there was a white car entered. It wasn't Japanese but the movie would say it was, no one would know the difference, and it would secure him entree into the lucrative Japanese market. In the final practice session, however, the white car broke down and had to be scratched. Frantically Frankenheimer searched around for a driver and team willing to paint their car white, paid them off and got it done. His cameramen had orders to film this car every time it went by. He also ordered lots of footage of spectators during the race: people eating, sleeping, kissing.

“If it rains Sunday,” he told them, “we are dead.

On race day his cameras were positioned everywhere. One hung from a helicopter. Another was mounted on an obsolete race car to be driven by the now retired Phil Hill at the tail of the race.

Preliminary footage, which would be spliced into actual race footage, was already in the can. It had been shot in bright sunlight, all of it, and Sunday morning dawned sunny enough, so far so good, but as the hours passed the clouds darkened dramatically, and less than two minutes after the race started stupendous thunder drowned out the noise the cars were making, after which the clouds dropped their load upon the race.

This tremendous first lap cloudburst wrecked seven cars, four of them clouting each other. One of those wrecked was the white car. What about Hill’s camera car? If it crashed, if it hurt someone, there would be additional lawsuits, colossal ones. And, worse, no more camera cars.

Hill got through, though of course his footage was no good. In such torrential rain neither was the helicopter’s.

When the real race ended John Surtees, the actual winner, was quickly hustled off the victory balcony, and his place taken by Garner and the John Wayne of Japan. The actor, who had a bouquet around his neck, now plucked flowers out of it, as Surtees had so happily and spontaneously done a moment before, and flung them down on the crowd. I was in that crowd and heard a good many Belgians trying to decide what Garner’s name was. He was apparently not well known in Europe, even though in Hollywood he was offered, so he said, 200 scripts a year. But later in the parking lot I saw him surrounded by autograph hounds. They must have decided by then that he was indeed somebody. This was the first time I had seen him so besieged since the picture began, and he looked relieved and happy as he signed on and on.

I flew to London and that evening met Sturges for dinner in the Rib Room of the Carlton Towers.

"Frankenheimer may have caught the circus aspects of motor racing," he said. "The gypsy life, all those hanger-ons at Monte Carlo. That's a valid side of motor racing. It isn't the side that interests me, but it may interest some people. Maybe a lot of people."

Sturges began to describe his own picture, which would be full of the quiet scenes that put the violence of motor racing in perspective: two drivers lapping the deserted Nurburgring together at high-speed in the night; a driver who can't sleep before the race, getting out of bed, driving out to the circuit and walking the course alone in the moonlight.

This sounded like the type film I'd written for Frankenheimer.

"You went with the wrong film," said Sturges.

Maybe. The idea made me wistful. But I had become a bit wiser now. It was possible that working with Sturges would have been no better, or even worse. Who could say? He seemed a decent, reasonable man tonight, but he was from Hollywood too. Anyway, the controlling element would have been McQueen, not Sturges, and from what I had learned of McQueen he was not a man one could rely on.

"You mustn't blame Frankenheimer too much," Sturges said. "Your script just wasn't his type. He didn't understand it. If you're looking for a film for Marilyn Monroe, and someone turns in a script for Ingrid Bergman, you're not going to be too interested, are you?"

Sturges was in his early 50s, a big man, baldish. He had already made thirty-five or so movies, some of them exceptionally profitable. And behind him, I had been told, he had left principally friends.

Frankenheimer had left principally the opposite. "People who last in this business generally don't act that way," said Sturges. "There are exceptions. Perhaps Frankenheimer is an exception."

By this time we had had quite a lot to drink, and were growing fonder of each other by the minute. Sturges spoke of his messages to me at the Beverly Hills hotel eighteen months previously, and apologized for being obliged to "drop that little lawsuit on you." He had thought he had a confirmed deal, he said, and so had announced the purchase of *The Cruel Sport*. In doing so, he had not sought to preempt Frankenheimer, who at that time had announced only his title: *Grand Prix*. "If he had had anything more than that—stars, a story, people, we would not have gone ahead with plans on the same subject. But I don't see where the announcement of just a title should close out something as vast as motor racing. So we went ahead, and then we found ourselves in this feud."

Everything now depended on getting out first, he said. Frankenheimer's film was being shot entirely on location, was being edited as it went along, and it was, despite the vast costs, on schedule to this point. Frankenheimer planned to finish shooting with the Italian Grand Prix on September 4, and then to finish editing, to score, print and distribute his film all within three months, and to open it the world over by Christmas.

Sturges said: "I couldn't look any bright citizen in the eye and say it doesn't matter who gets out first."

Still, he seemed confident that night. He planned to start shooting July 5 at the Nurburgring, and he began naming the people who had read his script and approved, including some of the more literate of the drivers, and even Enzo Ferrari himself.

We had been drinking Irish coffee for the last two hours, and the restaurant was closing. We went outside into the London night, shook hands and wished each other luck.

Who would win the race to make the racing car movie?

The answer came four days later. Warner Bros. canceled Sturges' movie. McQueen was ill. He had been working flat out since the previous November, had hardly had a day off for months, and had lost 14 pounds. His doctor had diagnosed exhaustion, and had ordered a month's rest—and *The Sand Pebbles* was not even finished yet. When McQueen was able to work again, he would have to finish that first. There seemed no hope that he could report to Sturges earlier than September 10, and in October the rainy weather would settle down over northern Europe, and the filming of an outdoor movie such as this one would become difficult, perhaps impossible. Besides, by then there would be no hope of catching Frankenheimer.

Sturges maintained that he would make *Day of a Champion* the following year.

Maybe.

It all depended on what sort of reception *Grand Prix* got. A bad movie might kill the market. A good one likely would soak it up.

The race to make the racing car movie was over. The winner and champion, it seemed, was John Frankenheimer.

Grand Prix was finished and out by Christmas, as Frankenheimer had planned, a fantastic performance, logistically speaking.

The critics were not kind to it, said it had beautiful images, yes, but too many of them and no characters nor story, absolutely nothing else but beautiful motor racing shots, and enormous noise.

Grand Prix was the beginning of the end of Frankenheimer's big career. He never had another hit, often could not command A-list stars or float films he wanted to direct. He began to drink. Some years later in an interview with *The New York Times* he admitted to having made career mistakes, and that his drinking problem "took its toll on me. When you have a problem like that, even when you're not drunk, is the most dangerous time because you make choices not in your best interests." At one point he moved to Paris and went to cooking school; he stayed five years. He took over a movie called *The Island of Dr. Moreau*, which was already a shambles, after the original director got fired. The star was Marlon Brando, who gave one of the weirdest performances ever seen on film.

To get work Frankenheimer found himself back in TV, where he directed some films which, by TV standards, were hits, and he was commended. A few years ago he at last got offered a potentially big feature film. He was 68 years old. The new film starred Robert DeNiro, was called *Ronin*, and it took him to the Riviera once more. Much of it was filmed in Nice, where the streets were blocked off to let him work, and once again he was plagued by furious neighborhood merchants who wanted to be paid for the business they were losing, and whose demonstrations got in his way.

Ronin was not the success he had been hoping for either.

John Sturges never made a racing car movie.

McQueen did, but with someone else. Several years after *Grand Prix* he starred in and partially owned something called *LeMans*. Ticket buyers—there weren't many—were treated to race cars from beginning to end. There must have been dialogue in the original script, but in the finished movie there was almost none. Being a big enough star at that time to have all his whims indulged, McQueen had ordered it all removed, saying: "I can tell the story with my eyes." Only he couldn't.

In time I wrote a motor racing novel. It was called *The Fast One*, and when it came out it was immediately optioned. In fact it went through a number of options, meaning money in the bank for me each time. Though never the finished movie I hoped for.

My story was about people not cars, and it was written in such a way that if it ever became a movie—I was aware of this as I wrote it—it would be relatively inexpensive to produce.

The first producer to option it assigned me to write the first draft screen play. But he could not get financing and his option lapsed. He was later convicted of being a major drug importer, and sent to jail forever. A second producer bought a second option. His principal fame was that he had once run the mile under four minutes. He brought me to Hollywood and put me together with a director named Ralph Levy, who had won Emmys on TV. Levy was a lovely man who came to my hotel every morning and stayed until dark. In a week's time he gave me a crash course in screen writing. Day by day we tightened my script, and the 4-minute miler then ran to the studios with it. But he could not get financing either.

Frankenheimer and McQueen, I concluded, had so poisoned the water that no one was going to finance a film on grand prix motor racing any time soon, and to this day no one has.

For my work on the Hollywood version of *The Fast One* I was paid altogether $39,000. I still have the script.

Much later I ran into Garner in a television studio in London. He was there plugging a movie, and I was plugging a book. We were not scheduled on the same interview program, and in fact mine was ending as his was about to start. He could not possibly have known I was even in the building, but when he saw me his face lit up and he came forward with his arms outstretched saying: "Bob, we have to stop meeting like this, once every 17 years." Movie stars are used to being recognized, to having their names remembered, but authors are not. So to have Garner recognize me, and remember also how long ago we had met, was an astonishing experience. During the making of *Grand Prix* I had found him a bit cold, a bit pompous, and had not been drawn to him at all, but was now.

What a change the sound of ones own name will make to a man.

Garner made the host of his show put me on stage with him as an extra guest, which at the very least meant extra publicity for my book. When the show ended I signed a copy of it for him, and we chatted a minute, before going off, once again, in our separate directions.

10.
Tenors and Sopranos

January 25, 2001, Connecticut

I look out my office window and it is snowing again. Big flakes. Wet. Heavy. I peer at the landscape through a white scrim.

We got home here four days after Christmas and the snow started coming down. It fell until it covered the lawn thick as a suitcase, then thick as two suitcases, one on top of the other. I was out shoveling most of the next day, and the next as well. As much snow as that weighs tons. I dug paths until my shoulders ached and my hands felt frozen. Driveway. Front stoop and walk. Paths to the garbage can, the mail box. The path to my office. It snowed twice more during the next week, though less. Then came another big dump, eight inches. In Nice I play tennis most days. In Connecticut most days I shovel snow, or so it seems. What are we doing here? Why didn't we stay where we were? The answer is that this house represents the major investment in our lives. The real estate agents say it is worth $2 million—present worth, not what we paid for it. One doesn't own one's possessions, they own you, and we are afraid to leave our house empty all winter lest the heat go off and the pipes freeze. This happened one year. What a mess to come home to. What an expense.

My office, which is in a separate building in the garden, is one flight up. The building is one third the size of the main house, and is barn-shaped, the same shape and style as the main house which it much resembles. It sits atop high stone walls that date back a hundred years or so. I don't know what the walls served for originally. An ice house, maybe. When we moved here it was a storehouse in total disrepair. Stone walls and a falling-in, lean-to roof. I thought the walls could be made into an office. I told the builder I wanted a wood shingle roof of the same shape and proportions as the main house, with, under it, windows all around. Inside, I wanted wood paneled walls, wherever there were walls, and a wood paneled cathedral ceiling. The result is this big, bright airy place. The nicest office I have ever had, and the roomiest. Plenty of storage space downstairs within the walls. I put in a wine cellar down there too, and for a time kept much old wine, but I have been depleting it lately. Left are a few bottles of first growth Bordeaux from 1959 and 1961, but not much else.

We have two and a half acres, about half of it woods. In summer you can't see other houses. In winter—this winter, anyway—all is white. At the bottom of the lawn is the Silvermine River, with woods on the other side. The snow is too deep to go out there, but from here the river looks frozen. Below my office windows the pond is frozen and white, its surface liberally laced with deer tracks. I noticed four or five deer out in the road this morning. They were running up and down driveways, running up to the doors of houses. They looked frantic and cold. There are too many of them. In summer they eat our flowers and bushes, but they have nothing to eat now.

I am a freelance writer, so as I sit watching the falling snow, I am alone. Hemingway was a freelance writer, and Shakespeare, and a good many others. In most of the ways that count, we are all the same. We do what we do alone. A writer, writing, is always alone. Even in a crowded newsroom in the old days with typewriters clacking on all sides, phones ringing, I was closed off inside my head and alone, and so were all my colleagues. The ability to pull a curtain down around our ears and eyes is all that ever made reporters—not to mention newspapers themselves—possible. The ability to do it on a grand scale day after day for months at a time is all that makes novelists and novel writing possible.

Even when not writing a writer tends, when tending to his profession, to go through life alone. I have had agents, editors also, who sometimes gave me the illusion that I was not alone, or not entirely alone. But the interests of these people are not always the writer's interests, their agendas and the writer's sometimes conflict, and the illusion does not last. I have had agents from the age of 28. And more editors than I can count—my twenty-six previous books were published in hard cover by fifteen different houses. I grew up planning to become Hemingway or Fitzgerald, to become as famous as they became, and have a single publisher my whole career long, as they did. But one by one I got over such notions, fame first. Fame strikes some and not others, much like lightning. And the Hemingway/Fitzgerald type fame is even rarer than lightning. It is not something that can be controlled, nor even earned.

And while it might have been nice to stay always with a single publisher, this cannot be controlled either. Some of my past publishers went out of business. Others were not interested in the type book I wanted to write next. One or two I got mad at because of the way they handled a certain book, and my next book I took elsewhere. Sometimes the editor I had been dealing with moved on to a new house, and I moved with him. More often they got fired. Editors, I have found, are frequently not there when needed. My last four book editors have been fired, my favorite editor in England as well. When this happens in the middle of a book that you are writing under contract, you and the book get assigned to some other editor, but in the end the book comes out with no one's prestige attached to it except yours, and no one in the house pushes it forward. Your sales, inevitably, are less than you hoped, and no one gets blamed but you.

The snow falls past my windows into the vast whiteness. Outside there is a silence one can almost see.

I had written a novel about foreign correspondents in Paris, and another about a pro football team much resembling the Giants. In *The Whole Truth*, I tried to write Paris and the newspaper into the book with as much intensity as if they were characters themselves, and in *Only a Game* I tried to do the same with the football background, to make it as intense a force as any of the players in the story. The idea was to make readers know what it felt like to live in Paris as a foreign correspondent, what it felt like to take all that punishment as a football player. I meant for the readers to live the experiences of the characters, to suck them in so deeply they would not want to get out, would reach the final page with regret.

But one of the results of this method, it seemed to me, was to use up my six years with *The New York Times* completely, and my six years with the Giants completely. I held back nothing for future use—all the knowledge and emotion I had acquired during those years gone—there was nothing left except a few extraneous pieces that hadn't fit anywhere. I worried about this. Twelve years of my life used up. Where were future novels to come from?

Because neither book had earned the equivalent of a year's pay, I had had to write a good many magazine articles on the side. I would take a week or two off from the novel and report and write them, then go back to the novel. I wrote for *The Saturday Evening Post*, *Life*, *Vogue*, *Esquire*, *Playboy*, *The Reader's Digest*, *The New York Times Magazine*. Some of these magazines paid $2000 an article, some much less. To keep switching focus required new energy each time. One's energy level had to be kept high. To keep mine high I sought and/or accepted assignments mostly on people and subjects that fascinated me, on which I wished to know more.

One Saturday we went to a matinee of La Boheme at the City Opera, and the young tenor, whose name we had not heard before, enthralled us. The whole performance did, but the tenor seemed exceptional. By the end he had me in tears. My wife was elbowing me in the side saying: "Stop that, you're making a spectacle of yourself, and of me."

According to the program the tenor's name was Michele Molese, and outside the theater afterward I spied a man carrying a violin case, assumed he was an orchestra member, and asked about the tenor.

"He's good, isn't he?" the violinist said. "He's an American. His name is Michael Mott."

Peggy and I sat down in a cafe opposite Lincoln Center, ordered tea, and presently here came Molese/Mott crossing the street toward us. He was carrying a satchel that contained sweat soaked underwear and his makeup kit, we would learn later. Singing an opera is at least as much physical exertion as playing a basketball game, we would also learn later. He was bareheaded, his hair damp and freshly combed, wore a topcoat, and walked beside a woman to whom he was talking earnestly. They stepped onto the sidewalk, and continued on.

I've got to meet that guy, I told myself. I want to write about him. I want to write about tenors.

At this point in my life I owned a number of complete opera recordings featuring Giuseppe DiStefano, whom I had heard in person only once. I loved the sound he made. I had been to the Met a few times. I had seen a single opera in Milan—I was there for the Italian Grand Prix at the time—and several in Nice where I once heard the tenor crack the high note at the end of the Flower Song in Carmen. He stopped the orchestra, sang the entire aria again, and this time hit the note squarely and brought down the house. Well, in the smaller theaters of Europe a star singer can do that kind of thing. One year Mario Del Monaco came to Nice to sing Otello. The day the posters went up I rushed to buy tickets but was too late. The best I could get was in the second tier, separate seats twenty boxes apart. At each intermission we hurried out into the corridor to discuss what we had heard. In Paris, after we had moved there, Del Monaco was announced to sing Otello, and I bought tickets, but he cancelled, and the role was taken by a young American named James McCracken. Each intermission, and there were three of them, lasted almost an hour, for the stagehands had some trouble changing sets. The last act started well after midnight but we stuck it out, McCracken was that good.

Three days after hearing Molese sing La Boheme I sat in an office at Life Magazine, and pitched my proposed article to two editors, one of whom was formerly an editor at Sport Magazine. I pitched it like a sporting event. Tenors could sing only every fourth day, just as a pitcher could pitch only every fourth day, I said. In between they had to rest their voices to the point where some wouldn't talk at all the day of a performance, and some couldn't talk the day after. Tenors made enormous amounts of money. They were the stars of nearly every opera, and had the most beautiful songs to sing. They were on stage two thirds of the time, and singing most of that, and if you sat closely you could see that they were dripping with sweat. The high notes were like the bar in a high jump. They had to get up and over, and sometimes missed. But if they made it, the sound could lift you out of your seat like a game winning home run.

The two editors were beaming, and I saw I had to be careful not to oversell this thing. A few more sentences and I would have the assignment.

Tenors came up through the minors just like ballplayers, I said. The Metropolitan Opera, LaScala, Covent Garden and Vienna were the big leagues. I mentioned Molese, who was young and new. I would focus on Molese, who had made it to New York, but not yet to the Met, and—

The editors were nodding with pleasure, so I stopped there.

I could not have gone on much further anyway, for that was all I knew about opera and tenors at that time. But few people in America knew much more. The two editors certainly didn't. There had been no televised operas as yet. The career of Pavarotti, who was to popularize opera and the tenor sound in the mass market almost all by himself all over the world, had barely begun. Placido Domingo's career was underway, and he had even made it up from Mexico to New York—he was the No. 2 tenor behind Molese at the City Opera. I didn't bring Domingo's name up now because no one had ever heard of him, including me.

The editors told me to go ahead with my article on tenors, focused on Molese.

So I made contact with the tenor. In New York we walked through the streets talking, and at one point he walked me into a record store, for his recording of Stravinsky's Persephone, with the composer conducting, had just been released and he wanted to buy it for me.

"Let the magazine pay for it," I said, withdrawing money from my billfold.

He asked the clerk to give us his artist's discount for this purchase the magazine was about to make, but the man refused him.

Already I judged Molese a strange young man. But then I didn't know any other singers yet.

I began to learn about them. Not only does the tenor play the hero-lover on stage but he often gets hero-lover adulation offstage. Sometimes he comes to have a hero-lover personality. This gets other singers so angry that a dozen new tenor jokes circulate around opera houses each season. They usually concern the tenor's fear of colds, his preference for singing instead of sex, or the popular notion that the vibration from high notes damages a tenor's brain.

I followed Molese to Tanglewood where he was to sing Verdi's Requiem with the Boston Symphony. I watched the rehearsal, watched the performance, Peggy and I both did, and in fact we spent most of the weekend with him, including a number of restaurant meals. During this time I learned as much as I was ever to learn about his background which, even though he was to become one of our closest and dearest friends, would remain murky to the end. He was New York born, went to high school at Mount St. Michael in the Bronx, was in the Navy at the end of the war, then went to Milan to try to become a singer. His father may or may not have been a ship captain. At Tanglewood I met the elderly woman to whom he was devoted, and who he always introduced as his mother. She attended all his performances, I was to learn, but in fact she was his aunt, and apparently it was she who had raised him. He carried a locket containing the faded photo of a young woman whom he said was his real mother, but it was years before he showed it to me. It was true that his name was Michael Mott. Many people called him Michael; everyone called him Molese. His passport read MICHAEL MOTT MICHELE MOLESE, no hyphens or parentheses, no AKA. There may have been Moleses in his family; it may have been his mother's maiden name. He certainly did not look Italian, for he had a fair complexion and fair hair, which he sometimes dyed so the color would show to advantage on stage, a job he did himself but was not very good at, for the dye job sometimes came out orange.

In Milan he studied and auditioned for years with no result. He was penniless. He haunted the Galleria, accosting every agent and impresario he saw, begging them to come up to his room and listen to him sing. He waited in anterooms to audition. "There were always a lot of young singers," he said. "They generated a terrific nervous atmosphere. There was such an electricity that even if you were the strongest man in the world you got nervous." At dinnertime he would go into a cafeteria, fill a bowl with hot water and, when no one was looking, pour in half a bottle of ketchup, which made tomato soup. Once he won a contest in the Teatro Nuovo over 99 competing tenors. This too seemed to lead nowhere.

I had gone into this assignment believing that a tenor, starting out, had it easier than other artists, writers for instance. He needed only to boom out an aria, clinch it with ringing top notes at the end, and all would rush to sign him up. But it hadn't been so for Molese, nor, I would discover, for most of the other singers I was to meet. People able to recognize talent are in short supply, it seems. Are almost as rare, perhaps, as talent itself.

At last Molese began to get jobs with small Italian companies traveling abroad. He worked his way back to New York via Dubrovnik and Tunis, and then Barcelona and Paris. Like all young tenors he was obliged to take risks, such as last minute substitutions for ailing tenors in operas he didn't really know and hadn't rehearsed. He once went on stage in Marseille in *Lakmé* with pages of the score wrapped like crib sheets around his swagger stick. During arias by others he could perhaps bone up on his own music to come. He got through that test, and all others, and here he was, the No. 1 tenor in the No. 2 company in New York.

While at Tanglewood I also interviewed Erich Leinsdorf, who had conducted the Requiem. "Dealing with tenors is life at its worst," he said. He did not think much of any tenor, it seemed. "The tenor's appeal is not musical, it's sexual," he said. "The best tenors have a quality, a timbre, that's essentially a sexual stimulant. That's why they're so rare. That's why they're so highly paid. They used to say that when Richard Tauber sang in Vienna there wasn't a dry seat in the house."

I interviewed Rudolf Bing, general manager of the Met, a cold, autocratic man feared by everyone in opera who had to deal with him. "The tenor voice is a disease of the larynx," he said. "The tenor with a secure top exerts a sexual fascination on the public—not just women, men too." I asked him about hiring young tenors, but he hired only established stars. "I'm not a collector," he said, "I'm not interested in virgins." And he dismissed me.

I was on to something here, or thought I was. At the same time I had begun to fear that an article focused only on Molese, might be rejected as too narrow. He was not a very big star as yet. In America no tenor was. Being a general interest magazine, *Life*'s audience knew nothing about tenors, and was not panting for an article on the subject. I would be paid $1250 for this article if accepted, but the kill fee, if it were rejected, was only $400. A fairly standard arrangement for freelance writers. Later on I was sometimes able to negotiate guaranteed fees, not then. I could not afford to write for kill fees, and I did not want to lose *Life* as a potential market.

So without informing the editors I decided to broaden my focus. I would write about several tenors, not Molese alone. So who else was in town? Well, there was Richard Tucker, who lived in Brooklyn, always had. And Franco Corelli, who was 6 feet 2, good looking, with good legs; in Italy he was known as "Golden Thighs." Corelli was as close to a male superstar as opera had at that time. And there was James McCracken, who had impressed us so when we heard him in Paris,

McCracken was on tour with the Met, but the tour had reached Rhode Island and he offered to stop at my house on the way back to New York. This was intimidating, but I agreed, and invited him to lunch.

He was a burly, florid faced man, and as I watched him get out of his car and approach our front door, he seemed rounder and shorter than I remembered—most singers, I was to learn, wore elevator shoes on stage, for the operatic stage is enormous. He weighed about 250 pounds as he sat at my table, and had an immense chest, which was where all that sound came from. Although only 40 years old, he had prematurely white hair.

During lunch, in response to my questions, he described his own struggle to break through. He was from Gary, Indiana, the son of a fire chief. He had sung bit parts at the Met for four years. Rudolf Bing, who did not hire virgins, would give him nothing better, so he quit and went to Europe with his wife, Sandra Warfield, a mezzo soprano, who soon got pregnant. They had very little money, and soon almost none. In Bonn they lived in a converted chicken coop. In Milan after the baby was born they lived in an apartment with the mattress on the floor and fruit crates for furniture. McCracken too auditioned for every impresario, every conductor who came by—his story was not much different from Molese's. For two years and two months no one hired him.

He could laugh about it now that he had contracts extending four years into the future: "There were an awful lot of tin ears out there."

My mother in law, who spoke no English, was living with us that year, and after lunch she came into the dining room and I introduced her.

"I don't speak French," said McCracken, "but I can sing it." And he reared back and let go with the opening phrases of *Samson et Dalila*. My dining room measured 13 feet by 11, and I thought the walls were going to burst. The voice of a soprano might crack crystal, but the voice of a great tenor is more likely to blast the picture window out into the garden. An embarrassed grin on my face, my ears ringing, I thought: "This is absurd, this is glorious, this is something only a tenor would do."

It was the first time I had ever stood beside a tenor singing, and later I compared it to the first time I ever stood on the field and heard two pro football teams crash together. I had had no idea it was done with such power.

One morning I went to the Met for a rehearsal of *Romeo and Juliet*. A dozen of us watched from the darkness: technicians, myself, a cleaning woman in a balcony who pretended to polish a balustrade. On stage the lovers, Corelli and Mirella Freni, were the only players in costume, and also the only ones not singing. Capulets and Montagues skulked about in street clothes, swords stuck in their belts. They sang their hearts out while Romeo and Juliet, protecting million dollar voices, spoke or silently mouthed whole arias.

And then Corelli unexpectedly sang a phrase. His voice soared out over the orchestra, over the chorus. It was as if amplifiers had been cut in—there are no amplifiers in opera. Corelli sang on, and so risked injuring his voice, just as an athlete who hasn't warmed up risks tearing a muscle. But it was as if he had to prove to those few of us out front who Franco Corelli was.

In the balcony the cleaning woman had ceased pretending to polish anything. She stood, mouth agape, listening to that great dark voice.

I listened suffused with joy. Surely no man ever lived who sang better than this.

When I came out, I went across to the City Opera where, in a small boxlike room, Molese was rehearsing for opening night. He stood with tie loose and jacket off in front of a score on a stand, and the pianist began. When the tenor's voice came in, it sounded, in that tiny, acoustically perfect room, like a radio with the volume turned up to the top. He sang one phrase, several, then flubbed the next, and said: "Oh, shit."

He started again. His voice rebounded off walls and ceilings. It filled every corner of that room, and my whole being too. Then I saw, rather than heard, Molese stop again, for his voice was so big it filled the room a moment longer.

"Oh, shit," he said.

Having missed another note, he stood there disgusted with himself but I remained enthralled. Surely no man in the world could sing better than this.

I sat in Corelli's apartment sipping Cinzano, and when I asked if he ever went to hear other tenors sing, the tall handsome tenor said no, adding with a grin: "I might lose my love for the lyric art." But his grin faded. He couldn't bear to listen to other tenors because he suffered too much for them, he said. Knowing how difficult a line was to hold, he began to feel sympathy spasms in his own throat and diaphragm. To go through that ten times in a night for someone else was more than he could bear.

Corelli too spoke of how hard it had been for him when he started out. Particularly he remembered his debut at La Scala. "I sing very bad that night, very bad." He was so bad that the conductor stopped conducting. "Just when I need him most, he put his face down in the score and leave me to finish alone." There was no applause, not a sound, and when the curtain fell no curtain calls, not one. All night Corelli could not sleep. Next day he went to La Scala to cancel all remaining contracts. This was refused. Since then he had had innumerable triumphs, but none had ever erased the memory of that debut. When I asked him what had been the high point of his career so far he couldn't think of one. "Perhaps one will come," he said.

I had arrived feeling somewhat afraid of him, for I had been told how temperamental he was. That he could and did hold high notes an unearthly long time I knew, for I had heard him do it. That his fans timed his high notes on stop watches, I had heard but did not believe. That conductors could do nothing with him, I did believe, for it was the talk of the opera world; he sang the music his way, not theirs. It was also accepted lore that he had once bit Birgit Nilsson on the neck because she was singing louder than he was, and holding her high notes longer. In Italy he was known to have leaped into a box to pummel a spectator who was applauding the soprano too enthusiastically. In New York one night he stood outside his dressing room in his underwear screaming at Renata Tebaldi. Another night, upstaged by a basso, he went at the man in earnest with a prop sword.

Was all this temperament, or nerves?

That night at least he had been a courtly and courteous host, and rather charming as well. When it came time to go he walked me all the way down the hall to the elevator and waited there until the doors closed.

In later years, when I had come to know him better, I would learn that Corelli was terrified every time he had to go on stage. At least once, standing in the wings with him, his wife had had to slap his face to make him do it. "Every tenor prays before a performance," Richard Tucker told me. "Because we open our mouths and sometimes what comes out is unforeseen."

Tucker was the next tenor I met, and this comment surprised me, for he had also been quoted saying about himself: "It's an awesome responsibility being the greatest tenor in the world." I met him for lunch at a new restaurant across the street from the Met. The manager rushed over to greet his illustrious client, and Tucker said: "Are you going to be open after performances? Good. I'll send you lots of people."

The manager beamed, and in a moment sent over a bottle of champagne. It is nice having lunch with people like Richard Tucker.

Most tenors tried to limit their performances to fifty a year. Tucker tried for seventy. He exercised strenuously every day and "my wife makes me rest. I'm married 31 years. We don't socialize more than three or four times a year, even though I love people—as people know. I still see my childhood friends. Only selfish people cut off their old friends.

"I'm not a prima donna. My makeup doesn't let me. Over the years I've grown and changed as an artist, not as a man. That's why I love and am loved by my colleagues."

I told him how much my wife and I had admired his *Aida* recording.

"Do you have my *Forza del Destino* recording?"

"Er, no."

"Do you have my Bel Canto record?"

"Er, no.'

"I can see you're not a Tucker fan."

"It's not that. It's just that I bought all the Scala recordings of operas, and you were only on one of them."

"Because you thought Scala was the best company, right. It's maybe third best. Give me your address and I'll have the records sent to you. I get them wholesale."

It was opening night at the City Opera and I stood in Molese's dressing room. His dresser, Jack, buttoned his knee length gold boots, while the tenor patted nervously at his makeup. He looked no more anxious to go out in front of the mob than a bullfighter did.

He began to complain about his makeup, about his throat which felt scratchy—he was awake half of last night. Suddenly he said to himself: "Any more complaints, Molese? Then shut up. You're doing exactly what you want to do." He paused, then said in a small voice: "The only thing is, tonight I don't want to do it."

He stuffed paper towels under the arms of his green brocaded jacket to soak up the sweat that was to come. The loudspeaker called: "Five minutes to curtain, everybody, five minutes."

Molese licked dry lips.

I watched him board the elevator which would take him down to the stage. He was alone and scared and I was awed by him.

The article duly appeared and all four of the featured tenors professed to be delighted with it. This is rare, ask any writer. It had never happened to me before, nor since either. In every profile I ever wrote the subject always objected to something, either a real or imagined error of fact, however inconsequential or, more often, to the way I had portrayed them in one section of the piece, if not all of it. No one ever likes to know the way others see him, apparently, not even performers who need the publicity to get contracts. Certainly I learned never to show subjects anything in advance.

But in this instance I picked up the phone and it was Richard Tucker. "I want to thank you for the article you wrote about me," he said. He invited us to an affair which we were unable to attend. He sent some more records. After that we would get postcards from him from various parts of the world. One came from Milan where finally, after a 30 year career, he sang at La Scala—Americans were rarely invited to La Scala. "Having a grand personal triumph here," he wrote, "warmest regards."

But with the other three tenors something much deeper developed, and I was pleased of course, even grateful, but also I could not have been more surprised. Close friendships with people I had written about simply had not happened previously.

McCracken invited us to Miami, where he was singing, all expenses paid. I couldn't permit that, but a few weeks later he invited us to Hartford, where he was singing *Otello*, and we did accept and drove up. In his fourth floor dressing room after the performance he looked drained, and I offered to carry his suitcase down four flights for him and did so. There was nothing in it but his costumes but they were soaking wet and weighed a ton.

Molese, who was singing in Italy when the magazine came out, sent a Christmas pannetone air express. All right, we could accept that. No way to send it back anyway.

We formed the habit of going out to dinner with the Corellis after performances. One night Loretta Corelli was wearing prominent dangling earrings, costume jewelry but very pretty, and Peggy told her so. With that the tenor's wife whipped the earrings off and handed them across the table because, according to her, they matched Peggy's dress better than her own. This threw into play all of the strictures of journalistic ethics. To accept gifts from sources was not permitted. But by now the Corellis were friends, weren't they? It felt like they were, but suddenly I wasn't sure they were friends enough. It was all so recent.

An ethical judgment had to be made about these earrings, but I didn't know what it should be nor, in case the decision should be to refuse them, how to do it politely. One could get a headache trying to think through questions like this. It was too much for me. Let Peggy cope with it, I thought, and I watched her try. She protested, she expostulated. The two women kept pushing the earrings back and forth. Finally Loretta reached over and fixed them to Peggy's ears. Much abashed, Peggy said thank you, and that was that.

Another strong memory of Corelli during this period is of riding in a taxicab with him at night through the city after a performance. We had just come from the Met which holds 3,800 people, and whose tiers of balconies go six stories high. Corelli had just filled this enormous space with sound, and he had to do it by singing out over a hundred piece orchestra, and a chorus of a hundred voices as well.

Now I was conscious of this potential sound sitting silent beside me. It was winter, the cab was buttoned up tight. What would happen if Corelli let that sound out now in that small enclosed space? Would the doors burst open from the force of it? I looked at him the way you would look at a man you knew to be concealing a lethal weapon. It was as if his voice could be used as a destructive force.

We rode on silently.

There was an uncommon generosity to tenors, I found. It was as spontaneous as it was sometimes disproportionate. However tense and temperamental around the opera house, away from it, in restaurants, taxis, wherever, they always wanted to pay. You had to fight them. You had to fight hard. In addition they always wanted to give presents.

These were men who were almost always lonely, it seemed to me—lonely even on stage with all those musicians in front and all those chorus voices behind, not to mention up to 3,800 spectators. Yes, they got tremendous adulation, but as you got close you saw that it didn't mean as much to them as you, and perhaps they, had imagined. As they perhaps had hoped. They seemed men who were not very sure of themselves, men in the grip of a basic insecurity that nothing seemed able to assuage.

We went to hear McCracken in *Aida* once. We didn't know him well yet, but afterwards we went out with him and Sandra, and he got more and more silent until finally he said: "You haven't told me you liked my performance." Another time in a cab Corelli began listing all the recordings he had made, and the contracts he had signed for additional ones. Why? He didn't have to tell me he was Franco Corelli, I knew that already. Then Loretta contributed the news that Franco was now a "millionario." She was wearing a mink down to the ground, so I knew that in advance too.

There were always crowds outside their dressing rooms, friends of theirs, friends of management, friends of friends. They would stand in the doorway dripping sweat, looking exhausted, but shaking hands, smiling. At the stage door on the way out a second mob always waited. These were people you saw night after night, the same faces night after night, opera goers every night apparently, standees perhaps, thrusting autograph books forward, wanting to touch their heroes, waiting at the stage door every night. But many of them seemed to the singers creepy, and they would get through them as quickly as possible. They would smile, sign a few autographs, and keep going.

Corelli and McCracken at least were married. Molese was alone. He lived in hotel rooms. Corelli, McCracken—Richard Tucker too—

apparently didn't like other singers very much. They seemed unable to get out of theaters fast enough once the singing was done, and I never knew them to socialize with colleagues. Whereas Molese's life was the theater, he surrounded himself with other singers, and when we would go out to dinner with him after performances he would almost always bring along the soprano with whom he had just shared the stage, and sometimes other singers as well.

With too few loved ones to tell him how well he had sung, and nobody when he was on the road, he latched onto us. As soon as we got to know him well he wanted us with him wherever and whenever he sang, which was impossible. He wanted us in Turin where he sang a series of *Turandots*, and in Dublin because he was singing *Werther*, which he considered one of his best roles. We told him we couldn't: we have children, Michael, we can't. This seemed to me a reasonable response, but his feelings were hurt and we had to work hard making it up to him.

We did follow him to a number of places, usually because I was able to get a magazine assignment in the neighborhood. In New Orleans where he was to sing *Lucia di Lammermoor* opposite Joan Sutherland, I interviewed Sutherland in her hotel room for an article on sopranos.

Molese had sat in on the interview.

"She was much taken by you," he said afterwards. "Did you notice? I've never seen her like that before."

"What?"

"It's true."

No, I hadn't noticed, I was working. I didn't believe it was true anyway.

They sang the performance together, and during the love duet, when he was facing the audience singing and she was facing him supposedly listening to his avowals of eternal love, he heard her say: "Don't sing so loud."

How to cut the you-know-whats off a tenor.

Once in Nice I stood in Molese's dressing room when the man came in with the money, cash in a paper parcel. This is the way it is done in Europe. The singers are paid in bank notes, great sheaves of them, and usually this takes place after the second act, or else the third act doesn't go on. So the only difference here was that the performance was over. Molese was sweaty, his makeup leaking. He was giddy as well, almost drunk with pleasure and relief, and he told me to take the money, count it for him, and put it in my pocket while he dried himself off and changed—no showers in the Nice opera house.

In Montreal he sang *Carmen* one winter, and we decided to drive up there to hear him, all five of us. We moved about the world a good deal at this time, often all of us together, but we were among the last in Greenwich to upgrade from black and white to color TV, and we had only one car, a Renault convertible with its little, very little, back seat—I have been hearing about the black and white TV and the tiny car ever since.

We started north, all of us crammed in tight, and a blizzard came down on us. At fifteen Theresa was already five feet seven inches tall, with hair three feet long, Suzanne almost as tall, they were wearing thick winter coats, and they fought all the way, even after Peggy took eight year old Leslie onto her lap to try to give them more room.

"Ow! She's sitting on my hair."

"Make her get off my hair."

I had an assignment for a piece on Fort Ticonderoga which is about halfway there, and this would pay our expenses, but I wondered if we would get even that far, for the snow was coming down hard and I could barely see.

At Ticonderoga we stepped out into biting wind and deep drifts, the others complaining that they had on the wrong shoes. We spent two hours there, and I did my interviews and collected the material I needed, and we drove on, past cars imbedded in snow banks, cars nose down in the ditch, the snow still falling thickly, the kids in the back still fighting, me unable to see, forced to drive ever more slowly.

In Montreal the next day the sun was shining. The sidewalks lay in trenches, with six foot snow banks to either side. We were walking toward the theater with Molese when little Leslie, who was a great tease, grabbed the tenor's gloves and ran off and rammed them into a wall of snow. We dug around for twenty minutes and never found them.

In Spoleto, Molese sang in an opera called *Il Giuramento*, by Mercadante, which hadn't been done in a hundred years, and between performances we drove to Assisi where a nun refused to let Peggy enter the basilica because she was wearing a short sleeved dress. While I ranted at the nun, Molese went into a store and bought her a kerchief to drape over her shoulders. The nun wouldn't let us in anyway.

In Toulon for *Faust* the sole rehearsal was the night before, a walk-through supposedly, for a singer is never supposed to sing so close to a performance. But the conductor didn't know the opera, hadn't studied it at all, apparently, and Molese got so angry that he began singing full voiced. There were only three or four of us out in the darkness, and he sang his entire part.

The next day he sang the performance, no problem. He seemed never to have vocal difficulties. At the City Opera he was the workhorse of the company. He sang nearly all the new productions, nearly all the opening nights, of which there were two each year, for the company had spring and fall seasons. Sometimes he sang seven or eight different operas a season, Puccini and Verdi mostly. He even sang Mozart, though his sound was Italian, and his voice, technically speaking, was much too big. His principal partner was Beverly Sills, and the No. 2 tenor, Placido Domingo, was still far back in his shadow.

One year the five of us went to Nice to spend Christmas with Peggy's family. Corelli was scheduled to sing *Tosca* there, and we knew this. Unfortunately Molese was already on hand, singing a series of *Fausts*.

We wanted to see them both, but this had to be concealed one from the other, which was not easy because we had no apartment in Nice as yet, and we and Molese were staying in the same hotel. Compounding the problem it was Christmas. Finally we had two Christmas dinners, one at midday with Molese and the kids, cooked by Peggy at her mother's apartment, one in the evening with the Corellis and their little dog, whose name was Pipi, in a restaurant.

Now came another problem. Molese was about to go out to the provinces to repeat the same opera with the same cast in a number of cities, and he wanted us to go off with him, at least as far as the first stop. We told him we couldn't.

"You want to stay in Nice to hear Corelli, don't you? Don't you?"

Terribly hurt, he turned away from us and went on to the next town alone.

Of course we wanted to hear Corelli. How would he sound in a theater so much smaller than the Met?

We almost did not hear him at all.

He had never sung in Nice before. For this performance prices had been nearly doubled, people had come from Paris and many other places. Every seat was full, but curtain time came and went and nothing happened. By the time thirty minutes had passed there was a great stir in the audience. What had gone wrong?

Although Corelli had been in Nice in advance of the performance he had refused to rehearse. He was big enough to get away with something like this, if he wished. But the result, as the orchestra waited in the pit, and the other singers waited on stage, was that Corelli, never having seen this stage before, or met the conductor or any of his co-singers, was gripped solid by terror. He would not leave his dressing room, and when the distraught impresario tried to reason with him, he would not make eye contact and only kept shaking his head.

About 45 minutes late the curtain finally rose. The pleadings and threats of the impresario, aided by Loretta Corelli, had finally prevailed.

The music started and Corelli sang. He sounded as he always did, better in fact, for the Nice house was a third the size of the Met, and when the first act curtain fell, the applause was tumultuous.

The intermission ended, and we all returned to our seats. Time passed, lots of time, the audience fidgeted and coughed, but Act Two did not start. Backstage the same charade was being played out a second time. Corelli did not even have much to do in Act Two, which was mostly the soprano's act. A few phrases ending in high notes, and Act Two, for the tenor, was finished. But in his dressing room he had removed his costume, packed his bag and was going home. The impresario cajoled, threatened, praised. Corelli was in great voice, he told him, had knocked them dead in the first act, what was he worried about? Everybody else told him how great he had been also—the conductor, his wife, everyone.

Finally an announcement was made in front of the curtain. Signor Corelli was not well, but had agreed to continue anyway, and he begged the audience's indulgence.

Act Two then went off normally, as did Act Three. The opera was over. I brought my car around to the stage door and went up to get Corelli. Now he did not want to leave the theater. I think he was afraid to show his face outside. I told him there was hardly anyone waiting at the stage door, and finally he followed me out to the car. In the restaurant he said scarcely a word, nor did he eat. He had the dog Pipi under the table, and presently he said the dog needed to be walked, he would go back to the hotel on foot. Watching him leave the restaurant Loretta snarled: "I have had just about enough of Signor Franco Corelli."

The next day they went home to Italy.

By then I had something else on my mind—Molese. We had somehow become his family, he depended on us like family, and I was worried about what he would see as our defection. How hurt was he? And so I sent him a telegram. He was then in Avignon, and the telegram read: "Sing well, come back happy, he is not in your class."

Fine. It made Molese, I learned later, very happy, so happy that he happily showed the telegram to everyone in the cast. I didn't want to hurt Corelli either, opera people do talk to each other, and I worried that the contents of my telegram would get back to him. I don't know if it ever did or not.

Molese could be temperamental too, a true tenor, and, as valuable as he was to the City Opera he got himself fired twice for exactly the type stunts Corelli seemed able to get away with.

One year the City Opera put on a new production of Massenet's *Manon*, an opera that is not performed all that often, principally because it is French, not Italian. Beverly Sills sang the title role, with Molese as her lover, Des Grieux. *Manon* to me is one of the three perfect operas I know about, the other two being *La Boheme* and *Otello*, for the *Manon* music is sumptuous and the story plays like a stage play. In addition this new production was glorious, being both beautifully staged, and beautifully sung. It made an instant superstar out of Beverly Sills. Unfortunately it did nothing much for Molese, even though he sang just as well as she did.

Manon is a soprano's opera. Des Grieux has only two arias, whereas Manon has five, two of them way up in the coloratura range that are show stoppers; her music seems to dominate the love duets as well. The reviews the next day were ecstatic especially for her. "With all due respect to Mr. Molese's work," wrote Harold Schonberg in *The New York Times*, "the evening was Miss Sills'." Not another word in the entire long review about the tenor.

And Molese steamed.

At that time Rudolf Bing never signed City Opera singers. There was no arguing with this blunt, stubborn man. But almost immediately he broke his rule by sending Beverly Sills a contract to move over to the Met, where Molese had not yet sung, beginning, I think, two years later. A record company signed her to record *Manon* too, mostly with City Opera people. However, she made no effort to get Molese onto the recording with her, and it was duly made with Nicolai Gedda in the tenor role.

The following year there was a new production of *Faust*, again with Molese and Sills. This time Schonberg praised principally the American baritone, Dominic Cossa.

Rudolph Bing broke his rule a second time. Cossa too found himself invited to sing at the Met.

Domingo, meanwhile, was beginning to attract attention. I talked to him at a cast party. He was a tall, fat young man, who seemed to me withdrawn and a bit surly, ill at ease when questioned, not in any sense the worldly figure he later became. He spoke little English, and when I tried to talk to him in Spanish he seemed to disdain me for it. Even then he pretended to be five years younger than his actual age, as he still does. In fact, though well into his thirties by then, seven or eight years younger than Molese, he was pretending to be much, much younger, making him seem what he was not, a very young up and coming tenor.

As a singer Domingo was, more than anything else, what is known as a dramatic tenor. He had strong, penetrating low notes. His top did not go as high as a tenor's should. So far as I know, he never attempted to sing a high C on stage. If the score called for one, Domingo would have the music transposed down a tone. Many singers do this. The audience almost can't tell. McCracken sang all the high C's as written, Molese too. Corelli had never cracked one, he told me once, but even he sometimes transposed them down. The high C could strike terror in any tenor's heart, especially on a night when, for some reason, he felt in less than top form. "I don't know where the high C is," Molese said one day. "I know where to go look for it."

On the other hand Domingo was a consummate musician. "Placido can go to sleep with a new score under his pillow," a prominent agent told me once, "and when he wakes up in the morning he's got it memorized."

Molese, perhaps seeing, or merely fearing, what was about to happen, did not like him. "He weighs 300 pounds," he said to me one day. "His voice is about this big—" holding up the tip of his little finger, "—most of it in his nose—"

Tenors could be extremely catty about other tenors.

Domingo went to Berlin to sing Wagner which, according to accepted opera lore, he should not have done so early in his career. His performance was not a success. This delighted Molese. "We may have seen the last of Mr. Domingo," he said.

Leonard Bernstein was to make a recording of the Verdi Requiem, but the scheduled tenor cancelled. Offered Domingo instead, Bernstein acquiesced. Who forced Domingo on him? This was never clear. Shortly after that, without ever having had a significant triumph, Domingo too signed to sing at the Met.

Opera is run not by singers but by agents, impresarios, record promoters, big donors, and by other, even more mysterious figures. Behind the scenes much went on, (and still goes on), that was secretive and murky. Like the world of boxing, which it much resembles, there is a great deal of money in opera, much of it in cash. The money moves back and forth in obscure ways, and it doesn't always stick to performers, many of whom get swindled.

Somebody, now, was pushing Domingo. The record companies? A powerful manager? Whoever it was exerted, clearly, a great deal of weight.

Some fighters get championship bouts, some don't. Domingo did, Molese didn't.

Molese was an extremely exciting singer to listen to. I thought this personally and I had seen also the way the crowds reacted to him in the various countries. There was a ping to his voice that few tenors had.

But Schonberg apparently did not like the way he sang, or perhaps the sound he made, and his reviews had got more and more uncomplimentary, until the day came when he complained in print about Molese's "pinched" high C.

Shortly afterwards, after hitting a high C that rang to the rafters, Molese stepped to the front of the stage, raised his hand to stop the orchestra, and announced to the dumbstruck players, and the dumbstruck audience as well:

"That pinched high C was for Mr. Schonberg of *The New York Times*."

So the company's general manager fired him for the first, but not the last time. As he went off to fulfill contracts in other countries, the tenor was happy. He had made his point.

Before long he was rehired, for the company could not do without him, and he behaved himself perfectly until he was invited to sing at La Scala and was sent a contract.

The only problem was that the dates conflicted with the contract he had previously signed with the City Opera. He went to the general manager and asked to be released. He begged, he pleaded. Scala was the holy of holies of the operatic world, as everybody knew, the summit of every singer's ambitions. They rarely used Americans, he had not been asked before, he might never be asked again if he turned them down now, he had to take it. Please, please, please.

Even the hated Domingo had never, at that time, sung at the Scala.

The general manager refused him.

Molese talked it over with me. I certainly did not know what to advise him. Finally he went anyway, walked out on his City Opera contract, and got fired a second time.

But was soon rehired again.

Late in his career he married a Greek mezzo soprano named Zoe Papadocki, who had also sung at the City Opera. She had once sung Carmen to his Don Jose, but had not lasted with the company. They set up housekeeping on a small farm Molese had bought—a vineyard, actually—outside of Stradella, about 40 miles south of Milan. We visited them there sometimes. He had about four acres under vines, and hoped to make something good, but he knew nothing about wine except to drink it, and I had my doubts.

They were both too old to want children by then. This did not stop them from taking in strays. Molese found a three legged dog somewhere, and brought it home and kept it for years. A painter he had met in New York left his wife and came to Italy to paint, but instead nearly starved. Molese hired him to paint murals inside his house, and fed him while he was doing it.

He never did sing at the Met. Of the four most important theaters he did sing at Vienna, and at the Scala, that was all. The cathedral of his own country ignored him.

My editor at NAL/World, Robert Gutwillig, had read my *Life* article on tenors, and it had set him thinking. Recently he had published a book called *Instant Replay*, the year long diary of a Green Bay Packers tackle named Jerry Kramer, who wrote it in conjunction with a writer named Dick Schaap. This book had been a big best seller based partly, Gutwillig believed, on its form. The diary form could be exploited further, he believed, and he planned a series of diary books, perhaps as many as ten. The diaries of a violinist, a golfer, a rabbi and—

He asked if I knew a tenor with a good story to tell. If so, did I and the tenor want to do such a book. If the answers were yes, then which tenor?

Gutwillig was about to publish my third novel which was about three priests in a New York parish. The Catholic Church was in ferment at this time, with priests suddenly leaving the ministry and sometimes the Church itself, something they had never dared do before—certainly not in such numbers. After foreign correspondents and pro football, the Catholic Church had seemed to me the only other subject on which I knew enough to base a novel. And so I had written it, and it was scheduled for publication in the fall. After running through about ten titles, I finally called it *A Priest and a Girl*—a rather poor attempt of a title I thought then and now My advance had been my biggest to date, $30,000, which to me at the time seemed an astronomical sum, almost enough to enable me to turn away from magazine articles for good.

Now Gutwillig was suggesting I do a diary book with a tenor. The idea pleased me. It wouldn't take all my time, and for a year I would be able to plunge ever more deeply into the world of opera that so fascinated me.

Which tenor? Not Corelli. He didn't speak English well enough, and I didn't speak Italian well enough. It would have to be an American, and it didn't take long to decide on the one I wanted. Richard Tucker was in his fifties and rather staid, so I ruled him out. Either Molese or McCracken then. As close as I felt to Molese, I opted for McCracken because he had the stronger story. Molese, after all, was alone, whereas McCracken had a wife who was also a singer, and a young daughter. Both tenors had starved in Milan, but McCracken had had a wife and baby to think about as well. In addition, the year ahead figured to be the biggest McCracken had ever had. He was scheduled to sing opening night at the Met, and a new production of *Pagliacci*, he had recordings of both *Pagliacci* and *Otello* coming out, and his wife, who had given up her own career to go to Europe with him and starve, was at last, after all these years, due to make her debut at the Met as well; next October they would sing *Samson et Dalila* together, and this might serve as the climax of the book.

From Gutwillig's office I phoned McCracken, who was at home in Switzerland. It took less than five minutes to persuade the tenor that the idea had value. He would get a tape recorder, and each night record his impressions of the day. Later we would meet regularly and hammer the book into shape.

Gutwillig was offering another $30,000 advance, which we would split.

That same day, or another, Gutwillig agreed to a second $30,000 advance for a novel called *The Fast One*, that I would write against a background of Grand Prix motor racing. I could do the two books simultaneously.

McCracken had agreed to start taping January 1. I would start on the new novel about the same time. *A Priest and a Girl*, which I thought the best novel I had written so far, would come out in the middle of all this work. Gutwillig thought it would be a success, and so did I. I was going to have a grand year. I figured to earn a minimum of $45,000 from the new contracts, a stupendous amount for a young writer, plus whatever *Priest* brought in above its advance.

I had never faced the future with such confidence. The year to come would be my biggest yet. Nothing could go wrong. What could possibly go wrong?

McCracken began on schedule, and soon sent the first batch of tapes. They started on New Year's day in southern Spain, newly booming at that time, where he and Sandra were looking over property for a possible investment. A singer's voice, he noted on tape, didn't last forever. It could, in fact, go at any time. He had to try to safeguard his future.

McCracken knew enough to include big events and small, the tapes would prove. One day on the beach he and Sandra and their daughter found and tried to rescue a bird coated in oil; in their hotel room they dabbed at its feathers with Q-tips and lighter fluid until it died. Another day as they waited for the ferry across to Morocco, they talked to a girl with a baby who was frantic because her husband was about to miss the boat, and they didn't have enough money to stay over another night; so Sandra gave Jim a sign, and he pressed money into the girl's hand.

Another nice touch, I thought, listening. The girl had no idea who he was, and he did not tell her. But I knew already how generous tenors tended to be.

The McCrackens went home to Zurich to the small house they had bought when they first began to get small contracts to sing, and there coped with mail, taxes, contract offers. Jim read financial data onto the tape, starting with his income (about $175,000 that year) and then giving a list of his expenses: travel, commissions, costumes, scores, coaches, accompanists, hotels, meals, tips, even the money he paid to claques—he called claques extortion. If you didn't pay they booed.

Jim flew to London for a new production of *Otello*, and also to meet with his lawyers, for he was suing the Decca Record Company (not the American Decca) for breach of contract.

I saw at once that this lawsuit would be still another thread running through the entire book, and I was pleased to learn of it. McCracken had signed an exclusive contract to record *Trovatore, Forza,* and *Turandot* but Decca already had these operas in the pipeline by Mario Del Monaco, and had never had any intention, the suit charged, of recording them with McCracken; the purpose of the contract was to prevent him from recording them with someone else.

Already the suit had cost him money, but he was outraged that any record company could do this to young singers and get away with it.

All this and more was on the tapes that reached me, and I listened, but even as I sent them out to be transcribed I saw what could be a major problem, and worried about it. Not the entries themselves. I was amazed at how intimate they were, and how detailed. Of course some were too long, and some too short. In places the drama might be heightened a bit. Here and there long inserts were needed. All of it would have to be polished without losing the sound of McCracken's speech.

The problem was something else, and I wasn't sure I saw any way around it. This book was supposed to be Jim's diary, but some of the entries were in Sandra's voice, and there was even one in the child's voice. If I said nothing this would doubtless continue. Could it be allowed to continue? I did not know of any diary in multiple voices. What would the editor say? What would the reviewers and the public say if the book went on this way to the end?

Would I have to tell the tenor to kick his wife out of the book?

Then I thought: they are both singers. They sometimes sing together. And Sandra's entries were often stronger, more insightful, more personal than Jim's. She was the one who spoke of trying to keep two careers going at one time, and about how good it felt when all three passports were in the same drawer. She was the one who described on tape Jim's debut as *Otello* at the Met when, after all those years of struggle, he was finally invited back, a leading singer at last. "I was in a state of shock most of the night," she dictated. "All I remember is that at the end of the big tenor-baritone duet at the end of the second act Jimmy has to sing a high B-flat, and to get up to it he has to take this enormous breath and sitting in the audience I took it with him and split my dress all the way down the front."

So that was my first decision: Sandra stays.

On March 14 Jim reached New York, collected his 43 kilos of excess baggage—costumes, boots, scores—and took a taxi to the apartment he was sub-letting on Beekman Place.

He was singing a series of *Turandots*, followed by a series of *Trovatores*, and he described all the difficulties and peculiarities of the too scant Met rehearsals, and of singing in that huge hall, which is more than twice the size of most of the opera houses of the world.

Regularly during this period we met and went over what we had so far. Several times the McCrackens drove up to my house and we worked all day. Mostly I probed for more detail so as to flesh out existing scenes further. What about Rudolf Bing, I would ask. He needs to be in this book. What do you have? Well, to help Bing out, Jim had once agreed to sing two different operas on successive nights, which no singer should ever do, in exchange for a double fee on the second one, which Bing "forgot" to pay him, until finally he stormed into Bing's office to demand the money. There followed a convoluted explanation by Bing, and McCracken shouting that Bing was a liar, and so was everyone else in the room. At which point Bing instructed an assistant manager to pay McCracken the money.

Only tenors, I thought, dared fight with the imperious Mr. Bing, but they fought with him all the time. Perhaps this was why he hated tenors so.

Also, I wanted to flesh out what in the movie world is called the backstory. I wanted details of their summer reconnaissance trips to Europe when both were still under contract to sing bit parts at the Met. I knew where the drama probably was, and I pushed for it. One year they bought third class tickets by ship, accepting an exceptionally small, windowless cabin on D deck, for they expected to offer to sing a concert at sea, and so get upgraded. But they couldn't get near the purser's office for two days, their cabin was like a tomb, and so they slept on deck. Finally they did get upgraded, and they sang their concert while the ship was pitching through a storm, hoping their high notes would come out and not their lunch. In Europe they hoped to audition for impresarios, and so drove hundreds of miles from one opera house to another, stopping to warm up their voices in fields, only to find that the impresario was on vacation when they got there, or that the house was closed for the summer.

Finally they both left the Met, went to Europe and nearly starved. In Bonn Jim sang Italian opera in German in a hall upstairs over a restaurant, because the opera house had been bombed flat during the war. From there he went on to Italy where the only job he could get was as understudy for Corelli and Bergonzi in Verona for $8 a day; this was followed by endless auditions in Milan where the entire operatic world seemed to be controlled by a single agent. Although this agent was always polite, even encouraging, Jim could not seem to get past him. One day he auditioned for the agent and the impresario of the Palermo company. His final aria was *Nessun Dorma* from *Turandot*, and by the time he finished the impresario was in tears, and he sprang forward and pumped his hand saying: "McCracken, you're truly a great tenor, what a pity I can't hire you."

Of course the breaks came finally, and I wanted to know about that too.

The McCrackens went off on tour with the Met, while I worked over the transcripts, and we next met in July at the Voile d'Or Hotel at St. Jean Cap Ferrat, on the Riviera. The typescript was up to 270 pages, and we went over this, working every morning under the olive trees. We clarified entries, we cut lines, and sometimes Sandra or Jim would dictate an addition. For instance, when we came to the entry about their first audition tour of Europe, Sandra said: "You mean that's all we're going to have about that."

"You mean there's more?"

"We didn't put in about Hamburg, or going home with the waiter at Innsbruck, or anything."

They decided to tape it that afternoon, and did so, lying in bathing suits in the sun beside the Mediterranean, passing the microphone back and forth. When I joined them they had finished, and they played it for me, and then began to tell stories not on the tape, and we all started laughing, and then I grabbed the microphone and began repeating into it these additional funny lines from that tour.

Their 24 foot cabin cruiser had been shipped down from Zurich, and Jim and I went to the railroad station where I served as interpreter to get it out of customs. As a reward, once we got it into the water, he let me drive; we went for a cruise around the cape, me driving, and I got stopped by the Gendarmerie boat for going too fast. On the night that Neil Armstrong first walked on the moon we watched on television at my brother in law's house, and when the space capsule touched down Jim suddenly began to sing. He sang "*Overhead the Moon is Shining*" and the blood rushed to my face and the hairs stood up on my hands it was so beautiful and so powerful.

Shortly after that the real world fell in on us all. The way it happened seemed almost operatic, like one of those scenes where the players are all singing gaily, and then someone rushes in with news that the soprano is dying.

In New York Gutwillig and his boss, Ed Kuhn quit, or were fired. At the same time the Met orchestra and chorus were threatening to go out on strike. This meant there might be no opening night *Aida* for Jim, no new production of *Pagliacci*, no debut by Sandra in *Samson et Dalila.* There might be no season at all.

I had rushed back to meet with the new editor for I had *A Priest and a Girl* coming out and needed to get him enthusiastic about it; I wanted to talk to him about the two contracts on which I was working, as well. He needed to be sold on all three books, and I tried to do it. He promised that

A Priest and a Girl would receive every push. However its first printing had been cut back to 12,000, I learned, and so, barring a miracle, its failure was already assured. There simply would not be enough copies on sale; many stores would have none.

After biting down on my lip I read to him from the typescript of the McCracken diary. He told me it was brilliant, and the following week even sent me a letter to this effect, begging me to keep up the good work.

But the letter didn't mean what it said, apparently, as would become clear.

McCracken, meanwhile, was pretending to optimism. The strike would not happen, he maintained. Had not Rudolf Bing phoned to guarantee his first month's performances, whether the house ever opened or not? Had not Bing told him to believe nothing he heard? But meantime he was receiving phone calls and messages from his agent, from Met singers and Met staff, all of them gloomy. More disquieting still, he began receiving offers from other agents and impresarios who understood that the Met season had been cancelled, that he was free to sing in their houses.

The tenor entered all this into his taped diary.

As the school year opened the McCrackens moved into a furnished house they had rented in Cos Cob, quite near ours. They put Ahna in school with our older girls, and we all waited to hear which way the strike would go.

Waiting, they came every day to my house, and we worked on our book. While the fine weather lasted and the trees slowly changed color we worked on the picnic table on my terrace. Later we moved into my study. There were regular entries on the state of the negotiations. Opening night was delayed one week, then two, three, four—the book began to develop the suspense of a murder mystery. One after another whole operas were cancelled out. On the night Sandra was to make her Met debut they reminisced about how they met singing Samson et Dalila in Norfolk, Virginia, how he fell in love with her white sweater, and she with his high

B flat—she had never heard such sound from a human voice, she said. Jim was 25 years old then, Sandra a year younger. The next day the raves, on the whole, were for Jim. It was the first time anyone had ever got better reviews than she did, she said, and she realized she didn't mind at all.

Now, on the night she was to make her Met debut as Dalila, the opera house was dark. "I cared too many years," she said on tape. "I don't see there's any use to go on dreaming."

They made other entries too during this period. One day I asked McCracken which he preferred, Shakespeare's *Othello* or Verdi's *Otello*. His answer was long, thoughtful and rather moving. It ended: "Every time I see Othello I find myself listening for the music. Does that answer the question?" Would he like to play Othello some day? "Yes."

In late November, with the Met still closed, we all went to Jackson, Miss. Each year the Opera Guild there brought in one or two name singers. Every one else on stage and in the pit were local enthusiasts. The McCrackens, who were to sing their first ever *Carmen* together, found that all the difficult parts had been cut because the musicians, of whom there were only thirty, were not able to play them, and the chorus was unable to sing them. None of these people knew the rest of the music very well either. At the Guild party one of the committee members bragged to Jim that he had never been to an opera before, and wasn't coming to this one. During the intermission the next night I heard a man brag to his wife that he understood a good deal of the words on stage because he had studied Spanish in high school.

For the McCrackens, an adventure of a performance, and the entries they dictated afterward were delightful.

It was mid-December in New York before the Met strike was settled. Opening night was still to be *Aida* with James McCracken, the tenor's first New York opening night, but his Met contract was supposed to be over by then, and he was expected in Barcelona where he was to sing *Otello* with Monserrat Caballe as Desdemona, followed by a *Samson et Dalila* with Sandra, and he declined to break this contract.

So they went to Barcelona and the Met opened without him.

On Christmas Eve Monserrat Caballe invited the entire cast to her apartment. They dined on Spanish delicacies and drank wine from her husband's vineyard. She had presents for every one, and then at midnight, after lighting the tree she said: "You like now I sing for you?"

And she did, and when she had finished Jimmy stood up and sang *Joy to the World.*

The McCrackens kept their diary open four days into the New Year so as to include in it their *Samson et Dalila.* They were in Barcelona, not New York, but they were together, and they were singing.

By then I was there too. Ostensibly I had come to collect the final tapes, but I had a message as well, though I couldn't bear to give it to them right away. We went to the opera together—Monserrat was singing *Norma.* After the first act we all trooped backstage to tell her how well she was doing, not staying for the rest of the performance because the McCrackens had a performance of their own the next day. As we were walking back to the hotel, and crossing a deserted square, the church bells started tolling midnight, and when the tolling stopped I gave them the message: the new management of NAL/World was engaged in canceling contracts that the Gutwillig-Kuhn team had put in place. Dozens had been cancelled, one of them our diary book. There was a clause in all the contracts that seemed to permit them to do this, they claimed. They were demanding their advance back—they had paid us $20,000 so far—and if they didn't get it they would sue.

They had cancelled *The Fast One*, my car racing novel, too. This was less immediate, for I had finished only a small portion of it so far.

Publishers have perpetrated this kind of thing from time to time. Harper Collins did it only recently: a new management cancelled about a hundred contracts signed under the preceding regime. Each time it happens everybody screams. But individual authors have no power at all. The agents, it would seem, have more, and could paralyze such a publisher, could refuse to send them any more manuscripts, but that did not happen in our case. In fact I've never heard of it happening.

The cancellations had occurred just before Christmas. I was in the position of a man who loses his job at the start of the holiday season, and wonders how he is going to pay for the gifts Santa is supposed to bring, not to mention next month's rent. In addition I was terribly embarrassed to have to face the McCrackens. We had a finished manuscript, no publisher and, soon to come, legal bills. The McCrackens were already enmeshed in a lawsuit, their dispute with Decca Records still moving forward, though slowly. The following year when the case would finally be called to trial Decca would settle on the courthouse steps, paying McCracken $120,000 plus costs. But this outcome was by no means clear as yet, and I could not be sure how he would react to still another suit. Lawsuits are emotionally and financially draining. They take possession of one's time and also one's soul. I did not know this then, but he did. He could have paid back his share of the advance easily enough, but I couldn't, especially now that I had no novel contract either, and no other assignments to fill the void.

It took the tenor about five minutes to think over his choices. He then said he would back whatever I decided to do.

And so the lawsuit began. It was two-sided.

Suit by them based on the clause that perhaps gave them the right to do what they had done.

Countersuit by us based on another clause by which this same right seemed precisely to be denied them.

Meanwhile our agent, Sterling Lord, went to other publishers with our manuscript, and also with my outline and first chapters of *The Fast One*.

No publisher would touch either one.

Their rejection letters followed one after the other, ten or more in all. These were due to the lawsuit in progress perhaps, but there was no way to be sure of this. If the manuscript and the projected novel had been good enough, surely they would have been taken anyway, would they not?

The rejections just kept coming, there seemed no end to them, and with each new one my morale plummeted further. I had suffered dozens and dozens of rejections in the past and not been stopped. But rejection was something I was no longer used to, this was a different me now, I had long since been weaned off rejection by success. And so each new one seemed crushing, another boulder on my back, impossible to carry or get rid of. Previous success had proven to be a mirage. One could not wave it around. It had no existence. It provided nothing solid at all.

One of life's great lessons. Past successes are in the past, and at times like that can not help.

Previously I had tried to write only what it pleased me to write. This was not always possible, of course, but mostly it was. Whereas now, on my way to the leanest year I ever had, I was obliged to take any magazine assignment I could get. I am not proud of an article I wrote for *Cosmopolitan* during this period. It was called *A Girl's Guide to Horse Racing*. An honest enough article but a subject that was silly. Three of my principal markets, *Life*, *True* and *The Saturday Evening Post* all had ceased publication, or were about to. Most of the major markets that remained had cut way back on prices. The horse racing article paid $2,000, a big price this year, and it was money we had to have.

Because of it *Cosmopolitan* thought quite highly of me, and I was assigned to write another piece to be called *The Girls of Las Vegas*. At least this one was fun to do. I was accorded a complimentary suite in Caesar's Palace, bet not one nickel in the casino, and got a chance to interview a number of girls with 40 inch busts, one of whom was a 24 year old actress who worked for a television comedienne who was one of the headliners that week. Their act was a series of skits in which the girl was sometimes allowed to get some laughs. To our interview she wore loose slacks and a loose sweater and looked like the girl next door, though the looseness of the sweater did not hide as much as perhaps she hoped. She seemed embarrassed by her bust, once cupping her hands under it, and referring to it as "this." People had difficulty taking her seriously as an actress, she said, with "this" staring them in the face. A truly beautiful girl, still very young, with big hopes for the future that I found touching. It was a grand interview until I asked how she had started out in show business.

Well, she had been a topless dancer at one of the other casinos.

My expression must have changed.

"What were you going to say?" she asked.

"Just that I wish I could have got to see—you dance."

The interview went downhill from there.

Cosmopolitan's editor, Helen Gurley Brown, had transformed what was once a literary magazine into a gold mine by offering sexual advice to teenage girls. Hemingway had written for *Cosmo*, and I had tried and failed to sell my early stories there. Now Helen and *Cosmopolitan* worked to change the sexual mores of American girls just as Hugh Hefner and *Playboy* had done for men.

In the changeover process Helen herself became a famous lady. In person she was demure, painfully skinny, not a bit sexy, and always totally focused on whatever man she was with, even me. The conversation was always exclusively about the man, never her, and she kept it that way. This was the same advice she gave the girls who read her magazine.

What did working for her do for my reputation? I had considered myself a serious writer, a serious man. To be so considered by the New York literary establishment was important to me. My presence now in *Cosmopolitan* testified otherwise. But it seemed to me that I had no choice. I had only the money I earned, not a nickel from anywhere else, and suddenly nothing was coming in. *Cosmopolitan* was a life ring, and I grabbed it. Certain of my colleagues appear to have worked years on books on no income, and I always wondered how they did it. Family money? Working wives? None ever made any such admission. When their books finally appeared their reputations were larger than ever, whereas mine perhaps had suffered. Reputation is a tricky subject, it can't be seen or touched, but it is there, it is important, and I would advise young writers to reflect carefully before working for something like *Cosmopolitan*.

In fairness to Helen Brown, she also let me write about subjects that interested me. I did a piece on sopranos for her—I spent time with Joan Sutherland, Birgit Neilsen, Anna Moffo, all women I admired; Birgit, who sang with God's own voice but who was about 50 at the time, told me I was one of the nicest looking young Italian men she had met recently. Where this comment came from I did not know. Perhaps it might have been pushed further, but I only nodded and thanked her. I wrote a full length profile of Beverly Sills, one of the first to be written about her. I did another on conductors: Thomas Schippers, James Levine, Julius Rudel and others. Today I was looking in my files and I came across many letters of praise from Helen—she appears to have sent me one after every piece. Probably she sent them to everybody. I rather liked her, she always paid well, and that year of struggling for contracts eventually passed. After I became a police official I sometimes ran into her at one function or another. I would offer her a ride home in my unmarked car, after first sweeping my coat back a few times to make sure she could see I was armed. I cringe to remember this, but I did it. In the car, sitting beside the detective who was my driver, I was careful to turn the police radio up, and I spoke to her over the various convulsions with which the city was beset at that moment.

Not my finest hour. Perhaps, without even realizing it, I was trying to make her pay for the real or imagined damage that working for her had done to my career.

But at the time of the lawsuit I had no career. The book world seemed closed to me. I was trying for magazine assignments everywhere but not getting enough of them, or else they didn't pay enough to keep us. I became frantic. At one point I considered getting a job. The French Government Tourist Board was looking for a director, and I actually interviewed for it, before becoming determined to hold out a little longer.

There were endless sworn depositions to sit through. The World Publishing Company's lawyers interrogated us, ours interrogated them. Behind the scenes the lawyers did whatever lawyers do, the bills kept coming, and McCracken and I each paid half. From time to time the tenor invited one or another of our lawyers to the opera, as if they would work harder for us once they had heard him sing.

In time, months and months of time, oral and written arguments were presented to a judge, who retired to deliberate. This took him only weeks and weeks. Finally his findings were published.

Our countersuit was without merit, he ruled. The publisher had had a perfect right to cancel the contract. Left intact was the publisher's suit for the return of the $20,000, which would be decided at trial. He set a trial date.

I felt like a man who had just been indicted. There would be a trial. Would this same judge preside? Probably. But he seemed already to have decided. I would have to find witnesses for our side, then hope they would get on the stand and testify as we wished them to. Would they do so? If they did, would they convince anyone? If I could even get them.

The World Publishing Company was a colossus. It owned NAL paperbacks, Harry Abrams art books, it published dictionaries and text books. It was itself owned by the Los Angeles Times Mirror, an even greater colossus. Would anyone in publishing be willing to stand up against it to save me? A trial would cost a fortune. Or we could appeal this preliminary decision. This would cost a fortune as well. Either way we might lose. If the same judge presided we would probably lose.

I paced. I could not sleep. I had to get myself out of this somehow. McCracken had paid his half of the bills without complaint. He had trusted me. I had to get him out too. But how?

I went to the man who served as chairman of the board of all Times Mirror publishing enterprises. His name was Martin Levin. I told him McCracken and I would have to appeal this preliminary decision, that we had no choice. It seemed to me I was lying to him; there was no possibility we would appeal. Nonetheless this was what I said. World would have to defend this appeal, I told him. My voice was strong, I believed. I looked determined, I believed. An appeal, followed by a trial would cost us all a good deal of time and money, him too. And it was giving his company a bad name. Unless he and I now could come to an agreement of some kind, the suit would go on.

To my surprise, he caved in at once and we settled on an agreement by me that World would get first look at my next three books. His lawyers produced a paper to this effect, I signed it, and the lawsuit was over.

By this time World's trade book division was a shambles, and the two men who had cancelled all the contracts were on the way out. Ultimately one of them committed suicide. The other went back to wherever he had come from, and disappeared from sight. But they had wrecked the company, which never again was a factor in trade book publishing.

And then Coward-McCann agreed to publish the diary book, now called

A Star In The Family. The advance was $10,000. So in the end we got the $30,000 that was promised at the start, the only difference being that most of the money had gone to the lawyers. Also, because Coward's advance was so small, our book was treated by their sales force as a small book.

I thought then, and still think, that it is a beautiful book. In advance of publication pieces of it were sold to various magazines, and when it came out it received, as they say in show business, nice notices—where it got noticed at all. It sold almost nothing. It contains a short introduction by me. "This is their book, not mine," I wrote. "It is funny, and also deeply moving. It will make you laugh, and in the next sentence make you cry. It is very human, and working on it was altogether the most pleasant literary experience of my life."

I hold to that to this day.

The McCrackens lived near us until after Ahna went off to college, so we were often together. I came to think we were the closest friends they had. We went to Paris with them, where Jim sang Schoenberg's *Guerleider* with the Boston Symphony, and for the second time in my life I stood in a tenor's dressing room when the man came in with the money. "Take it, Bob," said the tenor, sweat and makeup running down his body, "count it."

One year Jim had a new production of *Carmen* with Marilyn Horne. He came over every day for a week and went over the libretto with Peggy, getting the French pronunciation exactly right, and when he sang on stage he sounded like a Frenchman. I don't know any other singer who could do that. He had a fabulous ear. The four of us went to Bimini where we hired a boat and went out fishing. The captain was half drunk when we left the dock, and drank steadily all day. If he knew where the fish were he did not find them. We fished for eight hours in which we caught three mid-size barracudas and a mackerel that reached the boat half eaten by something else on the way in. It was rainy and cold the rest of the time, so instead of fishing we drank too much.

One year at the Met Jim sang all of the scheduled *Trovatores* until the one that was to be televised, which management gave to Placido Domingo. It made McCracken furious. He cancelled all remaining contracts with the Met, he didn't care how much this cost him, and refused to sing there ever again.

So both of the tenors we were closest to hated Domingo who had done nothing except accept jobs they wanted for themselves.

Finally, McCracken, along with a number of other singers, was invited to sing one aria in a televised Met gala. Five years had passed. He thought about this offer for a time, then accepted. Having come that far, and still being importuned by management, which badly wanted him back, he signed for the next season.

At the age of 61 he was scheduled to sing a series of *Trovatores*, but after he had sung the dress rehearsal he didn't feel well, and so saw a doctor who told him he was a very sick man, and should enter the hospital at once. He did not trust doctors and did not believe this one. Ignoring the warning he went home, where he fell down, quivered, and then didn't move. At Roosevelt Hospital it was diagnosed that he had had a stroke. He lay in a deep coma in intensive care. Sandra told no one what was wrong with him, even us, and when I asked when were visiting hours, for we wanted to come cheer Jim up, she advised us not to. He was "undergoing tests," she said, and he wouldn't be able to see us. She began canceling his series of *Trovatores*, but only one by one. Finally we went to the hospital anyway and embraced her in the hall, and she told us the truth.

I went into the room. Jim's breathing was being done by a machine, and I stood beside the bed holding his hand saying: "Wake up Jim, wake up." Behind me stood the distraught Sandra. She wanted to bring in his recording of *Otello*, his signature role, and play it into his ear as if this might cause him to sit up and open his eyes.

He lasted 16 days.

There was a memorial service in Alice Tully Hall. When Sandra asked me to serve as master of ceremonies, and to give the principal eulogy, I was not surprised. For some time I had thought not only that I was the best friend he had, but that I was one of the few. He certainly didn't have many. Although a smiling and apparently convivial man, he kept most people at arms length—they both did. Most times they seemed to pretend they were sufficient unto themselves which, to my mind, nobody is. Apart from us, they saw very few people socially, none of whom were other singers. On the road the local Opera Guild always staged parties that were more or less in their honor, but they rarely went to them. Between performances Jim would hole up in the local Holiday Inn, for he could rely on their big beds, and there was sometimes a pool. Mostly he stayed in his room. He would lie on the bed watching sports on television, conserving his strength like a prize fighter. Every three or four nights he would go out of the hotel and across to the opera house to sing.

I knew them for over twenty years. I knew them so well. In addition to everything else I had listened to their life stories over and over for more than a year, had I not? Who else knows that much about anyone else? And so it seemed odd to me that I had never felt as intimate with them as it seemed to me I should have. It was not Sandra who asked me to give the eulogy during the memorial service, she had their agent Tony Russo do it, as if afraid I might say no.

The famous concert hall was about three quarters full. From the stage I looked down and saw that many singers had come, one of them Franco Corelli. I read out the telegrams that had come in from other singers scattered all over the world, and then spoke for a time of James McCracken, both as a singer and as a man. Marilyn Horne sang. A children's choir sang. I introduced these various acts, and in between spoke of Jim again, and then opened *A Star In The Family* to a page I had marked. "He wasn't always the great James McCracken," I said, and I prepared to read a brief scene in his own words having to do with his early struggle to be heard, the time when Sandra was pregnant and Jim was being paid $8 a day as understudy in Verona, the only job he could get. It was a beautiful scene, I believed—we had written it together.

But I looked out into the audience and my eyes fixed on Corelli. This gave me pause. Franco's English was far from perfect. He might misunderstand what I was about to read, might be offended. But I had started by then, and could only continue.

"One afternoon about 5 o'clock," I read, "there was a knock on my door. I would sing *Aida* tonight; Franco Corelli was not well. Sandra and I rushed over to the theater. I was certain that the baby would come this very night, while I was on stage making my debut in Italy.

"They gave me an empty office as a dressing room. They brought in a costume. I got into it. They said they'd send me the makeup man in time, so I began to wait. Sandra sat by me. Missarolli, the head of the Arena di Verona came in and asked was I all right. Could I do it?"

"As curtain time came closer the nerves came on. I was waiting for them to send me boots and a makeup man and no one came. I kept going over *Aida* in Italian my head, and it kept coming out in German, because I had just sung it 12 times in German in Bonn and never in Italian anywhere. I was the understudy for *Turandot* also. I was ready for that. Why couldn't my debut be in *Turandot*?

"I wanted to go out of the dressing room to find somebody, find out what was going on; but Missarolli had told me to stay put and not let anybody know I was there. What did this mean? I worried that when the announcement was made that I would sing in place of Corelli — would they boo me as soon as I came on stage?

"Where was Corelli and what was wrong with him?

"Although I was his understudy, I had never met Corelli. The week before he had stepped into a small rehearsal room where I was singing with a piano. He didn't come in to hear me — he could hear me in the hall. He must have come in to see who my voice belonged to. I realize this and felt flattered. As if he had entered the room by mistake, he bowed quickly, and left without a word. I went right home and told Sandra, "Guess who came in to hear me sing today?"

"Now I was going to step on stage in Italy in place of this great Italian tenor. But I was still incommunicado in this little room and nobody was telling me anything. The makeup man still had not come and curtain time was already 10 minutes past. During the next 40 minutes I went through fear, excitement, frustration, anger and finally terrific disappointment. I knew I wasn't going on before they came to tell me. After the performance started, I took the costume off and we went outside and listened to Corelli sing. Sandra held my hand and whispered, `the audience doesn't know what it's missing.' By the time the opera ended we had convinced ourselves that Corelli had been afraid to let me go on in his place, that the management had used me to make Corelli sing, and furthermore that I deserved to be paid for the nerves I had gone through—though of course I never was. I got eight dollars that day just like always."

Closing the book I peered down at its cover. The hall was silent, and it remained that way because, for the moment, I was unable to speak.

The service ended with McCracken's recording of the death scene from *Otello*. For the last time his great voice boomed out over a concert hall, a way of reminding all of us, perhaps, of what we had lost. From the stage I saw that many people, listening, were in tears. So was I.

When the recording ended I went down the steps into the aisle and approached Corelli. We shook hands, but he did not smile, and after a minute he turned away.

He had quit singing by then. Unable to stand the nerves any longer, he had simply walked away from it. He was still in his fifties when he did this, his voice still working well. He became a voice teacher, and one of his recent pupils was the new blind tenor, Andrea Bocelli.

Most tenors do not live very long, so quitting perhaps saved Franco's life. Producing those big sounds puts a terrific strain on the internal organs, not to mention the heart and the brain. Opera singing is not good for the health. This is true of all singers, but particularly tenors. One could recite the names. Caruso was 48, Richard Tauber 50, Jussi Boerling 50, Richard Tucker 63, Gigli and DelMonaco 67. And now McCracken at 61. Molese, a year later, dropped dead in a supermarket in Italy. He was 62. We were sitting up in bed in Connecticut reading the newspaper, calmly turning pages, and came to the obituaries, and stopped suddenly, for there in the headline was his name.

With Michael gone too we were bereft, and did not go to the opera again for a long time.

Then one day we did go. This was in Nice, and the tenor on stage was a young American named Stuart Neill whom I had not yet heard of. A big, big voice. After the opera ended Peggy and I got into the car and actually started home, but suddenly I pulled into the curb saying to her: "I'm going to go talk to him."

There was a guard at the stage door but I gave him some fast English and pretended not to understand French, until he threw up his hands and let me pass. I knew where the tenor's dressing room was—how many times had I been in it in the past? I knocked, Neill let me in, and we talked. I told him how beautifully he had sung and asked him about himself. He would make his Met debut next season, he said. He was a big man. He said he had recently lost 80 pounds. He seemed extremely pleased I had enjoyed his singing enough to come backstage and tell him so in this foreign country where he knew no one.

We went down the stairs together and out the stage door, and the rest of the cast was waiting for him on the sidewalk. They were all going somewhere to dinner, as we used to do here with Molese; one night in a restaurant called Le Nautique on the port a Polish basso named Saciuk who had sung opposite him, and who was sitting across from me, suddenly began to sing. It was The Volga Boatman. He sang it all the way through, and every table applauded, none more than us. But Molese is dead and I don't know what ever happened to Saciuk.

As I watched Neill and the cast go off together I felt a pang. There are a lot of things in life which, having done them once, you can't do again, and following after young singers is one of them.

11.
Life in the NYPD

February 13, 2001, New York City

Because I am a few minutes early for my appointment at City Hall I cross Police Plaza and enter Police Headquarters. I do this for no other purpose than to breathe the air in there. As men in uniform enter and go out all around me, I pretend to be reading the bronze plaques on the walls, some of them green with age, the long rosters of slain cops. What I am really doing is allowing the remembered warmth of the police world to wash over me—yes, there is a warmth in that world if you are part of it, or have ever been part of it. I came into the police department as a deputy commissioner. I was 41 years old. It was the equivalent of joining the army as a lieutenant general. I lasted one year and seven days, at the end of which I was forced out almost in disgrace. I barely saved myself. For a professional writer it was a strange and, up to a point, fabulous experience. It was certainly unforgettable.

From the start, from one day to the next, I had authority according to the city charter over 32,000 armed men. Of course I was not expected to use it, and for the most part did not do so, not really. It was a high pressure, high exposure job, and most of what I learned from it I learned only afterwards, by looking back. The stickups, mob hits, and police funerals, of which I attended ten that year, I learned at the time, of course. Crime could be seen; often there were bodies on the floor, sometimes cops' bodies. It was what went on around me in headquarters that was so far beyond my previous experience that I never saw it clearly at all, never saw what men were doing to each other, what they were doing to me. Not until it was far too late. The police novels I wrote afterwards do contain some crime, some killings, but their principal focus is headquarters, and it was as I sat constructing them, brooding, that I finally saw headquarters clearly. What had caused me so much pain at the time almost made me laugh now, it was so obvious.

I never served here on Police Plaza. Headquarters at that time was one subway stop to the north, a low, ornate, almost Victorian building. A few years ago I tried to look in there too, again just to breathe the air, but it had been turned into luxury apartments, and the doorman turned me away.

In New York City then as now, the chief law enforcement officer, whatever the public may imagine, is the mayor. It is he who appoints the police commissioner whose job and career rest on the mayor's whim of the moment, whatever that whim may be. The police commissioner then appoints his deputies. The PC can be dismissed, perhaps ruined, any time the mayor wishes. The City Charter specifically states that no reason need be given. Same thing for the deputies.

The year I was appointed there were seven of us deputies, all nominally civilians, though three of the others were ex-cops, as was the PC himself, whose name was Patrick Murphy.

It was City Hall that engineered my near demise. I would have thought myself only a minor annoyance, if that, but City Hall evidently thought otherwise. It was probably someone else who swung the ax, but just as probably it was John Lindsay, Mayor at the time, who handed it to him. In high level politics people try not to leave their fingerprints around.

John Lindsey died just before Christmas—less than two months ago—aged 79. The obituaries remembered him as young, healthy and "handsome beyond reason." He filled City Hall with young men in their twenties who wanted to change the world, beginning with New York City. They were energetic, enthusiastic, idealistic and perhaps not too wise. Lindsay himself was a person of charisma, and of exceptional glamour, who took office as a republican, switched to the democrats, ran for president in 1972 and did not win a single primary—finished so far back in some of them as to be humiliated. He served two terms as mayor during which he spent and spent, taxed and taxed, and fiddled with the books so that the deficits would not show, and he left the city nearly bankrupt.

The obituaries I saw were not kind to him, which I mention in the hope that the reader will accept what follows as accurate, rather than bitter.

I saw a good deal of Lindsay. He met with Police Commissioner Murphy once a week, sometimes more often, came regularly to headquarters to be briefed, and there were other conferences at City Hall, or at the Police Academy on 20th Street, or in various of the precinct station houses, and many of these meetings and conferences I attended. Each time he entered the room my first impression was, isn't he gorgeous! I am being serious now. I think this was the reaction of every one of us as we rose to our feet to shake Lindsay's hand. Therefore the disappointment that followed was stupendous. First of all, he could never remember anybody's name. This was more than a blow to a man's ego. These were men he was working with regularly, after all, and if he couldn't remember their names it was unlikely he was remembering anything they told him.

In addition, he never seemed able to focus in on what the meeting or briefing was all about. He would sit there looking somewhat stupefied, then suddenly interject a question which probably had been asked by someone else and answered only a moment before. Or else he would throw in a joke which would make all of us laugh, and would also convince us for a while that he was both paying attention to the briefing, and absorbing it. It is hard to believe that any man with a quick wit can be stupid.

He gave the police department more intelligent support than any other mayor before him. He gave more men, more money, more sergeants, more equipment—-and he also waited outside the hospital room of every shot patrolman for hours on end. But the cops hated him totally and unequivocally because they judged that he did not know who they were and should have known, and therefore obviously cared for them not at all. With cops as with all other New Yorkers, that gorgeous facade woke everybody up each time, made everybody pay close attention, raised expectations beyond the level that any mayor could satisfy.

The first cop I ever knew personally was Sergeant David Durk, then 34 years old, a Jewish doctor's son out of Amherst. He was a man with ideas, a man on a crusade, and his impact on my life would be of a power and weight out of all proportion to anything either of us could have foreseen.

It was Durk's conceit that the NYPD—all the country's police departments—ought to be actively recruiting college boys to serve as cops. The average cop was blue-collar, sometimes an ex garbage man or stevedore. College boys would be better educated, and therefore easier to train. They would create another model on the street. They would show the ordinary cop that it was not unmanly to be concerned, to show compassion. They would be cheaper, for after a few years, long before the city had to pay them pensions, they would leave for better paying jobs. Above all, they would be less prone to corruption than blue-collar men seemed to be.

To preach this doctrine Durk had got a grant from the Justice Department, and a year's leave of absence from the NYPD, and he moved day by day through mostly Ivy League colleges recruiting. Being a cop was an absolutely succulent job, he preached. The siren and those red lights were fun. It was the only job where altruism merged with fun.

His imagery was vivid and it never flagged. "It's a safe, comforting feeling to believe you can do nothing. But either you are going to do it or no one's going to do it. Maybe you plan to join some conglomerate, and once you get to the top throw off your mask, saying, `It's me, Good Guy.' But sometimes you find the mask has fused with your face.

"There are other guys in the department who feel as I do. Not many. We're not even a significant minority. If you come in there will be more."

Life Magazine asked me to follow Durk into the colleges, and write about him, and I did this. Most times he seemed to win over every student in the room. At the end of each speech they crowded around him. He was like a Baptist minister making converts; if there had been a baptismal pool they would eagerly have jumped into it for him.

But the NYPD was not behind him, and there was no room for his recruits in New York, where admission standards were so appallingly low that 9,000 blue collar men were waiting in line ahead of them. They would have to wait years. He did succeed in a getting a few college boys accepted by the Washington PD, including Donald Graham, present publisher of the Washington Post, and James Lardner, of the Lardner literary clan. But outside the rooms and auditoriums in which he made them, Durk's speeches had little resonance, and in a year or two had been forgotten. Durk, I would learn, was not very good at following up on anything. He was an idea man only. For the most part he threw his ball into the center of the field and hoped someone else would pick it up and run for a touchdown.

He had a second crusade going. The NYPD was systemically,

endemically corrupt, he preached, and no one was doing anything about it. But he had no proof. He was in no sense a mainstream cop. Knowing nothing about the police as yet, I thought he was, but other cops regarded him with suspicion or even hatred. No cop in his right mind would commit a corrupt act when Durk was around.

Durk lived with his wife and two daughters in a rent controlled apartment on 70th Street just off Central Park. Patrolman Frank Serpico, supposedly his friend, was often there, as was I. Serpico would come in, lay his various guns on the mantelpiece, and get down on the floor with the little girls. When they were put to bed, he and Durk would argue. Whatever position Durk took on whatever subject, Serpico upheld the opposite.

Durk had wanted me to meet Serpico. Then he wanted me to meet other honest cops he knew. Durk fascinated me. Cops had begun to fascinate me. One night a producer named John Foreman was there. He claimed to be Paul Newman's partner. He said a movie about Durk was being planned, with Newman playing Durk. A few weeks later Newman's then favorite director, Stuart Rosenberg turned up. Durk wanted me to meet him too, said I had to be there. He wanted me to write the movie; that way he could better control what was in it. He introduced me to Rosenberg as his writer. The director, very polite, did not even blink.

But these people came and went and nothing happened.

Serpico was not a mainstream cop either. He was what was known then as a kook. He wore a bushy black beard and an earring, the better to entrap prostitutes and junk dealers. He lived in a tiny, cluttered, dirty, one room apartment in Greenwich Village, alone except for an enormous sheepdog, and two goldfish bowls, with so much tattered and broken furniture crammed in that one could barely move. A real Bohemian pad, I thought when I saw it. He carried at least two guns everywhere he went, sometimes three, and showed them to a succession of girlfriends because he had found it turned them on; most times he allowed the girls to think he was not a cop but a gangster. He was a loner. None of the girls lasted. He had almost no friends. He was perhaps excruciatingly honest. Mostly his principal character trait was something else. He did not want to get involved. In anything.

One day a fellow plainclothesman handed him $300, saying it came from a gambler known as Jewish Max, who was being protected by the precinct. Not knowing what else to do, and not wanting to get involved, Serpico brought the money to Durk, whom he knew from plainclothes school.

With Serpico's money in his hand, Durk was exultant. Here was the proof he had been looking for. Serpico's $300 was proof.

He now dragged Serpico from one agency to another. Serpico was reluctant every time; he did not want to get involved. Durk showed the money to officials and demanded action. He got none. He dragged Serpico to City Hall, spoke to one of Mayor Lindsay's bright young men, but they and Lindsay did nothing. He dragged Serpico to *The New York Times*, which at first did not react either. Durk brought in three or four other honest cops who had seen corruption first hand. Same result.

But finally the Times ran a three part expose that blew the roof off police headquarters and City Hall both. Lindsay formed a corruption investigation commission and filled it with his own men. It was laughed out of existence. A second, independent commission was formed headed by Whitman Knapp. The Knapp Commission would sit for about two years, and would expose plenty. The incumbent police commissioner, Howard Leary, sailed for Europe without even leaving a note. To replace him, Lindsay appointed Patrick Murphy, a name and person who meant nothing to most people, certainly not to me. If you had told me what was ahead both for both of us, a joint future, so to speak, I would have dismissed the notion as preposterous.

So Murphy took over the NYPD, and at the same time a magazine asked me to do a profile of Paul Newman. "Good," said Durk when I told him. "Find out about the film they're doing on me."

This was my idea too. The magazine assignment came in the midst of the World Publishing Company lawsuit against McCracken and me. I still had two books hung up in the suit, was still scrambling for jobs. This one would pay $1,600, money I needed. In general, profiles of actors were not difficult to do. More importantly, I would meet Newman, and when the moment was ripe I would ask him if he really meant to play Durk on the screen, and if the answer was yes I would propose myself as the screen writer.

Paul Newman, in a formal interview, turned out to be a poor subject, one of the poorest I have encountered. If asked a direct question his speech faltered, he became monosyllabic, almost inarticulate. The question could be anything. For instance: why did he choose to live in Connecticut? It took him so long to get the answer out that by the time it came, the question no longer seemed interesting. I was almost ashamed to have asked it. "Well, why live anywhere?" he said finally, which didn't seem too interesting either. To find out who he was and how and why, I soon saw, I would have to give him time to reveal himself in his own way and in words of his own choosing. This meant trailing him everywhere for an extended period of time. He was then 46 years old and at the peak of his fame.

"Hold this," he said, handing me a half empty can of beer.

Turning, he clambered over the back seat and out onto the tailgate of the station wagon, where someone handed him a microphone. This was in upstate Connecticut, where today Paul was campaigning on behalf of Joe Duffey, Democratic candidate for the United States Senate.

About 500 people who had been waiting in the rain in a shopping center rushed forward. From below the tailgate anonymous hands reached to touch whatever part of Paul Newman they could reach.

"Get in front of me, get in front of me," he started yelling to the bodyguards, five teenage boys recruited from local high schools and colleges. They traveled in the car ahead of us, and at each stop their job was to surround the tailgate so as to keep the predominantly female crowd off Paul Newman.

"Madame, that's very rude," Paul suddenly cried.

Annoyed, upset, he launched into his prepared speech: "If I seem to carry more weight than my credentials allow, just because I am an actor, I apologize. But I don't think I turned in my citizenship when I got my actors card. I'm here because I am a resident of Connecticut, and because I have six kids —"

A girl in the crowd — she couldn't have been more than 13 — called out: "would you like to try for seven?"

"—And when my kids," continued Paul, "put this old carcass in that six foot hole—"

"Oh, Paul," called out another female voice, "you could never die."

"—I don't want my kids to write on my tombstone that their father never had time to be part of his time."

After making a five-minute pitch on behalf of the liberal democratic candidate, Paul asked for questions from the crowd: "I'd like them to be of a political rather than of a personal nature."

But most spectators were struck dumb.

"Yes, I sleep in pajamas." Paul joked, trying to get them started.

"Feel free to insult me." More laughter. "It is my conviction that a man who doesn't have any enemies doesn't have any character."

Presently Paul clambered back across the seats.

"That woman you told off," I asked, "what did she do?"

"The full grope," muttered Paul. "There's the mini-grope, the midi-grope, and the maxi grope. That one was the full fold. The gropers aren't even young girls, they're middle-aged women. Young girls I could almost understand, but how can middle-aged women be so rude?"

To be mauled in crowds is something that pretty and/or pneumatic girls face all time. It came as a shock to realize that this 46 year-old concerned citizen had to face it too, and that obviously he didn't know how to shrug it off.

The station wagon nosed dangerously through the crowd. The windows were up. People were rapping on the glass, and peering in at one of us animals in particular, who stared straight ahead.

There were eight of us, sometimes nine in the station wagon. The campaign coordinator, a college sophomore, called across the seats to the driver who was no older: "The next stop please dispose of the trash buildup."

The boy at the wheel gave an elaborate sigh: "Dispose of it? I'll sell it—he touched it."

Everybody laughed but Paul Newman who, with an expression on his face that could almost be called sullen, said nothing.

The kids kidded about him. The adults in the car were thinking principally about their candidate, not Paul Newman. Paul wasn't even a particularly good speaker. He was extremely sincere, he knew what he wanted to say, and at some stops the words came out in reasonably good order, but in others they didn't. He didn't enjoy campaigning, he wasn't good at it, but had agreed to do it for 57 speeches in 57 towns for three straight days — strictly because he felt it was his duty as an American to participate in elections.

At lunchtime we stopped in a motel. The four adults were in one bedroom, the bodyguards and drivers in another, and sandwiches were brought in by one of the kids who at the same time handed Paul a paper to sign.

"The owner wants your autograph."

Paul was not only reluctant to answer direct questions, he also rarely signed autographs. But after hesitating, he signed this one. "Please tell her not to show it around."

Then he said to us: "About 35 years ago the convention was established that if you're a movie star you must sign your name to a piece of paper every 30 feet as you walk down Fifth Avenue. Well, I didn't agree to that convention, and I don't see why I should feel bound by it. To sign them is pretentious and smacks of arrogance, and to ask for them just gives people an excuse to be rude."

Now the campaign kid reentered carrying two plates of fried potatoes that we did not order.

"That paper you signed," he explained to Paul, "was a registration blank with lots of carbons. The owner gave a copy to the chef, so the chef sends you two orders of fried potatoes."

At the next stop the driver said to one of the bodyguards: "Hold his jacket."

"I don't want to hold his jacket."

"You don't want to hold his jacket? A thousand women would give their eyes to hold his jacket."

At last the day's campaigning was ending. We stopped in a gas station. It was nearly midnight. Someone had gone to fetch ice, a bottle of Scotch, and some hamburgers. Paul was standing beside the car when two young women drove up, recognized him and requested his autograph.

He leaned into their car saying: "I don't sign autographs, but I'll shake hands with you."

They drove away apparently delighted.

There were only three adults left in our car. During the ninety minute ride home we talked and drank. People had come up to him for autographs when he was standing at urinals, Paul said. Once when the Newmans were having dinner in a restaurant a man leaned over the table and invited them to join him and the woman he was with. Paul glanced over at the woman and she waved at him. "Thank you," said Paul to the man, "but I'm having dinner with my wife." The man kept insisting, Paul kept politely refusing until finally, startling the whole restaurant, the man snarled loudly: "Well fuck you, Newman."

By the time we reached Paul's house in Westport, the bottle was half empty. In the car headlights I saw him having a good deal of trouble getting his door open. His hand was not that steady, and the house was protected by elaborate burglar alarms that he might at any moment start ringing. The house was dark. There was no one inside to help him. Joanne Woodward, his wife, was at this moment coming across the country on a train, three days by herself, which she counted as a vacation. She did not have the recognition problem Paul had, even though she had won an Academy Award, and Paul, at that point in his career, had not.

We went fishing: Paul, myself, and A.E. Hotchner, the author, who was an old friend of Paul's. I drove up to Paul's house. It was 10 a.m. Joanne, wearing a brown and white dressing gown and slippers, handed me a cup of coffee, then put toast and eggs in front of Clea, 5 years old, their youngest daughter. It was, as always, hard for me to get used to seeing Joanne behaving like housewife.

Paul and I drove toward the river in his Volkswagen with the Porsche engine. He owned a number of these cars in various colors and on both coasts. They were as fast — and at least as expensive — as a Porsche, but as ugly and uncomfortable as a Volkswagen.

In his position I thought I would own a Ferrari, I said.

"But this is such a discreet car," he said. "You don't have people pulling alongside and waving at you through the window."

True, he didn't need a fancy car to prove he was Paul Newman, and when he parked his Volkswagen in among the Rolls-Royces at a Hollywood premiere, the crowd behind the police lines cheered, and this always amused him.

At the boat yard close to the mouth of the Saugatuck river Hotchner was waiting. Paul rented a rowboat, we dropped our chest of beer into it, Paul started the outboard motor, and we moved down river and out onto Long Island Sound. Soon there were no other boats within hailing distance, the sky was enormously high, and the sudden silence, when Paul shut the engine down, was not to be believed.

Sitting in the rowboat we bottom fished with worms for over six hours. We ate our picnic lunch. Paul told some obscene jokes. One of them, if I heard it correctly, was about the eagle that got raped by an elephant. Or perhaps it was the other away around. Hotch and I were both laughing. Paul told stories well, frequently acting out all roles. I had to keep telling myself not to be so surprised. He was an actor, was he not?

As we fished we talked about car racing, about death, about politics, about wine. Hotch propositioned Paul about starring in something Hotch was writing. Their friendship went way back, and Paul, declining, was exceedingly gentle: "You don't want me, Hotch, I wouldn't be right for it."

The subject died right there, Hotch saying no more about it all day.

It occurred to me that he had expected to be alone with Paul in this boat, free to push his proposition at length. If so, then my presence inhibited him, and perhaps he resented it, resented me. It occurred to me also that Paul might have invited me along for precisely this reason.

Paul yanked up his line, and at the end of it was a fish hooked through the tail.

"The reflexes of the man," joked Hotch. "If his fans only knew."

Then Hotch caught a bass, the best fish of the day. Paul and I went silent, watching him jealously. "We were having quite a good conversation," said Paul, "until this had to happen."

In one of the places where we anchored we caught nothing but tiny sea robins. They gobbled up all our bait. Paul, who thought we were catching the same fish again and again, began pitching them to the seagulls which caught and swallowed them on the fly.

"Killer Newman," said Hotch, "the terror of the deep. The side of him his fans never see."

We caught a good many flounders. Paul got the net bag, which was full of fish, tangled in the propeller. His language, as he worked to free it, was atrocious. Later we found ourselves in the shallows as the tide receded, and made jokes about our noble captain, Paul, who was cursing again, having run us aground.

At last it was late afternoon and we started back amid other boats. I noticed that each time one came within hailing distance, Paul's head went down and he pretended to be busy with the engine. With his famous face hidden, no one recognized him, there were no double takes or pointing fingers.

Hotch and I waved back at those who waved at us.

As our rowboat entered the river, Paul was standing up in the stern, steering with the pressure of his forefinger, a beer can in the other hand. In the voice of a news announcer, he suddenly said: "And here comes Paul Newman at the helm of his 56 foot cruiser. That's a bottle of Dom Perignon stuffed in his belt. Look out, he's about to eat some caviar—"

A week or so before, on the phone with a screen writer I had known for years, I mentioned I was doing a profile of Paul Newman.

"From what everyone says out here," the screen writer said, "he is one genuinely nice man."

"I know. I keep expecting it will stop."

"With him, I don't think it will."

I spent most of two weeks with Newman, and on the morning he was due to fly to California, knowing he was interested in car racing, I decided to make him a present of a copy of *The Cruel Sport.*

Only as I reached his house did I realize that the last thing he and Joanne needed as they rushed through the final packing, door locking and panic of departure was me and my small gift in the middle of it all. Furthermore, it was raining, and I tracked footprints into their kitchen, which was already crowded: the two men who would drive the Newmans, separately, to catch separate planes to Los Angeles; plus a cleaning woman; plus Joanne's stepfather who would look after the house in their absence; plus the five-year-old Clea who wasn't dressed yet; plus Paul who was half dressed, plus suitcases, plus Joanne, who was already screaming that they were going to miss the plane.

A scene known to any family that traveled. I've seldom felt more uncomfortable. Clumsily I handed over the book and turned to leave. "Wait," said Paul, "Come on in, no need to rush off."

He began looking into the book, grinning, pretending to be happy with it. He stuffed it into a satchel. "Great," he said, "I'll read on the plane. Come on into the bedroom while I finish dressing."

I protested, but he insisted, so I walked in past more suitcases and their unmade bed — Joanne would probably be mortified. I looked down at the bed and, feeling more uncomfortable than ever, thought inanely of the millions of teenage girls who would envy me this view of Paul Newman's rumpled pillows. Once, Paul ducked into the bathroom to pack his shaving gear. Rather than leave me standing uncomfortably alone in his bedroom, he went on talking from behind the door.

—While I stood there marveling at the simple courtesy of this man. A film star, of all people. We lived in a country and a period when scarcely anyone had time, much less inclination, to be nice to anyone else, but Paul Newman had time. I didn't think he was putting on a special show for me. There was nothing much I could do for Paul Newman.

Joanne and the child were gone by now. I tried to get away, but Paul protested that he still had 10 minutes. He got a key down off a shelf, opened the door to a screened in porch, and we stood outside, protected from the rain, talking about Christmas in New England.

This was my last chance to talk about Durk and the possible movie. Myself as possible screenwriter.

I couldn't do it.

Someone else had mentioned Durk some days ago. Paul did not react. He did not seem to know very well who he was. Years later, when I had learned much more about Hollywood, I would realize that producers and directors usually had development deals with studios. The two men who had invoked Paul's name to Durk, both of whom had worked with Paul previously, had been trying to get something new started. The way to do this was to throw Paul Newman into the mix. Mention Newman and everyone listened, got cooperative fast.

Happened a lot, I learned later. Another of the crosses on the back of Paul Newman. Happened to other movie stars too, of course. But Paul was particularly hot just then, and so paid a somewhat higher price than others.

About this time the New York cops went on strike in a contract dispute over money. Cops sat in their station houses or in their cars, refusing to go out on patrol. The new police commissioner, Patrick Murphy, who had been largely invisible until then, stayed invisible during the first five days of the strike. On the sixth day, he exerted maximum pressure, and broke the strike. The entire city was behind him by then, the strike running out of steam, and he gave officers down to the rank of lieutenant the power to suspend from duty and from being paid any cop who refused to go out on patrol.

The strike ended instantly.

Having no interest in the police commissioner or the department, apart from Durk and Serpico, I hardly noticed.

I spent my time calling on magazine editors, offering ideas, looking for assignments, the exact equivalent of the auditions an actor or singer goes through. One of my stops was at *New York Magazine* where the editor, Clay Felker, had seen my *Life Magazine* piece on Durk. Since I was obviously an expert on the police, he suggested I write a profile of Commissioner Murphy. Murphy was an idea man rather than a hero cop, Felker said. An intellectual. A former top cop in Syracuse, Washington and Detroit. A New Yorker whose biggest previous job in New York was command of the Police Academy. A modernizer. A corruption fighter.

I had known Felker for some years, and for six months when he was an editor at *Esquire* I had written a monthly column for him. Now he had floated *New York Magazine*, his own magazine at last. It was almost as new as Murphy was, and still paying low prices. For a profile of Police Commissioner Murphy he offered me $750.

I had to take it, and I went to meet Murphy.

I only saw him twice, following him on his rounds, which were mostly political, no excitement at all, spending most of two days with him. He turned out to be a smallish man who spoke in a monotone, who discussed crime, violence, degradation with studied detachment, as if he had read it all in a book. Nothing he said was quotable. Nothing he said seemed to excite him in any way, much less me.

Is two days with a man enough for a profile such as I had been assigned?

No. But I did not see the point of going back to him. He was boring. If my article was not to be boring, too, I would have to jazz it up somehow with quotes from others. Declining to visit Commissioner Murphy again, I did this, then started to write the piece. It was agony.

But at the end of that first day with him, as I stepped out of his official car, he had asked me to send him my resume. "Yes, of course," I promised, wishing to keep him cooperative. But I sent him nothing.

I phoned Durk. "What does he want?"

"Probably he wants you as the department press officer," guessed Durk. "Carries the rank of Deputy Commissioner."

My second and last interview with Murphy came one week later. At the end of it, the same. "I thought you were going to send me your resume," he said.

"Yes, well, I wondered what you wanted it for."

"If you would be interested, that is," he said. "Interested in working in the department."

I wasn't interested, but did not say so. Instead I talked to Durk again. "It must be that," he said. "Deputy commissioner. What else could it be?"

I still wasn't interested. Nonetheless, a week later I sat down and typed out my name, age, education and the titles of some of my books, sent it on to police headquarters, and forgot the whole thing.

The article on him was in, not a very good one, I thought, though Felker said it was fine. But weeks went by, and the article did not appear.

Then Serpico was shot.

He was making a drug bust. It was a clumsy bust, and he made it clumsily. He was trying to force open a partly opened door and a hand came out with a gun in it and shot him in the face. The bullet went in beside his left nostril and tried to come out his ear, but failed. He went down but not out. He heard everything from then on, but couldn't move.

By this time, still not wanting to get involved, Serpico had been forced to testify in court against other cops, thus breaking the police code of silence, and getting himself solidly hated by all cops. It was a junkie who had shot him; the junkie was captured the next day. But the fear inside the department was that a cop had done it. The story therefore, was potentially a good one, and Clay Felker immediately asked me to write it. I did so, visiting in the process Serpico's bohemian pad in Greenwich Village for the first time, and walking with him, his sheepdog and all his many guns out onto the disused and rotting piers that reached into the Hudson a block or so away. It was during these interviews that I learned, among other details, how much he resented David Durk, or perhaps hated him—the two emotions are not very far apart,

New York Magazine came out with Serpico's name on the cover, mine too, and the cover photo was an xray of Serpico's skull showing that the bullet, broken into pieces, was still in there.

This cover story provoked a number of reactions. They were instantaneous, and they were, to me, stunning.

First, the movie people, who had disappeared without a peep five months previously, descended en masse, waving money, flashing famous names.

And second, Commissioner Murphy's office called. He wanted me to come in and see him.

The movie people—agents, producer, studio—had a deal worked out within hours. Paul Newman would play Durk, we were told, Robert Redford would be Serpico. The director would be George Roy Hill, who had directed them both in two fabulously successful films, *Butch Cassidy and the Sundance Kid*, and then *The Sting*. Warner Brothers would bankroll a $5 million production, which was a big price at the time. My articles would serve as the basis of the screenplay. Durk, Serpico and I would split our share three ways.

Nice. The only problem was that Serpico balked, wouldn't sign. He didn't see why I should be in the deal at all, and he especially didn't want Durk in the deal. As he saw it, everyone was trying to make money out of his blood. When his agent tried to talk sense into him, he fired that agent and found another.

From his point of view the new agent did better. There was no way to cut Durk (and Paul Newman) out of the project, but to please Serpico my share got cut way down, leaving more money to Serpico, and of course to Durk as well. What they were to be paid and what I was to be paid does not matter now, as we shall see. Serpico agreed to these new terms. Durk agreed. Having no choice I agreed. Our agents and the Hollywood agents shook hands all around, and although no contracts were signed, we now had what in Hollywood counted as a solid deal. Contracts take ages to draw up. Films have sometimes been completed before contracts were signed. Once a deal has reached the stage ours had reached I have never known one to fail.

Warner Brothers took out a full page ad in Variety announcing the project.

And that was the last any of us ever heard about it. There was never even any explanation. This was a clear breach of contract under California law, where verbal contracts are binding, but we didn't know this. We might have sued. Most Hollywood people probably would have sued.

I declined an offer to write a book about Serpico, but a man named Peter Maas wrote one, entitled it *Serpico*, and afterwards Sidney Lumet bought the book and made a film out of it, keeping the title. This film, which starred Al Pacino, had some truth in it, not very much. Serpico/Pacino singlehandedly brings on the Knapp Commission, Serpico/Pacino single-handedly ends police corruption forever, Serpico/Pacino is heroically shot while making a brilliant arrest.

In the film *Serpico* came across as an unalloyed hero when in fact he had been a reluctant one at best, serving throughout principally as Durk's instrument. The movie made Serpico famous, not Durk. In the film there was no David Durk. No movie about Durk was ever made.

In response to the summons by Police Commissioner Murphy, I was again shown into his office. Again he got up from behind his big desk and came forward and shook hands. There were others in the room as well, his legal counsel, some high ranking cops with stars on their shoulders whom I did not yet know.

All spring I had sensed this summons would come. Even though Murphy's original feeler had been so tentative—that's all it had been, a feeler—even as the months had gone by, nonetheless I had sensed it would come, and sometimes I would wander along the tree-lined streets near my house wondering what I would say when it did. I was not a policeman and did not wish to be. I did not want or need a steady job. I was a writer and that's all I was.

Murphy's office, in its old fashioned way, was gorgeous. High decorated ceiling, brass chandelier, walls paneled in dark carved oak, a rug on the floor, red velvet drapes. His huge desk had once belonged to a previous reform commissioner, Theodore Roosevelt, who had gone on to the White House, leaving the desk behind. Roosevelt's portrait, painted when he was about 40, hung in a heavy frame over Murphy's marble fireplace.

I had forgotten how slight a figure the PC was, how low-keyed. He had thin gray hair. He talked. The other men in the room said nothing. I said almost nothing. Murphy made what was almost a speech. Without the support of the public the police can do nothing, he told me. Unless people trust the police, unless they are willing to come forward with information, are willing to serve as witnesses and jurors at trials, unless they are willing to believe police testimony—-the police are powerless. But we lived in a time, he said, when policemen were despised in this city. Police were often referred to as pigs. There were pig T-shirts, pig jokes. Assaults on cops had gone way up. A few days ago two cops had been shot in the back and killed as they walked down a sidewalk. Two others had been machine gunned in their radio car. There had been other attempted ambushes as well, and—

As a deputy commissioner I would be part of Murphy's cabinet, he said, a civilian adviser. I would supervise a staff of thirty three cops, with a car and driver assigned to me around the clock. My principal job would be to win the people back for the cops.

What did he see in me, I asked myself. Well, he had promised to stamp out corruption, and I had written two big articles about the department's most prominent accusers. Therefore, if he invited me into his inner circle, if he exposed the workings of the department to an outsider like me, he would perhaps buy himself instant credibility with the city. Perhaps he thought he was buying the good will of *The New York Times* as well, for he might not have realized that the Times' good will was not for sale. Besides, I had not worked there now in seven years. Later someone was to say to me, "Even your name was right," meaning that, in a department still dominated by men of Irish Catholic origin, my Irish Catholic name fit right in.

Murphy was a man with problems. He needed help, and perhaps imagined I could give it to him. Looking back, I can see what these problems were, though I didn't at the time. He wanted to reorganize and modernize the department in a business sense, and he wanted to—had to, in the face of the Knapp Commission—put an end to systemic corruption. But his immediate subordinates knew him as bookish Pat Murphy from the Police Academy. They had no great love for him, and were not interested in his new ideas which possibly threatened themselves. Their resistance could be depended upon, and they could block his programs simply by sitting on their hands. If he pushed them too hard, if the department ceased to function properly, if he lost control of it—then what? He had after all no job tenure at all. Turn the mayoral whim against himself and he was out, and the disgrace was not something a man could expect to live down. In one sense he had absolute authority over 32,000 armed men. In another, he had none at all. He had to subjugate the department first. He had to make believers of his subordinates and of the mayor and of the city. He had to prove himself to be forward-thinking, bold, hard-nosed, tough—and get his programs in place.

That was where I came in. I would have two jobs, not one, but no one ever spelled this out to me. Yes, I would be expected to win the public back for the police. Even more importantly I would have to find a way to build Murphy into a dominant personage, for this was what he was hoping for, build him into a man of such stature that he could command and be obeyed.

Did I want the job or not? I had come into the room undecided, and was still undecided, and I glanced around at the other men, at Roosevelt's portrait, even as the police commissioner in his low, quiet voice went on selling me on the department.

Any time a man makes a major decision he does so, most likely, for more than one reason—often for many reasons, some of them important and some probably silly. If, now, I should tell Murphy yes, what would my reasons be?

Civic duty would be one of them. I had always considered myself one of the good guys. If a man is offered a chance to do public service on this level and refuses, then he could no longer call himself one of the good guys, it seemed to me. So the pull of civic duty was certainly there, and it was strong. Too much exposure to Durk was perhaps partly responsible.

Durk, if he were here, would tell me I did not have the right to say no.

In his quiet way the PC was almost pleading. That he seemed to want me so much was intensely flattering.

And I was tired of being locked in a small room every day alone, as I tried to dredge words out of my head. The police department at the very least would be a vacation from that struggle. I would be around people, would see something new that might be interesting. I didn't have to stay long. A year. Two at the most.

I who had never got higher than corporal in the Air Force would start off as a deputy commissioner. A fanciful detail only, but it amused me, and at this point all details counted.

I was a New Yorker born and bred, had not only grown up in its streets, but had done every day of my schooling in New York City. I would be returning to my city, would be close to the hierarchy that ran my city.

And so I looked across at Murphy, but still I hesitated.

That I might write about the experience later did not, at that moment, enter my head, was not one of my reasons, did not influence me in the slightest. There were no books about the NYPD at that time. The department's hands were folded across its chest, and almost no inside information was ever given out ever. The NYPD was inaccessible. It was totally closed off from the city and the world. Secrecy was a way of life, was virtually total. As a result no appetite for New York cop stories had been whetted. No one was interested in the NYPD, and this included, to a large extent, me. I did not know what my job would entail, or what the department would be like from the inside, and could not be sure I would see or hear anything of interest. One thing I did know, books had to be based on grand events. One can't simply lump together family fights and isolated stickups. Events grand enough to make a book might never take place—certainly there had been none in recent memory.

Nor did I leap at the job for the money. True, the year just past had shaken my confidence in myself, but it was over now. Contracts had been signed with Coward-McCann to publish the McCracken diary, I had reestablished contact with the magazines I needed, and in the five months since January 1, I had earned about $20,000. Optimistically I could expect to double that before this year was out. And so, given that the new job paid only $28,500 a year—the PC himself got $41,000—I would if I took it be losing money.

Also, from what Murphy was telling me now, the law demanded that commissioners and deputy commissioners actually live in New York. I could keep my house in the Riverside section of Greenwich, but my official residence would have to be within the city limits.

Which meant I would have to find an apartment, carry two residences, which would be costly. I would have to buy suitable clothes, for I owned hardly anything. For seven years I hadn't needed clothes, had worked every day in corduroys and sweaters. On my rare excursions to New York to see or lunch with editors a blazer and gray slacks had been enough.

And except for Durk, I did not like cops. Cops to me were rude young men who gave you traffic tickets. I had no love for them, not even any respect for them, no interest in them or their world.

I hesitated a moment longer.

Then told Murphy I would take the job.

All the way home I asked myself: What am I in for? Why did I do that?

I had requested two weeks in which to finish the assignments I was working on. In that time also I bought one summer weight suit and two summer weight sports jackets, for the month was June, and New York City was going to be hot.

On the appointed day I appeared at Police Headquarters, which was then at 240 Centre Street. To the cops on guard at the door I introduced myself as the new deputy commissioner, then went as instructed into the basement to be fingerprinted, photographed and issued a gold shield and an ID card. I was asked if I intended to carry a gun. The idea horrified me, and I said no—unlike cops who were obliged by law to be armed at all times, deputy commissioners were not. About three months later I would change my mind, be thoroughly trained, and walk the streets with a .38 caliber Smith and Wesson in my belt. When *The New York Times* found out this caused considerable controversy, which did not die down for months. Reporters asked me why I now carried a gun and I told them I had had several death threats, which was true, and that in addition I was constantly going into dangerous situations with cops—also true. I explained all this, but it did little good. In any case my principal reason was something else, and I chose not to reveal it at the time. I had observed that the gun culture inside the department was very strong, that it was the gun, not the shield, that made cops go into dangerous situations. It was the gun, not the shield, that made them behave like cops.

And having noted this, I wanted to know what carrying a gun felt like. I wanted to be able to describe the emotion accurately, if ever called upon to do so.

I found, as all cops find, that being armed imposes a terrific burden. Because the gun is registered, meaning that, in effect, your name is written on it, you must carry it everywhere, lest it be stolen, for it can be used in crimes, and can then be traced back to its original owner, you. It is lethal, and must therefore be safeguarded from children, wife, everyone. You can never set it down without removing the bullets first. You must never let it out of your sight—which is almost impossible. I used to walk the streets worrying about being caught in a stickup or murder or some such thing. If I used it, what a scandal that would make!

In the police commissioner's office that first day I was sworn in by the department's chief clerk—I was made to pledge allegiance to the constitutions of the country, the state and the city. With this momentous event out of the way the department photographer posed me for the traditional photo: the warm, welcoming handshake from Police Commissioner Murphy.

My predecessor had been a career civil servant. I never met him. He was gone now, I did not know where. His job seemed to have been to keep the public from meeting or knowing anyone in headquarters. Anyone in any of the 75 precincts for that matter. Requests for interviews would go up through the chain of command and could be disapproved at each level. Few ever made it to the top. Requests to write articles or books were met usually with stony silence. The police department spoke with one voice, but most times didn't.

In my own office I met my three secretaries: a civilian woman and two cops. I met my chief of staff, an inspector—the equivalent of a colonel in the army. I met some of the others, three of them sergeants. I didn't know what any of these people did. I met my chauffeurs, both cops, who would alternate driving me wherever I wished to go, day or night.

No one seemed to regret my missing predecessor.

Seen from the outside the headquarters building was handsome. Four stories, long and narrow, decorated with pilasters, cornices and pediments. The roof carried a high, heavy dome in its middle. Built in the first years of the century, the building much resembled City Hall a few blocks to the south. And Patrick Murphy's office was gorgeous, as I have said. My own, though large enough, turned out to be as drab a space as any in which I have ever sat, and so was every other office in the rather rundown building, I was to learn. The walls of all of them had been painted institutional green, though not in several decades. Except for the nail holes, and the discolored squares around them, my own walls were bare, and I did not see how any decoration could improve them.

Suddenly there burst in on me a three-star chief named McGovern whom I did not know and had never heard of before today. McGovern, who was head of Internal Affairs, had a florid Irish face and a loud Irish voice. He just wanted to tell me how glad he was to meet me, he said loudly, and how happy he was to welcome me into the department. The enthusiasm he put into these remarks suggested that nothing had made him this happy in months. He called me sir or Commissioner three times in every sentence, and he promised that we would work beautifully together, that anything I wanted from him I could have, and if I ever needed help, just ask. I expected him any moment to invite me to his house. I had the impression that if I had told a joke he would have broken into uncontrollable laughter well before the punch line.

Finally McGovern went out. I had never experienced this level of obsequiousness before, and I was perplexed. McGovern was beloved by cops in the street, I would learn, because during his tenure he had not been able to find much corruption. He was one of those whom Durk had approached with Serpico and the $300; he had taken no action.

I went to lunch with Mike Codd, 54, the chief inspector, a tall, white haired man, the highest ranking uniformed officer, four stars. I was so little informed about the department that I didn't know whether to address him as chief or inspector, and so called him nothing. He called me Bob. So did Murphy, but no one else did. There were at this time fourteen one star chiefs, eleven two star chiefs, four three star chiefs, including McGovern, and then Codd on top. All were men in their fifties. All had been cops at least thirty years. All were men in front of whom ordinary cops trembled. Everyone of them, whether on or off duty, called me commissioner, or sir. Or else, sometimes, boss. This never changed in all the time I was there.

It took months before this ceased to surprise me. It was as if they were afraid of me, as I think now they were.

Prior to lunching together, Codd and I had met in his office. A coat tree stood in one corner, and I watched him remove and hang up his uniform jacket with its four stars on each epaulet, exchanging it for a sports jacket off the same coat tree. Cops were not permitted to drink in uniform, he explained to me. Wearing the sports jacket enabled him to go into a restaurant and order a tall one which, as soon as we had crossed the street and the waiter had seated us, he proceeded to do. Beneath the sports jacket his uniform trousers with stripes down the legs showed clearly enough, and so did the projecting tip of his holster.

Over lunch I tried to talk to him about ideas I had for improving the police image. To begin with, secrecy for the sake of secrecy must be ended. If the people knew better what cops were doing and why, maybe they wouldn't mistrust cops so much. The press, the people, should be told as much as we can at all times, I said. We'll open all the doors and windows, and—

The press hates us, Bob, Codd interrupted, the people hate us. Nothing can be done about that. Keeping the public informed about the police won't do any good. And answering questions about an investigation in progress is out of the question. You'd be telling the perpetrators what we know and don't know as well. You'd be compromising the investigation.

I mentioned a few other ideas I had, but he interrupted each time, advising me that no changes could be made in the way the NYPD operated, and I would only cause myself trouble if I tried. Best just to go along with the present method of doing things.

Finally I shut up. When lunch had ended I went back to my drab office and sat behind my drab desk in silence. From whatever direction I contemplated the future it looked so dull and uninteresting that once again I confronted the old questions: What have I got myself into here? What have I done?

The next morning I went to a press conference in the office of Burton Roberts, the elected district attorney of Bronx county. Full room. Print reporters seated, TV crews standing. Some detectives had broken up a Bronx stolen car ring, and from behind a big table the grinning, joking Roberts described the case, and took credit for it as if he himself had engineered the arrests perfectly, which he had not. Most likely he had not even known about them until yesterday. He showed tools and other paraphernalia the thieves had used to break into, break up, cars.

As I watched Roberts' performance, I realized that this was what always happened. The NYPD was allowed to take credit for all acts of corruption and brutality, for acts of stupidity too. But let cops bring a case to a successful conclusion, make one or more brilliant arrests, and the DAs moved in and grabbed the spotlight. Given such a one sided arrangement as this, it was no wonder the police image was where it was. Past police commissioners, past police commanders, had simply let them do it.

Why? Commanders of whatever rank, I soon learned, were terrified of elected officials, who had tenure whereas they did not, and they would take their every phone call, would obey to the limit of their strength any suggestion any one of them sent forward. Since I didn't know any of this yet, I saw no reason to be afraid of Burton Roberts who, it seemed to me, needed to be put in his place.

The arresting officers were ranged along the wall behind him. They stood in absolute silence, and Roberts waved in their direction from time to time, but when one of the TV reporters asked permission to interview one of them on camera, Roberts said this wouldn't be possible. Might prejudice the rights of the prisoners in custody, or their eventual conviction.

Clearly he had the spotlight where he wanted it. He intended to share it with no one.

But as soon as he had stood up, indicating that the press conference was over, I stepped forward and announced in a loud voice that this case had been broken by NYPD detectives, who would now be available to answer questions, and that furthermore, from now on any request by the press to interview any police officer of whatever rank would be honored whenever possible. Employing the same metaphor as with Codd at lunch, I spoke of open windows, open doors. Obviously there would be times when certain details would have to be withheld. To protect an investigation in progress, for instance, or to prevent the disappearance of a suspect, or to safeguard the rights of the accused. But in general the old policy of an unresponsive department, and of routine police secrecy was, I said, herewith changed.

The reporters clustered around the detectives, who seemed happy to be interviewed. Roberts, as I left the room, looked livid.

One of my sergeants, Ed Powers, had accompanied me to the press conference, and as we got into the elevator he said: "Whew!"

It took half an hour to drive back to headquarters, where one of my secretaries said, as I came in the door: "The PC wants to see you."

I went down there.

Murphy came around from behind Roosevelt's big desk. In the last half hour, he had taken calls from Roberts, from the Mayor, he said. "I guess you caused quite a stir up there." He was smiling. He seemed pleased with me. Roberts would get over it, he said. And he began to talk of another of his problems: how to communicate with his 32,000 men. He could send out T.O.P.s from headquarters, order them tacked on the bulletin boards in every station house in the city, but there was no way to make cops read them. The men didn't read the bulletin boards. They read the Daily News, and that's all.

This gave me an idea, but it would take a few days to work it out. I said: "Then we'll just have to try to reach them via the Daily News."

On May 19, three weeks earlier, (the date has stuck in my mind all these years; I did not have to look it up) black revolutionaries had machine gunned two cops as they sat in their car on guard outside the house of Manhattan District Attorney Hogan. Though the cops did not die, they took so many .45 caliber bullets through their uniforms that they were ruined forever as human beings. Two nights later two other cops were assassinated as they strolled along a sidewalk in the Polo Grounds housing complex, shot repeatedly in the back, and their guns stolen.

Since then hardly a word had come out of the NYPD. These cowardly attacks had caused the buildup of a great well of sympathy for cops and for the department, I believed. We ought to be tapping into that, I thought, but to do so I needed to know what was going on.

I went into the office of Chief of Detectives Seedman, which was adjacent to my own, and asked to be briefed on the investigations in progress.

Already I had made a mistake. In the NYPD the man with the higher rank stayed put. The underling came to him. I should have "invited" Seedman into my office; the invitation would have had the force of an order. Doing it the other way around signaled weakness on my part—uncertainty at least—and to such signals as this every man in headquarters was attuned, down as low as sergeants. I would realize all this only much later. At the time I knew nothing about signals. Freelance writers do not deal in signals. I could not imagine that anyone would count as important who went to whose office.

In the NYPD Albert Seedman was an anomaly: an educated man, a Jew, and a three star chief. He was stocky, smoked cigars, and had an irreverent sense of humor. He was one of the few high ranking cops who was not immediately obsequious to me.

I had not even concluded my request to be briefed on the investigations in progress before he was shaking his head: "That's sensitive information,

Commissioner. We don't give information like that to anyone."

Meaning me.

I pushed a little harder, but Seedman would tell me nothing. When I continued to question him he fell silent, and only kept shaking his head.

I went down the hall to Murphy's office, walked in on him and said: "He won't tell me."

"Oh no," the police commissioner said, "you're to know everything I know."

Everything? Of course I was surprised. My immediate thought was: I may have lucked into something here after all.

I went back to Seedman. Murphy must have phoned him in the interim, and when he saw me he shrugged.

"If he wants you to know, you can know."

Later, for reasons I will go into, Seedman and I would become friends, but not yet.

Murphy who, until then, had made few personnel changes and had put almost no programs in place, now fired McGovern, replacing the do-nothing internal affairs chief with a man named Syd Cooper, who in the middle of the night went out at the head of his men looking for radio cars in the coop, as the police euphemism had it—cops sleeping on duty. Moving from precinct to precinct he found cars parked in dark school yards, in a disused fire house, in parks under the trees, the cops inside sound asleep, not just one car in each precinct, but many. In one high crime precinct in Brooklyn he found seven out of ten cars in the coop.

When he heard Cooper's report, Murphy in his quiet way was furious. We had a meeting at which we talked over what to do. Present were Murphy, Cooper, Codd, me, some others. In certain of the precincts Murphy intended to sack the captains in command, he said. For months he had been preaching that precinct captains were accountable for their men. No one had taken him seriously, but now he would prove he meant business.

Should we, I asked the assembled group, make the information public, or not?

Absolutely not, said Chief Inspector Codd. We should keep this thing as quiet as possible. The numbers of cars and men caught cooping made the department look awful. With luck no one would ever know.

The other commanders agreed, of course. In every police discussion I ever attended everyone always agreed with whatever the highest ranking man put forth.

The story should be buried, they all said now.

Only Murphy was silent.

"I think we should hold a press conference," I said.

"No, bury it," they said.

"To bury a story like this is impossible," I said. "It will leak out, and when it does the department will look worse than ever."

A grudging concession from the others. "All right, but only a press release, and very short. Maybe it will be overlooked."

"I say we go public," I said. "The PC should go before the press and announce that cooping is corruption too, and he won't stand for it, and name the captains who are being replaced."

The opposition was instantaneous. "We've never done such a thing before."

"That's not the way we do things here."

"You can't change peoples' opinions about us."

I said: "The cops will read about it in the Daily News, and they'll think twice about cooping again."

Everyone looked to the PC. "Set up the press conference, Bob," he said.

Nervously, I did so. Suppose no one came. What an embarrassment.

But the conference hall was full, half a dozen camera crews, the rest print reporters. Murphy made his presentation, answered questions, and that night led all local news broadcasts, not to mention the next morning's headlines.

A day or two later he sacked the three-star chief of patrol. To replace him he took an obscure 41 year old inspector and jumped him three ranks over many others who had been waiting ahead of him in line.

Press conference.

Early on I saw that Murphy had a number of constituencies, some of which were sometimes mutually exclusive, or seemed so. Yet he had to try to appeal to them all—his men, his immediate subordinates, the mayor, the city itself—all at once.

Day after day the Knapp Commission was dredging up corrupt actions, corrupt cops. To counteract this Murphy had to find a way to praise individual cops whenever possible. Now a cop in Queens killed a robber and delivered a baby on the same tour. I called a press conference, at which Murphy congratulated him. An undercover policewoman, making a narcotics buy, had her gun stolen, pressed to her head, and the trigger pulled. When the gun failed to fire the suspect ran off with it. The girl screamed for her back-ups, led the pursuit, got her gun back and made the arrest. I suggested a press conference at which Murphy would promote her to detective on camera. He agreed, and I had her brought to headquarters. In my office she turned out to be just a little thing, about five feet two, and she could have passed for a high school girl. Wearing a thick veil to conceal her identity, she and Murphy went out to meet the press.

Next he sacked the deputy commissioner in charge of youth services, giving himself an empty slot. This was pre-Godfather days; not only were FBI agents forbidden to work against organized crime, but when J. Edgar Hoover insisted that the Mafia did not exist he was widely believed. Murphy knew otherwise. He changed the line to deputy commissioner for organized crime control, and called out of retirement a man named

William McCarthy, formerly the strictest cop he knew, to fill it.

At the press conference he took questions.

"Hoover says there is no Mafia."

Then as always the Murphy avoided any sort of snide or smart response. "In New York," he said in his quiet droning voice, "we are plagued with not one but five Mafia families. They control the docks, garbage disposal, the garment industry and much else."

"Are you saying Mr. Hoover is a liar?"

On TV, mostly because of what he was not, Murphy was surprisingly effective. He did not have the shoulders of a linebacker, was not emotional, did not raise his voice, was not overbearing. People who might have been afraid of the classic, hard-nosed cop, were not afraid of this slightly built man with the thin gray hair, who tended to speak in a monotone.

"I'm saying Mr. Hoover lives in Washington. He does not know New York, or what we're faced with here in New York."

Wherever in the city the PC now went he wanted me with him. We spent hours and hours together riding through the streets in his official car. We did not become friends. Murphy was not a man who acquired friendships. He was extremely reserved, aloof, and had no friends that I knew about. During these rides he always answered my questions, or responded to my ideas, and sometimes he discussed one of his pet projects or peeves. He did not think much of Hoover, for instance, nor of three of the five New York DAs. Some days he sat beside me working on papers and did not say a word. Other days other commanders rode along, having jumped into the car as the only way they could get to talk to him.

He put into place the neighborhood police teams—cops who would get out of their cars and mingle with the people of the sectors they served.

Press conference.

He instituted the model precinct concept—a single precinct where newly sworn cops would go to be trained on the street by hand-picked sergeants and commanders.

Press conference.

As if to give weight to whatever he had to say he was always flanked by three or four top subordinates, always Chief Inspector Codd, usually me as well. Since by then I had begun to worry about what was happening to my literary career, I was glad to sit beside him. I couldn't afford to drop completely out of sight lest editors forget my name. Appearing on camera beside Murphy would remind them of me, I hoped. But I would have to do more than that, I believed, though for a time I could not figure out what.

There seemed to be more reporters, more cameras at each of these press conference. A pair of Brooklyn anti-crime cops known as Batman and Robin, had compiled an arrest record few other cops could match. This time it was Murphy suggesting to me that he promote them to detective at a press conference. They came to headquarters dressed as the hippies they pretended to be on the street, bringing with them as I had requested all the guns and knives they had seized recently, dozens and dozens of them, so many as to completely cover the table behind which they sat to either side of the police commissioner. This was one of the most heavily attended press conference yet. But there was always something prim, almost prissy, about Murphy, and I saw that he would have been more comfortable if the two cops had appeared wearing coats and ties.

Afterwards he said as much. "No," I told him, "those are the clothes they wear on duty, and it's much more dramatic this way." And he nodded and went back to his office.

He began to use the press conferences to put forth his ideas for a more effective, efficient police service, trying to speak to all of his constituencies at once. The civil service laws must be changed, he said. It was insane that a candidate who had never finished high school could become a New York cop. The lowest limit ought to be two years of college. Those same laws prevented him from hiring, apart from the seven deputy commissioners, anyone for any job from outside; all he could do was promote from below, whether there was a man competent down there or not, and this was insane too. He was against capital punishment for he had never seen the slightest evidence, statistical or otherwise, that it deterred crime. He urged congress to pass meaningful gun control laws, because New York was awash in guns. And there ought to be national standards for police training. America had 40,000 police forces, whereas most other advanced nations had seven or eight, and they trained their cops in national police academies, whereas, outside the major cities, most American cops hadn't been trained at all.

One week we had four press conferences in five days. It became impossible for high ranking subordinates to doubt that Murphy had taken command of the department, was steering it down new roads, and that they had best embrace his programs, put them into practice, and make sure they worked.

On television the PC had become a constant presence, not only during his own press conferences, but during talk shows as well, occasionally on a major network during prime time, regularly on the Sunday morning shows, whose producers wanted him whenever he would agree to appear.

In this way Murphy became a personage in the city. Preoccupied by his presidential campaigning in Florida and elsewhere, Mayor Lindsay had not yet noted what was happening behind his back.

All this time, especially at night, I went into station houses, talked to cops, sometimes rode with them. I believed I needed to know what cops did, and how. I went to crime scenes, ducked under the yellow tape, watched what was happening, talked to detectives, victims, suspects in handcuffs. I went up on dark rooftops with cops, watched them prowl about under the New York stars, guns in one hand, flashlights in the other, looking for the man with a gun that some citizen had reported to 911 but who, in my presence, was never there. Once I went into a bank vault with men from the bomb squad. Bombs set to go off had been placed in safe deposit boxes. I watched these men, who wore civilian clothes, slide the boxes gingerly out of the drawers, carefully open them, then defuse the bombs inside. The detectives on the case were cowering behind the vault door, which was six inches thick, and when it was over one of them said to me: "Commissioner, you got balls." I don't think so. I had wanted to see how it was done. It hadn't felt dangerous to me. The lieutenant bent over the bombs hadn't even removed his hat and coat.

I was trying to learn about the department, about law enforcement. Absorbing Murphy's theories wasn't enough. I wanted to see everything. I was learning as fast as I could.

Murphy was asked to make the keynote address at a bar association meeting in Town Hall. I wrote the speech in which he would denounce revolving door justice, and then, as any writer might have done, I stood in the back of the hall to make sure he did not change one word of it. Part of that particular speech later appeared as an article on the Op Ed page of *The New York Times* under his byline: By Patrick V. Murphy. This pleased him. Well, it pleased me, too.

He began to be asked for many other speeches. I wrote them as well.

He began routing me copies of nearly every memo he sent out to subordinates.

He went to a convention of the International Association of Chiefs of Police in Anaheim, California, and the other chiefs rose and applauded as he entered the hall. He was now the No. 1 cop in the country after Hoover, or perhaps before. Magazines sent journalists to write profiles. I sat in on most of the interviews, and unlike his manner when I had first met him, he answered their questions freely and in depth, even volunteered personal information about one of his brothers who was an alcoholic. *New York Magazine* put his picture on the cover, and suggested he run for mayor.

Once he said to me, "We've never had anything like this before, Bob." I was in thrall to him, but looking back I see now that he was in thrall to me, too.

There were executive conferences at least once a week. One week I came in a bit late, and looked for an empty chair. "Sit here, Bob," Murphy said, patting the place beside him, and I did. No doubt eyebrows went up all around the table as eighteen armed, middle aged men rearranging the status of the police hierarchy in their heads. The chair I was sitting in was a signal, and they were evaluating it. Evidently I fit in much higher than they had thought. But to me nothing significant had occurred. There had been an empty chair beside the police commissioner, and he had invited me to take it, so what.

I did not know what power consisted of in an organization of this kind, or how it was accorded or, once it had been accorded, how to use it. Later this chair incident made a good scene in one of my novels, for by then I had had time to recall and mull over my police experience, see it with a clarity that had been entirely lacking as it happened. But at the time the chair beside Murphy had had no value to me that I was aware of.

I began to send him memos recommending actions and decisions he should take in the coming weeks, sometimes explaining when and how he should do them. Some of my suggestions were slight, some heavy, and I watched as one by one he implemented them. The Knapp Commission had shown that gambling enforcement was the single most corruption prone police activity. I had studied many cases. They showed that bookies, runners and such were arrested repeatedly, some of them more than 20 times, without ever serving a meaningful jail sentence. I wrote him a memo. He should announce, my memo suggested, that the NYPD would no longer enforce the gambling laws, and that the 400 plainclothesmen assigned to gambling would henceforth be turned against street crime. I thought the city, and the legislature as well, would accept this. I thought no one would attack Murphy over it. The risk seemed to me small, and in my memo I outlined ways to make it smaller still.

"Do it, Bob," he said.

It became Christmas, six months since I had been sworn in. Cops who ran afoul of department regulations risked losing pay or vacation time. Because of the Knapp Commission police morale had reached its lowest ebb ever. Why not decree a Christmas amnesty for all minor infractions, I suggested, make the cops smile a bit?

He did this too, Merry Christmas to everybody, and when someone praised him for it I heard him say: "It was Bob who got it through."

The newly appointed deputy commissioner for organized crime control, this decorated ex-cop whom Murphy had brought out of retirement to run the most sensitive department units, came into my office, stood before my desk, and said: "Can you get me in to see the PC? He keeps saying he doesn't have time to see me. I really need to see him."

I told him I'd try. The man was going out of his mind, I told Murphy an hour later. He should make room for him as soon as he could.

Murphy's secretary called him and set up an appointment that very day.

Considering all the ways that power and influence within the NYPD were measured, it is possible to speculate that I had risen, for this brief—very brief—period, to the rank of No.2 man in the department, behind only Murphy himself.

Did I realize this at the time? Once, being driven to a crime scene in Brooklyn in my own private police car I remembered all those years in Europe, remembered what it was like to be an outsider everywhere I went. So that I said to myself: this is my town. I was born here. Here is where I belong.

Yes, I felt confident and heady that day, and many others also. But did I realize anything deeper than that? No, not a bit.

The downhill was steep, rather swift, and I never saw it coming. When it was done, when I was back home being a writer again, I felt ashamed of myself. Guilty too. I hadn't been shrewd enough or smart enough to hide my cards. What I was guilty of was being a fool. I deserved what I had got. There was no one to blame but myself.

But looking back, I am inclined to think that the target had never been me at all, but Murphy.

One Friday evening after Murphy had left the building, the Knapp Commission sent over the photostat of a dinner check from a midtown restaurant. The dinner had been consumed by Chief of Detectives Seedman, his wife and another couple. Seedman had not paid this check, which was for $84, meaning he had accepted a gratuity, or perhaps a bribe, for which, being a cop, he could go to jail.

A meeting was hurriedly called. It attracted to the office of First Deputy Commissioner William Smith most of the high ranking cops left in the building, none of whom, apparently, had eaten in a decent restaurant lately, because $84 to them seemed an outrageous sum. At that price it couldn't be a gratuity, it was a bribe. What favor had Seedman sold that was worth so much?

Seedman had always been considered a wheeler-dealer. His appointment by Murphy, whose regime was dedicated to ending corruption, had seemed to many people shocking. Now the Knapp Commission, of whom everyone present in Smith's office was terrified, had caught him in this act that was certainly a crime. What else did Knapp have on him, and what, this Friday evening, did Knapp expect them to do about it?

They decided to suspend Seedman from his functions immediately, in effect calling him guilty, and announce this to the press and the world. The Police Commissioner at home was consulted by phone. He either agreed, or was talked into agreeing, and the order went out.

I at this time was in my car being driven home to Connecticut for the weekend. When I learned what Smith and his group had done I was appalled. Immediately I phoned Murphy at home and poured out to him all the reasons I thought a terrible mistake had been made. This decision, based as much on the size of the dinner check as on anything else, had been done much too quickly, with no time taken even to consider other options. No one who had dined in midtown lately was going to think $84 much of a gratuity—if in fact it was a gratuity at all. There could be other explanations. If Seedman was known to be a crook, okay. But if not, then a quick and mindless reaction of this sort in no way suited the situation. They hadn't even consulted Knapp to ask why the restaurant check had been sent over, or what Knapp thought it meant. What did these decisions of Smith et. al. do to the image of the department, the image of Patrick Murphy as well? Did Knapp need only to hiccup to provoke a reaction like this? What kind of signal did such a reaction send to Knapp, and to the city? On a human level Murphy was ruining a man's career and life. He couldn't do that without more evidence than had been produced so far. If Seedman was exonerated, how did he ever give him back his authority?

There was another reason I did not go into, though perhaps Murphy saw it coming better than I did. Seedman was a Jew in an Irish Catholic department, and this was going to smack of anti-Semitism to many. Murphy anti-Semitic? How was he going to weather that one?

I begged him that night, and also in several phone calls the next morning, to soften the decision, to explain, to leave himself—and Seedman—a way out. I wanted him to come in and face the press—face the city.

He spoke to me from his house on Staten Island, each time in a small voice sounding crushed. He felt so terrible about what had been done, he said, so terrible for Al Seedman, that he couldn't face what I was asking him to do, please don't ask it of him.

I kept after him, and finally at midday Saturday he did come back into the city. There was a press conference, at which he said what I wanted him to say.

Ultimately the Jewish groups descended on the mayor, and through him on Murphy, and when no evidence against Seedman was found, he was quickly reinstated. He took my wife and me out to dinner and paid for it, and from then on kept me apprised on all investigations. He and his wife came to our apartment to dinner a time or two as well, yet he never called me by name. He called me Commissioner to the end.

Since events had proved me right, I won that battle big, and within the department, and with Murphy, my star rose exponentially. I doubt it rose with Smith, Codd and the others. In the long run it doesn't necessarily pay to be right.

A month or so later allegations of corruption against Detective Eddie Egan, one of the few department heroes—Gene Hackman, who portrayed him in *The French Connection* got the Academy Award for it—reached First Deputy Commissioner Smith. An investigation was begun, and the First Deputy ordered Egan's locker searched. Although no other evidence against him was found, his locker did contain an unregistered gun, a hypodermic syringe, and a small amount of other drug paraphernalia, evidence the detective had seized and failed to deposit with the property clerk.

Egan went on trial for this carelessness, or oversight, or whatever it was, in the department trial room in front of the Deputy Commissioner of Trials. Found guilty of all charges, he was reduced to patrolman. But when this verdict reached Smith for approval, Murphy being absent that week, he overruled the trial judge and dismissed Egan from the department with loss of all pension rights. The First Deputy believed Egan was dirty. In addition, this man who thought $84 an outlandish sum to pay for dinner for four, resented all the money Egan had surely made—in fact he hadn't—off *The French Connection.*

I was away that week also—I tried to make my time off coincide with Murphy's because when he was absent the department languished. Nothing happened.

When I came back and learned what had been done to Egan, and the flimsy reasoning behind it, I wrote a long memo with copies to everyone criticizing the decision. To dismiss one of the few police heroes when there was no evidence to back it up was a mistake on the public relations level, and it wasn't fair to another human being. Why make us, the hierarchy, look bad over a not very bright detective like Egan? Furthermore, the courts were going to call this decision too harsh, and his rank and pension rights were going to be restored.

This in fact happened. Right again. But as I look back I am appalled that I would write such a memo in an organization like the NYPD, make solid enemies of First Deputy Commissioner Smith and whoever he may have consulted before making his decision. Me, a newcomer to the department. Me against them. For as long as I had Murphy's confidence Smith couldn't hurt me, no one could. But would that confidence last?

On a night late in January two more cops, one black, one white, were assassinated. This was in the East Village, a poor, high crime precinct. They were shot in the back as they walked along, and their guns stolen. These mad attacks had to be stopped and, once again, one way to help do it was to elicit sympathy for the slain cops, and for other cops everywhere, particularly in the black community, and I went on television holding up one of the bloody, riddled coats. I told who the cops were, and what had been done to them, and poked my fingers through the bullet holes, and begged for information and sympathy from the public.

I was appearing on television more and more lately, usually from crime scenes, for somebody had to tell what had happened, and Murphy never went near crime scenes. Neither did Smith, Codd or the others. Sometimes I was the only high ranking person there, though often Seedman came as well, and it was at this time that one of my sergeants, Ed Powers, a man older than I with more than twenty years on the job, said to me: "The number one rule of the headquarters hierarchy is to stay away. If something heavy comes down, let a sergeant handle it. If someone is going to make a mistake and wreck his career, let it be a sergeant."

Later I would base an entire novel, the one called *Man With a Gun* on this premise, but at the time I did not yet take it to heart.

A few days after the assassinations a letter to the Daily News claimed credit—once again—for the so-called Black Liberation Army, which we knew to be a violent offshoot of the already violent Black Panthers. By then, in addition to having been briefed on the NYPD investigations in progress, I had read an 85 page FBI report which had tracked these people from San Francisco to Utah to New Orleans to New York, as they ambushed and sometimes killed cops, while financing themselves by robbing banks.

It was a Saturday when the letter was received. The investigation was being conducted out of the Ninth Precinct station house. Seedman was there, I was there, but no one else from headquarters. "There isn't a cop in the country who's safe until we catch these guys," Seedman said.

I agreed, and suggested he and I go on television and tell what we knew. My response to almost every problem had been, and continued to be, to get it out into the open. Previously Chief Inspector Codd had warned me not to show the cop's bloody coat on TV. I had simply overruled him. There was no overruling to be done today, for Seedman agreed.

Now it must be understood that Mayor Lindsay's chief claim to fame, almost his only one, was that New York had stayed calm when the black ghettos of other major cities had gone up in flames. Lindsay had actually walked the streets of Harlem in the night calming people down.

And here we were, Seedman and I, indicting a segment of the black community in front of cameras. Not so much Seedman, as City Hall saw it. I.

The reaction of City Hall was immediate. Contacted by *The New York Times*, sticking to the City Hall line, Police Commissioner Murphy more or less disavowed everything Seedman and I had said. The Black Liberation Army perhaps didn't exist. This made the Times, now, consider me untrustworthy and unreliable.

A few days later, nonetheless, when even more evidence had piled up, evidence so strong that even Lindsay would have to accept it (though he was not consulted in advance) Murphy agreed to a press conference at which he would declare that, yes, the Black Liberation Army did exist, and was responsible now for four New York cops murdered and two others ruined by machine gun bullets. Seedman had posters prepared showing the photos of the suspects, and listing their past crimes and suspected present crimes, and showing their relationships to each other.

But at the last moment, with the reporters and camera crews already waiting in the conference room, Murphy's phone rang, and it was District Attorney Hogan, whose office would have to prosecute these people, if they were ever caught, and he begged Murphy not to go ahead with the press conference. It would make convictions more difficult, he said.

Murphy promised to reconsider, then hung up, and for the next half hour we argued about what to do. The usual heavyweights were present; so was every high ranking cop in the building who had a law degree. The purpose of the press conference, I kept insisting, was to enlist the assistance of the public. To ask the public to help us catch the killers we were after. At the same time we would be warning cops across the country to be careful.

Finally Murphy called Hogan back and said he felt obliged to go ahead with the press conference. Hogan responded sadly, according to Murphy: "That isn't the way we used to do things here."

A few days later I received a call from a reporter in St. Louis. Cops there had got into a shootout with some black guys last night. Were these perhaps the men we were after?

Within minutes Seedman was in contact with the St. Louis police. Yes, the suspects had been in possession of what might be police guns. Seedman read off the serial numbers of the slain cops' 379 guns. Yes, those were the guns.

So I appeared to have exerted the correct pressure, done the right thing still again. But almost at once I was called to city hall by Tom Morgan, the mayor's press secretary, formerly a freelance writer like me. I had even met him at a dinner party once some years previously.

He talked to me like a father for half an hour. He said that any emphasis we (the police) might give to these murders or to other crimes was creating an atmosphere of fear. Next summer the whole city might explode into violence. Since the situation was touchy, how wrong of us it was ever to talk about the Black Liberation Army or the Panthers, or anything like that. "What purpose does it serve," he said "to make people afraid?"

I said that in fact our purpose was otherwise, but he was unreceptive of this argument.

All of the details that I and others had given on television were wrong, he said, he did not believe any of them.

Well, I told him, I had spoken to eye witnesses. But he was unreceptive of this argument also.

He told me I was becoming a celebrity and he thought this was terribly wrong. I should be faceless, as he was. I should never have gone on the Dick Cavett Show or on Eyewitness News. He had the rank of administrator, and although the police commissioner outranked him, the PC's deputies, meaning me, did not. All the mayor's top advisers were faceless, and proud of it. He was against our dumping guns out on the table, or showing posters of murderers. Any dramatic presentation or press conference was bad style, likely to be misinterpreted, and possibly unprofessional. He was against the visual in principle. His own approach with Lindsay was never to offer anything visual. He believed in a low key, low profile approach, creating no controversy whatever, and that's what I should believe in.

I might have told him, given Lindsay's dismal showing in the campaign so far, that his low-keyed strategy did not seem to be working. But I forbore doing so.

I told him there could be no effective police work without the cooperation of the citizenry, Murphy's idea, adding that they were never going to cooperate until the police were credible. But he brushed this argument aside. I pointed out that I was in a extremely visible position, and this seemed to wring from him a grudging admission that I did have the right to disseminate facts to the press.

He stated that politics should be left to the politicians. The police department should not get involved in politics of any kind. Murphy's court and prison and civil service speeches were wrong. Our system of government left this kind of change to the normal democratic process. It wasn't the job of the police to get involved. Politics was not the job of the military arm of the civilian government, his phrase.

He patted me on the back, and I left.

So I had been warned. But Morgan's arguments and attitude seemed to me so asinine that I did not take this warning to heart.

I did, however, type out a two page memo to Murphy summarizing the conversation. "I have no way of knowing," the last paragraph read, "whether the flack is coming from Lindsay, or from Morgan to Lindsay, or just from Morgan. I don't know whether Morgan is purely a technician, or whether he has actual input into the mayor's thoughts and programs."

When I reread this memo today I see it from Murphy's point of view, not my own. I may have been as naive as a bride back then, but he wasn't. He would have seen that the weight of Morgan's criticism was not directed wholly against me, perhaps not really against me at all. That the principal target was perhaps himself.

My memo was in no way intended to shock him, but I think now it did worse. I think it paralyzed him. I shouldn't have sent it. Why did I ever send it? Because now he was going to listen to every criticism of me that came his way. And his principal worry would be to protect not me but himself. He was perhaps already thinking he might have to get rid of me.

Lindsay had come back from Florida, or wherever he had been. Having declared for the presidency, he had been campaigning, would continue campaigning, in all the states with early primaries. As a newly switched democrat he had a lot of ground to make up. But he was awfully handsome, was he not, and he could be funny. What more was needed?

He would go off on the road again almost at once, but for a few days he was here among us. His top subordinates, whose lives and fortunes dangled from his own like trinkets from a necklace, had returned too. The campaign was not going well, and they would all have been worried. They hung close around Lindsay, and he—they—could not have liked what they saw. In the press and on TV, Murphy had become the sun, and Lindsay the moon orbiting around him. The mayor had been eclipsed. The police commissioner, the mayor's creature, had usurped the mayor's place in the minds and hearts of New York. Lindsay's advisers would have advised him to do something about it before it was too late.

I was aware of Murphy's new stature of course, and was proud of my part in the making of it. I was also too unpracticed in the art of big city politics to see this as any threat to him, or to me either.

He himself did see the threat, I believe. Though he never said anything overt about it, he did call me into his office where he asked if I couldn't get some of the other commanders on television from time to time, Codd, Bill Smith.

So they were jealous, I reflected. They see my supposed fame, and they want some. Fame to which, as they see it, I have no right since it is their police department I am trading off, not mine.

This idea confused me.

I told Murphy I had tried to turn the press toward one or the other of them many times, but the press wasn't interested. They weren't running the place, as he was, nor looking for murderers, as Seedman was. As the press saw it, these other commanders weren't doing anything that viewers or readers found interesting.

"But isn't there some way you could—"

He had never asked anything like this before. "I'll try," I said, "I'll keep trying. But I can't make the press want to talk to them."

He nodded, then switched the subject slightly: "On the other hand, your name is in the paper nearly every day."

This was true. The reporters asked questions, and quoted my answers.

I told him I couldn't help that. Talking to reporters was my job. "Anyway," I added, "getting my name in the papers doesn't mean anything to me. My name was in the papers a thousand times before I ever came into this department. And I was on television dozens of times before now as well."

I wondered even as I left him if he understood what I had said. Between touring with the Giants, and touring for my books, of course I had been on television dozens of times. There had been multiple reviews of my books, and I had had a thousand bylines in *The New York Times* alone. But I am not sure now that he had understood me at all. It was never clear to me how sophisticated Murphy actually was outside his own peculiar area of expertise. Perhaps he thought I was exaggerating, or even lying. If so, then his opinion of me had just dropped down through the floor.

I decided to lie low for a while, to stay out of everybody's crosshairs.

But about now I began to note that decisions were coming out of various headquarters offices, and memos were being sent around, that I learned of only afterward. This had not happened before.

I sent a memo to Murphy asking him to take note of this. An oversight, surely, I suggested. I really should be kept apprised of what was happening in headquarters.

I didn't realize it, but my descent had started, and would gather speed.

The chief of personnel shifted some commanders, and some narcotics detectives. I sent him a polite but firm memo. I must be notified in advance, it said.

Three days later Chief Inspector Codd issued a number of orders reorganizing the department in a significant way. I learned of them only after calls came in from the media. The memo I sent him, looking back, was stupid, but I had begun to see what was happening, and was trying to fight back before it was too late. "Henceforth," my memo to Codd ended, "no orders other than those of an emergency or completely routine nature, will be issued by you without prior consultation with my office as to significance and timing." And I sent copies to the PC and the Chief of Patrol.

That evening President Nixon came to New York for a fund raising dinner, landing at the Wall Street heliport about 6 p.m., accompanied by his wife, by a hundred or more aides and Secret Service men, and by the

White House press. These landings were always a circus, and I went to watch this one. New York firemen dragging hoses and carrying axes entirely surrounded the pad. In the street waited a truck that was a hospital operating room on wheels. Police launches idled on the river. Police helicopters made a screen into which the White House helicopter would descend. Secret Service men with sniper rifles watched the rooftops and the river itself.

There were hordes of cops on hand, and many dignitaries who waited to greet the president.

Codd came up to me, and he was sputtering. "I don't have to take orders from you, Bob, and I, and I, and I—" He was so angry he could hardly speak. "—And I won't."

"Mike," I said to this ramrod straight, white haired, 54 year old four-star chief: "Either I'm to know what goes on in headquarters, or it's a waste of my time and the city's money for me to be here at all." And I walked away from him. Into our midst a few minutes later dropped the president's helicopter, and Nixon jumped out and began shaking hands on his way to the motorcade in the street.

When I saw the police commissioner the following day he laughed and said: "Well, you certainly ruffled the Chief Inspector's feathers."

So it was possible to imagine I had got away with it, though I don't suppose I had.

As far as the city itself was concerned, I was still trying to stay out of sight.

Then a cop was shot to death with his own gun inside the Harlem Mosque on 116th Street where he and his partner had gone in answer to a 911 emergency call.

I raced up there. It was midday, sunny, warm. In the street a riot was in progress. Cars were being overturned and set afire by dozens of bands of youths, while TV crews leaned in close, filming. A police helicopter, unarmed of course, was dive bombing the rooftops across the street, trying to scare off more youths who were hurling debris down onto the spectators and rioters below.

The ranking cop present was Inspector Michelson, a black man—his rank the equivalent of colonel—who administered the three precincts that constituted the Harlem division. Much later Seedman arrived, but no one else from headquarters ever showed up.

The hordes of reporters and TV crews were inflaming—no pun intended—this thing, it seemed to me. So was the helicopter. In an effort to calm the situation, I began urging the TV crews to withdraw, they had their pictures, the youth gangs would get tired of wrecking the street if they were not being filmed. Naturally I got filmed making this request; the more I made it the more I got filmed. At some point also I suggested to Michelson that the helicopter be withdrawn, as it was only making the mess worse. This was only a suggestion, and he took it as such, for the helicopter hovered above us a good time longer.

That night there was a long and acrimonious meeting in First Deputy Commissioner Smith's office, at which Murphy was not present, to decide what information to make public. I never saw the slightest venality in any of these men. All seemed totally honest, and as honorable as they knew how to be. But they were at all times stolid, unimaginative, and when forced into a corner, as they felt themselves to be now, they became fearful. This case was Black Muslims, it was Harlem. It was cops perhaps defiling a mosque. To them the subject under discussion was not murder, it was perhaps political, and it was certainly racial. Any action they took might prove wrong. Better to do nothing. Better to stay away. This was the message their police genes were screaming at them. They should say nothing, stay out of it, make no statements.

Except for Seedman and myself all of them were agreed. They would close up the department. They would shut the windows and doors tight, as tight as they always used to be in the past. They would offer no explanation of what had happened in the mosque, or why, would offer no support for the slain cop—in fact the cop did not die for several days—would not even mourn him. Nothing. I argued as forcefully as I could without screaming that, in the absence of a statement, the cops on the scene—the department itself—would look guilty of brutality, or unlawful acts, or who knew what else, but I got nowhere. Seedman, who had all the facts known at that time, as did I, seemed to feel as I did, but did not help.

By phone Police Commissioner Murphy backed the others. No information of any kind would be given out.

In fact Murphy made no public statement for nearly a week, at which point he made a lame one. In the black community at least, nothing he said sounded credible.

And he had silenced me. I was not allowed to talk to the press about the dead cop, or the Mosque case, and for this I got roasted in *The New York Times*, whose reporter, Eric Pace, accused me of covering up police misconduct, of deliberately giving out inaccurate and misleading information. Of lying to the press.

I called up the reporter, and told him he had been grossly unfair: "You know I'm not allowed to give you information."

"If you don't like it," he replied, "then tell me what I need to know."

The Sunday morning talk shows wanted Murphy, but he refused them, and stayed out of public sight.

A letter came to him from a "concerned citizen." It contained sentences that were ungrammatical, words that were misspelled, and it was unsigned. Murphy sent it to me with a note that read: "The flack against Bob's comments in the street is very strong."

A new department phone directory had just been published. My office had been sent four copies, not enough. When my duty sergeant asked for more he was refused. To straighten this out I walked in on the Chief of Personnel, a man named Lonergan, and told him we needed additional copies. “You get four,” he said. His eyes were fixed on the desktop. I tried arguing with him. He wouldn’t look up. He kept saying: “You get four.”

I stood before his desk a moment longer. Finally I slunk away.

This had gone beyond phone directories, I realized. I saw these people as testing the situation, and also me. How weak was I? How far could they go? Clearly they were not afraid of me anymore. In a place as obsequious as headquarters, this was, to say the least, alarming. I didn’t know what to do about it. What could I do about it?

Complain to Murphy? Unwise, to say the least. I tried to gauge how dangerous the situation had become, but couldn’t.

The police academy commander, a one-star chief whom I knew slightly, sent a confidential memo to Murphy. Relative to the length of my hair, he wrote, he had taken a poll during four division level training sessions in four different boroughs. According to the poll, cops on all levels believed in uniform appearance standards, and felt I should conform to them too. My hair, worn in the style that was current that year, reached my collar, covered my ears, and had caused no comment whatever during the previous ten months. “If Deputy Commissioner Public Affairs sacrifices his locks,” the memo concluded, “it might enhance the Police Commissioner’s image in the eyes of the men. At any rate, I am sure his doing it would obtain great publicity.”

A few weeks ago no ambitious commander would have dared send forward such a memo.

It had reached Murphy before the Mosque murder. He had held it nineteen days, and sent it to me only now.

I wrote him an angry note which, once I had cooled down, I did not send.

By this time Mayor Lindsay was back in New York, and he was not in a good mood. Nor were any of the people around him. He was not going to be the next president of the United States. In every primary he had entered he had been soundly drubbed. His approval rating in New York City had dropped alarmingly also.

To strike back had perhaps become a need, even an imperative.

Strike back at me? This does not seem likely. Strike back at Murphy through me?

Press Secretary Morgan, or a crony, went into the City Hall pressroom asking reporters there to sign a petition to the effect that I had at times given them misleading information, and at other times had withheld information they needed so as to keep it for my own personal use later, that I had favored some reporters over others, that my conduct was unprofessional and that I should be removed.

I had never had any dealings one way or the other with City Hall reporters.

When a sufficient number of reporters had signed, the petition was sent to police headquarters. First Deputy Commissioner Smith was chortling when he waved it at me.

I was vain enough, naive enough might be more accurate, to suppose no one but him could possibly take this petition seriously.

Murphy never said a word to me about it, but surely it shook him up. Obviously City Hall wanted me gone, and better me than him. He must have seen this clearly.

I didn't. I preferred to believe it would all blow over.

Another month went by during which Commissioner Murphy made no speeches, no press conferences, no public appearances of any kind. When J. Edgar Hoover died, making Murphy, now, indisputably the No. 1 law enforcement officer in the country, he made no comment. He even went out of the country for a time.

Inside headquarters nothing was happening, there was nothing much for me to do, so at mid morning each day I would go out of the building, and into Little Italy where I would sit in one of the coffee bars over a cappuccino, and brood. Maybe I should just quit. But I hated the idea of being driven out. Maybe I should hang on and see what happened next.

These conflicting thoughts batted themselves about in my head, until one evening as I prepared to leave my office, I decided to take home all my personal papers and files, all those memos that had passed back and forth, all the crime reports and Knapp Commission reports, and the 85 page FBI report on the Black Liberation Army. Whatever was to happen to me, I would at least have this stuff, and might do something with it later.

During my first three months in headquarters I had kept no notes, no diary. I had had no intention of ever writing anything about the one year or two years, whatever it would turn out to be, that I might spend in the police department. But so many strange crimes and events had already taken place in those early months, were still taking place, that I did start a diary, and after that I made entries in it nearly every night. Now a year had gone by.

I decided to take this diary home with me too.

With a pile of papers a foot high in my arms, I almost staggered out of the building to the curb, where I waited for my official car to come by. I stood under a scaffolding, because for some time the headquarters building had been disintegrating overhead. If there had been no scaffolding, then cornices or bird droppings might have fallen on me. Or perhaps the entire NYPD. As I waited for my car a city official came by whom I knew slightly, and he stopped to shake my hand and say what a great job I had been doing. He just had to tell me, he said. I was Murphy's most inspired appointment, he said.

I wondered, as I thanked him, if he was the only one in city government who thought so. Then my car came and I was driven uptown to my apartment.

When the police commissioner returned from abroad he called me into his office, and began what sounded like a prepared, nervous speech. First came praise. For the second time I heard him say: "Bob, we've never had anything like this before. It's been really remarkable."

But—

But this ought to be like a marriage, he said, and it isn't anymore.

It seemed to me I knew where this was heading, so I moved to cut him off. "I'm going on vacation tomorrow," I told him. "In two weeks I'll come in and resign. Is that what you want?"

He looked relieved.

I phoned my then agent, Sterling Lord: "This thing is coming to an end," I told him. "See if you can get me a book contract."

I spent most of my first week of vacation brooding. Finally I decided I could not do what I had told Murphy I would do. If I came in on the fourteenth day and resigned I did not see how this could play to my advantage, and so when the first week ended, I phoned my office. It was Sunday. There was almost no one in headquarters. I told my duty sergeant to send out a one line communiqué. I resign. Was this a betrayal of Murphy? Maybe. But at this point I felt my loyalty to him was at an end. I owed him nothing.

At home in Connecticut our phone started ringing immediately. One reporter after another. My resignation led all the local newscasts that night, and was on the front page of *The New York Times* the next morning: DALEY OUT IN POLICE RIFT. To every reporter who called I praised Murphy and blamed the district attorneys and "others" in the administration, who, I said, were not interested in the openness I had tried to bring to the police department.

Looking back from this vantage point I can see, I think, the way the minds worked in City Hall. Murphy had become too popular, too out spoken. It was Murphy who had to be reduced in size. It was Murphy who had to be silenced, and he couldn't just be fired. His dismissal would have created a firestorm. The quietest, most practical way to silence Murphy would be to get rid of me. This should result in no publicity whatever, which was good. Murphy would take the hint and henceforth shut up. He would never again cut into the mayor's stardom.

But the ploy backfired slightly. The firestorm was out there, caused, to my surprise by me, and Murphy received orders from City Hall to contact the press, claim he had fired me, and denounce me in any other way he could. He did this until I called him at home and asked him why, adding that I was saying only nice things about him.

"You are?" he said.

After that, when the press called him, he was mostly conciliatory.

He did, however, send someone into my office to empty out my cabinets and seize every piece of paper to be found—not many, luckily. So saving my files turned out to be a good idea, because I was able to write books out of them for the next twenty years.

Though he had become indisputably the No. 1 law enforcement officer in a country that desperately needed leadership of his type, Police Commissioner Patrick Murphy, during the next several months, never raised his head, was scarcely mentioned on TV or in the newspapers, and as soon as he had found a job that would take him out of the maelstrom and out of New York, he resigned, leaving emptiness behind him. He lived more than thirty more years, was rarely heard from ever again, and he exerted no further influence whatever in the law enforcement field. He was simply gone, and to this day has never been replaced.

By the middle of the week following my resignation I had received a contract for an Inside the NYPD type book for an advance of $60,000, more than twice my NYPD salary. This book, which I called *Target Blue*, I wrote in the next six months. It came out almost 600 pages long, and most of the events in it, as I described them, I saw more clearly than I had seen them when working inside headquarters every day. The book's ending came out a bit muddled though, I believe. But how could I have made clear to readers what had happened between Murphy and me when I did not yet see it clearly myself?

And would not, until many years later when the identical situation reoccurred.

The then mayor, Rudolph Giuliani, had appointed a man named William Bratton as police commissioner. New techniques were implemented by Bratton, crime in New York fell precipitously, and in the media this was credited not to the mayor but to Bratton. Commissioner Bratton was seen to be such an open and attractive man that his every movement on and off duty became documented on television, and in the press. He was seen even at book parties. Apparently Mayor Giuliani could not take much of this. His solution was not to fire the popular Bratton, which would at the least have dimmed Giuliani's appeal, but instead to drive from office John Miller, the man who held my old job, thus sending Bratton a strong—very strong—signal. Bratton immediately fell silent, as Patrick Murphy had done so many years before, and a few months later found another job, as Murphy had done, and resigned.

The night John Miller resigned I called him up and we talked about Mayor Lindsay in my day, Mayor Giuliani in his. We had some laughs together. Politicians don't change much over the years, we decided.

I have been standing in the lobby of Police Headquarters for some time. I gaze up again at the memorial plaques. I read some of the bronze names. 1930, I note, was the only other year that matched mine in slain cops, ten.

That had been in the depths of prohibition, a joke to many Americans. Not to those ten young men, though.

These days the number of dead rarely exceeds two or three.

It is time for my appointment at City Hall—it is with Mayor Giuliani himself, who has asked to see me—so I go out and cross Police Plaza a second time. I have come in from Connecticut for this meeting. Giuliani and I have known each other many years. He and the wife he is currently divorcing, Donna Hanover, have been to dinner at our house. You would call us friends, I suppose. I know what it is he wants, and am not sure it is what I want. City Hall is about 200 yards away, and as I walk there I try to imagine what he will say to me, and what I will say to him in reply.

12.
Mayor Giuliani and *Prince of the City*

February 13, 2001, New York City (cont.)

As City Hall comes in sight I note that the park in which it stands has been divided almost in two by a stout wrought iron fence. This separates it from the benches and trees, from the people eating lunches out of paper bags, from the city that rises up high to all sides, and that supposedly it serves.

To me the fence comes as a surprise. What used to be the entrances to the park closest to City Hall, paths entering from either side, have been blocked off by great iron gates, and if you managed to crash your car through one of them you would ram into the retractable barriers that lie just inside. Hydraulically operated, they come up out of the ground and when they are up, as they are now, look capable of stopping a tank.

All these precautions leave a vast open space in front of the handsome domed building, a kind of parking lot where, today, a handful of official cars are parked. During my time this area sometimes swarmed with demonstrators and signs. Not anymore. The public is now on one side of the fence, the dignitaries on the other. The days when people could get close to the mayor, close to City Hall are over.

A pity. The locked gates and tank traps were put in by the present mayor, Giuliani. Would terrorists really try to assault City Hall, plant explosives, assassinate Giuliani. The mayors I used to know, Lindsay first, and then Abe Beame, entertained no such idea. But then they lived, though only a brief time has passed, in a different world. How did we ever get from there to the point we have reached now?

I identify myself to the cop in the booth. When he asks who I have come to see I do not give Giuliani's name. Instead I mention, as instructed, someone I do not know and never heard of before today. The purpose of my visit is politically sensitive, apparently. Reporters prowl the corridors inside, and Giuliani would prefer that no one knows about any meeting between us.

As mayor, Giuliani has been the rarest of creatures, a blunt, undiplomatic man, who behaves in almost all cases not as a politician but as the prosecutor which he was when I first knew him, and which he remained for many years afterward. He is a republican in a democratic city. He fights with nearly everyone. He says what he thinks and does what he pleases. If an action seems correct to him he orders it, apparently giving no thought whatever to the enemies he will make.

But the result has been a New York City that is cleaner and less crime ridden, that works better and costs less—all of this under the thumb of one man, for in New York these days no one speaks out publicly but him.

Last fall he was supposed to run for the senate against Hillary Clinton. Diagnosed with prostate cancer, he abruptly quit the race, and at the same time announced an alliance with a divorcee and left his wife.

A short time ago Hillary Clinton signed a contract to "write" her autobiography. That is, a ghost writer would write it. She must have agreed to tell all, for her advance, according to press reports, is to be $7 million. So Giuliani has decided to "write" his autobiography too, and also a follow-up book on how to manage a city like New York. He too has apparently promised to tell all, but he doesn't have as much to tell as Hillary Clinton so, again according to press reports, he is to get only $3 million.

Now all he needs is a writer such as she has got. For reasons that will become clear he thought of me. There were a number of phone calls between his agent and mine. He wanted to see me, I was told. Finally, today's meeting was arranged. In it he will make his case, I will make mine, and we will either go forward or not. Either way it will be good to see him again. He was part of the triumph that made my career. Made his career too, I believe. I have not forgotten, and I know he has not either.

Having entered City Hall I give the receptionist the same name I gave the cops outside and, while waiting, glance at the nearby walls on which hang portraits of former mayors. They continue along the entire corridor, going back to 1800 or before. Among them is Lindsay, of course, but also Beame who followed him, whom I knew a bit better and liked a good deal more.

Lindsay was one thing, and Abe Beame was the exact opposite. Except that both were mayors, and both were New Yorkers, they had nothing in common at all. Lindsay the Wasp, Beame the Jew. Lindsay may have been the tallest mayor ever, and he was one of the youngest. Beame, five feet two, 67 years old when elected, was the shortest and oldest. Beame was low keyed, unpretentious, undramatic. No glamour, no charisma at all. But an honest, dogged, modest, hardworking former accountant trying to cope with a city about to default on its bonds.

One day Beame went up in a police helicopter, and it crashed, but he lived.

And said nothing dramatic to anyone, including me when I tried to talk to him about it.

The helicopter had taken off from the Wall Street heliport into the late afternoon of the first day of summer. There was sun over Staten Island.

Then suddenly, no sun anywhere, only blackness. A ferocious rain beat down on the machine, and the wind, like a giant's hand cupped over a fly, pushed it down, down, down. Beame, in the co-pilot's seat, watched the stick quivering in the pilot's fist. The pilot couldn't hold the helicopter in the air. The descent took an entire minute, perhaps more, a long time for terror. Here came the water rushing up to meet them. As he struggled to keep the helicopter from flopping onto its back before it struck, the pilot's knuckles, Beame noted, were white.

The machine smacked the water at a twenty degree angle, and hard enough to tear off its rear rotor. It teetered, righted itself, floated. Finding themselves still alive, the other four men aboard, one of them Deputy Mayor Judah Gribetz, became euphoric, almost hysterical. They began cracking jokes.

Most of the jokes had to do with how other politicians might now play up the event. A massive news conference at City Hall, perhaps. No, a song and dance act on the pier. They were laughing uproariously. But as the rescue launch reached the pier where presumably press and public were waiting, Beame turned to Gribetz and said: "No jokes, Judah."

Later I asked Beame what had happened.

"How should I know, I'm not a mechanic."

Had he been scared.

"I was in good hands."

It was no good trying to dig drama out of Abe Beame.

I wrote two long profiles about him for *The New York Times Magazine*. I spent days and days with him. I liked him a lot, and I think he liked me. After the second article appeared he wrote me an extraordinary—for a politician—letter in which he said that if I ever needed anything that was within his power to give I had only to ask. The Times Magazine then as always paid very badly. If I had accepted these two assignments it was because I had wanted to get close to Beame. I thought I could perhaps cozy up to him and then, if the moment presented itself, suggest to him that I belonged back in the police department. I wanted to be invited back, and a word from him would do it. I wanted to be vindicated. However, I could never bring myself to ask him. It didn't seem right. Even after receiving the letter I couldn't do it.

Beame died two days ago aged 94. His funeral was this morning.

The man whose name I gave at the desk comes running out into the rotunda. He has a cell phone in his hand. The site of the meeting has been changed, he tells me. Mayor Giuliani has left for Jacoby Hospital in the Bronx where some injured cops have been taken. We will meet instead at Gracie Mansion, the mayoral residence, which is at 87th Street and the East River. At this hour of the afternoon a forty minute drive. I'm not particularly surprised. A bit annoyed, though. Politicians are never on time. Giuliani didn't used to be a politician, but he is one now. Well, at least Gracie Mansion is on the way home.

"You're to know everything I know," Police Commissioner Murphy had said to me. But there was one secret, the department's deepest, that he did not tell me or anyone. It was this secret that changed my life, and Giuliani's as well.

The Knapp Commission was a public thing. Everyone knew its investigators were out there, and that they were focused exclusively on cops. But a second investigation was also in progress. It revolved around a narcotics detective named Robert Leuci. Working out of the U.S. Attorney's office, Leuci had agreed to wear a wire and to gather evidence against corrupt prosecutors, bondsmen, judges, federal agents, lawyers. He was "sickened," he said, that the Knapp Commission should go after cops only, when the whole system from top to bottom was corrupt.

How did he know this? Because he had been guilty of several minor acts of corruption himself, he said, and he named them. He would do the investigation, but he was not going to work against cops. And for a time he did work exclusively against other parts of the system, nailing the people he said he would nail, and some important mafia figures as well. Sometimes this was at great risk of his life.

Leuci had thought he could control the investigation. He couldn't. Ultimately, he was forced to turn against cops too, then against detectives in his own unit, then against his friends, and, in the end, even against his partners. It was Giuliani, a 29 year old Assistant U.S. Attorney working on the Leuci cases, who did most of the forcing. It was Giuliani, based on his own knowledge of the streets of Queens where he had grown up, who looked at Leuci and thought: this man is guilty of more than the few more or less benign acts he has admitted to. It was Giuliani, young as he was, who finally broke Leuci, forced him to admit to all he had done in the past, forced him to name names. "You're asking me to put to death my best friends," Leuci cried at one point.

Yes.

By then the future mayor was directing the entire investigation, and was personally prosecuting some of the cases in court, as well.

Leuci had belonged to the Special Investigating Unit of the Narcotics Division, a group of elite cops with city-wide jurisdiction and almost no supervision who worked only against the kings of the drug trade. They were a swaggering lot. They were good, and knew it. They arrested great numbers of major dealers, seized undreamed of amounts of heroin and cocaine. They were incredibly effective. They picked their own targets, went when and where they pleased. Someone once called them the Princes of the City, for they operated with the impunity and arrogance of renaissance princes. They could apply the law or not, as they chose, lock this man up, let this other man go. They were immune to interference from anyone.

But in order to make all those arrests and seizures, and to obtain all those convictions in court, they routinely planted illegal wiretaps, regularly gave drugs to junkies in exchange for information, and many many times they perjured themselves on the witness stand to make convictions stand up. They also stole, at times, suitcases full of drug profits. They watched the Knapp Commission investigation but were unworried. "Durk can't hurt us, Serpico can't hurt us," one said to Leuci one day. "Those guys aren't cops. The only way they can hurt us is if they turn somebody who's been in bed with us."

Of the approximately 70 detectives who served in the SIU, 52 were indicted. Most went to jail. A number of others were implicated but in the absence of corroboration, not prosecuted. The grateful prosecutors—and Giuliani too was grateful—chose not indict Leuci, who was allowed to finish out his 20 years in the department, a pariah hated by almost everyone.

Considered purely on a law enforcement level, overall results were close to perfect. On a personal level they were tragic. Two of Leuci's partners killed themselves with their service revolvers. Leuci himself came very close to doing the same. Two other detectives, hounded by prosecutors, died of heart attacks; both were 42. In the final act of the tragedy Leuci, on the witness stand, was forced to testify against a partner whom he had loved more than any brother, forced to accuse the partner of criminal acts in which he himself had taken part. Testify, in other words, not only against the partner, but also against himself.

After leaving the department I had been introduced to Leuci at a cop gathering. By then he was no longer undercover, had had some publicity, and had begun testifying in court. As I shook his hand I imagined I knew his story. He was a corrupt cop, and I wanted nothing to do with him.

About a year after that he phoned me. He wanted to see to me, he said. He wanted to tell me his story. He begged me to listen to him. He begged me to give him half an hour—fifteen minutes.

He was so persistent, and sounded so needy, that I agreed to see him, and the next day he came to my house. "We were the princes of the city," he began.

But the princes came to a bad end. His story, it seemed to me, was as sad as any I had ever heard. All those great detectives gone wrong. All those deaths, those ruined lives. Long before his recital ended I had begun making notes.

At this time my principal occupation was writing books—or so I believed. Since leaving the police department I had written three novels and two non-fiction books—but none of them had become best sellers, so I was writing also for magazines to make up the income I needed. One of the markets for which I wrote frequently was *New York Magazine.* I knew its needs and its editor, Clay Felker. Leuci's story was one Felker would want. It was a New York story, a big story, and it had a news peg as well, for within a month would occur the final trial in which Leuci would testify, this time against his partner.

Leuci's hope was that I would write a book. He wanted the world, especially the cop world to which he belonged, to understand what had happened. He wanted to explain. He wanted to try to make other cops, other people, see what he had been through, what he had been forced to do, how much he had suffered. A book, he said, would do all this.

We sat looking at each other.

I envisioned, I told him, only a magazine article.

He said he would be grateful even for that.

I wrote the article. I got $2,000 for it, which was a good price, though sometimes Felker paid me more. It was published under the title: The Cop

Who Knew Too Much, and it caused much comment.

I was waiting that month for another book project to come through, but this wasn't happening, and perhaps it never would. I had to get something else going, and the response to the Leuci article was so positive that I asked my agent to show it to publishers as a book outline. I thought some publisher would jump on it, and in my head I was getting ready to accept an advance of $100,000—$75,000 at least.

But one house after another turned the idea down. Finally there came a single offer. It was from Houghton-Mifflin, and the advance would be $25,000 only. Not enough to pay for the time it would take to write the book. Nor from such a book could I expect any subsidiary income. I did not see it as a possible movie. It did not seem book club material.

The book project I had been waiting for had nothing to do with the police. For months I had been dickering with Juan Trippe, founder and for 41 years CEO of Pan Am. Trippe was the first and last aviation tycoon in history, and Pan Am spanned it all, from the primitive to the jets. His story, the Pan Am story, was a saga about which I already knew a good deal. Such a book would be about the heroic early flights and about fortunes being risked, about flying boats and the invention of long distance navigation. Most of all it would be about the tycoon, Trippe. I knew many Pan Am people, and had ridden Pan Am planes all over the world, so the subject was congenial. Trippe especially interested me. In the past I had met plenty of famous men, but no tycoons. I was eager to know what this giant of the business world was like. I saw I was going to have to pay money for access to him and Pan Am, but I was willing to do this.

Finally I signed 2 contracts to write such a book. One contract was with Random House. The second was with the Pan American foundation, this being another name for Mr. Juan T. Trippe. In exchange for access to him and to Pan Am records, the Foundation would collect 15 percent of my royalties. No in depth book or even magazine article had ever been done about Pan Am, nor about the the secretive, you could almost call him mute, Mr. Trippe. Random House expected a big best seller. So did I. The MS came out over 800 pages long, including 200 pages of source notes, and took me three years to write. But the book never became a best seller—Mr. Trippe's doing entirely, I have always thought.

I'll get to that.

The book's eventual title was *An American Saga*. It was not a paid company history. The independent author, me, had to pay to write it. Well, the Random House contract was for an advance of $120,000, big money in 1976 and my biggest contract to that date. And surely hundreds of thousands more would come in later. I figured I could pay 15 percent to Trippe's foundation and still come out ahead. All editorial decisions would be totally, completely mine. He could not later order one word to be changed.

I was eager to meet Mr. Trippe. I had known bullfighters, racing drivers, actors, singers but never a man like him. What would he be like?

I was 46 when I met him, he was 77. In all we had about 50 interviews. My wife and I were invited several times to dinner at his apartment near Gracie Mansion, overlooking the East River. I dined with him a number of times at the Cloud Club on top of the then Pan Am building. He and Betty came once to lunch to our house in Greenwich, he invited himself, in fact. I think he wanted to rate the value of the project we were engaged in by rating our house, rating how we lived. And that lunch was the only time I ever saw him show any emotion, and when it happened I was surprised.

He was a terrible interview. Multiply that by 50. He would not permit me to tape our conversations. His answers when he gave them, were sometimes long winded, but often far afield of whatever I had asked him. Some questions, even questions having to do with events 30 or 40 years in the past, he would not answer at all, looking at me over his hands, then saying: "I'm a businessman, I don't give away information like that."

He seemed to be protecting secrets that were no longer relevant, even, in some cases, no longer secret. Habit? This was the man whose nickname from his time at Yale was "Mummy."

In 1939 the Pan Am board of directors, fed up with his secrecy, with never knowing what he was up to, deposed him, putting in Sonny Whitney to run the company. Trippe was obliged to move to an office at the other end of the hall. For all the months this interregnum lasted he sulked, hardly spoke a word, until at the end of that time the board realized that over the years he had written almost nothing down, had never confided in anyone. It was impossible to figure out where anything was, what plans he may have set in motion. The entire company was in his head. The board had no choice but to dump Whitney and give him his airline back, and after that his power was never questioned. I once asked John Leslie, a vice president and member of the board why, during the decades that followed, no one ever resisted him and John said: "But he was right all the time."

The interregnum must have been agony for Mr. Trippe , the traumatic experience of a lifetime, but when I asked him about it he said only "Whitney wanted it so I gave it to him." That isn't the way it happened but it was all he would say on the subject.

In our interviews he mentioned presidents he had had to deal with. Apart from that he never boasted, never crowed about how big or important he once had been. He never got enthusiastic about any of his own accomplishments or Pan Am's, either. Nor did he praise any of the men whose work, objectively speaking, was as vital as his—Hugo Leuteritz, for instance. Never mentioned him. Leuteritz was the radio man who virtually invented long range navigation, which was what made possible all that crossing of oceans. He worked 19 years for Pan Am, then quit in protest, so he told me, against Mr. Trippe's high-handed ways. Leuteritz lived to be 95, the last of the founding pioneers to pass on. Going through his things afterward, his son found a few hundred shares of Pan Am stock, worthless of course, which his father had kept to the end as if unable to bear throwing them away.

No matter how dramatic the event being discussed, Mr. Trippe in our interviews never offered any revealing anecdotes about himself or anyone else, or smiled or laughed or showed any particular emotion. The anecdotes and details that are in *An American Saga*, and there are many, I had to get from others. No, I can't say I ever knew him, and there were days I wondered if anybody did.

Crossing the Pacific in 1935, was possibly the most dramatic event in the company's dramatic history. He said nothing worth quoting on any of that. The takeoff of the inaugural flight was to be broadcast live on all the radio networks. Half the dignitaries in the country would be in attendance, and 50 million or more listening in. The China Clipper would be obliged to find and land on a series of pinprick islands lost in thousands and thousands of miles of open ocean. In other words Mr. Trippe was risking everything with this flight. The night before takeoff he phoned Leuteritz. "Hugo," he asked, "are you sure of your navigation?" Leuteritz said: "Relax, Juan, we've tested it and tested it. It works." But this anecdote came to me from Leuteritz, not Mr. Trippe, who would not admit to any worries, any misgivings on that day or any other. I asked him a specific question about Wake Island once. Wake is the top of an underwater mountain. It is a sand spit in the shape of a hairpin the two arms of the hairpin barely two miles long but in some places only a hundred yards wide. No one had ever lived there. It has no water, almost no vegetation. It's highest point is 12 feet above sea level. Between the two arms of the hairpin is a rather small lagoon. Mr, Trippe sent a shipload of men and supplies to Wake to build a hotel and all the rest without knowing if flying boats could even land there. "Suppose," I said to him, "it proved impossible to land on that lagoon." He answered: "We could have landed off shore on the lee side." But there is no lee side to Wake. It was the lagoon or nothing.

I came to see Mr. Trippe as a colossal gambler. In his quiet, undramatic, stubborn way he was as much a daredevil as any of the bullfighters or racing drivers I had known. Even Las Vegas never saw bets as high as his, and he did it not once but over and over. Crossing the Pacific in 1935, of course. Buying those first jets before most of the world's airports could even land them. He once spent millions of dollars for powerful new jet engines for which he had no planes. The idea was to force Boeing to build him the plane to go with them, the plane he wanted but Boeing didn't. With so many engines on hand he couldn't back down, so Boeing would have to.

He had started as a pilot in air races in the rickety planes of World War I. This he talked about willingly enough, but without any particular emotion—fear, for instance.

The only emotion I ever saw from him came during the luncheon at my house that I spoke of. He was long retired by then, but someone phoned to tell him that a regularly scheduled helicopter carrying Pan Am passengers from JFK to midtown had crashed on the roof of the Pan Am building. Debris had killed a pedestrian in the street. He turned from the phone with tears in his eyes, and I thought he would start to cry. In an anguished voice, speaking mostly to himself, I heard him say: "It's the end of New York Airways."

During the writing I went to Wake Island, flew in from Hawaii on the once a week supply plane, a C 141. I had conceived the notion that I would begin and end the book with descriptions of this tiny atoll a thousand miles from anywhere which Pan Am had colonized, had put to use for the first time in history, and had turned into one of the most famous islands in the world. It was so famous that the Japanese, once the war started, absolutely had to have it. They attacked it within days of Pearl Harbor, overwhelmed the small marine garrison, and recolonized it themselves. And then for the rest of the war they starved to death by the hundreds. The island could not be supplied. Cargo vessels were vulnerable to American submarines, and supply by air was impossible—the only planes in the world that could reach it were the Pan Am flying boats. A few days before I got there a Japanese burial squad landed, dug up the bodies of 786 soldiers, cremated them amid the ruins of the old Pan Am hotel, and took the ashes back to Japan.

I found the hotel's foundations easily enough and stood in the ruins myself, and without much difficulty conjured up a vision of the China Clipper tying up out front after ten or more hours in the air, the well heeled passengers trooping up toward the hotel where cool drinks awaited them on the veranda. And after that a good night's sleep in imported American beds in a hotel that was almost of luxury class.

The ruins of the pier are still there too, concrete pillars jutting up out of the water like rotting teeth. And off to the side is a concrete ramp that slopes down into the water. If repairs were needed the fat, wet flying boats could be winched up the ramp onto dry land and attended to. The present Island personnel will talk of the ramp if questioned. It is known to them as the Pan Am ramp. No one I spoke to seemed to know why.

Waiting for my plane out I walked along the beach which is littered with rusting, half swallowed military junk, and listened to the silence and gazed off into the vast distance.

I saw Wake then, and see it now, as a symbol of the daring, the imagination, and the hard, hard work that had made Pan Am into the colossus it became, the first and also for so many years the greatest airline the world had ever known.

Few people worked on Wake when I was there. A six man Air Force detachment was in command. Probably there are less now. Soon there may be nobody. Wake has no value for weather forecasting which is done by satellite today, nor as a refueling station—today's great planes overfly it. Leuteritz's radio direction finders are obsolete. Before long, most likely, Wake will go back to being the uninhabited desert island it once was.

The island had erupted from the ocean floor who knew how many eons ago. Juan Trippe and Pan Am had given it sudden extraordinary fame. Now the rather small island had evolved into little more than a rather large monument—one that commemorated more than anything else the hour of the hundreds of men who had first put it to use, the hour of the Pan Am flying boats, the hour of the vision and ambition of Juan Trippe. It would be visited in future by very few persons, and perhaps in time by no one at all. No matter, it is there, and will remain there, and its status as monument will last for as long as aviation has impact on the affairs of men.

And that is how my book ended.

According to the contract I had signed with Trippe he had the right to read my finished manuscript, but not to change it. He began demanding changes anyway. I refused. He went to Random House and in his quiet, tenacious, stubborn way threatened lawsuits. He went back there day after day quietly threatening. He used up everybody's time. After agreeing over my protests to certain innocuous changes, the publisher finally got fed up and sent the book to the printer. But it was too late. With the Random House lawyers still afraid he might sue, the decision was made, by whom I don't know, to publish the book, as they say in the trade, quietly. Worse, the press and the critics had heard about all this. If Mr. Trippe was editing the book, which he seemed to be doing, controlled the book, which was what it looked like, then obviously it was a corporate sponsored puff job, and not to be taken seriously. My 800 page fully documented in depth and highly entertaining study of Pan Am, the first ever written, was not even reviewed in *The New York Times*. It never earned back its advance either, a considerable loss for Random House.

Shortly after it came out Juan Trippe suffered a stroke from which he did not recover, though he lingered another seven months. He died April 3, 1981 in the same New York apartment in which I had sometimes dined with him. He was two months short of his 82nd birthday. His funeral at St. James Episcopal Church on Madison Avenue at 71st Street was well attended. The church was crowded, I saw, but not full, with none of the dignitaries present that he would have drawn in his prime. He was a man who had outlived his fame. And almost his airline.

Trippe was one to be the most exasperating persons I ever met, and one of the least attractive. A man who told off waiters. He told me off once too, accused me of being a communist. Where this idea came from I cannot imagine. Also he was boring. A famous negotiator, he had many times stalled Boeing, Douglas, Pratt & Whitney and other great firms, driving them crazy. Just as he had kept stalling me. Nonetheless, when Pan Am died in 1991, it hit me hard. I had bought a small amount of Pan Am stock. Like Leuteritz I could not bear to part with it, and instead watched its value diminish day by day until at the end there was nothing left.

But all this was in the future. For the moment, Trippe was still stalling, and I needed a project to tide me over until such time as he was willing to sign a contract—if, in fact, he ever was.

But Houghton Mifflin was offering only $25,000 for the book that would become *Prince of the City*. I had two daughters in college. We lived well, but not luxuriously. Double digit inflation had not yet set in. I needed a minimum of $50,000 a year to get by.

Finally I thought: I know the police department. This is my type material. I know most of the people in it already, I can do the book in three months probably. Of course I can, it will be easy. Take the contract.

But *Prince of the City* did not turn out to be easy, and it did not take three months. Because I was dealing with real people's lives, and was not going to change any names, I had to be absolutely accurate, meaning there was an enormous amount of checking and double-checking to be done.

But more than this, the story turned out to be so full of moral ambiguity that hardly any scene was what it seemed to be, and at the start of each one I had to ask myself who is the good guy here, who is the bad guy. Often I was unable to tell, and I would stare at the page unable to start. Month after month went by, and I struggled. I wrote scenes one way, and then another, and then, sometimes threw away what I had written and began again.

My starting point was Leuci. For some weeks he almost lived at my house, but everything he said had to be checked out. I had to interview each one of the prosecutors involved, including Giuliani, not once but many times, and then when I got stuck go back to them again. Most of them were decent men who had seen the individual tragedies happening, and sometimes had been moved to tears. But one or two seemed as cold and as heartless as anyone I had ever known.

I had to find trial minutes, typescripts of clandestine tape recordings, rap sheets and other documents. I went to Washington to interview federal people, and also Patrick Murphy, for I needed to know how much had he known about Leuci, and when.

I had not seen him in five years. For most of those years he had been the director of something called the Police Foundation, whose good works were difficult to discern. Murphy's secretary followed me into his office and, as if on cue, reminded him that his next appointment was in ten minutes. "Take all the time you want, Bob," he told me. I saw no warmth in him, no memory of all those hours we had spent together. Taking the hint, I left after ten minutes. He did not ask me to stick around and chat.

When my manuscript was finished I saw that it needed an introductory chapter that proved difficult to write. I saw also that the construction of the first half was all wrong and would have to be done over.

Turning the MS in at last I felt only one emotion, relief, and thought: this is the end of it.

Now I had to make some money. I could not afford even a single day off, and I started on the Pan Am book the next morning.

Houghton Mifflin, as was the custom in the industry, sent copies of the MS to the book clubs, and the paperback houses. Previously Leuci had acquired an agent, Esther Newberg of ICM, who had prepared a contract with Leuci that I had signed. It was agreed that, because the advance was so low, I would keep it all. After that Leuci was to get one third of print royalties, if any, but two thirds of movie money, if any. I didn't care about movie money; I was certain there would be none. Also, according to this agreement, it was up to ICM to try to sell the movie rights.

Let them, I thought, they'll find there's nothing there.

I was wrong. A few nights later Robert Bookman, ICM's man in Hollywood, called: "I have a movie offer for $300,000," he said.

When I could breathe again, I said: "Take it."

"No, I think I can get more."

A few nights later he phoned again. "I have an offer for $500,000."

"Don't take it," said I, "try for more," for greed takes possession of a man's soul more quickly than I would have thought possible.

He laughed. "No, this one I'm taking." It was not an option, he explained. It was an outright sale.

Sterling Lord, my own agent, called. A paperback house had established a guaranteed floor of $500,000. This meant there would be an auction.

The house with the floor would have the final bid, and topping rights over any other bid. Eventually these paperback rights would sell for $675,000. Houghton Mifflin would keep half, we would get the rest.

And still another call. The Book of the Month Club had made *Prince* a full selection for $100,000. Again Houghton Mifflin would keep half.

More money was to come in from the *Reader's Digest* Condensed Book Club, and from foreign sales—ultimately Leuci and I would split about $1,200,000. I had never before even dreamed of so much money. With my share I bought a Porsche and a Chinese rug for our living room, then incorporated myself as Riviera Productions Ltd. which immediately created a pension fund, into which went every other cent, and nearly all the movie money that followed in later years as well, and I never touched any of it until this year when the law said I had to. Leuci, I'm afraid, did not save very much of his.

Leuci and I went on tour, five weeks, 16 cities, 96 interviews, the longest tour of my career. This was possible because to interviewers Leuci was a curiosity. A corrupt cop who had tried to atone not only for his own misdeeds, but for those of his colleagues as well, who had broken the police code of silence, who had put other cops in jail, who had caused two of his partners to commit suicide. One interviewer said to him: "Detective, I want to know just one thing, who is your psychiatrist?"

"I am," I said, for at that moment I realized that's what I had been. "Next question," I said.

Throughout the tour Leuci was relaxed and happy. In interviews he was effective, and in private he was charming, and often funny. Also, I learned, he was afflicted with what he jokingly referred to as the Italian Malady—he tried to make nearly every woman who crossed our path, of which there were many, often succeeding, apparently. Young or old, short or tall, fat or thin, he did not seem to care. He carried a hair dryer in his valise, and worked on his hair a lot. I watched all this and was mystified. Portago had been a great womanizer too, but he was dead. Leuci was the only other one I ever knew well, and years later, when I wanted to write a womanizer into one of my novels I went to him for information on how such men operated, and how their minds worked.

Prince of the City was supposed to be directed by Brian DePalma, who was hot at that time, and the star was to be John Travolta, who was even hotter. I met with DePalma, and he had a script done by a playwright named David Rabe, who invented a whole new story. But DePalma was involved in a number of other projects, and seemed unable to get started on this one. At length the studio, Orion, fired him.

The new director was Sidney Lumet, who almost immediately phoned asking to meet me. This was flattering. Heady stuff, in fact. I went into New York to his office where he shook my hand, gave me a twenty minute speech and dismissed me. The speech described how he and Jay Presson Allen would write the screenplay of my book, and how he then would film it. In the course of the speech I managed to interject very few words, and even fewer complete thoughts. Once when he paused for breath I said I was surprised to find him interested in *Prince* at all, since he had covered some of the same conflicts and emotions only a few years ago with *Serpico*. But he was having second thoughts about Serpico, he said. A good film, but a bit simplistic. Serpico had not been guilty of anything, whereas Detective Leuci had experienced guilt from beginning to end. It was this guilt that had attracted him, Lumet said. "Give a Jew a story about guilt and—"

In the book three prosecutors, the last of them Giuliani, share nearly equal time. Surely, I interjected again, speaking fast before he cut me off, he would combine the three into a single character in his film, lest the audience become too confused to track the story. No, he said, he would keep all three. He would keep all the different detectives too.

"All of them?"

"Yes."

Since I had found it a terrific problem to keep so many people separate in the readers' minds, this seemed a mistake. I had had to use a number of literary techniques not available to a man working with film. But Lumet did not ask my advice then or ever, so I did not give it. There was no time to give advice anyway, for now he shook my hand a second time, and a moment later I found myself in the street.

He vetoed Travolta, opting for a more modest actor named Treat Williams to play Leuci, and this was perhaps a mistake too. Williams was a fine actor, but not box office. Except for Jerry Orbach as one of Leuci's partners, all the other actors would be total unknowns, or nearly so. Great faces, but not box office either.

Soon Lumet was ready to begin shooting.

Now it must be understood that when an author sells $4 worth of typewriter paper for half a million dollars, and then comes onto a movie set where he watches all those people working, all those millions more being spent—and all because of him—this is a strange experience. Exhilarating and rather delightful, but weird. So I phoned Lumet and asked permission to come on the set for the first day's shoot. "I wish you wouldn't, Bob," he said, and gave me another long speech about disturbing the actors. Disturbing him, I think he meant.

So on the last day of filming I ignored him and just went. When he saw me he ran forward, almost kissed me on the lips, and thanked me for coming.

When the film was shown I saw that Lumet had tracked the book almost word for word. If the reviews for the book had been excellent, as good as any author could wish, not a single bad one, nonetheless this was as nothing compared to the reviews Lumet got. The film's reviews, his reviews, were ecstatic. One read them in every newspaper, every magazine. I never saw better ones for any work of art.

So it was a famous film, a serious film, but it failed to make money. As a result it got only one Academy Award nomination—for Lumet and Allen's screenplay—and this did not win. Counting the rough cut, and the various previews, I saw the film a total of five times, including once in Nice dubbed into French. I thought then, and still think, that Treat Williams should have been nominated as best actor, Lumet as best director, and the film itself as best film. But in Hollywood no one wants to sign his name to a financial failure. Films that don't make money are rarely considered for prizes. I think to this day that *Prince of the City* is a great film. Certain scenes in it are absolutely brilliant. Its only flaws, to me, were the ones I had expected from the beginning: too many prosecutors, too many detectives. A viewer tended to get lost. That is, the story was not quite as accessible as it might have been.

Some years later Lumet bought a second book of mine, a novel called *Tainted Evidence*. I was delighted, believing he would film this one word for word too, treat it with as much respect as he had treated *Prince of the City*, and I waited while he wrote the screenplay himself. My novel was about a woman prosecutor trying to manage a career, a family, an amorous detective and a case no one else wanted. Lumet started by changing this woman into a man. After that he changed nearly everything else until his story did not resemble mine at all. Not in a single detail. Then he changed the title to *Night Falls On Manhattan*.

I did not wish to go on the set of this one.

I was paid a total of $450,000 with which I bought the apartment in Nice I described earlier. An author, it seems to me, should spend the money and keep his mouth shut. He has no right to complain.

Two other prosecutors, Nick Scoppetta and Mike Shaw had nurtured

Detective Leuci, and the cases he developed, through all of the long and dangerous undercover phase which lasted in all fourteen months. Although he worked in the same office as the other two men, Giuliani never even met Leuci until the night the detective was nearly killed, and his cover blown.

But as Scoppetta and Shaw now moved on to other, bigger jobs, Giuliani took over the cases Leuci had developed, and also Leuci himself, meaning he became the sole emotional support of the increasingly fragile detective. As he began to understand the stresses Leuci had lived under for so long, and that often had him not only close to being murdered, but close to suicide as well, Giuliani found it impossible not to care for him, and to admire the courage that had brought him to this point. But increasingly he sensed all that the detective had kept hidden until now about his partners and himself, all he had hoped never to disclose. Fearing for Leuci's future, Giuliani became determined to force these dark secrets into the open. "There's a cancer inside you," he kept telling him. "It has to be cut out or you will die." There could be no doubting the young prosecutor's sincerity. "Let one detective come through that door and verify these allegations against you," Giuliani told him, "and I won't be able to save you."

Finally Leuci cracked, and Giuliani was able to break open and destroy the nest of great detectives that was the SIU. At the same time, with the help of others among the prosecutors, he managed to save Leuci himself from prosecution.

A great number of convictions resulted from Leuci's disclosures. In law enforcement circles this gave Giuliani a gigantic reputation, and made possible all that would follow.

Even before Leuci had finished testifying Giuliani had been appointed a deputy attorney general and been moved to Washington. When the post of U.S. Attorney for the Southern District of New York became vacant, although he was by then No. 3 man in the Justice Department, he asked for this other job, and got it. Politically speaking, U.S. Attorney was one step down—perhaps several steps down—from what he had had, but Giuliani saw where this new job could be made to take him, and it was where he wanted to go.

I know a woman to whom Giuliani spoke during his early years. One day he would be U.S. Attorney in New York, he told her, and after that he would be mayor.

The first part of that boast was now fact. In New York he was boss, could direct scores of assistant prosecutors, and more scores of New York based FBI agents, at whichever targets he chose. He seemed to choose almost exclusively people who would make headlines. Mafia chieftains. Corrupt politicians previously considered untouchable. White collar criminals with access to expensive lawyers. The arrests he ordered and that his men made were sometimes spectacular—he seemed to stage manage them for effect: Wall Street brokers who could have been asked to come in and surrender, for instance. Instead, he ordered them dragged out of their fancy offices in handcuffs in front of their employees and co-workers. He was sometimes accused of violating the civil rights of some of these people but he shrugged this criticism, all criticism, off.

He got himself noticed in New York. No one spoke for his office but himself. He gave, over the years, hundreds of press conferences. Very soon there were few TV newscasts in which he did not appear, and no cocktail parties at which he was not talked about. He did for himself, if you will forgive the comparison, what I had once done for Police Commissioner Murphy. He became a television star. No one, so far as I know, helped him, and several times, watching his performances, I found myself wondering how he had known how to do it.

He ran for mayor, a republican in a solidly democratic city, and lost, ran again four years later and won, and four years after that he won again. The law limited him to two terms, so he looked around and saw that a Senate seat would become vacant; he would run against Hillary Clinton. That was when he found he had prostate cancer, and abruptly quit the race and his wife, in order, as he put it, "to be with the woman I love." Not a new phrase, much less a new idea.

I have reached Gracie Mansion.

Like City Hall, it stands at the northern end of a park, and it is separated from the park by iron bars, also like City Hall. It is a noble old Federalist house built, I believe, in 1796. It looks comfortable, and perhaps it is, or could be if it were really a house rather than a showpiece. The ground floor is mostly big public rooms that are mostly empty. Paintings on the walls, a few wooden armchairs in an ornate, period style. It is as if the furniture has all been pushed back or moved out to make room for a reception or a dance.

Around me as I cross through some of these rooms the house is silent, and feels empty. The mayoral apartment is upstairs. I do not know what Giuliani's domestic arrangements are these days. I am told that Donna and the children still live here, but if they are present overhead I cannot hear them.

I was in this house several times for conferences when Lindsay was mayor, but never during the time of Abe Beame. The unpretentious Beame never liked Gracie mansion much. I guess such big rooms felt too ritzy to him, and on he weekends would often go home to his apartment in Brooklyn where he could feel comfortable.

I am led to the far end of the house, and into another public room that is almost equally empty, and am asked to wait. In this room there is a sofa with a coffee table, and along one wall a bookcase containing mostly very old volumes. For a time the mayor's chief of staff waits with me making small talk. Once he offers me a choice of either a soft drink or a coffee.

When I ask for a beer, he goes out and comes back with one.

He assures me Giuliani is in the house somewhere. It won't be much longer. I wonder if the mayor is resting. He's still being treated for prostate cancer, and his stamina, he has said, is not what it was.

Other people come into the room from time to time, shake my hand and go out again.

On one wall is a painting of Lafayette. I walk over and look at it. Then I walk to the window overlooking a big lawn, with, at the end of it, part of the East River.

I have never been much good at waiting for people, or things.

When I first met Giuliani he was 33. He had gone into private practice, and was working for a New York law firm, a stopgap job until a republican got back into the White House and he could return to Washington. We had a number of interviews during the writing of *Prince of the City*. I found the future mayor an excellent subject. He listened to the questions, answered frankly, and he remembered details. When my manuscript was finished I asked him to vet that portion of it in which he appears. He agreed, and I sent it over. Presently we met again and discussed the notes he had made. In one place he said my description of one of the other prosecutors was a bit harsh, and I agreed to tone it down somewhat. In other scenes he added details I had not known about. Some were vivid, and I went home and wrote them in.

The gestation period between manuscript and finished books is long. On publication day about a year later Houghton Mifflin hosted a party in a midtown hotel. Giuliani, who was invited, sought me out. "I'm Rudy Giuliani," he said as we shook hands. As if I had forgotten. But there was a diffidence about him then, which the mayor of New York City these last seven years has not displayed.

When he was appointed U.S. Attorney and came back to New York we began to see something of him. He and his wife, Donna Hanover, who anchored the nightly news on Channel 11, and whom we had not yet met, came to lunch at an apartment we kept then in New York. Donna was a delight, a very pretty young woman with solid journalistic credentials. She had started her career in Danbury, then moved on to Florida, which was where the future mayor met her. Giuliani had already been married once. His upbringing had been rigidly Catholic, he had once wanted to become a priest, and at that point he was still a believer, meaning he could not marry again within the church, unless he could get his first marriage annulled. Getting an annulment out of Rome is no easy thing to do, but he had managed it and their marriage had taken place.

I remember another luncheon some years later. We were living then in Ridgefield, and the Giulianis, who had driven up to Danbury where Donna had started her career, had stopped by our house afterward. There were several other guests including a prominent assistant district attorney. The two prosecutors had not met previously, and I thought this might make for some interesting conversation, but in fact there was no conversation. Instead Giuliani talked. And talked and talked. Hardly anyone else got to talk at all. He had had some solid successes as U.S. Attorney by then, he seemed more sure of himself than he ever had before, more self centered too, and he talked of himself almost the way film stars tend to do. When he got started on law enforcement he did not talk cases as much as he talked of ethical behavior, his own and everyone else's. He tended to see the law in terms of good and evil, right and wrong, so that at one point Donna interrupted fondly to remark that "Rudy always wants to wear the white hat." I remember thinking: I never thought of him quite that way before.

The Giulianis lived then on East 86th Street, not 200 yards from Gracie Mansion. I always sent them my books as they were published.

Finally Giuliani was elected mayor. Shortly afterward a new edition of *Prince of the City* was to be published, and I called him and asked if he would be willing to write an introduction. He responded at once. Of course he would write an introduction. He would be delighted to do so.

We met in an office the Republican Party kept in midtown. I put a tape recorder on the table and Mayor Giuliani began to talk. Once again he talked more of morality and ethics than of anything else. *Prince of the City* was a very moral book, he said. Yes Detective Leuci had testified against cops who were criminals, and for this cops hated him and called him a rat. But whose definition of morality are we to accept? Are we going to allow criminals to decide what is moral and what is immoral? Does the police wall of silence take precedence over what is best for society, over what is right and what is wrong? Next he considered the same ethical question from a different perspective: a child who brings a gun to school. Is it wrong for another child to inform the teacher?

Clearly he had not prepared for this interview, had not decided in advance what he wanted to say. I got him to speak of his first meeting with Leuci, which he described, and then about the book itself. "It's a beautiful book," he said with feeling. "I've read it straight through four times." This might have been taken for arrant flattery except that it was a statement to which he was willing to sign his name. Nonetheless it was such sincere and effusive praise that for a moment or two I was unable to speak.

I transcribed his remarks, put it all in order, and sent it to him for approval: introduction by Mayor Rudolph Giuliani.

And the days started to pass. The printer's deadline neared, and the publisher would not okay the introduction unless Giuliani initialed every page. I began phoning him. The secretary kept saying he was busy but would surely get to it later today or tomorrow.

Finally I phoned Leuci. "You call him. Perhaps he'll listen to you."

Leuci by then had divorced his wife and was living with a series of live-in girl friends in Rhode Island. He had written a number of police novels which I thought very well done, though they didn't sell all that well. He now had heart trouble and had already had two angioplasties.

He called back later to say he had had Giuliani on the phone: "I don't care what you're the fucking mayor of, I said to him. Sign the goddam thing and send it back."

I laughed, not doubting for a minute that Leuci could and would address the mayor of New York in just that way.

The introduction came back the next day, every page initialed.

The door to the room in which I am held captive opens and the mayor's chief of staff reappears to say: "The mayor will see you now."

We cross the hall and enter a somewhat smaller sitting room. It looks comfortable. Upholstered furniture. Paintings on the walls. The big window, I note, offers the same view of the lawn and the river that I have been studying for the past thirty minutes.

I note also that a number of other people are present and they look comfortable, as if they have been chatting together comfortably for a long time while I waited next door. Giuliani sits alone on a sofa, and immediately he jumps up and comes forward. I have seldom in my life been greeted so warmly. For a moment I imagine he is going to embrace me. He doesn't quite. But the effect of this, despite the long wait, makes me glad to see him too. Maybe his greeting is no more than the practiced warmth of the polished pol. Maybe not, also.

An irreverent thought occurs to me: every time I see this man he seems a different person.

He introduces me around: his agent, his publisher, his press secretary, and one or two more whose names and functions I do not quite catch. A dialogue starts between Giuliani and me, and for the next half hour all these other people remain watchful and silent.

"How does one go about writing such a book?" Giuliani begins.

Sitting in Gracie Mansion, which few other people have been inside, talking on intimate terms with this important personage whom other people see only through cameras, or from a distance, makes me privileged, I suppose. But I am focused on what I am there for, and I give him specifics. We would decide on a chapter about, say, his police commissioners, I tell him. Particularly Bratton. The tape would be running, and I would ask him: "What went wrong between you and Bratton?" And we would talk about it, and about the police, maybe for hours, maybe again the next day too, and when the whole story was down on tape, all the details, I would write a draft and—

"Bratton," he interrupts, "Bratton was one of the worst mistakes I made as mayor," and he begins a five minute denunciation of his former PC. According to the media, the mayor states, it was Bratton and his new ideas and techniques that collapsed the crime rate; whereas in truth all he did was implement ideas and techniques Giuliani had fed him—and then afterwards he took credit for them.

I let this pass.

"We would have to find a strong opening chapter," I say. "A good one might be to describe the way you felt the morning after the election. You've just been elected mayor. You must have felt the terrible weight of it. You must have had a moment of panic. I'm mayor, what do I do now?"

"On the contrary," Giuliani says. "I knew exactly what I intended to do as mayor, step by step."

He had prepared himself down to the smallest detail, he informs me. After losing so narrowly the first time, he had watched Mayor Dinkins make one blunder after another, had watched the polls as well, until soon it became clear that in the next election he would win easily. So he had begun meeting with experts in every field—one of them Bratton, by the way—brain picking them all, mixing their thoughts and ideas in with his own, until he was ready with the policies, programs and people he wanted, and he began putting them in place the morning after his victory. "So there was no panic at all," he says with a smile.

"All right, it's a good story that way too."

"I think we should begin with last year," the mayor says abruptly. "In the course of last year my life turned completely around. I learned I had prostate cancer and my marriage came to an end and I left my wife. That was some year. You can't get much more dramatic that that, can you?"

His prostate cancer and the treatment he has been following are public knowledge, but his marital problems are not. He does not go into detail about them now, but if they are to be part of the first chapter he will be obliged to. He must know this. He does, doesn't he? He would have to put in enough details to fill a chapter—a first chapter. This is something that, in his place, I would not be willing to do—a long marriage is awfully personal—and I am a bit surprised to think he might.

I say: "We could try that as the first chapter. See how it works out."

Or else he has no idea of the amount and intimacy of the revelations that this first chapter should entail. That the whole of such a book should entail.

And how does Donna's right to privacy fit in? Writing about his marriage would be the equivalent of exposing himself in public—her too. Does he realize this or not? I begin to imagine hours of conversation with him, followed by writing reams of copy, only to have him at the end realize he has exposed himself, blue pencil it all and ask me to start over.

I can see problems ahead. Am I sure I want to get involved in this thing?

His deadline is August of next year. Eighteen months from now. But he would like to start immediately, he says.

"Before your term ends?"

"Yes, tomorrow. Soon anyway."

"I don't see how you can," I tell him. "Doing such a book takes too much time. You're the mayor of New York. You don't have that kind of time."

He says he guesses he could accord me five or six hours a week.

I picture myself sitting here in Gracie Mansion, or in City Hall, sitting around all week waiting till he is free to talk to me. The five or six hours might occur ten minutes at a time. In any case, writing a book takes much more than five or six hours a week.

Also, Giuliani now suggests, I should follow him around for a day or two, see what a mayor does.

"Yes, of course," I respond. "I'm certainly in favor of that. But it would have to be a week. Maybe two weeks, maybe more. We would be waiting for unusual, dramatic things to happen, and you can never tell when that would be." Then I add that the best time to follow him around would be next summer, not next week. When the streets are hot, and tempers are short, and violent events sometimes occur.

Do I want to do this book? I sit opposite him and keep asking myself this question. I suppose I at least want to be asked. Why? I don't exactly know. Will it make me seem stronger, richer, more important? In whose eyes? Mine? Someone else's?

"If we get together on this book," I say now, "I see no difficulty completing it well before your deadline. Especially since, after January 1, your time will be your own. I don't see either where my own current schedule poses any problem."

But the fact is, as I informed his agent a few days ago when she phoned, and as I inform him now, I live half the year in the south of France. Furthermore, I'm leaving four weeks from now, and not coming back for almost four months.

It occurs to me that this may sound to him like a declaration of independence, or even an ultimatum. I might tone it down a bit by offering him the weeks before I go, so as to get the book started. But I have other things to get done before then, and choose not to do so.

Or I could offer to forego the trip entirely. If I really wanted the job this is what I should do, probably. But it is an option I do not consider for a moment.

"Why do you want to write this book?" I ask him.

Of course one reason must be money. On January 1 he will be out of a job, with no political office that he might run for opening up in the next few years. He will have to earn his living some other way. He will have alimony and child support to pay. So he has decided he will write this book, which will earn him less than half what Hillary Clinton gets, but more by far than most professional writers earn in a lifetime.

But he does not mention money.

"I think I've had an interesting life."

"Yes you have."

He pauses. "And writing it down might enable me to see it clearly."

And you would make your mark one last time, as well, I reflect.

These are my own feelings too, of course. Why else, dear reader, have I written the book you are holding in your hands? Everyone who writes such a book feels the same. But I do not articulate these thoughts to him, nor the thought that follows either—that basically I'd rather concentrate on my own memoirs than get involved with his. At the age I have reached there is a certain measuring of time, of resources, of priorities. Or perhaps only of possibilities. Always there are choices to be made: if you choose to do one thing, you will be obliged to give up something else.

How much do I want to give up for Rudy Giuliani?

Then comes another thought, which I also do not articulate. My head is already crammed so full of facts, of memories, of books written, of a life lived, that I sometimes wonder if there is room left for anything more. Can I cram Giuliani's life in there too? To reduce what I am trying to say to an analogy that may sound silly, I have had to memorize eight or ten new pin numbers in the past year alone. How many more before my head starts refusing them?

"It can't be an I, I, I, me, me, me kind of book," I tell him. "You would have to write about your defeats too, your disappointments, your mistakes."

"Mistakes?" he said. "You mean like endorsing Mario Cuomo? How's that for a mistake?"

Cuomo, a democrat, was the incumbent governor of New York, and Giuliani endorsed him over his own party's candidate, George Pataki. But Pataki won.

This type mistake isn't what I mean at all, but again I let it pass. After a moment I remark: "You probably have a good many other stories to tell I don't even suspect as yet."

"Yes. For instance, I had breakfast in the White House with President Reagan the morning he was shot.

I gather he is trying to impress me with the richness of the material he is ready to put at my disposal. But I know so much about him already, as he must realize, that he doesn't have to dangle additional bait.

He adds a few more lines about the breakfast. It was a crime conference. A number of others were present too. Then Reagan went out and got shot.

We go on talking for a good time longer. Giuliani is still projecting enormous warmth, which I warm to. Of course I do. Finally comes another warm, warm handshake from the mayor and the meeting ends. I drive home.

When I get there I receive a call from Esther Newberg, whom Leuci brought into my life and who is my agent now. How did it go? she asks.

It could not have gone better, I tell her. I would be very surprised if he picked anyone but me. What I really mean is that he would be crazy to pick anyone but me.

Esther cannot tell me how much I would be paid, nor even whether the publisher would pay me, or Giuliani out of his $3 million. These and many other details would need to be settled before I would sign on, I warn.

As I hang up I am still not sure I want the job. Rudy does interest me, and I admire what he has done to make the city more livable. But the same question keeps surfacing in my head. Do I really want to put myself, for the next year or so, at the behest of this man? Of any man?

And yet the idea of frequenting City Hall again is appealing, frequenting Gracie Mansion. Frequenting Police Headquarters again is especially appealing.

I don't know what I want.

The next day: Connecticut

Giuliani regrets. He wants someone at his side immediately who will stay there until the book is done.

Which is not me.

In a way the news is pleasing: now I don't have to decide.

Nonetheless I feel a pang. Yesterday I had a rather concrete glimpse into my past. If you go back over your life as I am doing in this memoir, you will experience many pangs, many things and people that are gone from your life, a past that may seem more beautiful looking back than perhaps it was at the time, but that in any case you cannot have again.

13.
Scrambling: Wine, Spanish Galleons, Hollywood

March 1, 2001, Connecticut

When I came out of the police department—suddenly, as I have described—I was faced with the need once again to make a living as a freelance writer. I was 42 years old, a novelist who had not yet had a hit and I was worried about it.

I could perhaps get a contract for a police novel, I thought. I had an idea for one—one idea and one only. It had come to me at the last of the ten Inspector's Funerals I attended that year. As always, the entire police hierarchy was lined up in the street outside the church, Mayor Lindsay and other political figures as well, flanked by hundreds of cops in white gloves, all waiting for the hearse to arrive, and for the coffin of the slain hero to be lifted out and carried inside. The church, which was in Brooklyn, was a modern one, with a flat roof.

By this time the Black Liberation Army had assassinated four New York cops and machine gunned two others not quite to death. I was standing in the second row, behind the mayor and the police commissioner, and I looked up at that flat roof and thought, why kill one or two of us at a time?

If you really want to make a statement, why not be up there on that flat roof with rockets and grenades? Why not decapitate the entire department with one stroke? The mayor and all those politicians too.

I thought this would make an interesting climax to a novel, and so now, months later, I put a plot together, wrote up an outline, presented it to my then publisher, and waited to be offered what I needed: a contract that would carry us for the year. The title I put on this outline was: *To Kill A Cop*.

My then publisher decided this story was of no interest, and advised me to forget about it and go on to something else.

I have been out of work at least once every year of my professional life. Most writers are. Every time you finish a contract you are out of work, and I say this in an attempt to show what a writer's life sometimes looks like to the writer himself. I complained about this once to an editor of mine named Michael Korda, who replied: "Well, would you rather work in a car wash?"

If there was no interest in *To Kill a Cop*, what then?

At this time an editor named Larry Freundlich, who loved wine, was looking around for a writer who would be interested in an idea he had for a novel with a wine background. My then agent, Sterling Lord, told him I had written a few pieces about wine, and put him in touch with me. You ask what agents do for their ten percent. They do this kind of thing. Sometimes.

My first exposure to wine had occurred at the reception following my wedding in Nice. In America at that time no one in my family, or in the circle in which my family moved, the sports circle mostly, ever served wine, not with meals or any other time, nor knew anything about wine. But my new father in law, who was Swiss-born with a French wife, and who kept a restaurant in Nice, had, following the birth of their daughter, bought some bottles of the great 1929 vintage for her eventual wedding, and at the reception he opened these and poured them into all the glasses, until he came to mine. But my drink of choice at that time was milk. I cannot even tell you the name of the wine he served that day, for I put my hand over my glass and refused it.

When we got back to America, married, there was a second wedding reception at which my mother served, in an effort to please her new French daughter in law, some muscatel. With dinner. God!

But all this had piqued my interest, and I began to taste wines, and to learn about them. Very quickly interest turned to love, and in time I began to write a few magazine pieces on wine when I could, one of them for *Esquire* about the drinking, in 1966, of a bottle of 1806 Chateau Lafite at a restaurant called La Beaumaniere at Les Baux, an experience that turned out to be so strange and ceremonial that it took me twelve manuscript pages to describe it.

A few years later *Life Magazine* sent me to Rome to write about a wine scandal there. Certain firms, including one of the biggest in Italy, were concocting wine out of dregs, ox blood, water of course, plus various chemicals. Called *sofisticatori*, the Italian word for it, these people were sophisticating wine, and I interviewed, among others, a colonel of carabinieri called Naso, who was head of the anti-sofisticatori police. It made for an amusing article. What it may have done to the Italian wine trade or to Naso's career, was not my concern.

I didn't think much of Editor Freundlich's suggested plot, but the wine background that he wanted was congenial, provided I could set the story in Bordeaux, a place I had been to, and wished to see more of. There is a strange beauty to the Bordeaux wine country. In a novel set there I thought I would be able to do a lot of scenery painting, and it was easy enough to think up a plot that pleased me: a dishonest Bordeaux shipper dealing in adulterated wine, (as in Italy), a hard-nosed young businessman exiled to Bordeaux to run his conglomerate's chateau, a love story as well, and in the midst of all this, nosing around, an agent of the Brigade des Fraudes.

Freundlich offered me a contract. A rather small one, I thought then, and still do, but I took it. I would call this novel, I decided, *Strong Wine Red as Blood*, a terrible title everyone has always told me, though I'm still not convinced.

Novel contracts do not pay expenses. Since I still knew relatively little about the wine country, and nothing about the social life of the chateau owners, I would need to spend time in Bordeaux, so I looked around for other assignments which would take me there.

The Bordeaux wine harvest starts each year about October 5. It was then late September and I went to Clay Felker at *New York Magazine* and suggested that I go to Bordeaux and write a report of that year's vintage. This seemed to me a far-out idea for a magazine focused on New York, and I never thought Felker would go for it. But America was just becoming interested in wine, Felker as always wanted to be on top of whatever was trendy and new, and his response surprised me. His enthusiasm surprised me even more. By all means, he said, go do it.

Bordeaux resembles Paris in miniature. Though its population is only 210,000, it has similar Grand Boulevards, similar handsome old buildings, and wonderful gardens. It has steeples and towers dating from the middle ages, and an old, old cathedral, whose earliest walls date from the eleventh century.

But I had work to do and not much time for admiring the sites.

Bordeaux is sixty miles inland, and most of the best vineyards are quite far north of town. The Garonne, which passes through the city on its way north to the sea is soon joined by the Dordogne to form the River Gironde which swells and swells until, in some places, it is seven miles across—with vineyards stretching inland along both banks for thirty or forty miles.

I could not describe the year's vintage without first learning about it. I had a few appointments made from New York. Mostly I drove up to chateaus, knocked on doors and asked questions. I talked to cellarmasters, to owners, most of whom had rarely been interviewed before, some of them never. The wine business was only just waking up from a long, depressed sleep, and reporters and journalists for the most part did not come by.

Thierry Manoncourt, who owned Chateau Figeac in St. Emilion, and whom I did not know, heard I was in town and issued an invitation to lunch. As I came through his door he greeted me in pidgin English. A few memorized sentences—that's all he had. But he was so eager to get publicity for his wine that he was willing to suffer a luncheon that might have been conducted in nearly absolute silence. When I answered him in French an expression of stupendous relief came onto his face, which brought a smile onto mine. He opened five or six bottles of Figeac from various years, and we sampled them, and talked about them all through lunch.

Manoncourt became something of a friend, and we lunched with him at Figeac every year after that.

Wine does not live forever, but under certain conditions it can live a very long time. It was Chateau Lafite Rothschild, I had heard, that had the oldest bottles, and a special method for storing them. I went down steps, down corridors into the deepest part of the Chateau's cellar. It was as dark as catacombs down there, and as cold. Finally I came to the last room. It was almost a cave. The bottles lay in stone sepulchers, rows of tombs, each one filled with sand, on top of which, well nestled in, lay bottles from the great vintages of the nineteenth century and before. The 1797 vintage seemed to be the oldest, though the light was so poor it was difficult to be sure. A single bottle—the date was chalked on a board imbedded in the sand.

There was only one bottle left from the 1806 vintage, as well, the vintage I cared about most, and I gazed down at it for a time and remembered what it had tasted like—what this bottle here would taste like too, most likely.

A taste that not many people alive today had ever known.

Presently I came up into the sun again, blinking, and gazed around at the walls and towers of the chateau itself.

I drove across to Chateau Petrus in Pomerol to interview Christian Moueix. We met and talked standing out amid the vines. Petrus, which was virtually unknown until well after World War II, is now the most expensive of all Bordeaux wines, a triumph of marketing by the Moueix family, I have always thought. As if to prove its excellence Christian took me into the shed where the new wine was kept, siphoned some out of a barrel, and had me taste it. Petrus harvests somewhat earlier than other Bordeauxs. The wine in my glass was thirteen days old.

Not many people have tasted a thirteen day old Petrus, either.

I hope that what I have written—the Figeac, the sepulchers, the 13 day old Petrus—does not come across as petty and pretentious, the vinous equivalent of name dropping. I don't mean it to sound that way. Rather, it is an attempt in each case to recapture for myself an experience out of the past that to me was a delightful surprise. I am talking about pleasure, and about the thrill of discovery. I am trying to share the memory by putting it down on the page.

The Bordeaux people I met displayed none of the arrogance of most of the subjects I had interviewed previously, the athletes, actors, politicians and the rest. Mostly the wine people invited me into their houses, and started pulling corks. They had wine to sell. Their cellars were full. They were not only gracious, they were also honest—too honest, perhaps. The current harvest, I was told, had problems. In future years, they would learn better, no problems would ever be mentioned, and as wine began selling again these same people would praise every new vintage to the skies. The best of the decade. The best of the century. You had only to ask. And then, they hoped, write it up the way they said it. I did vintage reports for

New York Magazine for the next five years. They never appeared before November 20th, sometimes as late as December 15th, but that was soon enough, for there was no risk of being scooped. Almost no one else was writing about wine at all.

Nowadays the results of each harvest are known all over the world before all the grapes are even in.

Year by year my wine circle widened. I met a man named Alexis Lichine who, it was said, had done more to get wine into stores in America, and to popularize it, than any other single person. Lichine was a twice divorced Russian born American, educated partly in France, owner of a grand apartment on Fifth Avenue in New York, owner also of Alexis Lichine & Co., a Bordeaux wine shipping firm, owner of Chateau Prieure Lichine, and part owner of Chateau Lascombes, both of which are in Margaux, a director of Chateau Haut Brion, and author of two books on wine including *Alexis Lichine's Encyclopedia of Wines and Spirits*, which for thirty or more years reigned as the bible of the industry.

For all of this he was a man who knew how to spend money and was perpetually short of it. In time he was forced to sell his part of Chateau Lascombes, and all of his shipping firm, his name with it. What he would never sell was his beloved Prieure which he had bought for $50,000 around 1950, a time when no one wanted it or any other wine property, and the rain came through gaps in the roof.

He had since built the chateau itself into one of the most comfortable manor houses in all of the Medoc, full of antique furniture and paintings, and year by year had bought up parcels of land and replanted until he had achieved as substantial a holding as any of his neighbors.

Obviously Lichine was a valuable source of information for someone like me, and in time when we went to Bordeaux he would ask us to stay with him in the Prieure. Lichine had certain other qualities I have not yet mentioned. He was lonely, and he was an insomniac. One lived in his chateau as a virtual prisoner. He never wanted to let us out of his sight. And at night he would beg us to stay up a little longer and watch television with him.

Chateau Haut Brion was the first of France's great wines to be known by name, and for centuries it had been the most prestigious in all of Bordeaux. But in recent years certain others had found ways to become more and more publicized, Petrus for example, and to sell their wine at ever higher prices until, now, Haut Brion was lagging behind. As a director of the chateau, Lichine conceived the notion that a book about its fabulous history would bring back some of that forgotten fame, and he decided I was the man to write it, all expenses paid. Since I was still working on *Strong Wine Red as Blood*, and needed to come to Bordeaux several times more, Lichine's offer, particularly the expenses part of it, sounded to me very good indeed.

He produced a contract, which I signed, and with that he installed us in the Chateau Haut Brion which was fully staffed, but not being lived in at that time. The original chateau, a rectangle with four towers, had been built in 1550, a true castle, with a major addition in the style of Louis XV tacked on about 200 years later.

We lived in a suite in the old part, the bathroom being in one of the towers, and I went every day into the city to research the chateau's history in the two archives, the Departmental at 13, rue d'Aviau, and the Municipal at 71, rue du Loup. I found some wonderful things, including the death warrant of the nobleman who had owned it and who, in 1794, for the crime of being an aristocrat, had been dragged out of the chateau and guillotined.

We had the run of this huge empty chateau, and at each meal sat opposite each other at this huge table in this huge dining room, ministered to by the staff, with a fresh bottle of 1964 Chateau Haut Brion set out twice a day, and in my head from time to time I would stand off and look at myself sitting at lunch or dinner in this great old chateau, me, and I would remember as a boy kicking an old football around the streets of the Inwood section of Manhattan, and I would snicker. I believe Peggy, though her background was closer to Haut Brion than mine, did the same.

But when I was some distance into writing the book a change in the chateau hierarchy occurred.

It had been owned since 1934 by Clarence Dillon, a multimillionaire Wall Street banker. A Texan who did not drink wine, or anything else, Dillon had bought the chateau, as he said to me once, because he wanted a rose for his buttonhole.

Now 93 years old, he had long since passed the chateau on to his son Douglas, formerly Ambassador to France under Eisenhower, and Secretary of the Treasury under Kennedy, and now Douglas decided to hand it over to his daughter Joan who was my age, who had once worked as an underling on the Paris Review, and who at present was married to the Prince of Luxembourg, making her a princess. Joan was a contemporary in almost every respect of Grace Kelly, richer than Grace by far, and possibly, since Luxembourg is a much bigger place than Monaco, more of a princess, but whereas Grace had become one of the three or four most publicized women in the world, Joan was still passing through life unnoticed.

Immediately she decided to redecorate the Chateau Haut Brion, to reserve it exclusively for her family, and apparently she did not like either Lichine or the book project he had put in motion. Especially she did not like the draft of my manuscript that Lichine showed her, and she scrawled uncomplimentary comments all over the margins. Lichine was embarrassed, I was embarrassed. A settlement was reached, my contract was bought out, and that was the end of that. Well, it was nice while it lasted.

Later, when the prince of Luxemburg had died, Joan married the Duc de Mouchy and became a duchess.

In fairness to Joan, when I was preparing *Portraits of France* some years later, I asked her permission to include in it the long passage I had written about the Pontac family which had founded Haut Brion, and owned it for 240 years, and this she graciously accorded.

Lichine died in 1989, aged 76, and was buried by special permission amidst his vines. As this is written his tomb is still there. But his son Sacha was obliged to sell the Prieure to pay death duties, and I wonder how long the new owners will keep Lichine's name attached to the chateau and to the wine. How long will his tomb be allowed to take up valuable space where grapes could be made to grow? I suppose similar questions could be asked by or about almost anyone. Once I am gone how long will I be remembered?

Reading back on what I have written I see I may have given the impression that wine had become my consuming interest at this time. It had not. I accepted many other assignments from many magazines on many subjects: singers, politicians, actors. I wrote a long essay for *Playboy* about people who were in love with taking risks. I was learning a lot, seeing a lot, working longer hours than most writers I knew, and I was making a living at it, not much more. One year, the year of Haut Brion and *Strong Wine Red as Blood*, I wrote two books and nine magazine articles. I was writing much too much, and often I thought of those writers I had studied in school, the same ones students still study, perhaps, Faulkner, Fitzgerald, Hemingway. Compared to them, was I doing it wrong?

But they were not pure artists either. Hemingway had a rich wife—a series of them in fact—and did not have to worry about money. Faulkner wrote as much as I did, perhaps more, including work on movies. Fitzgerald sold himself to magazines, and died too young. You have to make a living. Ask any writer and he will tell you the same. You save your money now and you put your soul into a novel when you have bought some time and can afford to do so.

Writing articles about wine is not the same as writing other kinds, the principal difference being that most interviews take place around dinner tables. Of course they are not really interviews at all; rather they are conversations from which a reporter can glean information.

But there can be distractions that make it hard to keep one's mind on the job. During dinner at the Chateau Angludet, Peter Sichel once served us an 1876 Chateau Lafite. For a time, sipping it, I forgot what I was there for. It was Sichel's habit always to serve very old wines which he would decant first. The decanters waited on a sideboard behind him as we sat down to dinner. He would pour one wine, and we would talk about it, and then the next, and so forth. Only at the end would he tell us what we had been drinking.

One of the other guests on this particular night was Edmond Penning-Roswell, a renowned British wine expert and columnist, who looked up from his glass and said: "I say, Peter, cough mixture, that." Sichel turned to me for my opinion. I did not think the wine tasted like cough mixture at all, but hesitated to contradict the famous Penning-Roswell. "It tastes like the 1806 Lafite I drank once," said I. Sichel smiled, and showed the bottle: an 1876 Chateau Lafite.

I was patting myself on the back for an hour.

Another time we were invited to lunch at Chateau d'Yquem, indisputably the greatest sweet wine in the world, by one of the owners, the Count de Lur-Saluces. With the foie gras, and again with desert he served several fairly recent Yquem vintages, at which point, mostly just to make conversation, I mentioned that the previous week I had drunk his 1937 vintage at a birthday party for Alain Chapel, one of France's most celebrated chefs, who had been born the same year as the wine.

As soon as I had spoken I could have bitten my tongue.

Most of the best chefs in France had been at this luncheon, several of whom, including Andre Daguin and Roger Vergé, had been seated at my table, and all agreed that the wine had not shown particularly well.

"And how was it?" asked Lur-Saluces.

"Well, er, er—"

What was I supposed to say? From the way I stuttered he knew the answer without being told, would see through any outright lie, but he was waiting for me to say something.

Finally I toned the chefs' verdict down as much as I could, which did not fool Lur-Saluces a bit. Immediately he summoned his butler to the table, and said: "Bring me a bottle of my 1921."

So he poured the 1921 Chateau d'Yquem into our glasses. "And how do you find this one?" he asked.

I assured him it was magnificent, and he put the bottle down, beaming. But in fact I was so embarrassed I had to force myself to drink it, and hardly tasted it at all.

Sometimes, going into these chateaus I learned, or thought I learned, more than I was supposed to, and usually it was information I could not use.

I stopped at a chateau in the Graves which had recently been purchased by a middle-aged Englishman, and he invited me in. Presently his wife joined us—a much younger woman. A woman in her early twenties, or less. Everything in the living room in which we sat looked new. There was wall to wall white carpeting that had hardly yet been walked on.

The Englishman was cordial, but also nervous. His young wife sat silent and smiling at his side. We talked of his wine, which he did not seem to know much about, while the questions I really wanted to ask him ran through my head but could not be addressed. Who was this man, and what was he doing here? I never found out, but a few years later I noted that the chateau had been sold, and new owners were living there.

We were invited to lunch in St. Emilion at a first growth chateau on the outskirts of the village. Many of Bordeaux's so-called chateaus are only villas, and some are no better than farmhouses, but this one was a real chateau, and architecturally it was a jewel. But we were met at the door by the owner who, looking harried, told us lunch would be delayed because he had to fetch his kids at school. Waiting in his house, we admired the wood paneled walls, the paintings, the antiques. Obviously he was a man of great taste. The room was dominated by a handsome 17th Century portrait which he later told us was one of only five or six De La Tours still in private hands.

At lunch, explaining why he had had to fetch his kids he told us only that his wife was absent. But we had already heard the story from someone else, and it was not an edifying one. To us it had sounded somewhat incomprehensible as well. His wife, it seemed, had just run off with a ski instructor. This was a man of about 40, handsome, rich, and part of the old French nobility as well—he was a Count. Furthermore, he produced one of the finest St. Emilion wines, some said the very best of the properties in or close to the town. He was a gracious host too, and he took me down into his cellar and allowed me to pick the wines to go with lunch, even as—once again—questions filled my head that had nothing to do with his wine, or the article I had come there to write. How could a woman with any sense trade all this, her small children too, for a ski instructor?

A story like the above should have a moral. I don't know if this one does or not. I do know that if you keep hanging around strange dinner tables you will come upon strange stories. This is especially true in Bordeaux, one of the few places, almost the only place, where strangers invite you regularly into their houses, and sit with you for long periods drinking wine.

What Felker had seen as trendy and new, every other editor saw now too, and I was asked to write wine articles by a number of publications.

The Times Magazine asked if I knew of a chateau that made great wine but was unknown to the public, and if I did would I write a piece about it.

As it happened I did know of such a chateau. Now it must be understood that in the Bordeaux wine country most of the regions have published official classifications of their wine. The most famous of these is the 1855 classification of the Medoc wines. The status of each of them was decided then and there once and forever, even though, today, some of the names on it were not making wine anymore, and some others were making it on different parcels of land altogether.

One of the names not on the 1855 list was Chateau Gloria, because at that time Gloria did not exist. Gloria was the invention of one man, Henri Martin, 73 years old when I met him, a barrel maker's son who sometimes described himself as a peasant with a peasant's love of land. During all of Bordeaux's down times, and there were many of them, Martin would go to owners of classified growths and say: I notice a parcel of your land lying fallow. Since you're not using it, would you consider selling it to me?

Often enough the answer would be: sure, why not?

In this way Martin put together a property composed almost entirely of land that had belonged in an earlier life to classified growths. In other words, he now had in all but name a classified wine. A very very good wine lacking any official pedigree, and therefore selling cheap.

I went to see Martin—he invited us to lunch, naturally, and we tasted a good many of his wines. I wrote my article, which was duly published. Within hours every bottle of Chateau Gloria in New York was gone from the shelves, and within days Martin's sheds were empty too.

I mention this because it was the only article I ever wrote, though I tried many times, that actually managed to help someone. Martin himself was so grateful that he notified the Times editors that a barrel of Chateau Gloria, the equivalent of about 225 bottles, was on the way to 229 West

43rd Street. The Times forbids the accepting of gifts, even strange gifts like barrels of wine, and the editors were obliged to work fast to stop the barrel from being loaded onto the plane. Martin did not send a barrel to me. I can't be sure, but if he had I think I might have drunk it. He really made an excellent wine, his daughter and son in law still do, and to this day Chateau Gloria is my favorite Bordeaux. Well, Chateau Figeac too.

The wine boom in the magazine world preceded the sales boom in liquor stores by several years, although when the latter did hit, it was in a big big way. The prices of all wines rose exponentially, and in 1979 another bottle of the 1806 Lafite that I had written about in *Esquire* went on the block at an auction in Chicago. This was thirteen years after I had paid $60 for mine in a restaurant, and it was knocked down for $28,000.

I went to Rioja in the north of Spain where vegetables grow between the rows of vines, and the fermenting vats, which in Bordeaux are inside the sheds, are outdoors here, necessarily so, because they are huge things, big as apartment houses, five or six stories high, higher than the buildings in the town.

In his encyclopedia Lichine called the best Riojas the equal of any red wine except the finest Burgundies and Bordeaux. He also called Riojas one of the most reliable wines in the world. Now I found this out for myself. I visited eight or ten bodegas, and talked to people, sometimes in my halting Spanish, and every wine served was splendid, one of them a Federico Paternina from 1896 which stuck me as being as perfect a wine as one could ever hope to drink.

I went to Burgundy for a wine tasting or wine contest, or whatever it was, at the home of a woman named Lalou Bize-Leroy, her home being a castle—I don't mean a chateau, but a done over and very comfortable medieval castle. Madame Bize-Leroy, who was then about 40 years old, with a beautiful 14 year old daughter who later that evening helped serve at table, owned a major Burgundy shipping firm, and a number of Burgundy's best wines, including part of Romanee Conti, the rarest and most expensive Burgundy red, and Montrachet, the most famous and almost as expensive white, all of this inherited from her late father.

There were about forty people present, most of them renowned French chefs, plus a few reporters like me, and also Madame's husband, an amiable man identified to us as a mountain climber; he seemed a bit out of it, an appendage. In any case Madame dumped him soon after. While waiting to be summoned to the table we stood around on the gravel outside the castle sipping Montrachet from crystal glasses, and when the summons came I watched to my horror as most of the others poured what was left in their glasses of this coveted, almost priceless wine out onto the gravel. This seemed sacrilegious to me. I drank mine down, and followed the others inside.

I was assigned a table, and as I took my place I saw that beside me was Paul Bocuse, at that time and still the reigning monarch of French chefs. I talked to him several times in the course of the evening. He seemed a raucous man. His restaurant was one of the most sophisticated places on earth, but he, it seemed to me, was not.

During dinner came the blind tasting we had been gathered for—in flights of five we were served 25 extremely expensive Burgundy wines all of which came from the same commune, Gevrey-Chambertin. We were asked to identify wines that did not differ much one from the other, and how could they since certain of the vineyards were separated one from the other only by a tool shed or a footpath. Each flight represented a single vintage, the oldest vintage served being 28 years old, and each came with a scorecard on which we were supposed to write down what each wine was. These were all Bize-Leroy wines. Otherwise, no hints.

You can say, if you wish, that tastings such as this don't prove anything, are actually silly, but if you get caught in one there is nothing to do but smile, while pretending to an expertise you do not feel. What I felt was daunted. I was in way over my head. All these wines were made within yards of each other, great wines of course, but pretty much all tasting the same, and they kept coming, and we all wrote down what we had guessed, and around me nearly every three-star chef in France was guessing too, Vergé from Mougins, Haeberlin from Illhaeusern, Troisgros from Roanne, Senderens from Paris, and of course the great Bocuse beside me.

When the scores were totaled the winner was a guide-book journalist, and second was the wife of a two-star chef who, it turned out, chose the wines for her husband's restaurant. Most of the great chefs did badly. I myself identified four wines correctly, which actually was pretty good, for the great Bocuse got none right at all, and I watched him rip his cards up in disgust and throw them on the floor.

Well, well, well.

I went to Reims to write about champagne, and at dinner our host served a 1914 Bollinger champagne, still fizzy, still alive, and the man next to me raised his glass to the light, sipped from it, and then said: "Let the war begin." And for a moment all of us were back in 1914, the war had indeed begun, all that slaughter, much of it very near here, much of it before the champagne we were drinking was even in the vats.

There is so much pleasure out there to be discovered, to be amazed by, to learn about, and to love.

I finished writing *Strong Wine Red as Blood*, turned it in and it was published. Life is long, no single triumph carries you very far, even a great triumph, and *Strong Wine* for me turned out to be, commercially speaking, a rather small one.

Furthermore, it was now done, and I needed another contract. Being on good terms with Editor Freundlich, I brought out my *To Kill A Cop* outline.

He read it, said do it, so I did. My time in the NYPD was by then five years in the past, but I imagined a police assassination and a disgraced Chief of Detectives who hopes that if he can break the case he might save his job, and I led up to the climax I had thought up outside the church in Brooklyn as the coffin of the slain cop was lifted out of the hearse.

By the time this novel was finished, it seemed to me I had used up everything I knew about the NYPD. There was nothing left. My police career was definitively over. That I would eventually write many more police novels, all of them set more in headquarters than on the street, never occurred to me. My first, I believed, was also my last.

What I needed, once the novel was done, was still another contract, and since I imagined I had nothing further to say about high ranking cops or the department, I looked outward for an idea, not back.

Diving on a Spanish Galleon

An item in the paper caught my eye. A treasure hunter named Mel Fisher claimed to have found the remnants of Nuestra Senora de Atocha, a Spanish galleon lost off Key West in 1622 with, he also claimed, $600 million in gold and silver in its hold. But a day or two later there was a second item: his oldest son, his daughter-in-law, and another diver had been killed in a terrible accident.

I phoned *The New York Times* Magazine to say there was a big story here, and I wanted to write it.

I did write it, then used the article as an outline for a non-fiction book, was given the contract I was after, and then spent much of the next year flying to and from Key West, where I interviewed Fisher, drank and dined with him, interviewed all the divers, and many times bummed rides in speedboats 40 miles out to the so-called wreck site, which was a stretch of empty sea marked by a few buoys under which divers had found stray clumps of coins, a silver bar or two, a few bronze cannons, and some rusted arquebuses welded together by the sea. Not the galleon itself, as Fisher often claimed. Not nearly.

Fisher had no money, had already been looking for this galleon fifteen or so years, and he paid his bills by finding gullible investors and selling them contracts in the treasure he intended to find that year. Each contract represented a percentage of whatever would be brought up—a percentage of the treasure, not money— and the contracts ended each December 31. Most years nothing was brought up. A few of the gullible were rich and could afford the hype Fisher sold them. Most weren't. His divers, youths with air bottles on their backs, sometimes went months without being paid.

Fisher was a con man. Was he even an honest con man? I never knew. Honesty, in a man like Fisher, depends on faith. If he truly believed the treasure was there and he would find it, then he was honest enough. But did he? I came to know him well, but could not decide.

When he had money he sent his divers to sea, and they dove, and sometimes found this or that. He never had enough money for repairs. His gear was rusty and sharp edged—not something you wanted to be close to in a bouncing sea. His boats were in deplorable condition, and some were either downright dangerous, or unsuited to the uses to which he put them, or both. The vessel that sank taking three people to their deaths was a Mississippi River tugboat that had no business being out on the Gulf of Mexico. Another was a former cargo ship, a steel hulk with no engines. Fisher had it towed out to the wreck site and anchored, and it served as a kind of headquarters at sea. The divers slept on it. So did I, and sometimes in the morning was surprised to find it still afloat. I was at sea with the divers in all seasons in various kinds of weather, and also went spear fishing with them for dinner in the shallow waters of the Marquesas Islands. Twice on successive days small sharks swam past me.

They didn't scare the divers, who had encountered bigger. Did they scare me? Yes.

It was an exciting and sensuous story to work on. I was aware of sun, sea, wind every day, and if the weather was fine I slept on deck under the stars. I was aware all day of the surface of my skin, and the weight of my body. I was aware of the sea air, the temperature of the water, of breathing in and out, of being alive, and when the experience was over I often thought of Korda's remark: would I rather have been working in a car wash?

There was a second part to the Fisher story, and then a third part that I will get to in a moment.

Fisher had working for him a historian named Eugene Lyon, who was another who rarely got paid. Lyon, who had a doctorate from the University of Florida, had spent months in the Archivo de Indias in Seville, poring over 350 year old documents relating to the loss of the Atocha. It was Lyon and the documents he had found that had put Fisher over the wrecksite.

Because there was a possible scam involved, I went to Seville to check out Lyon's research. I stayed a week in John Fulton's house, which was usually full of indigent young bullfighters, and from there each morning I would take the bus downtown to the archives, and spend the day going through the bundles of documents called legajos that Lyon had worked in, until I had found and verified every detail he had cited, and as I held the handwritten old documents in my hands, as I read reports and descriptions that men dead three centuries had written, the tragedy of the Atocha became vivid to me, and the men involved became vivid, until I could feel their bafflement, their grief, their pain.

It was as pleasant a week as I have ever spent, and afterwards, as I started to write the book, I decided to turn the story into two searches, not one, Fisher's in Key West, and Lyon's in Seville.

I had already begun writing the book as I went along, certain, because Fisher seemed so certain, that the wrecked galleon and the bulk of the treasure would be found any day. But it wasn't. Finally I could wait no longer. The National Geographic gave Fisher a reception in Washington. The Queen of Spain came, and Fisher gave her one of the bronze cannons Fisher's son Dirk had found just before his death. I put this rather mystical ending on the story, it would have to do, and turned it in, and the book was published. Peggy had a great title for it, I thought: Deep Blue Gold. But Random House in its wisdom overruled us both, and called the book *Treasure*.

Ten years to the day after the death of Dirk Fisher came the third part of the story, its true ending, the one I had hoped for, and waited for as long as I could. For ten years Fisher had somehow kept the search alive, and now one of his divers forty feet below the surface of the sea, swam up on the Atocha's rotting timbers, and its treasure hold, which was still intact, still full.

I went back down to Key West, talked to everybody, wrote a hundred page epilogue, and the book was republished, though in paperback only.

Hollywood

The years immediately after the police department were difficult. To stay afloat, I wrote constantly. I don't think I ever tried to write too fast or sacrificed quality. What I did do, because I had to, was work non-stop, work all the time.

Then came *Prince of the City*, everything changed, and as I began to write novels with the police headquarters background I had learned so well, each of them very different from all the others, I began to be very well paid. My advance for the first of these post-Prince books, *Year of the Dragon*, was $110,000, and it rose ultimately to $350,000 for *Tainted Evidence*, so that I was able to give up magazine writing altogether. All the novels during this period brought in additional money as book club choices, and in foreign sales, most were bought outright by Hollywood, and nearly all were at least optioned, one or two of them several times.

I was also asked to write a number of screenplays, for which I was well paid also, though none of my scripts was ever filmed.

My Hollywood vogue finally ran out of course. In Hollywood no one's vogue lasts forever. In all there were, as I have already written, eight outright movie sales, six of which were actually filmed, and I was able to bank, mostly in my pension account, nearly four million dollars.

Once I got caught in a bidding war between Sylvester Stallone and Dustin Hoffman, two of Hollywood's biggest stars. Both were backed by studios, and the novel both wanted was called *A Faint Cold Fear*, a story about the cocaine wars set partly in New York, partly in Colombia. The bidding rose to $875,000 payable on signing, with various subsidiary clauses promising, if the film were made, to lift me into the seven figure range.

For me, though surely not to Hollywood, this was the biggest deal imaginable. Now all I had to do was decide between the two bids—between the two renowned actors.

I had met Hoffman some years previously, and liked him. Now I talked to him on the phone, and liked him, and later spent a hour with him in his trailer on Riverside Drive where he was shooting a scene from a picture called *Billy Bathgate*, and liked him again. He said he had read the manuscript on a yacht in the Caribbean and had called his people ship-to-shore, ordering them to get him this property, he had to have it. He mentioned one scene toward the end of the novel that he had especially loved, and told me with great enthusiasm how he intended to play it.

How little praise it takes to turn an author's head. What author could turn down a man who talked like that?

Stallone, I decided, would play my protagonist naked to the waist, torso greased and glowing. In most scenes he would most likely be wielding a sub-machine gun. So I decided on Hoffman, whom I counted a serious artist, and who seemed to recognize good literature when he read it. Hoffman, I thought, would make a film that I would be proud of.

His backer was Twentieth Century-Fox who hired a producer who came to New York to meet me, and a director who was already in New York whom I also met, and who was ready to start work at once, and the most expensive screenwriter then extant as well. In all, the studio must have disbursed at least $2 million, maybe much more.

Hoffman spent nothing. This did not prevent him from controlling the project, which Fox executives, kowtowing as always to stars, let him do. Hoffman's first move was to blackball the chosen director, perhaps for no other reason than to show the studio who was boss. When five other names were given him, popular directors who might be available if one acted quickly, he was too busy even to consider them for some months. The producer begged him for a meeting, but he did not have time for that either. The expensive screenwriter, meanwhile, turned in first one draft, then another, both of which I read. Neither seemed to me particularly good, and the producer did not like them. Fox would have to put up more money to hire someone else. There was still no director approved by Hoffman.

Enthusiasms cool fast in Hollywood. Despite having spent $2 million, or whatever it was, Fox decided to close the whole thing down, to walk away. How they explain such decisions to their stockholders I do not know. In any case, the picture was never made.

When I had chosen to go with Hoffman I had been unaware of his then reputation, though plenty of people threw it in my face later. Dustin Hoffman was the only man in Hollywood, it was said, who could turn a go project into a development deal. He is a bit older today, less in demand, and probably less arrogant than he was then. Still, I would hesitate a long time before doing business with him again.

14.
Return to Modena

March 12, 2001, Nice

We got here yesterday, and this morning, trying to shake the jet-lag out of our bones, hit tennis balls for two hours, running for them, trying to hit them hard. We belong to the Tennis Club de Beaulieu, eight red clay courts. The sun was bright, there was no snow here, and the vast towering cliff face that hangs over the town, that seems to be trying to push the town into the Mediterranean, rose, as always, high up behind court eight.

Afterwards we had lunch on the club terrace outdoors in the sun, then spent an hour in the supermarket stocking up on groceries. French supermarkets are now very like American ones, except that here there are a hundred varieties of cheese on sale, and about the same number of sausages and salamis.

Also on sale is wine, so I stocked up on that too.

No one can have it all, but it has always seemed to me that one can have more than most people are willing to settle for.

April 5, 2001

We left Nice this morning for Bologna in our rented Renault with our friends the Goujons—Pierre is one of the Riviera's foremost architects. In Bologna we will meet our daughter Leslie, a graphic artist who is there attending a convention, and we have tickets to the opera tomorrow night. We drove south on the autostrada at speed, not intending to stop, but then the signs for Modena started to appear and I asked the others if they would mind stopping there for an hour or so.

Now we walk through the streets of this city where I once spent so much time with Phil Hill. I don't know how Modena seems to the others, but for me it feels almost like returning to the scene of an old love affair. Phil and I were just starting out on our careers, and we hardly knew each other as yet. We both had rooms in the Hotel Fini, and we ate in the Ristorante Fini on another street—hotel and restaurant are now so expensive I am not tempted to try either. One afternoon we went to a French movie called, I think, *Les Amants*, because in it Jeanne Moreau was reputed to bare her breasts. In those days a young man would go a long way to see bare breasts, but that scene had been cut out of the version shown in Italy. We laughed about this afterward.

We had a number of long conversations too, sometimes about death which Phil, like all front line drivers in those days, risked nearly every day, and did not mind talking about. Later I wrote a column about him. He thought he had a good life, and that risk was the price he must pay for it. The column ended: "Death is like furniture in a familiar room. He knows it is there, but he has not looked at it in a long time." I thought this comment very clever of me, but I'm not sure now it was accurate. I think now that Phil looked at death constantly, tried to avoid it constantly. I think as a result, champion though he was, he won fewer races than he might have. One year the British Grand Prix was run from start to finish in pouring rain. He finished second and afterwards, soaked, exhausted and with considerable bitterness, he described letting the eventual winner go by him: "he had his arms all crossed up. I didn't see how he could keep the car on the road, and I said to myself: `I'm not going to kill myself just to become world champion.'"

Of course he became world champion anyway. But in many races he had to contend with people who drove faster than he did, but who, in some cases, did not live out the season.

In retrospect those few days here in Modena seem to have been exceedingly pleasant. But I remember also how short of money I was, and that I was worried the whole time about getting in to see Enzo Ferrari. A month's income rode on getting in to see him. Suppose he wouldn't see me, what then?

So obviously it didn't feel that wonderful at the time.

Phil Hill does not live in Modena anymore, and the me of that year no longer exists either. But the 12th century Romanesque cathedral is still here, and Peggy and I step into it. It is one of the least known in Italy. One of the most fabulous and beautiful too, both architecturally—inside it is built on three levels—and for its decorations. I must have come in here with Phil, for we did some sightseeing together, but don't remember it at all. This time I wander around inside for thirty minutes or more, which is very nice, but not the same as it must have been then.

I am somewhat tempted to write Phil a letter—a postcard at least: "Thinking of you here." Something like that. But I don't do it. I don't know why exactly. Perhaps I am unwilling to confront the long vanished Phil with the long vanished me. He is 73 years old, one of the few who got out alive. I still have his address and phone number somewhere. He still lives in the same house in Santa Monica, I have been told. He writes for enthusiast magazines sometimes. He goes to many motor racing gatherings where he is treated as a hero. He spends much of his time trying to get his son started as a racing driver. I haven't seen him in over twenty years.

We get in the car and go on to Bologna.

15.
Giuseppe Verdi

April 7, 2001, Bologna

Tonight we attended *Il Giorno di Regno* at the opera here. *Giorno* was the second opera Verdi wrote, and it was such a colossal flop he thought his barely begun career was over. His reputation was ruined, no one would want anything from him ever again. He was inconsolable.

I know exactly how he must have felt. Exactly. So does every artist in every discipline.

We have all had to start out in life, which is never one triumph after another, not even for Verdi.

Il Giorno di Regno is a comedy, and since that first time, it has hardly ever been done anywhere. I have never met anyone who has seen it, not even my friend Tony Russo, who has been a singers' agent for forty years. Listening to it tonight we were enthralled. We found it so absolutely delightful that I wondered why Verdi, once he became the powerful Verdi, never forced promoters to give it a second chance.

He didn't. And he never tried a comedy again until he was 79 years old. *Falstaff*, his last opera. He went out to the sound of laughter. Would that we could all do that.

16.
Notes from Hungary

May 1, 2001, Budapest

I sit on a bench on the edge of the Danube reading the International Herald Tribune, looking up from time to time to watch the sun drop behind the Buda hills opposite. Presently the sky becomes streaked with red. It's not a glorious sunset for the hills are too high, but it is very nice. The Danube is very nice too, half a mile wide here, not the Hudson, but deep, fast moving, rather grand.

I came to Hungary two days ago hoping to find something of the France I first knew. Europe back then was desperately poor. Much had been destroyed. No new constructions had gone up in fifteen years. Hardly anyone had a telephone. The few cars dated mostly from before the war. There were almost no traffic lights. The stores had little stock. If you admired a dress or suit in a window and went in, they would take your measurements and you would come back for it in two weeks time.

To me, aged 23, Europe was exotic and strange. I was enchanted by everything I saw. I was too young to recognize the poverty, the struggle. I never understood why some things were so expensive. The first purchase

I tried to make in Nice was a chocolate eclair seen in a bakery window. Not the New York version, but a French one, the real thing, and I went in. But I had very little money, which had to last, and the price quoted was too high. I wanted it but I didn't buy it.

France today, all of western Europe is supermarkets, smog, people in a hurry. People making money. Expensive cars parked on sidewalks because there is no place else to put them. Traffic jams. A ferocious death toll on the roads. Spain, the last to join the club, is no different. Yes, even Spain.

I expected Hungary to be the old Europe, for it had just come out of fifty years of Russian oppression, had it not? I thought it would be run down and seedy. Much dust. Few cars. Peasant women wearing black. Animals pulling plows in the fields.

The old Europe was what I wanted to see again if I could, before it was gone forever.

But Hungary is not it. From Budapest, superhighways radiate out in all directions, and there is a McDonalds on every corner, so it seems, Burger Kings too, hotels by Hilton, Hyatt and Marriott that rise straight up, ATM machines every fifty feet—one bank boasts on a billboard I saw yesterday that it has 300 throughout the city.

In most rest rooms one pees into automatic self flushing urinals.

Everyone seems to speak English.

When I first came to France I had to eat what the people ate; I was told not to drink the water and to wash the salad first, but didn't believe it, and didn't do it. I drank their water and loved their food. I slept on hotel beds that bore the sags and lumps of thirty or forty years service, but slept soundly nonetheless. I didn't mind that the bathroom was always two flights down. I changed my travelers checks on the black market at whatever rate I could get, and if I wanted to talk to anybody I had to do it in French, which I set about learning to speak, a hard job, terrifically hard, but what a thrill finally to communicate in a language and culture not my own.

Hardly anything then resembled home. Traveling was adventure, and the differences you encountered stayed in your head for the rest of your life.

How far do you have to go today to find a people, a country, whose accomplishments and aspirations are different from what you see everywhere else? To find the adventure of which I speak? Is there any longer any such place? Very soon the learning of another language is going to seem the silliest waste of time imaginable. The homogenization of the world advances at a furious speed, it can't be stopped, and before long going to Hungary will be no different from going to Idaho. It's almost that now.

My daughters knew the old Europe as children, and to a greater or lesser degree remember it. But my grandchildren don't, and can't even suspect what it was like. To them it will be as if that Europe never existed. A whole world will have been lost. It is not so much this lost world that I regret, but rather, I think, that I can no longer expect any applause for having learned to cope with it when it was there. Which is a pretty shallow regret to have, isn't it?

I look across the Danube at the other half of the city. I still hold the Herald Tribune in my lap, but it is now too dark to read it. The lights have come on over there, and around me as well. The river has become glossy. Excursion boats drift by. They're all lit up, houses moving. Aboard are tourists sitting down to dinner, gypsy musicians, and guides spouting spiels. I can't hear the music or the guides, or see the tourists; the boats are too far out. But judging from what I have seen and heard in the streets, the tourists are mostly Austrians and Germans. A few Americans too, perhaps.

I fold the paper and go back to the hotel, turn the television on—mostly just because it is there—and flip through stations, of which there are many:

German, French, English, Hungarian of course. Wherever you travel, you now bring your programs with you. I come upon a bullfight in Seville and realize I am watching TV Española. Bullfights start late in the afternoon, and Seville is at the far side of this same time zone, so it is still light there. The spring feria is on. I watch the final bull of the day's program. The matador is Antonio Rivera Ordoñez. It takes me a minute, then I realize this is the son of Francisco Rivera, called Paquirri, who was killed in the ring in 1984, and the grandson of the great Antonio Ordoñez himself.

The bullfight ends. I turn the TV off. I have to shake myself to remember I am in Hungary.

May 4, 2001, Vienna

From Budapest to Vienna takes three hours by car, super highway all the way. The border is one of the last in Europe where you must actually stop and get your passport stamped. Don't have to get out of the car, though. Does anyone remember when customs guards of every nationality made you open all your suitcases? Sometimes you had to carry them inside a shed first, and then watch the guards thrust their hands in among your clothes. I remember. To me it doesn't seem that long ago. When the guards' hands reached the soiled laundry and rummaged through it, how the women used to cringe.

We have never been to Vienna before. I went to many many countries and cities when I worked for the paper, but not all of them. Not nearly.

We are here with our friends George and Julie Rusznak, who escaped from Hungary after the failed revolution of 1956, the one that was put down by Russian tanks. They met in a refugee camp outside this city. She was 16 years old, he was 18. She was to be sent to Canada, he to the United States. To stay together they got married, then raced to the American consulate to hand over their papers and await their visas.

Today we went looking for the hotel in which they spent their wedding night, but couldn't find it. They didn't remember where it was. This was because in it they spent one of the shortest wedding nights on record. Almost at once there came a knock on the door, and they were ordered to prove they were married. They couldn't. The Americans had their papers.

They were made to spend their wedding night sitting up in chairs in the lobby. They had only enough money for the one night, so when morning came they went back to the camp, she into the women's side, he into the men's.

They got to America newly married, two frightened teenagers with no money and not a word of English. Today they own property in Santa Barbara and Palm Springs, but spend much of the year on the Cote d'Azur, where I sometimes play tennis with George.

I once asked him why he had wanted to come to America.

"Because I understood that the streets there were paved with gold," he answered. "And you know something? It's true."

We arranged to stop here on the way home because Domingo was scheduled to sing *Pagliacci* at the Vienna State Opera. Julie Rusznak adores Domingo. It was she who arranged to buy the tickets, paying scalpers prices. This was weeks ago, but when we reached Vienna we learned Domingo had cancelled. An excuse was given, but you mustn't bet your house on the truth of it, whatever it was. Julie was terribly disappointed, I less so. I heard Domingo sing the part some years ago, after Molese had sung the *Cavalleria*. Another time I heard Domingo sing the *Cavalleria*, with James McCracken singing the *Pagliacci*. Domingo was very good both times, but I have seen others I thought sang better, and I have never understood the size of the success he has made.

The performance was last night. Domingo's replacement was a strong-voiced Czech tenor named Janez Lotric who was every bit as good, I thought, as Domingo would have been. I said as much to Julie, but I'm not sure this consoled her.

And that I trust is the final appearance—or non appearance—of Domingo in my life.

17.
Still Another Strange Place to Have Got To

May 5, 2001, Nice

There came a day, some years ago, when I found myself strapped into a kind of canvas sling behind the machine gun in the open side of a helicopter gunship, scooting along above the hot, flat jungle known as the Chapare, which is the principal coca-growing region of Bolivia. We were looking for clandestine landing strips, clandestine laboratories. We were about 500 feet up, well within small-arms range. The wind blew through my hair and the racket was deafening.

I watched our shadow moving below, moving fast. The tops of the trees were mauve, like cauliflower. Then for vast stretches the jungle disappeared. It had been scalped. Slash and burn. Long trees lay every which way on their sides, and amid them, beside them, grew the new coca bushes. The trees were like giant straws strewn over the ground out of a box.

There were eight of us aboard, some American DEA agents, some Bolivian narcotics police and yours truly, a novelist looking for a plot line.

A good deal has been written relative to novel writing, some of it by my colleagues in the profession. Something about realism as opposed to estheticism. Should novels be researched or invented in the author's head? Should everything in them be totally imagined? Or should they, for their own good, make use of some of the techniques, rules and energy of modern journalism?

All I can tell you is the way I have done it.

In New York some years ago, walking along Mott Street with a Chinese police detective, I ask what a Chinatown gambling den looks like, feels like, smells like, because the chapter I am facing tomorrow ought to be set in one. I can't get in to see for myself. They peer at you through peepholes, and if you're not Chinese the steel door stays shut.

The detective points down steps from the sidewalk. "That's one down there, he says. We'll raid it."

"What?"

"You and me. Come on."

The detective darts down the steps, bangs on the door and, when it opens a crack, he bulls his way inside, waving his police shield, hollering in Chinese that this is a raid. Despite many misgivings, I follow him in. It never occurs to me not to, for I need to learn whatever I am about to learn.

Trestle tables covered in green felt. Piles of loose bills. Joss sticks burning. Smoke. Odors. Twenty or so Chinese gamblers.

The mayor has ordered the police to leave Chinatown gambling dens alone—I know this as well as the detective does. I should not be here, I tell myself. It is like barging uninvited into someone's house. But instead of leaving I try to look in all directions at once, committing the whole place and everyone in it to memory: the chips, the bowls of buttons for fan-tan, the position of the cash desk, the faces. The gamblers, off-duty waiters most likely, have backed against the wall. They have just had a terrific shock to their nervous systems. Perhaps they will be arrested, dragged out in handcuffs, forced to make bail, pay lawyers.

The Chinese cop walks along the line like a Gestapo man, shoving his face into theirs, threatening arrests he cannot make. They are obliged to stand there and take it, humiliated by him and by their own fear. I have never seen 20 humiliated men in one room before. I wonder how they would feel if they realized they were taking part in a novel.

Suddenly the detective turns to me with a grin. “Seen enough?”

Back up on the street, I feel shamed. But grateful too, and next morning as I begin the next chapter of the novel that will be called *Year of the Dragon*, I feel more grateful yet. My character, a Chinese undercover detective, Luang, has tailed someone into the gambling den. He is alone, unprotected, and...

The job of the novel at its highest level is to illuminate the human condition. Entertainment is fine, and the transference of ideas is nice too, but the novel, like all art, has as its supreme goal to engage the beholder’s emotions, to make him or her laugh and cry and suffer and triumph and—one thing more—understand. At least this is what I have always believed.

But how is it to be done in our time when the audience is so fragmented and so busy? By writing small? By imagining stories that, being pure invention, cannot possibly be as exciting as the ones appearing in any day’s newspaper? How do you make an emotional connection with an increasingly blasé, increasingly beleaguered reader?

That is what the debate comes down to, it seems to me. Not realism versus imagination at all, but getting read.

On the second floor of the commissariat on the Rue Gioffredo—this is here in Nice where that year’s novel is set—I’m studying reports by detectives of raids on bars owned or frequented by organized crime. The French police hit such bars regularly, randomly, line everybody up against the walls and interrogate them—not on suspicion of crimes committed but on general principle. This is known as keeping tabs on the underworld. Who was there in the company of whom on a specific date and what explanation did they give? Were girlfriends with them? If so, what are their names and where do they live? When a crime eventually is committed, it gives the police a head start. As I page through the files, my novel in progress, to be called *The Dangerous Edge*, begins to change direction in my head.

I have been learning about French cops for weeks—that's where my ideas for scenes come from; I do not make them up out of nothing. I went out to dinner with a commissaire from the Sureté Urbaine whom I did not know, and by the dessert course believed I understood much more about him than he probably imagined. His attitudes, perceptions, suspicions I recognized from New York. This guy is a New York City detective, I told myself. He doesn't have a word of English, but that's what he is. Even his jargon was familiar. Criminals to him were *les animaux*, for instance. How often had I heard New York cops call criminals animals? The structure and strictures that controlled him were similar, too.

If I can put all that down, and this town down, I thought, readers will feel themselves living in the world of the French detective. The experience will become part of them.

When I went into the NYPD in 1971, already the author of 10 books, I found, as I have said, that the Department was not what I had thought it would be. The men were different from what hundreds of books, movies and television shows had led me to believe, and the tensions and emotions under which they lived were very different. To begin with, there were two police departments. There was headquarters and there was the street.

Headquarters, where officers fought so hard for career advancement that they had little time for fighting crime, was in many ways the more interesting of the two.

And then I came back out into civilian life and was faced with the need once again to make a living. I realized I was the only professional writer ever to have seen so much of the New York Police Department from so deep inside and, following *Prince of the City*, I began to see ways to use that experience—ways I had not previously imagined.

Some years ago John Ford stood up at a convention of directors in Hollywood and identified himself. "My name is John Ford and I make westerns." This was oversimplifying it. His westerns were much more than that, he must have hoped and believed. To paraphrase Ford, I became a writer of cop books. I imagined they would be exciting, if only because the police world was exciting. In addition I knew, or had access to, stories no one else had ever written. I was hoping that if I wrote them well enough their theme would be seen to be profound—in fact the most profound theme of all, good versus evil, and how difficult it can be sometimes to know which is which. Obviously such a theme is viable forever.

But I quickly used up the stories I had witnessed personally, together with the intimate details I had so carefully observed. My framework—the police world, police mores—I could keep using, but what did I fill it with? I needed cases, characters, plots, details. What to do?

Well, how about raiding Chinatown gambling dens, and combing French police files. How about a good sex crime?

I sit against the wall in the Manhattan District Attorney's office while the rape victim's story pours forth. Present are the assistant DA whose business this case has become, and the detectives who brought the victim in. The rape is so recent that she is still trembling, and she holds back nothing: what he said, what she said, what he did, what she did. Details more lurid and at the same time more tragic than the reading public has ever read before, because no one, not this author nor any other, could ever possibly have imagined them. Her voice cracks, she weeps—my heart goes out to her, but also I am elated. I have been listening to rape victims all week. My notebook contains lines of dialogue, indeed whole scenes that can be transposed almost directly to the printed page. I believe I have come to understand as much as any man can what rape to a woman is like—and I know just how I will portray it in the novel that will be called *Hands of a Stranger*.

But there is another emotion at work here, and I discuss it with the assistant DA afterward—she feels it as strongly as I and is just as confused by it. I have felt it every time I have stood inside the barriers that surround a crime scene, and so has she. So have most cops. To peer closely at the extremes of human behavior is fascinating. It makes the blood run quick. For me there is also a certain discomfort. I am always aware that I am working the tragedy of others, profiting from someone else's pain, and many times, as with the rape victims, invading their privacy as well.

Cops and district attorneys can take refuge behind the law. A novelist cannot. Is that something I should worry about? How many novels would there be if novelists worried too much? My justification is this: I need it.

I don't like the word reporting very much. Reporting is what you do when sent out to cover a water-main break. How many gallons per minute are going down the street? Surface stuff. The word research is not satisfactory either. With regard to book writing, it suggests an author locked in a library studying other authors. The death of emotion. But sometimes, because there is no other, I have used the word research. I have used the process—my version of it—on nearly every book.

The word novel also ought to be examined more closely than it is. It means new, and imposes a command upon the writer. The novelist must each time find something that has not been written about before, or at least not in his way; and at the same time, if he is to write about it for three or four hundred pages, he must know it with terrific intimacy. In a novel the emotion is in the details—I have said this so many times. I do not mean the enumeration of trademarks or the specifications of hardware. I do not necessarily mean even how something looks and sounds as much as how it feels, and I have always imagined that it is the novelist's job, if he does not already know how something feels, to go find out. Whether a service revolver is .32-caliber or .38 is not particularly important, though an author has an obligation to get it right. I am not writing police procedurals. What is important is how much a cop's gun weighs on his life. How does he safeguard it from his children? What does he do with it when he goes to the beach? What code of conduct does it impose on him even when he might be out on a date with his wife? If he should shoot somebody with it, how does he react? And what sort of investigation does he have to endure afterward?

In novel writing you must get in close, as close as possible, closer than might seem possible. You must get close to the French police, close to the rape victims, you must somehow get into the Chinese gambling den. Write about what you know all of us were taught the day we started our first short story. There should have been caveats, though usually there weren't: but it has to be new, our teachers should have told us, and you have to know it with terrific intimacy. If you don't know something intimately enough, then go out and get close and don't come back until you do.

Yes intimacy is hard to come by. It is achieved by having been there, either having lived the story yourself (which is good for only one or two books) or else by having hung around for days, weeks, months, watching whatever special world your protagonists will belong to, watching how real people behave in light moments and under stress, watching for the unexpected details—the ones that eventual readers will recognize as real when they see them, the ones that will make a character or a scene come alive rather than lie dead upon the page. That will evoke in readers the emotion that you as author are trying for.

It takes enormous amounts of time and sometimes mileage, and there are many failures. I went to Hong Kong and Bangkok to work on *Year of the Dragon*, which was about a New York City precinct captain, his career in the balance, trying to cope with the sudden surge of organized crime in his Chinatown precinct. Hong Kong was where this crime was coming from. How, why? He would have to know, and so I would have to know.

I had made appointments from New York. One was with the Hong Kong police commissioner, an Englishman. He turned out to be as cold and close-mouthed as anyone I have ever interviewed. He did not see me as a former police official but as a pressman. He did not like pressmen, he made clear.

That's a ridiculous question, he said.

Your supposition is entirely wrong, he said.

If you're going to ask questions of that nature, I won't talk to you, he said.

I had come 12,000 miles and the interview was over.

One learns to improvise—frantically in this case. After much effort I was able to make contact with lower-ranking officers who, fortunately, had nothing against former deputy commissioners, or pressmen either.

The lesson I learned on that novel was the same as on all the others. You simply must get in close. Which, difficult as it may be is the easiest part of the job, for then comes the writing, the transforming of the research into art, the transforming of truth you have found into truth in a permanent form.

In the end most research gets thrown away. It does not fit. You cannot use it. One of my novels, *A Faint Cold Fear*, is about two New Yorkers in South America—he is a cop, she is a newspaper correspondent—both caught up in the principal law enforcement crisis of those years: cocaine. In the planning and then the writing, I went to Bogota and also to Medellin, home of the Medellin cartel, the so-called murder capital of the world, where I spent most of my time looking over my shoulder. I went to Lima and La Paz, and then I was in the helicopter with DEA agents and Bolivian cops riding 500 feet above the Chaparé.

And they had put me behind the machine gun, don't ask me why. Perhaps to allay my supposed fears. Proof that no one expected any shooting. Certainly not. No, señor. To get an author killed was out of the question. The muzzle of the machine gun, which I tried to think of as a decoration only, dangled between my shoes, as if searching for anything below that might move.

I felt a number of emotions, all of them familiar from work on other books. Surprise was one—how did I get here, me, to a place and situation as rare as this? And confidence. My notebook was full, I could remember back over the entire trip, and my doubts were gone—this new novel was one I would be able to write. Sheer physical pleasure was a third emotion, and I mean more than the pleasure of sun and wind and scenery. I was in some small danger, about the equivalent of driving 90 miles per hour on an open highway, and my skin tingled.

A faint cold fear, if you will.

No, I did not spot any airstrips or labs. The others did, and pointed them out to me.

See it—there!

Where, where?

The men to either side were shouting over the noise but I could not understand what they were saying, and I had only a vague idea what I was looking for. But then the jungle ended and suddenly we were over marshes or grasslands—impossible to tell which from the air. Some empty dirt roads. Occasional houses with thatched roofs. Streams that moved so slowly the water was red. There were rivers everywhere. Tortuous things doubling back on themselves. I could see every bed they had ever run in.

But the novel I had planned contained no big helicopter scene, and at first my real-life ride seemed to lend itself to nothing important in a fictional way—no moment of discovery, no crisis. I would have to discard it. The plot continued to go elsewhere, as if of its own accord. Was I to be left with the memory of a nice day over the jungle, and that's all?

But as I neared the end of the writing an idea occurred to me. The more I pondered, the stronger it seemed. The helicopter ride was not to be wasted after all. It could be made into a climax, I saw—not my actual ride of course. Normally that is not the way the process works, and in real life nothing climactic had happened. To researching novelists climactic events rarely do. But suddenly it had begun to suggest scenes, including one in particular.

As it took shape in my head I saw that it ought to occur not in Bolivia at all but in Colombia. Suppose I transposed it there—I now knew what it was like to hover over that kind of country, to drift, to drop down. I had sensed the awful menace of that machine gun. I knew how heavy it hung in its mount—you can't sit behind one and not move it about a little. Even more important, I had learned how law enforcement minds worked in Colombia, what certain men in certain situations would likely do. So just suppose that...

18.
CELEBRITY:
SOME NOTIONS ABOUT FAME

May 10, 2001, Nice

My birthday once more.

And the end of 365 days of rummaging still again through my head. I have tried to remember it straight, and tell it straight, but doubtless there are pages and pages of self justification, self aggrandizement in here. It would be a miracle if there weren't.

A number of celebrities populate this book. They are not there for that reason, but rather because they are part of my story. The celebrities I have known are in many cases already gone, and in all cases will be replaced by other celebrities within hours or days. The truest thing about celebrities is that they are replaceable.

I have been interviewed five or six times by Larry King, once when I was in Los Angeles, a remote pickup, the two of us 3,000 miles apart. Of course that was before he became an interviewer of presidents, but it was the same guy, and why presidents of the United States, France and other places became so anxious to go on with him is a something that baffles me.

I was always trying to sell a book I had written, but they weren't. In some mystical way he had become as big as they were, though with a difference. History will remember the presidents for a while, but I doubt it will have much time for Larry King.

I have been interviewed also by Johnny Carson. First I cooled my heels for an hour or more in the Green Room, pacing the floor, worrying about whether I would get on the show at all. Writers, always the last of the night to be interviewed, sometimes didn't. If that night's show ran long someone would peer into the room, thank me for coming and tell me to go home. It had happened to plenty of writers in the past.

But I did get on, stepped across the cables and sat down beside the famous comedian, who began asking me about some magazine article he had read. Now on that particular night the show had run not long but a bit short, and I saw that I might have as much as ten minutes on camera nationwide. Still, ten minutes isn't much time if you have a book to sell. I couldn't afford to waste one second talking about someone else's magazine article. So I ignored Carson's question entirely and launched into a discreet, I hoped it was discreet, pitch for my book. This was rude, but I was playing for what seemed to me high stakes. He was polite, and let me speak. No jokes. During the commercial break the two of us stared straight ahead out over the audience, two men with completely different agendas. We had nothing to say to each other.

When Carson decided finally to retire he was immediately replaced by two other comedians, and they are the men people speak of now.

One year I spent considerable time with an actor named Elliot Gould, who was soon to appear on the cover of *Time Magazine*. In America this is the consecration of celebrityhood, though one might ask oneself why. Gould was a nice enough fellow. I sometimes enjoyed being with him and sometimes didn't, same as with everybody. But almost immediately after the *Time* cover Gould's star fell completely out of the sky. I never knew why, and I wonder if he did. When he works at all these days it is in supporting parts. A good many people, Gould for one, get a taste of fame, but usually it doesn't last, and because taste is possibly the most fleeting of our sensations, it leaves nothing behind, not even—forgive me—a taste.

Some people imagine writers are celebrities. They are not. Writers are people who lock themselves in small rooms for months at a time, and don't come out. When finally they do come out, they do not get recognized at cocktail parties, much less on the street, and the two questions they get asked most are:

"What kind of books do you write?"

And: "Have I read anything you've written?"

In a country of 300 million people, a sale of 50,000 hardback copies will most likely land a book on the best seller list, and a writer who can sell 20,000 is in the top ten percent. There are book clubs and paperbacks as well, of course, and public libraries. But on the whole, Americans do not much read.

So most writers, me for one, respond to these questions with embarrassment, and begin mentioning films their books have been made into. We are all searching for that little flash of recognition, and a film title just might get it.

"Oh, I saw that film," is not exactly the praise a writer might hope for, but most times it is the best he can expect.

Unlike real life heroes, a writer does not mow down villains with his sub machine gun. He does not even, like an actor, pretend to do so. The action, such as it is, takes place only in his head, where it is invisible.

In addition, nearly everybody imagines he or she could write a book too if only they wished, and they tell writers this often enough. "But I don't have the time to sit down and do it," they explain. Some do do it, and a few even get published. Writing remains—this has been said often enough—the only business outside of prostitution in which the amateur competes with the professional.

Even inside the publishing business there is a pecking order that causes writers some distress. The big money goes to authors like Hillary Clinton and Rudolph Giuliani who, by literary standards, are not even real, while real writers, most of them, barely make a living.

Once in Nice there was a book fair. Rows of stalls were laid out on a lawn off the Place Massena, and crowds milled about staring in at the authors, each one sitting behind a counter behind a pile of his latest book. There must have been fifty of us in fifty stalls, all put there by our publishers, in my case by my French publisher. Book fairs are no place to sell books, but we were all trying to score points with the firms that paid us.

The fair lasted two days, during which only one of us made substantial sales. He was at the end of the row, where he was besieged by oglers and buyers. His name was Daniel Ducruet, and he had been the bodyguard, then the lover, then the husband of Princess Stephanie of Monaco. But he happened to get tangled up, literally, with a strip tease dancer from Belgium, and a paparazzo concealed in a tree and using a long, long lens photographed them cuddling nude in the swimming pool of a luxurious and otherwise empty villa. When these photos appeared in an Italian magazine, Ducruet found himself out on the street. So he decided to become an author, why not. He had now written a book trying to explain himself.

The crowds around his booth were really impressive. Leaving my own pile unattended I went down there to have a look at him. For some minutes I watched him sign his book and hand it out to admirers, and I heard several women murmur that he was real cute. In the course of the fair I sold, I think, ten books. I don't know how many he sold. I was afraid to ask.

Most writers, as my wife is inclined to say, talk only about themselves.

Most I don't find very interesting. I have known relatively few, have never frequented writers' hangouts, and the ones who never talked about themselves unless asked were the ones I cared for most. James Michener, who did not get published until he was 39 years old, I liked enormously. We went to bullfights with him in Spain, and once shared a picnic in a woods in the Pyrenees. He was good fun at a fiesta. Another time he stayed overnight at our house, and in the morning Peggy was mortified to see that she had forgotten to put out towels. "Tell her," said Jim when I apologized, "that I've been drying my face on my socks for years." He was always lavish with his praise. He praised me in two of his books, one of them Iberia, in which he also called Peggy the most beautiful woman in Europe. Michener helped also a number of other people I knew personally who were not writers, and he gave away $35 million or more to various charities, a sum four or five times what I have earned in my entire career.

Writers are rarely rich men, though Michener came to be. So did James Clavell, an admiral's son, who as a young man survived three years of near starvation in a Japanese prison camp, and who as an older man sold one of his novels, *Whirlwind*, for $5 million for U.S. rights alone. When he talked about this afterwards he sometimes got as giddy as a girl. He had a villa on the Cap Ferrat near here, in among the billionaires, and for a time we saw a good deal of him.

James Jones was another rich writer who was always generous to young ones trying to get started, including me, and I have always considered *From Here To Eternity* the supreme work by an American in my lifetime.

But all these men have died, and I don't see much of any writer anymore except, occasionally, James Salter, an ex-jet fighter pilot who, to my mind, writes the most beautiful prose of anyone working in the English language.

I have met Hemingway, met Faulkner. I suppose this sounds a bit impressive, for both were Nobel Prize winners. But both were I think, wildly overpraised, and both were drunks who ended badly. I also knew Norman Mailer and in fact once did a book with him. It was called Bullfight. He did the prose, with which went about a hundred of my photos. But the editor tried some funny business--he decided not to pay me, though eventually he was forced to--and when I tried to ask Norman for help he wouldn't take my call, nor did he choose to return it. I have never owned a copy of this book, but now, looking back, I am curious about it, and rather wish I did. The editor later went to jail for providing his celebrity friends with drugs, and when he got out he committed suicide. This is one of the sad, sad stories that completely passed me by. I have no sad stories to relate about myself. I have been, obviously, very lucky.

A mean spirited reporter with a mean spirited question recently accosted Paul Newman. "So, Paul," he asked, "what's it like to be 75 years old?"

To which the former sex symbol replied: "This may be the best time."

Not for everybody, surely. For him, perhaps. And for me? Maybe. This has surprised no one more than me. I grew up thinking that a man fifty was over the hill. Might as well lie down in the box and pull it shut.

Not true. The future is not unlimited, but then it never was. It is unlimited enough. There is still so much out there to be discovered, to see, to do, to learn. There are still other stories I'd like to write down.

Today, my 71st birthday, Peggy and I are going out and play tennis, and after that talk to our daughters and grand children on the phone. Grand children are a delight--why did no one ever tell me? And tonight we will go out to dinner, oysters and a bottle of Sancerre, most likely. And not a big restaurant but a corner brasserie. I mean, I don't see this as a champagne kind of birthday. Nothing to celebrate but finishing this memoir which, like all books, is months or years from being published, for the process is long. Maybe at dinner we'll talk about what comes next, or maybe we won't. We'll have to see.

Made in the USA
Lexington, KY
10 December 2017